Ministries of Song

Ministries of Song

Women's Voices in Ancient Syriac Christianity

Susan Ashbrook Harvey

UNIVERSITY OF CALIFORNIA PRESS

University of California Press
Oakland, California

Suggested citation: Harvey, S. A. *Ministries of Song: Women's Voices in Ancient Syriac Christianity*. Oakland: University of California Press, 2025.
DOI: https://doi.org/10.1525/luminos.257

Library of Congress Cataloging-in-Publication Data

Names: Harvey, Susan Ashbrook, author.
Title: Ministries of song : women's voices in ancient Syriac Christianity /
    Susan Ashbrook Harvey.
Description: Oakland, California : University of California Press, [2025] |
    Includes bibliographical references and index.
Identifiers: LCCN 2025007455 (print) | LCCN 2025007456 (ebook) |
    ISBN 9780520422681 (hardcover) | ISBN 9780520412378 (paperback) |
    ISBN 9780520412385 (ebook)
Subjects: LCSH: Syrian churches—Liturgy. | Women's choirs—
    Religious aspects—Christianity. | Women—Religious aspects—
    Christianity. | Hymns, Syriac—History—To 1500. | Syriac Christians—
    Social conditions. | Church history— Primitive and early church,
    ca. 30–600.
Classification: LCC BX107 .H37 2025 (print) | LCC BX107 (ebook) |
    DDC 264/.208828163—dc23/eng/20250825

LC record available at https://lccn.loc.gov/2025007455
LC ebook record available at https://lccn.loc.gov/2025007456

GPSR Authorized Representative: Easy Access System Europe,
Mustamäe tee 50, 10621 Tallinn, Estonia, gpsr.requests@easproject.com

34   33   32   31   30   29   28   27   26   25
10   9   8   7   6   5   4   3   2   1

For Sebastian P. Brock and Frances M. Young

CONTENTS

ILLUSTRATIONS

ACKNOWLEDGMENTS

Toward the end of the twentieth century, Sebastian Brock, Robert Murray, and other notable Syriac scholars began to bring the anonymous Syriac dialogue poems to the attention of scholars. These quickly garnered interest for their lively presentation of biblical stories through an ancient literary form of contestation and debate. I, too, was fascinated. What caught my attention, however, was the prominence these hymns granted to biblical women, and the realization that women's choirs would likely have been singing them. I began working on these issues fully a quarter century ago. Answering my questions turned out to be a complicated process, with many circuitous detours along the way. Any project of such long duration yields great debt. It is my honor and delight to express my thanks here. Lists never convey the full significance of exchanges nor the depth of appreciation involved. Although inadequately stated, in each instance my gratitude is deeply felt!

Research for this book was generously funded at different times by the John Simon Guggenheim Foundation, the American Council of Learned Societies, and Brown University. At Brown, specifically, the Cogut Institute for the Humanities, the Royce Family Chair for Teaching Excellence, the Program in Early Cultures, the Dean of the Faculty Office, and the Office of the Vice President for Research all contributed generously and graciously.

A number of student research assistants helped at different points. I am grateful especially to Evan Strouss, Abby Linn, Hannah Moser, Gabriella Reyes, and Aliosha Bielenberg. Paul Michaud prepared the original manuscript with careful attention and good cheer. All have been lively, inspiring companions.

For some years now I have participated in a loosely defined project on comparative late antique hymnography (Jewish and Christian, in a half dozen ancient languages). The impact of this remarkable group of colleagues on my research has been profound. Thomas Arentzen, Maria Doerfler, Uffe Holmsgaard Eriksen, Georgia Frank, Sidney Griffith, Kevin Kalish, Derek Krueger, Laura Lieber, Ophir Münz-Manor, Gerard Rouwhorst, Michael Swartz, Erin Galgay Walsh, and Jeffrey Wickes all have given copiously of their time, wisdom, and scholarly knowledge, all with unimaginable generosity.

Although music does not survive for the hymns discussed in this book, the ancient sources have much to say about it. I have found it tremendously helpful to talk with experts in both Greek and Syriac chant traditions. For Greek, I thank Spyridon Antonopoulos, Alexander Lingas, Sevi Mezera-Mamali, and Photini Downey Robinson. For Syriac, my gratitude is especially to His Eminence Mor Polycarpus Augen Aydin, Gabriel Aydin, Tala Jarjour, George Kiraz, and Eve Sada. My counterpart for the modern study of Syriac women's liturgical singing, Sarah Bakker Kellogg, has been a particular source of inspiration and insight.

I owe special thanks to Sarah Bassett, Adam Becker, Mary Cunningham, Stig Frøyshov, Darlene Brooks Hedstrom, Patricia Fann Bouteneff, Daniel Caner, Jeff Childers, Jonathan Conant, Susan Einbinder, Carrie Frederick Frost, Ephrem Ishac, Robert Kitchen, Margaret Mullett, Stratis Papaioannou, Ute Possekel, Ashley Purpura, Teva Regule, Alberto Rigolio, Samuel Rubenson, Eva Stehle, Robin Darling Young, and my colleagues in Brown University's Religious Studies Department, particularly Mark Cladis, Jae Hee Han, Nancy Khalek, Ross Shepard Kraemer, Michael Satlow, Janine Sawada, and Daniel Vaca. Tina Creamer and Nicole Vadnais have managed numerous logistics that would otherwise have been the death of me, always with calm efficiency and endless wisdom. Toward the end, the incomparable Karen Bouchard at the Rockefeller Library guided me through the labyrinthine maze of image locations, permissions, and formats, always with warmth and enthusiasm.

I have been helped at crucial points by the opportunity to present my work in invited lectures and at professional meetings, workshops, and conferences here and abroad, always with invaluable responses, ideas, and exchange with others. Each encounter moved things forward and encouraged me. It is an extraordinary blessing to be part of such a supportive community of scholars.

Ross Kraemer granted me the immense honor of reading the entire draft and being willing to talk about it in endless detail (!). Gerard Rouwhorst kindly read drafts for the first three chapters, catching a number of problems. I am deeply grateful to both, and to the anonymous readers at the University of California Press for their encouragement and helpful guidance on the manuscript. Susan Einbinder and Darlene Brooks Hedstrom seemed never to tire of urging me forward. At the Press, Eric Schmidt was an invaluable source of encouragement and advice, starting fully ten years before the book's completion. Margo Irvin and Jyoti Arvey picked up Eric's role with unfailing kindness and efficiency, with Jyoti as a constant and trustworthy guide through the production process. Cynthia Fulton, Stephanie

Summerhays, Paige MacKay, and Marian Rogers oversaw the final stages with gracious care, while Greg Fisher managed the indexing with scrupulous attention.

All remaining problems are my own responsibility.

Once again, my family have been my constant strength. My husband, Jim, has not only lived with this book along with me (cheerfully enduring its sprawl across multiple rooms in the house), but also attended numerous of my lectures about it, accompanying me near and far in various adventurous travels. Our daughter, Julia Claire, is an inspiration at every turn, and, so, too, Alexandra Demasi. My mother, Patricia Ashbrook, never lost her enthusiasm for the project. I cannot imagine having done any of this without them.

Two further debts remain to state.

For nearly forty years I have served as tonsured chanter, choir singer, and, for some years now, as choir director, at St. Mary's Antiochian Orthodox Church in Pawtucket, RI. This choir, including some members now passed away, has been an unfailing source of strength and comfort for me. In the years I have worked on this book, I have often considered parallels, analogies, and insights between a choir in a small parish context now, and those of late antiquity. The resonances are woven into this book, even with due humility for the insurmountable differences in time and place.

Finally: at heart, this is a book about different kinds of teachers, female and male, known and unknown, from the distant past. It is dedicated to two teachers, Sebastian Brock and Frances Young, from whom I have been learning over many decades. Their gifts to me (as to many others!) have been immeasurable. May their luminous wisdom continue to guide us long and well.

There is no standardized form of transcription for classical Syriac, an inconvenience for us all. I have utilized a simple system to facilitate reading and render my text more accessible to the nonspecialist. It should suffice for scholars who wish to pursue philological inquiries. Inconsistencies are inevitable, alas, in both Syriac and Greek. Sometimes it has been easiest to retain conventional spellings. Sometimes the reader will note inconsistencies between quoted texts and my own usages. I beg the reader's forbearance: there were no satisfactory solutions.

Introduction

A Forgotten History

Now Syrian women sing praises with their hymns!
—JACOB OF SARUG, "ON MAR EPHREM"[1]

SINGING WOMEN

In his homily written to celebrate the great saint Ephrem the Syrian (d. 373), Jacob of Sarug (d. 521) recounts that Ephrem himself recruited the women's liturgical choirs that, by the time Jacob preached during the late fifth and early sixth centuries CE, characterized Syriac churches in both the Roman and Persian Empires. In this homily, among other important considerations, Jacob offers a paradigm of human salvation exemplified in the dynamic between women's voices, silent or singing. The first mother, Eve, Jacob explained in chanted verses, tied "a cord of silence" around the tongues of women. With Mary, mother of the Son of God, the bonds were loosed. The turn did not simply grant speech to women; it granted them song. Jacob imagined Ephrem's voice summoning women to sing his hymns:

> Your silent mouth which your mother Eve closed,
> is now opened by Mary, your sister, to sing praise.
> . . . .
> Until now your gender was brought low because of Eve;
> But from now on it is restored by Mary to sing Alleluia.
> . . . .
> Uncover your faces to sing praise without shame
> To the One who granted you freedom of speech by his birth.[2]

Elsewhere, in a festal homily on the nativity of Christ, Jacob recalled the moment when the Virgin Mary, having agreed to the miraculous events to come, prepared herself to receive the conception of the Son of God. Readying her body and soul for such an unthinkable task took diligent effort on Mary's part. As she worked, Jacob imagined, she sang hymns of praise, *qalai shubha*, to her Maker.[3] This singular salvific moment of human-divine relation, to Jacob's mind, was marked by this action: a woman singing.

In both instances, as if to underscore the point, the liturgy in which Jacob performed his homily would have framed his words accordingly. For immediately before the homily and directly following, by his own description, the sound of women's singing would have filled the church. Holy hymns sung by women's choirs "with glorious voices" (*madrashe men nakpatha b-qalai shubha*) taught the congregation and in turn led them, male and female, in their own singing forth of faith and praise.[4]

Women's singing has not often been the vehicle through which Christians have told their story, taught their believers, or expressed their worship. Or, rather, women's voices have not often been utilized in this way when historians present Christian history and practice. Yet ancient Syriac Christianity presents the possibility of thinking with such a model. What might we see if we look from this vantage point?

Between the fourth and seventh centuries CE, during the period known as late antiquity, women's liturgical choirs were a notable feature of Syriac churches in both the Roman and Persian Empires. The singers were variously described as consecrated women known as daughters of the covenant (a Syriac office of service to assist the bishop in the civic community) or deaconesses or consecrated virgins. Regardless of their different designations, these choirs had the distinctive ministry of singing *madrashe* (pl.; sing. *madrasha*), hymns by which the basic teachings of the church were expressed. Additionally, they led the congregation in their singing of refrains, responses, and hymnodic prayer. These Syriac women's choirs were officially designated in ecclesiastical canons, supported by church leaders such as Ephrem and Jacob of Sarug, and historically attested in hymns, homilies, chronicles, and hagiographies that referred to, described, praised, and considered their ministry. While the evidence for these choirs is not abundant, and its assessment can be problematic, it is qualitatively extensive and historically incontrovertible. Women's liturgical choirs continue as a living tradition into our own time in both the West and East Syriac churches.[5] The long historical arc is impressive.

A further feature of ancient Syriac worship was the content of hymns, sermons, and other forms of liturgical poetry. In late antiquity, these were largely given to teaching stories of the Bible, often presented through the imagined voices of biblical characters, including women such as the Virgin Mary. These imagined women's voices were sung in poetry variously performed by singing voices either male or female, depending on the poetic form, role, and portion of the liturgy in which they appeared.

Because Syriac liturgy designated a distinct role for women's choirs, and because Syriac liturgical poetry often presented the imagined words of biblical women or saints, (real) female voices of the liturgical present and (imagined) female voices of the sacred past sounded forth in high relief. Women's voices mattered for the purpose, content, and expression of late antique Syriac Christian worship. This, in short, is the premise of the present study.

What was important about late antique Syriac women's choirs, and why? Could Syriac Christians have done something completely and unilaterally different in comparison with the more dominant Greek and Latin churches of the same period, where choirs of nuns or consecrated virgins served other roles? Or have these other traditions of women and sacred song also been misunderstood or misrepresented? What, in fact, can be known about Syriac women's choirs? What can they teach us?

SYRIAC VOICES

Syriac was a form of Aramaic that appeared in the first century CE in the region of Edessa (Şanlıurfa), in present-day southeastern Turkey. Growing rapidly thereafter, it soon emerged as a major Christian language of the eastern Mediterranean: a region corresponding roughly to present-day Syria, Iraq, Lebanon, eastern Turkey, Israel, Palestine, Iran, and parts of India. Its dialects were used on trade routes as far west as Gaul and as far east as China. Beyond its homelands in the Middle East, Syriac served as the language of liturgy and scholarship for religious communities founded by Manichaean and Christian missionaries in south and central Asia, and along the ancient Silk Road, for centuries.

Throughout the two millennia and more of its history, Syriac has been a language used by minority cultures, always in multilingual and multicultural contexts. During late antiquity, the period explored in this book, those larger cultures were principally Mesopotamian, Semitic and Hellenic in their longer histories, and Roman (both Greek and Latin) and Persian in their contemporary forms. Unlike some of the other "minority" Christian languages of the period, Syriac blossomed in a brilliant era of literary and scholarly achievement that continued well into the Middle Ages. It was not only influenced by the literature of the dominant cultures in which it was spoken, but also influenced their literatures and intellectual traditions in turn. Similarly, it was affected by and affected in turn the cultural and religious practices of other language traditions. The material of my project demonstrates both the depth of interaction between cultures that Syriac allowed, and the distinctive qualities that gave Syriac Christianity its particular luminosity in late antiquity.

Women's voices present a particular challenge in the study of this history. Over the course of late antiquity Syriac Christianity produced an impressive cadre of women saints and martyrs, both historical and legendary.[6] Compelling evidence also testifies to the active engagement of Syriac women in civic and domestic religious life, whether as laywomen, consecrated virgins or widows, deaconesses, ascetics, or nuns. Yet no known text in Syriac and written by a woman survives from the ancient or medieval period. This textual silence is troubling, but not necessarily trustworthy. At least one early Syriac manuscript offers an indication of possible female authorship.[7] Literacy was certainly cultivated in female monastic contexts, as sometimes for upper-class women. Not only are there numerous literary depictions of women engaged in religious reading and writing, but a sixth-century manuscript preserving a (partially damaged) colophon appears to indicate commissioning or ownership by an abbess named Maryam, perhaps intended for her nuns.[8] A great deal of ancient and medieval Syriac hymnography and hagiography was preserved anonymously, and it is entirely possible that women were among the authors. Scholars confront a similar though less severe lack of women's writings in Latin and Greek.

The Syriac situation is further compounded by the violence that has afflicted its regions over centuries. Much has been lost or destroyed, including in recent decades. The vast majority of surviving Syriac manuscripts have been preserved and transmitted in either (male) monastic or ecclesiastical libraries. These contexts to a certain extent favored selective preservation: particular types of manuscripts (liturgical, biblical, ascetic, ecclesiastical, theological, hagiographic) were chosen for transmission by and for learned male communities. Such circumstances were not conducive to preserving material pertaining to women's lives, nor to identifying female authors—or even male ones; in addition to the anonymous extant Syriac literature, many texts are wrongly attributed to several particularly beloved saints—for example, to Ephrem, Rabbula of Edessa, and Jacob of Sarug among West Syrians, and to Narsai and Isaac of Antioch among East Syrians.[9] It is entirely possible, even likely, that women produced or composed some of these texts.[10]

Still, the ostensible silence might lead one to think that women's voices were not important in Syriac Christianity. This would be a mistake. Not only were women's choirs a regular feature of Syriac Christianity, but, as noted above, the developing Christian culture was one that highlighted women by attention to the women of the Bible. Late antique Syriac liturgical poetry presents numerous biblical women from both the Old and New Testaments as favored exemplars of the life of faith, explored through a number of exegetical techniques. These often took the form of imaginative narrative expansions of the biblical text, frequently with fictive speeches by the woman in monologue, or in dialogue with another character (usually male) from the biblical account. These speeches far surpassed—in length as well as substantive content—what was attributed to women in the biblical stories.

Different liturgical participants presented these imagined stories and conversations in diverse liturgical forms: clergy, deacons, deaconesses, and male and female choirs all chanted, intoned, and sang these biblical accounts, and congregations of women and girls, boys and men, sang responses in return. Through rhetorical construction and ritual performance, then, gendered voices retold, expanded, and taught biblical stories to the larger Christian community as a means of holy instruction for doctrinal, moral, and ethical formation.

In many respects, all of this was part of a larger religious culture common across the eastern Mediterranean. During the period that is the focus of this study, the retelling of sacred stories was a much-loved activity among pagans, Jews, and Christians. Tales of gods and goddesses, and ancient, revered sagas, were the subject of public art and household decoration.[11] Variations on these stories were presented in the theaters and performances of singers, musicians, actors, and dancers; they provided the practice texts for schoolboys in their study of grammar, declamation, rhetoric, and oratory. Both school exercises and theatrical performances favored imagined speeches and dialogues to explore the characters and personalities of divine and legendary figures.[12] Similarly, extracanonical narrative literature abounded for biblical figures among both Jews and Christians, as did an exuberant iconography in synagogues and churches. These works explored the voices and thoughts of biblical figures well beyond what the canonical texts contained (indeed, the notion of "canon" itself was hardly set during this period). Throughout the Mediterranean world, expanded and retold sacred stories provoked apparently boundless enthusiasm, through a wide diversity of media. The Syriac interest in biblical stories was part and parcel of this shared culture.

Still, much about this situation was unique to Syriac Christianity. Only in Syriac Christianity did women's liturgical choirs gain regularized, normative status, in the assignment of a teaching ministry in song. These were not choirs of nuns assigned to chant the Psalms, like the choirs used in Greek and Latin churches on particular feast days or special occasions. The Syriac contribution was more robust in nature, including the teaching ministry of the madrashe and their generous attention to the stories and imagined words of biblical women, whether or not the Bible presented any such speech (and generally, for female characters, it did not). Over the course of late antiquity, women's voices—real and imagined—were an important part of daily, weekly, and festal Syriac worship, in addition to occasions of domestic and civic importance such as funerals, natural or political crises, and celebrations of good fortune. This conjunction of female voices, real and imagined, is the focus of this study.

LEARNING FROM SYRIAC WOMEN

In the chapters that follow, I will argue that Syriac women's choirs, female laity, and the biblical women whose voices they represented and whose stories framed their singing contributed significantly to late antique Christianity and to Syriac Christianity in its historical duration. Hence they have much to teach us. Their evidence contributes substantially to our understanding of Christian history more broadly, as well as to Syriac Christianity in particular.

In the case of the women's choirs, the evidence matters first for what it demonstrates about women's contributions to the collective ritual life of ancient Christians. The presence of women's choirs changes how we understand women's liturgical roles, pointing to forms of leadership women exercised (often unrecognized as such), and to how gender differentiated types of religious authority. Scholarship on liturgy often reductively spotlights the ordained male clergy. But liturgies were complex occasions even in their simplest forms; a variety of ritual agents and authorities were involved—not in competition, but as mutually necessary. Women's choirs cast this rich mosaic of participation in high relief.

Secondly, the choirs bring the role of the laity into fresh light. Bishops and clergy occasionally instructed their congregations on the significance of the women's choirs and how to receive them. Women's singing often framed and in certain respects shaped the participation of the laity. We have much to learn about the laity and their liturgical experience through study of these choirs.

Thirdly, Syriac Christianity offers a different history than that of Greek or Latin churches. Although these interacted, responded to one another, and contributed to the larger history of Christianity, as did churches of other languages, each offers distinctive aspects. Syriac Christianity was not marginal. It was a center of creative literary, liturgical, and theological activity. Women's voices real and poetically imagined demonstrate these creative qualities.

These three areas of consideration represent three historical voices often missing from our understanding of Christian history: the voices of women in a choral ministry, the voices of participating female laity of all ages and social status, and the voices of non-Greek or non-Latin Christians. These voices, often occluded by historians and by the sources they use, are made visible—if not audible—by the evidence regarding late antique Syriac women's choirs. As such, they present a fourth contribution: recognition of liturgy as an often untapped resource for the study of late antique social history.

Again, biblical women and women saints as they were treated in late antique Syriac writings have much to teach us. These stories were a lively, dynamic, highly creative aspect of ancient Christian life. Biblical women were used to demonstrate, but also to problematize, normative roles and behaviors. They were utilized for the moral and ethical formation of Christians both male and female. Their literary expressions occupied some of the most brilliant and vibrant writers in the history of the Syriac language, and produced some of its most glorious literature.

In their liturgical poetry, ancient Syriac authors honored their women's choirs and honored women of the sacred past. In both instances, these women were praised for their voices: the choirs were praised for loud, bold singing; and biblical women and saints for bold, wise speech. Yet in neither case do we have access to the women themselves. These choirs are wholly anonymous in our sources. No female singer was identified by name, nor was any choir singled out for mention.[13] Nor can we know the women whose stories the Bible purports to tell, and whose voices were invented in hymns and homilies about them. These figures were wholly constructed, whether as heroines, villains, or ordinary women. And in the absence of Syriac women's own writings, we lack the perspective of women themselves on these voices celebrated by Syriac liturgy and liturgical practice. Yet real women lay behind the stories and the unidentified voices that sang them; further, women were among those who heard. In many respects, the voices this book considers stand as placeholders, gesturing toward women whose own stories lie beyond our reach.

The voices studied in this book will not bring us to significantly greater knowledge about women and their lives in late antiquity, although I hope they offer a contribution in that direction. Feminist scholars of antiquity have increasingly recognized the limitations of seeking such knowledge, even where we have extant writings by women or documentary material about them. Rhetorical conventions govern all our surviving evidence, no matter the language. As Suzanne Dixon has argued, genre determined what was included in any given text, how the material was treated, and what was excluded. The audience was invariably male and inevitably elite, even when form or context might appear to speak to all; the purpose was always ideological.[14] Hence literary and documentary representations of women are precisely that: representations. They are "unreliable witnesses," in the words of Ross Kraemer.[15] Real women, as Elizabeth Clark has admonished, vanish before our eyes.[16]

In this absence of evidence, I begin from the sounds of presence: Where, when, and how were women heard? If we are to hear any echo of the (missing) women of Syriac Christianity, a twofold methodological move is required. First, we must start from that social location where women's voices were heard often, repeatedly, loudly and clearly, in public, and as publicly significant: Christian liturgy. That is, I propose liturgy as a historical location of social consequence, and liturgical poetry as a site for serious social, political, and cultural negotiation. Liturgy was not a separate sphere disconnected from ordinary life; rather, we need to view it as part of social history. Second, I use the term "liturgy" in its most capacious sense, to include the full array of collective worship practices: not only the eucharistic celebration on Sundays, but any and every gathering of the collective Christian community involving prayers and hymns; and further, including also the ritual practices of daily lives—the prayers and singing that punctuated work at home, in fields, or in civic or monastic domains. Liturgy as a broadly construed category is the working context of this book's exploration; as such, it will yield helpful perspective.[17]

I will argue that the sounds of women's singing framed and inflected the voices of biblical women and women saints presented in liturgical poetry. Singing voices and voices sung intersected in terms that resonated throughout the social worlds of women, whether ecclesiastical, domestic, civic, or monastic. In every instance, it is crucial to approach liturgy through primary sources other than liturgical *ordines*, commentaries, or manuscripts. These sources are important, to be sure. But we will also gain by attention to how liturgy was represented and described in other kinds of literature—chronicles, hagiography, and letters, as well as hymns and homilies, which may not always match the technical liturgical information. Such sources may provide better glimpses of how people actually did things, or their attitudes or perspectives, in terms that better illumine the social world of the participants.

Moreover, since much of the surviving evidence is literary, literary analysis forms a primary through-theme and methodology in this study. What were the literary strategies, tropes, conventions, or traditions present in a given text? How were these deployed? What is the work these literary portraits accomplish? In the instance of choirs, certainly the portrayals provided authority for their liturgical participation and presented them in support of male ritual agents and officiants. In the case of laity, the depictions signal not only ritual but also moral and ethical order, as well as underscoring the import of laywomen as liturgical contributors. Biblical women and saints, as noted already, were utilized toward the moral formation of the community.

Yet, for each of these perspectives—choirs, laywomen, women of the sacred past—more was accomplished than those basic agendas. Within a historiographical record intrinsically patriarchal in nature (written by and for men), the sounds and voices of women intrude, just as they intruded in late antique society. Jacob of Sarug complained about the sounds of professional women mourners in city streets; Thomas of Marga tells us that village monks complained about the sounds of women's weaving. Yet ancient Christians in villages and cities alike took notice of the sounds of psalmody issuing from the homes, huts, or monastic dwellings of ascetic women, whether consecrated or not.[18] Women's voices mark, interrupt, add to, enrich, and fill out the historical view visible to us from the past. More than this, they are generative in the possibilities they open when we grant them our attention.

This book, then, seeks to do several things. It seeks to recover this often-ignored or unknown history of women's contribution to Christian worship. It seeks to explore what the choirs and their hymns can tell us about late antique civic life. It seeks to expand our repertoire of female sacred stories. It seeks to center liturgy as a resource for social history. Finally, it seeks to remember voices we have lost.

PRACTICALITIES

Several terms do heavy lifting in the course of this study. Here are my working definitions.

By "choir," I mean *a group who sing together in a form distinct from the surrounding group.* Distinction might be set by location, clothing, or rehearsed performance (however basic or informal). A choir could be as small as two or three persons who nonetheless lead certain sung portions of the liturgy, guiding tone, tempo, and melody; or it could be a large, more clearly organized and trained group such as the cathedral in a major city would need. It might be formally or informally constituted within the local community; its identity was functional rather than an institutional designation.

By "authority," I mean *a quality of significance recognized by others as legitimate, morally weighty, and collectively affirmed*. Sometimes authority was granted by institutional means: a ritual, a hierarchical designation, a practice from oral or written tradition. Or it could be gained within a community by accrued or enacted moral status.

By "laity" ("people"), I mean *nonordained persons* as distinct from ordained clergy. The term most often designates those who were married or part of a "secular" household. In this sense, the laity were not the same as a liturgical congregation, which could include persons of every class and status: ordained, consecrated, monastic, ascetic, or secular. It is also the case that monastics and consecrated widows and virgins were all "laity" insofar as they were not ordained clergy.

Finally, by "sacred," I mean *having an overt intersection with the divine*. I use the term "sacred stories" rather than "myths," for example, when referring to stories that carry the revered traditions of divine-human relationship, whether pagan, Jewish, or Christian, and whether or not they are contained in a particular collection of writings (e.g., a canon, the Bible). Pagan sacred stories did not have a canonical literary form, although Homeric texts sometimes served that purpose. For Jews and Christians during late antiquity, it is more accurate to speak of a "canon of sacred stories" rather than a canonical text (the Bible). Few people could have owned or had access to such a text, but many people were knowledgeable in the sacred stories of their religious tradition. Moreover, textual boundaries were malleable. There were many sacred stories about Achilles that are not in the *Iliad*; there were many revered, even ritually celebrated stories about biblical figures that are not contained in either the Jewish or Christian Bible.

Next, this book is organized in three parts. These correspond to the three perspectives represented by the Syriac women's choirs: the choirs themselves, the liturgical poetry and its performance, and the laity. In each part, I will treat both the singing voices that illuminate that perspective (chapters 1, 3, and 5) and the sung voices that contribute to our understanding of it (chapters 2, 4, and 6). There was a dialogue between the singing voices of choirs, clergy, and laity, on the one hand, and the sung voices of biblical and other holy characters, on the other. What we can learn is substantially deepened in every case when we keep the exchange of singing and sung voices as a constant dialogue.

Chapter 1 addresses when, where, how, and why women sang in ancient Mediterranean religions broadly, whether pagan, Jewish, or Christian. Within this overall view, what is the evidence for Syriac women's liturgical choirs, and what was distinctive about their ministry and authority, both within Syriac Christian communities and in comparison with their Greek and Latin counterparts?

Chapter 2 analyzes the short but striking literary characterizations of ancient Syriac women's choirs: in the fourth-century hymns of Ephrem the Syrian, and in two Syriac sources of the late fifth or early sixth century that attribute the founding of Syriac women's choirs to Ephrem himself—the homily by Jacob of Sarug "On Mar Ephrem" and the anonymous Syriac *Life of St. Ephrem*. Each of these sources used different imagery, justification, and authority to account for Syriac women's choirs and their importance. I contrast these literary portraits with several prominent non-Syriac accounts of women's sacred song: Philo of Alexandria's presentation of the (Greek, apparently Jewish) Therapeutrides, Methodios of Olympos's (Greek, Christian) *Symposium* with its dramatic all-female cast and closing choral performance, and Jerome of Stridon's (Latin, Christian) description of the heavenly choir of women martyrs and saints at the end of his *Letter to Eustochium*. Despite shared themes, there are illuminating differences between these, not least between an existing practice and utopian projections.

Chapter 3 considers issues of gender and performance: When, where, and how did women's voices sound in Syriac liturgical celebrations? What were the performative logistics for choirs and congregations? What were the poetic forms for the imagined voices of biblical women and women saints, and what were their modes of presentation?

Chapter 4 analyzes especially prominent poetic portraits of biblical women in Syriac hymns and sung homilies. I focus on the Old Testament figures of Sarah the wife of Abraham, Tamar the daughter-in-law of Judah, Rahab, and Ruth (as Syriac authors read them); and from the New Testament the Virgin Mary, Mary and Martha of Bethany, the Sinful Woman, the Canaanite Woman, the Samaritan Woman, and the Hemorrhaging Woman. The complex portrait of Eve follows these. I argue that these portraits inflected the work of women's choirs and female laity typologically and theologically, as well as literarily.

Chapter 5 turns directly to the laity as liturgical participants, including women and girls. What were the forms of their contributions, and what was their authority? I consider liturgical participation as ethically and morally formative, following models from Ephrem the Syrian and Jacob of Sarug, attending to their notions of the impact of sound on one's disposition, both individual and collective. I discuss two major biblical (lay)women—the Virgin Mary and the Sinful Woman (Luke 7:36–50)—presented by Ephrem and Jacob as models for priesthood.

In chapter 6, I consider liturgical listening. What kind of participatory agency did liturgy allow for the listener? How did performance impact the listener's reception of sacred teaching? Consideration is given to the stock characters and scripts with which biblical stories were retold, and how these presented wives, mothers, daughters, and widows. What was the impact when the living voices of liturgical participants offered these imagined voices of the sacred past in response to late antique realities? Gender permeated what one heard, how one heard, and how one granted value or meaning in the liturgical exchange.

A short afterword glances at the overall history of Syriac women's choirs: from the scarce but richly textured evidence of late antiquity to the absence of historical evidence from the twelfth through the nineteenth century to their reemergence in the twentieth century and their revitalization in the twenty-first. The work of Syriac women's choirs in the present differs in many respects from that of late antiquity. The continuities as well as the contrasts are significant, and hopeful for the future.

Western scholars of Christian history have often overlooked Syriac Christianity, focusing instead on the better-known Greek and Latin traditions. In part, this has been due to a genuine lack of access to Syriac sources. The past fifty years have seen a near revolution in this regard, yet many people, including scholars, remain unfamiliar with Syriac literature. Hence I have chosen to quote abundantly from the ancient sources. Their words shine with luminous eloquence, even in translation.

Finally, a word on "women" and "gender" as categories of historical inquiry. Both have yielded extensive bibliographies in recent decades, transforming how historians do our work, what we seek, whom we recognize, and how we tell our stories. As will be apparent throughout the chapters that follow, I am much indebted, in particular, to the critical theories and methodologies that feminist scholars have offered.[19] In writing about women in ancient Christianity, however, in no way do I mean to reduce historical persons to essentialist notions of binary genders, male or female. Nor do I think the ancients thought so reductively. Rather, I hope to demonstrate that ancient texts allow for more complex readings, even within the totalizing discourse of patriarchal hegemony. Above all, as current historiographical commitments evolve toward more inclusive perspectives, I do not want to lose sight of the women: not of the past, the present, or the future.

This is a book about missing voices: Syriac voices often missing from our scholarship regarding ancient Christianity, women's voices lost from our historical records, and biblical voices absent from the sacred stories that underlie both that history and its memories through the treasured legacy of scripture. In any history, of course, much is lost. Many voices go unheard and forgotten. In the present instance, however, we have a historical record of women's voices singing, and women's imagined voices sung. That record survives. It enables us—however tentatively—to recognize, if not to reconstruct, something of what has disappeared. It is my hope to honor these missing voices, and, by what is written here, to remember what has been forgotten.

1

Singing Voices

Women's Ministry, Women's Authority

The women's choirs of Syriac Christianity first appear in occasional hymns of Ephrem the Syrian (d. 373) during the fourth century. In his second hymn on the resurrection of Christ, for example, he acclaimed their sound and urged the congregation to let the women's songs fill their ears.[1]

The timing and nature of Ephrem's witness are important. Syriac women's choirs come into view at a particular historical moment and for a particular task. Ephrem composed his remarkable hymns in response to urgent need in the Christian communities of Nisibis and Edessa: the education of the faithful during the volatile circumstances of his day. Ephrem indicates that women's choirs performed these hymns and were essential to their effective pedagogical work.

Late antiquity was a time of dramatic religious change in the Roman Empire. Finally legalized in 312 under the emperor Constantine I, Christianity soon rose to political and social domination. Constantine granted Christians imperial favor, showering them and their churches with political, economic, and social benefits on an astounding scale. These policies continued under his successors. By the end of the fourth century, Christianity had been declared the state religion of the Roman Empire—an empire extending from Britain to Persia, both north and south along the Mediterranean Sea—and had spread well beyond Roman borders, especially to the east, to Persia, India, and beyond.

Church historians speak of this era as the time of Christianity's "triumph," but the reality was chaotic. In a matter of decades, Christianity had grown from a small, sometimes persecuted sect to a dominant force in the Roman Empire. Converts flooded into churches as the social structure fluctuated to accommodate the change. Church leadership scrambled (with considerable imperial help) to stabilize

FIGURE 1. A wealthy Edessan family with names in Edessan Aramaic script. Moqimu, funerary couch mosaic, Edessa, 3rd cent. CE. World History Archive/Alamy Stock Photo.

and standardize an infrastructure, including biblical canon, confessional creed, sacramental practices, and liturgical order. Above all, they scrambled to educate: about the Bible and its correct interpretation, about right beliefs as opposed to wrong ones—"orthodoxy" as opposed to "heresy"—and about devotional practices.

Liturgy became, quite literally, the church's school. In cities, towns, and villages, Christians gathered daily for morning and evening prayers, and for the eucharistic liturgy on Sundays and feast days. Every gathering was occasion for instruction. Indeed, one of the strongest characteristics of late antique worship—something that would change in later centuries—was its pedagogical focus.[2] In this situation, song became a tool for teaching and learning. Along with traditional musical expressions, new forms of presentation developed. Distinctively in Syriac, however, performance of new hymn forms was granted to women's choirs, presenting them with a new role as liturgical performers and teachers. The combination would prove to be an enduring and distinguishing aspect of Syriac Christian history.

In this first chapter, I will survey the evidence for the ancient Syriac women's choirs. Chronology is important, and so, too, awareness of inconsistency in what the sources present. Scholars of Christian history have often emphasized formal offices, canon law, and liturgical rubrics when considering the authority, role, place, and function of different groups within Christian liturgy.[3] But such emphasis on formal structures is anachronistic for the unsettled circumstances of late antiquity. I will argue that the evidence for Syriac women's choirs requires us to rethink how we understand the practice and experience of ancient Christian liturgy, and how it impacted the social world of its adherents. Such a view will not overturn the long-term impact of Christianity's patriarchal legacy. But it will decenter the traditional scholarly focus on a male-centered liturgy, to allow a richer, fuller account of what took place. That account will make visible a quality and level of women's contributions that scholars have largely missed.

Syriac women's choirs were part of a larger culture of religious singing across the ancient Mediterranean world. Beginning from the shared perspective will draw the qualities of difference into view. We must start, then, by asking: When and why did women sing in sacred contexts? How did their voices matter?

SINGING WOMEN IN THE ANCIENT MEDITERRANEAN WORLD

Religion in the ancient Mediterranean functioned relationally: religions bound the members of a community to one another through inherited traditions of actions, stories, and social and political order; and they bound the human and divine domains through constant ritual practices, individual and collective, domestic and civic, rural and urban. The proper functioning of religion cultivated beneficial relations in both domains: within human society and in the human-divine relationship. Its reach was comprehensive and normative. As such, religion delineated a place and role for every member of the community. These were demonstrated by and through the rituals in which people engaged, and by and through their manner of participation. While the religious systems of the Mediterranean tended to be hierarchical, with some actors and roles deemed to be more powerful, more valuable, or more important politically or socially than others, every role was critical to the well-being of the whole.[4]

Girls and women played numerous roles in the religions of the ancient Mediterranean.[5] They were priestesses and prophetesses. They were participants in processions, assigned to carry ritual implements important for the occasion. They were weavers of cloth for statues or temple adornments; patrons who donated important cultic items; devotees who spoke or sang prayers, prophecies, invocations, lamentations, or other forms of ritually significant words. They were faithful worshippers who cleansed or purified bodies, spaces, or cultic objects. Sometimes the context was exclusive by gender; sometimes both males and females were included. Depending on the immediate occasion, the ritual action might take place in a home, at a temple or shrine, in a field, or in a civic space. Each mode of participation and each location offered activity that was valued by the larger community. Among girls' and women's most frequent contributions was that of song.

Choirs of girls or women were familiar components of religious activity in Greek and Roman cultures, regularly distinguished—and thereby separately valued—from choirs of boys or men, and from the combined singing of local civic communities. Throughout the history of ancient Greece, for example, choirs provided a socially permissible means for female presence, participation, and speech in the public sphere.[6] Thus did Kallimachos summon girls and women to sing at the annual Thesmophoria festival for Demeter in Alexandria: "Sing, virgins, and mothers join the chorus: 'Demeter, all hail, nurse of many, giver of full measure.'"[7] Sometimes described by male authors in disparaging terms, these choirs were yet recognized by all as necessary for proper religious activity.[8]

For major festivals, choirs were organized ahead of time for training; dance often accompanied song. These periods of training were an important means of education for young girls. The metrical and melodic word patterns as well as the rhythms of movement aided memorization of the hymns, inculcating fundamental social and ethical commitments along with sacred stories of gods, goddesses, and human–divine interaction.[9] At Delos, Delphi, and Thebes, choirs of young girls sang and danced in honor of Apollo and Aphrodite. On Samos, choruses of girls and boys performed cultic worship for Artemis.[10] Pausanias spoke of the choirs of girls and women who sang in honor of Eileithyia at Olympia. Plutarch wrote of the women of Elis singing invocational hymns to Dionysios. Diodoros of Sicily described the women's rites sponsored by many Greek cities biennially for Dionysios, during which groups of matrons offered hymns of praise.[11]

In performance, choruses sang the sacred stories of their communities: their histories, their relationships with their divinities (female choirs sang for both male and female deities), and their collective memories. Such stories spoke to the community, and for it; they negotiated a past that was meaningful to the present. They modeled the community's future.[12] The singing inscribed female voices and female presence into the full fabric of community life, granting girls and women a culturally authoritative place. Even when men and boys predominated as ritual leaders and performers, such activities required the participation of girls and women and, often, their singing voices. At the same time, it was precisely such collective ritual that naturalized gendered social norms. Female voices sang their own circumscribed places and roles, at once affirmed and constrained in their collective worth.[13]

Roman religion seems to have gained appreciation for the significance of female singing beginning in the third century BCE and continuing thereafter, and perhaps under Greek influence.[14] When the emperor Augustus convened the Secular Games in 17 BCE, a choir of twenty-seven boys and twenty-seven girls sang a hymn composed by Horace in alternating verses.[15] The processions, prayers, and singing of Roman matrons were a crucial part of devotion to the goddess Juna Regina.[16] Under the early Roman Empire, the cities of the eastern provinces included *hymnodoi* (hymn singers) among their prized civic associations. They commemorated them in inscriptions and civic documents in places like Smyrna, Pergamum, and Ephesos. The evidence contains limited but sure attestation of women's cultic singing in this distinguished capacity.[17]

Other voluntary associations included hymn singing among their cultic activities. Early Christian communities such as the one encountered by Pliny the Younger in Bithynia in the early second century CE resembled such associations, in part because of their practice of gathering at dawn, men and women together, for the singing of hymns and sharing of a meal.[18] But the trained, polished performances of choirs carried a different sonic valence than the collective singing of groups or communities, whether of single or mixed gender. Choirs presented an authorized voice of sacred content, through a medium of heightened speech, rendered more distinctive by a ritually significant occasion.[19]

The possible exception for female choirs during the Roman period may have been in formal contexts of Jewish temple and synagogue worship. Yet there is evidence for the importance of women's participation in Jewish communal worship, and particularly in hymnody.[20] The Hebrew Bible included memory of women's singing and, possibly, women's choirs for important celebrations in Israel's sacred past (e.g., Ex 15:20–21; Jd 21:21; Ez 2:65; Neh 7:67; Ps 68:26; 2 Chr 31:18, 35:25; Jer 9:17–18). The recollection of Miriam leading the women in song at the crossing of the Red Sea in Exodus 15:21 was especially prominent, discussed at length in Philo of Alexandria as well as rabbinic texts.[21] Miriam's model was also significant for Christian writers, and indeed for the Syriac understanding of women's choirs, as we will see in due course.

Jews of the Greco-Roman era worshipped in a variety of communal venues: in *proseuche* (houses of prayer) established in diaspora communities, synagogues in the Land of Israel, and, until its destruction in 70 CE, at the Jerusalem temple.[22] Practices differed by locale, but there seems to be consistent indication of women's presence and participation, especially in collective prayers and song. There were certainly elements of Jewish worship, as for all Mediterranean religions, that were exclusive to men. However, these did not overshadow the evident valuation of women's voices in worship assemblies of different kinds. There is much that we do not know about the actual performance of hymns, whether in the Dead Sea Scroll communities, the early synagogues of Judea and Galilee, or the temple itself.[23] Best known is Philo of Alexandria's striking presentation of male and female singing among the ascetic Therapeutae of Egypt.[24] Scholars remain divided as to whether the Therapeutae were a historical community or whether they were a literary construction composed by Philo for philosophical purposes.[25] Still, it is worth noting that Philo did not question the validity of women's singing in sacred choral formation.[26] On the contrary, his depiction accords with gendered choral practices otherwise prevalent across the ancient Mediterranean, especially in the practice of double choirs.[27]

The picture for Jews changed in late antiquity, when we have a greater diversity of data but face major problems of historical reconstruction. Detailed rabbinic references to liturgical practices present a minefield of problems, both with respect to dating and because they are apparently irreconcilable with the tantalizing remains of elaborately decorated late antique synagogues as sites of regular religious meetings.[28] A rich corpus of Hebrew, Aramaic, and Samaritan hymnography known as piyyutim began to emerge by the late fourth century, showing interesting parallels to the surging vitality of Christian hymnography of the same period in Greek and Syriac.[29] Yet there is no sure evidence regarding performance, apart from internal textual indications of responsive refrains (for the congregations? for choirs?).[30] How exactly to piece together these disconnected components remains a challenge, including the questions of when, how, and in what capacities women were involved.[31] However, as with broader Mediterranean custom, women's religious singing was also located in other registers of Jewish activity: in domestic devotion, in contexts of birth and death, and in those of communal song for festival celebrations.[32]

A strong consensus has emerged among scholars that we can best understand developments of Judaism and Christianity in the Roman Empire not through an idea of "influences" in various directions, but rather in terms of broader shared notions of piety, and broader shared cultures of religious expression, whether music, prayer, hymnography, or other aesthetic modes.[33] Certainly here is an important instance: a regular activity of religious singing was normative for all religious persuasions across the ancient Mediterranean. It occurred daily and on special occasions in cities and villages, in domestic, civic, rural, and cultic locations. It provided a continual presence of female voices in public contexts, a factor often overlooked by scholars when considering women's places and roles in the ancient world.

In fact, scholars have often given more attention, and somehow more credence, to the moral disparagement with which ancient authors characterized female musicians or singers of the theater, brothel, or banquet than they have to this constancy of religious song.[34] Female performers were part of these widely popular yet socially problematic contexts, as also were male musicians and singers.[35] Often the requisite performers were slaves, and their sexual activity was an expected component of their status.

Early Christian leaders condemned such musical activity, whether by male or female performers. But early Christian writers also conflated these entertainment performances with traditional religious practices, refusing to distinguish between

FIGURE 2. Slave woman with harp. Bishapur Palace, mosaic floor pavement, Bishapur, Iran (Sasanian era), ca. 260 CE. Louvre Museum/© 2005 GrandPalaisRmn (musée du Louvre)/Franck Raux.

contexts or occasions when discussing their rivals. Their characterizations utilized the strategies of rhetorical invective, including gendered stereotypes and sexual slander, as a means for discrediting other religions.[36] So, for example, Tertullian scorned pagan liturgy for closely resembling theater performances in their ritual and musical elements.[37] Elsewhere, he opined that a pagan husband would have nothing to sing to his (Christian) wife except for "some piece, no doubt, which is popular in theaters and pothouses . . . [,] some song which sounds in the throat of the devil himself."[38] By contrast, he insisted, Christ rejoiced in Christian marriages where husband and wife shared in song: "Psalms and hymns they sing to one another, striving to see which one of them will chant more beautifully the praises of their Lord."[39] John Chrysostom's vicious caricature of Jewish festal celebrations employed the same rhetorical tropes when he likened synagogues to brothels and theaters, and the musical aspects of Jewish festal processions to performances of public indecency.[40] Needless to say, John's descriptions of Christian festal processions were the polar opposite. These he presented as occasions of sober majesty, even when filled with joyous acclamations and song—and this despite his vivid complaints about rowdy liturgical behavior.[41] Basil of Caesarea, for one, scolded his congregation when Christian celebrations of Easter included drunken mayhem replete with immodestly dressed women who danced while singing "obscene ditties."[42]

For ancient Mediterranean communities, musical performances carried moral resonance. Women's singing might provide the measure of piety in instances of rightly performed religious ritual, or of impiety on occasions of scandalous activity.

FIGURE 3. Elegant women with musical instruments, either a theater scene or a banquet. See Gavrili, "A New Approach." Maryamin mosaic, Homs, Syria, 6th cent. CE. Public domain.

Gender and performance were fundamental means for moral coding, whether in written or other forms of public discourse. Thus, rhetorical conventions utilized gendered religious expression for purposes of praise or blame.[43] For example, Livy would famously use the behavior and decorum of women at sacred gatherings to disparage the arrival of the Bacchic rites at Rome. In sharp contrast, he employed these same descriptive elements to celebrate and affirm the arrival of the cult of the Great Mother from Asia Minor.[44]

Separate male and female choirs could present the image—and sound—of the pious, well-disciplined, rightly ordered social community, as in a fresco from the temple of Isis at Herculaneum. The fresco portrays an elaborate altar at the front of the scene where a priest performs a sacrifice. He is flanked behind by a male choir on the left and a female choir on the right, standing in impeccable lines, attentive to a man (the choir director?) standing in the center as the scene pans back to the temple entrance.[45] As noted, Philo's depiction of the male and female choirs of the Therapeutae offers a similarly idealized portrait where the voices of men and women expressed unison on earth and together with heaven.[46]

In turn, and by contrast, when Christian bishops wished to depose the controversial bishop Paul of Samosata in 268 CE, they relied on just such morally freighted depiction to discredit his ministry. Gathered in synod, they condemned

FIGURE 4. Double choir, men on the left and women on the right, in a ceremony of the cult of Isis. Wall fresco, Herculaneum, 1st cent. CE. Museo Archeologico Nazionale, Naples, Compania, Italy. Peter van Evert/Alamy Stock Photo.

Paul's Christology. But, further, they disparaged his worship services as disordered: a women's choir sang hymns that glorified Paul instead of Christ, while the congregation behaved indecorously, shouting, clapping, stamping their feet, and waving handkerchiefs.[47] The account is well known from Eusebios of Caesarea's *History of the Church*, and is often cited as a key instance of Christian opposition to women's liturgical singing. But one should note how Eusebios crafted the episode. The "heresy" of Paul lay in his Christology. Yet the scandalized bishops (and Eusebios's account of their synod) focused on Paul's behavior generally, and then specifically in the Easter liturgy, where "he arranges for women to psalmodize him in the middle of the church on the great day of the Pascha."[48] The women's singing receives only this scant mention, where it is clear that the hymns dedicated to Paul, rather than the women singing, were the real problem. Nonetheless, as Eusebios presents the episode, gender and performance are strategically highlighted categories by which to condemn the renegade bishop. A counterfoil here would be the choir of virgins depicted by Methodios of Olympos (d. 313) in his *Symposium*, chastely singing the hymn of Thekla in honor of virginity.[49] I will discuss Methodios's depiction as well as that of Philo's Therapeutae in more detail in chapter 2. But it is important to note that Christian authors, like others of the ancient Mediterranean, might depict women's voices to indicate virtue or vice, piety or impiety, depending on their purpose.

Female religious singing was an ordinary sound of daily life in the ancient Mediterranean world: appropriate, familiar, and beloved. Organization as choirs provided a formal, institutionally authorized mode of performance that further highlighted female voices. There was a delicate balance here between containment and valorization. Religious ordering provided a designated place and role for female voices, marking their sound as crucial to the community's wholeness even while delineating contours beyond which that sound should not stray. The notion of right order (Greek: *taxis*) was fundamental to ancient Mediterranean societies, a notion at once inclusive and hierarchical.[50]

CHRISTIAN SONG

For Christians, singing was basic to worship from the very start. New Testament epistles both described and encouraged the singing of hymns at the gatherings of Christ followers (1 Cor 14:15, 26; Eph 5:19; Col 3:16). The book of Revelation envisioned hymn singing as part of the ultimate eschatological celebration (Rev 5:8–10, 15:3–4). In every form of earliest Christian literature, from a rule book such as the *Didache*, to the letters of Ignatius of Antioch, to the apologists such as Justin Martyr or Tertullian, to extracanonical literature such as the *Protogospel of James* or the *Acts of John*, hymns are mentioned and singing prescribed whether for individual, domestic, or collective moments.[51]

The earliest surviving Christian hymn collection is the *Odes of Solomon*, dating probably to the mid-second century. Extant partially in several languages, it survives almost complete only in Syriac.[52] It is in fact the earliest nonbiblical Syriac text we have. In their chiastic form and to a certain extent in their content, these odes resemble the biblical Psalms. Some identify the odist (or singer) as a prophetic liturgical presence.[53] Beautiful and enigmatic, the *Odes of Solomon* are a harbinger of the hallowed place that Syriac Christians would grant their liturgical song. Baby Varghese starts from these odes when he charts the development of early Syriac liturgy as something best followed through examination of its hymnography.[54]

Changes to poetic form and performance marked a major turning point for Christian singing in the fourth century, and Syriac apparently led the way. The greatest Syriac hymnographer, Ephrem the Syrian, offered a kind of revolution when he developed the form of sung poetry called the *madrasha* (pl. *madrashe*) for liturgical use. Earlier Christian hymns were sung either by a solo cantor or by everyone together. Ephrem's compositions used short stanzas or verses (usually four to six lines) punctuated by a brief, repeated refrain. A chanter or choir sang the verses, and the choir led the congregation in the refrains: a sung dialogue took place. Similar forms would appear in Latin with the hymns of Ambrose of Milan, and in the emerging Greek kontakion, brought to glorious heights in the sixth century by Romanos the Melodist, himself much influenced by the Syriac poets Ephrem and Jacob of Sarug. Interestingly, the Jewish *piyyutim* emerging in this same period also used the pattern of verses and refrains. But it seems to have appeared first in Syriac with Ephrem.[55]

The fourth century marked a new stage of development as Christians gained public visibility and greater political and social impact. Their liturgical activity expanded, with increasingly structured expression; services multiplied in kind, form, and duration.[56] Late antiquity brought the elaboration of sacred time with the establishment of the great feasts of the Christian year—Easter, Christmas, and in due course other celebrations of the life of Christ, the Virgin Mary, and martyrs and saints of Christian history. Vestments, incense, candles, processions; jeweled liturgical instruments such as crosses, book covers, chalices, patens, ewers, wine strainers, fans, lamps, and chandeliers; church decoration with mosaics, frescoes, and tapestries; architectural diversity—any and all forms of adornment increasingly enhanced Christian worship as the size and scope of congregations and services grew. The appearance of trained choirs, professional chanters, and dedicated hymnographers took place in this context.[57] Congregational singing continued, now ritually intersected into a veritable symphony of liturgical song in new forms for new purposes.[58] In Syriac churches, women's choirs were notably present as the sonic landscape expanded.

SYRIAC WOMEN IN CHRISTIAN MINISTRY

Syriac women's choirs grew out of other generally recognized forms of women's ministry in late antique Syriac churches. Like their counterparts in other Christian communities, Syriac Christians from an early period designated ministries for women as consecrated widows and deaconesses. Evidence for these offices appears in rule collections that circulated across the different languages of ancient Christianity, for which the Syriac versions provide some of our earliest manuscript witnesses.[59] Inscriptional evidence is also extant in Syriac for women's offices, particularly the deaconesses, along with abundant literary attestation in letters, hagiography, and historical chronicles.[60] In the case of deaconesses, it seems likely that the office lasted longer in Syriac-speaking churches than among Greek or Latin Christians, perhaps into the twelfth century, though it may not have been actively exercised at that time.[61]

From the Syriac evidence, one might characterize the early Christian office of widow in terms of concern for public propriety: how to provide an acceptable social location and (meager) economic means for Christian widows, such as would allow them to refuse remarriage and serve the church instead.[62] Syriac church canons mandated that the local church award their keep, in addition to that of orphans and the poor; their seating in church accorded with that privilege. In turn, the widow should serve the church through the offering of her prayers, either in her own home or else at her designated place in church during liturgical celebrations. Only occasionally was she directed to other ritual actions, such as anointing the baptized.[63] By the sixth century, this office fades. The practice of the church's provisions for widows, orphans, and the poor continues, but the sense of a special consecration or designated ministry is no longer evident.

For deaconesses, the Syriac evidence is abundant and also at some points distinctive.[64] The Syriac version of the *Didascalia Apostolorum*, parts of which probably date to the third century, pronounced the deaconess to "stand in the place of the Holy Spirit," as the bishop stood in the place of God the Father and the deacon in the place of Christ the Son.[65] The underlying logic was immediately clear in its ancient context, for the Syriac word for "spirit," *ruha*, was grammatically a feminine noun. Indeed, prior to the year 400, Syriac authors most often referred to the Holy Spirit in the feminine gender, and there was some theological exploration of the image. In the *Didascalia*, the imagery allowed the presentation of a fully Trinitarian account of the primary Christian offices that included an authoritative role for female presence.[66] After 400, Syriac writers began to refer to the Holy Spirit almost exclusively in masculine forms. No ancient source refers to or explains this change. Perhaps it was due to increasing pressure toward the standardization of teaching and expression that accompanied Christianity's legalization and rise in the Roman Empire over the course of the fourth century.[67]

As elsewhere in late antique churches, the role of the deaconess for Syriac Christians was essentially threefold: she assisted at the baptism of women and girls; maintained order in the women's area of the church building, preventing the presence of the unbaptized during the eucharist; and provided doctrinal and spiritual instruction for women, especially in their homes. All of these were instances where ministry by male clergy might be unseemly. Baptism required ritual anointing of the entire (naked) body, as well as its full immersion in water. Since most baptisms were performed on adult converts until well into the sixth century, the need for female ritual assistance remained high throughout late antiquity. The deaconess would anoint the candidate prior to immersion and receive her from the font afterward, clothing her in a white baptismal garment. The deaconess could provide ministries of mercy, such as care for the sick or distribution of the reserved sacrament, in addition to offering spiritual counsel. Canonical sources sometimes placed the deaconess among the ranks of clergy, but most often not.[68]

In the case of both widows and deaconesses, Syriac canon collections that included the *Apostolic Constitutions* and the *Testament of Our Lord* show a tightening of restrictions and increasing curtailment of activity over the course of the fourth and fifth centuries. Occasional local canons mention the assistance of deaconesses with practical aspects of liturgy: pouring water and wine into the chalice, placing incense in the censer, lighting candles, cleaning liturgical instruments and also the sanctuary. By the sixth century and thereafter, the head of a female monastic community might also be ordained a deaconess.[69]

Widow and deaconess were the most prevalent offices for early Christian women generally. Over the course of late antiquity, these offices gained sharper delineation in church canons (whether Syriac, Greek, or Latin) and an increasingly restricted range of activities. The pattern fits the broader picture of Christian history during this period. For Christians throughout the Roman and Persian Empires, the fourth century brought a time of pronounced impetus toward standardization of structure and doctrinal expression. Facilitated by imperial support previously unthinkable, church councils provided normative rulings on matters of organization, functionality, governance, and pastoral guidance. These circulated widely across the Roman Empire and provided strong models for synodical gatherings beyond the borders, especially in Persia.

In this broad historical context, canonical and documentary evidence for women's ecclesiastical offices shows an emphasis on practical ministry by women for women, including a kind of logistical support for the male clergy. Stipulations that widows must pray in church do not integrate that function into the order of services. Designated places for seating, an assigned place in the order of distribution of communion or gifts, or preparation of liturgical instruments are indications of behavioral order rather than distinct contribution within the ritual sequences that comprised the different worship gatherings. Visitations to women at home, attention to and instruction of catechumens, care for the sick or needy, were ministries that occurred outside the church assembly proper.

Here, for Syriac Christianity, is where the evidence for women's choirs takes its distinctive turn. A conviction that women's liturgical singing was a significant form of ecclesiastical participation is apparent from two important vantage points in ancient Syriac texts. First, women's choirs were often described as consecrated virgins known as daughters of the covenant (*bnat qyama*), a Syriac designation associated with, but distinct from, the diaconate. Secondly, hymn singing and liturgical participation were commonly mentioned as basic components of ascetic discipline, especially efficacious with vows of celibacy. In what follows, I attempt to map the developments for when and how women's choirs appear in the Syriac sources. Throughout late antiquity, the terminology is inconsistent. In addition to "daughters of the covenant" (*bnat qyama*), these choirs are identified by other words for consecrated virgins: they are "chaste" or "holy" or "pure" women (*nakpatha, kanikatha, dakyatha*), all of which could be technical terms signifying an avowed celibate vocation.

In the course of the fifth century and thereafter, matters were clarified to an extent through canons or guidelines put forth by local synods and prominent bishops. Yet, even then, ecclesiastical terminology varies for these women. Inconsistency in terminology and in practices was a given for ancient Christianity.[70] What remains consistent, and, I think, important for our appreciation of what these choirs meant for ancient Syriac churches, is the twofold association of women's liturgical singing with the daughters of the covenant and with the practice of an ascetically disciplined devotional life. These associations, I suggest, provided a serious religious authority for the choirs, institutionally granted by their canonical affirmation beginning in the fifth century, but already widely accorded in the fourth within the Christian community because of the respect garnered by those pursuing a life of ascetic piety. Finally, evidence for choral training and rehearsing, scarce though it is, contributes to a picture of established contribution, valued by liturgical agents and congregations both.[71]

SYRIAC CHRISTIAN MINISTRY: DAUGHTERS OF THE COVENANT

Syriac women's choirs were often identified as daughters of the covenant (*bnat qyama*), a consecrated identity among Syriac Christians dating perhaps from the late third century and lasting for some centuries thereafter.[72] Concrete evidence for the covenanters, both male and female (*bnay* and *bnat qyama*), first appears in the early fourth century. It suggests that members of the covenant took vows of celibacy and simplicity, generally at the time of baptism, and worked in the service of their local bishop. They appear to have held a special place of honor within the local congregation, representing a kind of elite spiritual heart for the local Christian body.[73]

Concerns about vows of celibacy dominate the earliest surviving evidence for the covenanters, Aphrahat's *Demonstration* 6, "On the Covenanters," written in 336–337 in Persia.[74] Those fears recurred in literature for clergy and monastics for centuries thereafter.[75] Aphrahat's treatise is perplexingly enigmatic as a source. On the one hand, it presents an entire text devoted to those with this title. Clearly, Aphrahat spoke to a familiar and well-established group. Yet the treatise lacks social details. Speaking primarily to sons of the covenant, Aphrahat explicates the meaning of the vow, or covenant (*qyama*), to which those with this title were consecrated.[76] He urges a life of faith characterized by prayer, piety, and scrupulous moral perfection. Daughters of the covenant are directly addressed only in one section, *Demonstration* 6.7. Throughout, Aphrahat's major concern is protection of the celibacy vow through an emphasis on covenanters (both male and female) as virgins espoused to Christ. An eschatological tone prevails as he exhorts his audience that any alternative to their vow would be adultery against their heavenly Bridegroom (6.6, 14, 19). Envisioning a variety of possibilities, he follows the apostle Paul in 1 Corinthians 7:9, suggesting marriage between a son and daughter of the covenant if they desire to live in partnership rather than exposing themselves to temptation beyond their strengths. Otherwise, he advises strict separation of the sexes (6.3).

At the same time, Aphrahat admonishes the covenanters to maintain a humble public decorum with modest self-presentation. The mention of grooming, clothing, and adornment indicates that he is addressing persons of some wealth (6.8). He does not discuss a formal ministry, although his discussion evokes covenanters as townspeople whose work on behalf of the church is somehow public. And what was their work? For Aphrahat, it seems to have been a publicly evident way of life, fully apparent in their civic context, by which their celibacy was embellished through stringent moral conduct and acts of charity (6.1, 17). Noteworthy in this regard are Aphrahat's occasional musical references. These do not directly indicate liturgical contexts, but rather the devotional piety of practicing ascetics.

Thus Aphrahat speaks of the sons of the covenant as "children of the Good One." They are constantly vigilant against Satan's attacks, using the basic tools of ascetic discipline to defeat unwanted desires. Devotional singing is one such weapon. "If [the Evil One] tries to come to them in sleep, they are attentive and keep watch, singing songs and praying."[77] This singing has its celestial counterpart, for Aphrahat stresses the eschatological rewards for faithful celibates: "Those who enter the [heavenly] kingdom are glad and rejoice and dance and sing praises. For those who do not take wives are ministered to by the watchers of heaven."[78] When he speaks of the daughters of the covenant, he also refers to the musical quality of their ascetic piety: "Instead of the groans of the daughters of Eve they utter the songs of the Bridegroom. The wedding banquet of the daughters of Eve is for seven days, but [the daughters of the covenant] have a Bridegroom who never goes away."[79]

Sweet voices, of course, might also indicate moral danger. Aphrahat does not hesitate to remind the sons of the covenant that "[women] are the weapon of Satan, and through them he fights against the [spiritual] athletes. Through them he plays music at all times, for they have been like a harp for him from the first day."[80] But the voices of men were no less dangerous. Aphrahat admonishes the daughters of the covenant sternly: "You virgins who have betrothed yourselves to Christ: if a covenanter says to one of you, 'I will live with you and you will serve me,' you should say to him, 'I am betrothed to a man of royalty, and I am serving him.'"[81] For Aphrahat, absolute devotion to Christ was a performed practice requiring voiced manifestation. Like devotion, temptation was vocally expressed and vocally displayed. The resonance of holy song, the ascetic's weapon against the unholy music of Satan or words of Satan's avatars, underlay Aphrahat's evocation of trial by dialogue.

Other fourth-century Syriac sources identify the covenanters, male and female, in the context of their civic communities. While an explicit ministry is not mentioned or described, martyr texts for both West and East Syriac persecutions, under both Roman and Persian circumstances, identify sons and daughters of the covenant as figures targeted for harassment, torture, or execution, along with bishops, priests, and deacons. Instances of rape or sexual violation of the daughters of the covenant were noted among the atrocities of the persecutors. In the eyes of the civic, political realm, then, whether for Roman or Persian officials, covenanters were a visible public presence, easily targeted and distinguishable, along with the clergy, from the laity.[82] In martyr lists where multiple ranks are cited, the listing follows the taxonomy inscribed through liturgical order: bishops, priests, deacons, deaconesses (if mentioned), sons of the covenant, daughters of the covenant, laity.[83] The same order was indicated in texts that describe public liturgical processions, whether for celebrations, supplication in times of crisis, funerals, or other civic occasions.[84]

In Persian instances, the virginity of the daughters of the covenant could be a particular point of contention.[85] Several Persian martyr texts present a verbal contest between a daughter of the covenant and her tormenters over this chosen condition. The instance of Martha, daughter of Posi, is an example. Her persecutors offered her marriage as an alternative to death, even if she would not renounce her Christianity. In an extended verbal exchange with her interrogators, Martha stated her political loyalty to King Shapur II. However, she insisted on replacing human bonds with divine ones, citing God as her true father (rather than Posi, her biological father), and Christ as her true bridegroom, whose betrothal she would not rescind. Her final statement culminated with a description of the second coming of Christ as the fulfillment of the marriage vow for herself and all who were thus divinely espoused.[86]

Aphrahat and the martyr texts agree on the covenanters as a discernible civic presence. The account of Martha indicated a visible marker in clothing. Addressing her persecutors, she stated flatly: "I am a Christian, as my clothing shows."[87] Together, these texts attest that the covenanters were recognized in the public sphere by dress, comportment, and an asocial choice of celibate living arrangements.

Fourth-century sources signal a second context where covenanters were prominent: the liturgical life of the local church. Ephrem the Syrian speaks of the covenanters directly in two texts that survive only in Armenian, but articulate a web of imagery consonant with Aphrahat's and appear to be foundational for the understanding of this office. According to Ephrem's *Memre on Nicomedia* 8, the covenanters, male and female, stood apart among the congregation. Their covenant was enacted in a life adorned with prayer, fasting, peace, virginity, and chastity. The consecrated women, moreover, stood at morning and evening prayer, and on feast days and commemorations. With uplifted arms and radiant faces, their prayers were especially treasured, and, he implies, especially effective. As Aphrahat and the Persian martyr Martha had done, Ephrem tinges these references with eschatological overtones: the consecrated virgins await their heavenly Bridegroom with eager devotion; at death, they are prepared to enter their celestial bridal chamber with joy.[88] In a similar vein is a hymn surviving in Armenian composed by Ephrem to celebrate the consecration of a daughter of the covenant.[89] Again, her joy and radiance are extolled, her loyalty to her heavenly spouse acclaimed, and a life adorned with fasting, prayer, and purity exhorted. Again, the eschatological wedding feast is awaited. The hymn itself presents the liturgical context with luminous wonder.[90]

Ephrem is also the earliest source to mention women's liturgical choirs as an identifiable component of worship services. In *Memre on Nicomedia* 8, noted above, he praises the holy virgins (probably a small group) standing apart in prayer at the liturgy, whom we might understand to constitute a choir. Elsewhere, he is explicit on this point.[91] His wording often implies that the singers were consecrated virgins, a state he affirms without the title "daughter of the covenant" in a number of hymns, for example, in *Hymns on Virginity* 25:

> King Solomon took fully a thousand
> wives—a very licentious thing!
> Our glorious Lord made disciples of myriads of myriads
> of virgins—a powerful, splendid thing![92]

In some instances, he refers to the liturgical song of young girls and boys "resembling harps and lyres . . . together in innocence . . . scatter[ing] halleluiahs like blossoms."[93] The term "virgin," then, might also refer to the young unmarried, especially in instances like the Easter liturgy where Ephrem joyfully lauded the participation of the entire congregation.[94] Ephrem praised all who offered their singing voices in worship, as in *Hymns on Nativity* 22: "O peoples sing praise on the feast. . . . Sing, O Church, with a voice!"[95] But now and again he drew attention specifically to the choir of virgins: "May the chant of chaste women please You, my Lord."[96]

Because their vows were often taken at baptism, and because in the early church baptism represented a commitment of utmost sobriety, modern scholars have sometimes thought the designation of "covenanter" was incumbent on every baptized Syriac Christian.[97] Rather, with the emergence of more evidence, it is clear that the covenanters were a choice group that signified the highest level of commitment within a congregation. They represented the congregation, standing in its place, so to speak, in the presence of God, offering their prayers *with* the whole but also *on their behalf*.[98] The term *qyama* (from the root *qoph-waw-mim*, "to stand, to take a stance") carried precisely this double sense of meaning: covenant, and also stance.[99]

Early in the fifth century, Syriac sources began to identify daughters of the covenant with women's liturgical choirs, drawing together the two prominent areas of association indicated in fourth century texts: public visibility, and sacred song that was both an ascetic practice and a liturgical offering. At the same time, as ecclesiastical canons began to appear that designated liturgical singing as a duty for covenanters and especially for daughters of the covenant, the task of liturgical singing took on a more authoritative dimension by virtue of being exercised within and through an identity now presented as an office. Canonical citation inflected the singing with institutionally granted authority, even as the assigned singing granted different resonance to the office—a sacramental quality, beyond practical ministerial duties. For female covenanters, this identification of their ministry with liturgical song would be particularly important, enhancing their status within the worshipping community.

SYRIAC WOMEN'S SERVICE AND SYRIAC WOMEN'S SONG

In the early fifth century, a short set of West Syriac ecclesiastical canons ascribed to Bishop Rabbula of Edessa (d. 435) granted direct attention to the sons and daughters of the covenant, in addition to clergy (priests, deacons, deaconesses, *periodeutae* or traveling clergy, and chorbishops or [unattached] "country" bishops who circulated between villages) and monastics.[100] The Rabbula canons are the first Syriac source to offer specific delineation of the ministries, behaviors, and social and liturgical locations inclusive of the covenanters. In these canons, covenanters both male and female are assigned to separate living spaces within the civic community, either with relatives, others of their office, or, in the case of sons of the covenant, with the clergy (canons 2, 10, 22, 42). They are assigned to observe a life of poverty and abstinence (canons 11, 12, 19, 23, 24). The clergy and sons of the covenant are admonished to avoid financial or political engagement and to abstain from secular employment (canons 5, 6, 7, 8, 9, 14, 25, 26, 34, 41). These restrictions indicate that the covenanters were supported financially by their local churches, and that the presiding bishop would supply further supporting funds if needed (canons 12, 19). The sons of the covenant are to assist the clergy in providing care for the needy (canons 11, 12, 16, 24). Covenanters male and female are instructed not to walk alone in public (canons 18, 37); canon 37 places the daughters of the covenant under the supervision of deaconesses when walking in public areas.

Moreover, the Rabbula canons assigned the covenanters specific liturgical duties. The sons of the covenant were to chant the Psalms, and the daughters of the covenant to sing the Psalms and the madrashe, the teaching hymns of the church (canon 20). Both should be "constant in the [worship] service (*teshmeshta*) of the church," and attentive to "the times of prayer and the [singing of] psalms by night and by day" (canons 20, 27). Other canons in this collection prohibit the clergy and sons of the covenant from exploiting the daughters of the covenant for their own household needs. They are forbidden to "compel by force the daughters of the covenant to weave garments," and they are forbidden to be served by them (canons 3 and 4). These canons, then, present the establishment, safeguarding, and financial support of a ministry for the daughters of the covenant that was largely liturgical: a ministry of instructive song.[101]

Loosely related to the Rabbula canons was the magisterial *Life of Rabbula*, written shortly after Rabbula's death in 435.[102] Here, Rabbula is portrayed as a bishop who implemented visionary ecclesiastical discipline throughout Edessa and its environs, reforming and reinvigorating the religious, social, and political dimensions of the region. In the narrative, an important part of Rabbula's work was providing instruction and guidance for the covenanters, both men and women, and the account of that instruction is similar to the content of the Rabbula canons. In this instance, the narrative specifies that the daughters of the covenant assisted in the charitable work of the church, mentioning their service at a new women's hospital under the supervision of a deaconess.[103]

The Rabbula texts appeared at roughly the same time as the *Teaching of Addai*, an epic romance portraying the origins of Edessan Christianity in the time of the first apostles. The picture this text provided of the earliest Syriac Christian community represents the ideal underlying the fourth-century depictions of the covenanters, clarified and to some extent codified in the Rabbula canons and the *Life of Rabbula*. In this ideal, the *Teaching of Addai* presents the covenanters living in the civic community as the heart of the Christian congregation, visibly displaying a way of life that resulted in practical ministry as well as liturgical devotion:

> As for the manner of life of the whole *qyama* of men and women, they were modest, honorable, holy, and pure; apart from defilement they lived in solitude, modesty, honorably in diligent [worship] service (*teshmeshta*), relieving the burden of the poor, and visiting the sick.[104]

Two other late antique sources underscore the significance of the sons and daughters of the covenant for local Syriac churches. One is a list of biblical readings to be used when a man was tonsured as a *bar qyama*, preserved in British Library Add. 14528 and dating to the sixth century.[105] Ten possible lections are identified (some may have been listed as alternatives). Interestingly, the wedding parable of the wise and foolish virgins (Mt 25:1–13) is not included among the gospel passages, although hymns and texts about the daughters of the covenant frequently allude to this parable. Instead, the gospel passages for this service of tonsure are stern admonitions that discipleship requires the believer to renounce all family ties (Mt 10:24–39, 19:27–20:16; Lk 14:25–15:10).[106] These are combined with other Old and New Testament readings exhorting a life of spotless moral probity and spiritual warfare.

The second source is a funeral *memra* (metrical homily) by Jacob of Sarug, preached in the late fifth or early sixth century on the occasion of the death of a daughter of the covenant.[107] The homily is a sustained meditation on death as a marriage banquet for the one betrothed to Christ, offering consolation to the mourners by imagining the joy to which the woman has now passed. There is no concrete discussion of the woman's life, and little detail of her ascetic regime other than praise for her vow of virginity. Jacob, like the account of Martha the Persian martyr, mentions a distinctive dress, for which he describes a black cloth bound round the head as an indication of mourning over the crucifixion. This he calls a sign belonging to the "covenant of virgins," a mark of their betrothal to Christ.[108] The memra appears to address a mixed audience of ascetic companions (presumably other covenanters) and family members, with imagery and words of consolation suitable for both.[109] Its language marks the covenanters as cherished precisely because they remained part of their civic community even while separated out in their service to the church.

A number of Jacob's tropes, images, and sentiments from this funeral memra reappear in an anonymous burial hymn cast as a dialogue between a newly deceased daughter of the covenant and her mourning community of sisters.[110] The hymn bewails the loss of her sweet song, even as it remembers her joy in offering her voice in prayer. Grief is expressed through the imagined dialogue with and through the somber singing of her bereaved companions.[111] The tropes reappear in a similar funeral hymn ascribed to Narsai of Nisibis, and continue into present usage in a modern Syriac burial service for nuns.[112] What echoes across this funeral tradition is a sense of shared joy at singing together, whether in the present or in the life to come:

> May the Lord, who has separated you from our company,
> Give you joy in the bands (*gude*, "choirs") of chaste virgins there,
> And may he cause the grief of your sisters to pass away,
> And may they rejoice along with you at the resurrection.[113]

These texts, for the service of tonsure and for funerals, are reminders of the type of public status covenanters held in a civic context: fundamentally defined by a relationship of service to the church rather than relationship to a family by blood or marriage, and marked by a vow of celibacy that carried public weight.[114] The status of consecrated virgin or celibate (for some covenanters had been previously married) provided a quality that framed and distinguished the work of covenanters, whether charitable assistance or liturgical service. It is this sense of distinctive public status in a fully civic context that is important for their work of singing in civic, nonmonastic churches.[115]

Syriac sources present a general account of the daughters of the covenant similar to those women known elsewhere in late antiquity as *asketriai, kanonikai, subintroductae,* or *syneisaktoi*: consecrated virgins in the service of the church.[116] These, too, held a special status in local congregations by virtue of their vow of virginity. They also appear to have provided practical assistance to clergy and bishops, including dedicated liturgical participation. Aphrahat's admonitions against cohabitation between sons and daughters of the covenant recurred in fifth-century Syriac canons, demonstrating that spiritual marriage was sometimes practiced (or at least sought), as also in the case of the *syneisaktoi*.[117]

In fact, the ministry of the sons and daughters of the covenant seems most like that of the *philoponoi* of Alexandria. For these, a ministry of charitable work and liturgical service, especially singing, was explicitly designated under the direction of the bishop—although the sources do not specify an involvement by women.[118] Whereas the title of consecrated virgin, like the practice of spiritual marriage, appears to have generally died out as convents for female monastics became common in the fifth century, the covenanters and the *philoponoi* continued. What made the difference, undoubtedly, was the emergence of (often local) church canons, assigning specific ministries to these offices that distinguished them from deacons and monastics; and, particularly for the covenanters, their liturgical ministry as choirs. For the covenanters (and, it seems, the *philoponoi*), the role of civic ministry sometimes assisted that of the diaconate but did not replace or replicate it, so that the two offices coexisted for a very long time.[119] Nor were the covenanters eclipsed by the rise of monasticism, although gradually the terminology became interchangeable.[120] Sons of the covenant sometimes continued into clerical ranks. Daughters of the covenant might remain in their office for life.[121]

The Rabbula canons explicitly assigned a liturgical ministry for the daughters of the covenant, requiring them to participate in the daily services of the church, to chant the Psalms and to sing madrashe, teaching hymns.[122] The madrasha was the form of hymn, sometimes translated "teaching song," that Ephrem developed extensively during his storied career and that will be discussed in detail in chapter 3.[123] Significantly, sixth-century Syriac sources attribute the establishment of women's liturgical choirs to Ephrem himself, as his chosen vehicle for the performance of his madrashe in civic worship contexts.[124] Thus the anonymous Syriac *Life of Ephrem* presents his founding of the choirs:

> [Ephrem] prepared troops for battle against those heresies of which we spoke previously. He appointed teachers among all the Daughters of the Covenant who regularly came to the holy, catholic church, and taught them hymns. Evenings and mornings they would gather in church before the liturgy on the feasts of martyrs and funeral processions and they would sing.[125]

Jacob of Sarug affirmed the tradition in his homily "On Mar Ephrem": "[Ephrem] introduced women to doctrinal disputes, / with [their] soft tones (*raphyatha*) he was victorious in the battle against all heresies."[126] Elsewhere, Jacob encouraged Christians to listen closely to the "madrashe sung by the virgins with glorious voices," which "the wisdom of the Most High has given to the congregations," sung in the divine liturgy between the Psalm verses and the lectionary readings.[127]

Important in these accounts is the clear indication that Ephrem trained these choirs and rehearsed them regularly, even every day. Like the anonymous *Life*, Jacob described Ephrem teaching and rehearsing the women's choir as an eagle amid a flock of doves and partridges who "learn[ed] from him a sweet song with a pure melody. / He taught the swallows to chirp, / and the church resounded with the pure voices of pious women."[128] Since these descriptions were written more than a century after Ephrem's death, we can presume the authors were drawing on their own liturgical experience: choirs required training if they were to be effective liturgical participants. This aspect of women's choirs has not been acknowledged by scholars, but carries important ramifications for our knowledge of women's education and leadership in their local communities. What kind of skills were needed for liturgical choral ministry?

Training is indicated in the fifth-century East Syriac canons from Persia ascribed to Maruta of Maipherqat. Here *chorepiscopoi* were mandated to persuade parents in all the villages to "set some of their sons and daughters apart."[129] These the *chorepiscopos* should mark by prayer and a blessing of the laying-on of hands to consecrate them as covenanters. "Educated in doctrine and instruction," these covenanters should then be assigned for service in churches and monasteries.[130] Specifically turning to the daughters of the covenant and the deaconesses, these canons further required every village and town church to have "an order (*taxis*) of the sisters (*d-ahwatha*) . . . instructed in the scripture-lesson, and particularly in the service of the Psalms."[131] Further, a deaconess, selected from among the daughters of the covenant, must serve as supervisor.[132] In the sixth century, the West Syriac canons of Johannan bar Qursos (John of Tella) similarly prescribe that parents who have dedicated their children to be covenanters must supply them with suitable garments and send them to monasteries for proper instruction.[133] The East Syriac Synod of Mar George I in 676, Canon 9, mandated that daughters of the covenant should be distinguished by tonsure and dress, and identified the most important work of these women as the chanting of the Psalms at the offices of the church, as well as the singing of hymns (madrashe), especially in funeral processions (but not at the cemetery), at the memorial services for the dead, and at vigil services.[134]

These canons reference a training process that required basic literacy and more. Sources for the training of male liturgical agents indicate mandated study of the Bible, exegesis, doctrine, and the services of the church, including hymnody.[135] The liturgical curriculum at the famed School of Nisibis was a three-year program.[136] Local churches provided less formal but nonetheless necessary instruction.[137] In other words, for those women and men who served as liturgical agents—as readers, chanters, singers, in addition to the diaconate and clergy—it was important to understand correct church teaching, as well as to perform one's ecclesiastical function well. It was not enough to be able to sing in a polished way; one had to know the content one was singing, and to understand it rightly.[138]

An example is included in John of Ephesos's sixth-century account of the wandering recluse Simeon the Mountaineer. Simeon stumbled upon a seminomadic "heathen" village at the eastern edge of the Roman Empire. His first act in their conversion was to round up eighteen boys and twelve girls whom he tonsured as sons and daughters of the covenant. These he schooled in scripture and singing for some years, first together and then separately, when their ages became a problem for shared learning. "Loud choirs" filled the mountains thereafter, as a liturgically rich Christianity took root among the people. On his deathbed, Simeon still took delight in the singing of the women's choir, and also in the tradition of teaching that his students carried forward: "These disciples of his also had become grown women and men, and they were themselves now becoming readers and daughters of the covenant, and they were themselves teaching others as well."[139] John's narrative is important for its portrayal of covenanters as foundational to the liturgical life of the Christian community. But it is also significant as an account of the education necessary for their work of liturgical song to be effective: an education extending over years, and valued by the church as a community.

The training of women's choirs, then, included religious study in addition to musical rehearsal. Other kinds of sources may fill out this picture. There is strong Syriac evidence for women's literacy as part of ascetic training in late antiquity, including the ability to read scripture, hagiography, and ascetic and theological literature, and the ability to chant psalms and prayers of the daily offices with knowledgeable skill.[140] The sixth-century widow Euphemia provided exactly this kind of instruction for her daughter Maria in the city of Amida, where their religious knowledge and the sound of their psalmody were widely admired in the civic community.[141] John of Ephesos passed long hours of spiritual direction with the widow Caesaria the Patrician, a correspondent of the patriarch Severos of Antioch; her personal library surpassed seven hundred volumes of theological writings, and her liturgical recitation also earned John's praise.[142] Over the late sixth and early seventh centuries, the solitary Shirin was renowned throughout northern Iraq for the sound of her long hours of psalmody and sung prayer services, and also for the breadth and depth of religious reading through which she instructed the crowds of faithful who approached her for spiritual counsel.[143] She was regularly visited by other (male) monastics and local families, especially mothers and children, but also abbots and church leaders. Hagiography of women saints mentions reading together as a valued practice of women's monasteries, taking place at sung prayer services as well as other times of communal gathering.[144]

This picture from hagiography is supported by slender but intriguing manuscript evidence. Dating from as early as the fifth and sixth centuries are a number of Syriac manuscripts containing collections known as the "Book of Women," including the biblical accounts of Ruth, Esther, Judith, Susannah, and sometimes Thekla, the companion of Paul (in Thekla's case, taken from the apocryphal *Acts of Paul and Thekla*).[145] The damaged colophon for one of these collections, British Library Add. 14652, dating to the sixth century, seems to indicate that the manuscript belonged to, or was commissioned by, an abbess named Maryam.[146] Here was exactly the kind of manuscript women's monastic reading involved.

The East Syriac nun Hanah-Isho oversaw the education of her brother, the future saint Rabban Bar-ʿIdta, over the course of many years and in two different schools. She saw that his training included liturgical music, hymnography, and the order and occasions of services.[147] The role of mothers and sisters in the education of young boys was a common theme in Syriac hagiography, as in Greek.[148] It points to a culture where women valued and cared about serious religious education, including knowledge of liturgy and its music, in addition to the classical curriculum. They themselves had to have appreciation for this kind of knowledge if they were to guide their youth to its pursuit. Such background should inform our reading of the evidence for Syriac women's choirs.

Syriac canons on women's liturgical singing are quantitatively small yet qualitatively substantial. Their attention to the daughters of the covenant and a ministry of music is consistent in both West and East Syriac sources, and consistent with our evidence from other kinds of texts. While occurrences are not numerous, they indicate a codified tradition and an institutionalization of women's liturgical choirs that held their contribution in some reverence. At the same time, canon collections provide inherently problematic evidence. On what authority was a given set of canons promulgated? Over whom did they have governance? Who knew the canons were operative? How were they distributed and implemented? How were priests or bishops educated in canonical knowledge? As a possible scenario, the Maruta canons directed that the chorepiscopos should read the canons twice a year to the covenanters.[149] The *Life of Rabbula* may have depicted just such instruction in its passages where Rabbula addresses the sons and daughters of the covenant.[150] Were canons recopied by tradition, automatically, or were they actively kept in service? These are questions we cannot answer.

The Rabbula canons, for example, survive in at least seven manuscripts, dating between the sixth and nineteenth centuries.[151] But the later manuscripts significantly reduced these canons, especially those pertaining to the covenanters.[152] Canons addressing daughters of the covenant diminish over time. Local practices varied, depending on local circumstances. Yet the persistence of these canons through different synods and canon collections accords with the testimony of other texts. While the evidence of ecclesiastical rulings is problematic, women's liturgical voices continued to be marked as fundamentally integral to a fitting and effective liturgical life.

Our late antique sources indicate that the Syriac women's choirs were trained for their assigned task and regularly rehearsed. There seems to be no discussion of their musical talent as such, no reference to their voices as more beautiful than those of others nor to such a quality as a criterion for participation in a choir. There is an intriguing canon from the collection of Jacob of Edessa in the seventh century mandating that local nobility should not be permitted to read or sing at church services or festivals, but only the readers and singers "who are experienced and who read beautifully, and . . . whose voice is good." The ruling continues by explaining that untrained voices confuse the readings and offend the congregation.[153] Tensions, then, could erupt at the local level between prominent citizens or aristocratic families, and trained liturgical specialists, some of whom may have come from humbler social backgrounds. The canon is a clue, perhaps most importantly, to the audibility as well as the visibility of liturgical performance. Poor or "confused" singing was a trial for the congregation.

A liturgical commentary attributed to George of Arbela, and probably dating to the ninth century, twice likens the women's choir typologically to those who enslaved the people of God in the Hebrew Bible—a puzzling characterization. The commentary compares the seated laity at evening prayer to the humiliated Hebrews, stating that the women's singing signified the enemy captors, Babylonians or Egyptians.[154] The same commentary states that the women's singing was a method of teaching doctrine (*yulpana*). How should we understand this source? On the one hand, it appears to witness to a strong practice of women's choirs. On the other, it appears to undercut that witness. What lay behind its ostensibly negative imagery? Was there anxiety over an authoritative liturgical role for women at the time? Or was it annoyance (long suffering?) in the face of poor liturgical singing? Was the author *complaining*? In the absence of additional comment, we cannot know.

Christian women's choirs appeared at the historical moment when Christian liturgy was going through an era of dramatic expansion and elaboration, as noted above. But only in Syriac do we have evidence for a deliberate cultivation of a female teaching ministry exercised through song that served the larger local community. Now we must ask how the Syriac evidence stands in relation to the broader practices of the Greek and Latin churches.

WOMEN'S VOICES IN SACRED SONG

In some respects, Syriac women's choirs performed tasks shared by women in the larger Christian community. The chanting of biblical Psalms in private prayer, monastic offices, or in the liturgy, for example, as well as singing hymns in any liturgical event, involved ancient Christian women across the Mediterranean world. From the fourth century onward, Christian singing often included choral as well as congregational song, for women as well as men. In this regard, Christians continued the practices and habits inherited from prior religious traditions, as discussed above, in which public religious activity included and sometimes even featured the singing of girls and women.[155]

Yet modern historians often follow the position of Johannes Quasten in presuming that women were generally forbidden to participate in liturgical singing after the legalization of Christianity in the fourth century.[156] To be fair, Greek and Latin church leaders sometimes admonished women to keep silent in church, following the New Testament injunctions to that effect (1 Cor 14:34–35, 1 Tim 1:11–12, 1 Pet 3:1). Such passages are not without ambivalence, however, and are often prescriptive rather than descriptive in tone. Eusebios of Caesarea's account of Paul of

Samosata's expulsion from Antioch in 268, as noted above, did not criticize the women's choirs in Paul's church but rather the hymns Paul directed them to sing in honor of himself rather than Christ.[157] Cyril of Jerusalem exhorts that women should maintain absolute silence in church, in a passage addressing catechumens preparing for baptism.[158] It is not clear that the passage precludes singing by the baptized, although scholars have assumed it does. Isidore of Pelusium urged that women be forbidden to sing in church, on the grounds that people "misuse the sweetness of melody to arouse passion," an opinion shared by Jerome.[159] But that may have been precisely the problem in such cases: the women were singing, too well it seemed.

The rhetoric of women's singing as morally dangerous was deeply embedded in Mediterranean culture. The sirens' song from Homer's *Odyssey* 12.52 remained a potent image; there is no surprise in finding Christian variations on this motif. The Syriac *Cave of Treasures* included the story that the debauched daughters of Cain seduced the sons of Seth with lustful song and dance.[160] In another Syriac treatise on virginity, angels were thought to be immune to the "wounds" of "sweet tones."[161] Both Ephrem the Syrian and Narsai of Nisibis described Satan's seduction of Eve as a musical one.[162] The danger of music, especially when performed by women, was a trope among authors of every religious persuasion. Libanios, the famed fourth-century pagan orator of Antioch, boasted of his impeccable virtue during his student days: "I made it quite clear too that the singing girls—Scylla's heads, or neighbors perhaps more dangerous than sirens—who have wrecked the career of many a man, sang to me in vain."[163] Similarly, Jerome admonished the widow Furia, "Drive out the singer like a criminal. Cast from your house all women lyrists and harpists, the devil's choir whose songs are the deadly ones of the sirens."[164]

Yet, as we have seen, women's voices could be rhetorical markers of vice *or* virtue. Severos of Antioch mentioned disagreement as to women singing the doxology, but stated that even the apostle Paul did not prohibit women from *singing* and cited the precedent of Moses's sister Miriam in Exodus 15 to support women's liturgical participation by song.[165] The sources demonstrate differences in practice. Ambrose of Milan mentioned women's singing positively, directly taking issue with the Pauline admonition that women must keep silent in church (1 Cor 14:34); he advocated the singing of psalms as beneficial for all people.[166] Paulinus of Nola mentioned women's choirs singing psalms and hymns, both in heaven and at the shrine of St. Felix.[167] Asterios of Amaseia advocated that people should give generously to the holy virgins who sing psalms, rather than to pagan revelers singing bawdy tunes.[168] Victricius of Rouen praised the choir of virgins in his own community. Celebrating the arrival of relics sent by Ambrose from Milan circa 396, Victricius's sermon extolled, "You, too, holy and inviolate virgins, chant, chant [cf. Ps 47:6] and in your choirs dance on the paths that lead to heaven."[169] Is he referring to women's choirs chanting the biblical Psalms, or other hymns? Is the call to dance metaphorical or literal? The citation is made in passing, at the very least indicating that the singing virgins were not a controversial or problematic aspect of the liturgical order in his setting. Leontios of Constantinople praised the women's choir in the Palm Sunday liturgy as holy women who "have just sung to us through the mouth as if through the spirit."[170]

Extant textual evidence hence provides a complicated picture. The occasional admonition that women keep silent in church must be reconciled to steady mention of women's religious singing. Cyril of Skythopolis recounted the hagiographic tale of a penitent named Mary, who had been a chanter at the church of the Anastasis in Jerusalem. There she had become a cause of scandal, for which sin she fled to the desert.[171] The detail that this Mary was a chanter stands out more for its implied plausibility (that a woman was serving as chanter) than for its implication that her singing was the source of the sin.

Certainly, women's choirs accompanied the rise of monasticism in the fourth century, as women's monastic communities took primary responsibility for their own liturgical practices. The letters of Basil of Caesarea and Gregory of Nyssa's *Life of Macrina*, for example, describe such choirs of nuns and their psalmody as prominent in the daily discipline of Cappadocian convents.[172] Here, however, the women's singing may have been devoted specifically to the biblical Psalms. As such, the practice was part of the ascetic discipline of the monastic life. When Gregory describes the funeral for Macrina, he explains that he ordered the women's psalmody to control their otherwise excessive grief over the loss of their beloved founder and leader.[173]

Ascetic literature refers often to the training of nuns, and of avowed virgins, in the practice of psalmody. Athanasios of Alexandria directed that families with a virgin daughter should send her to a convent where the abbess would "teach her the order of the singing tones. With them she shall pass the night watching and shall [then] return to her house."[174] Jerome, too, despite his concerns about women singing in church, advised that psalmody was the best way to train young virgins at home.[175] The chanting of psalms was as fundamental to a woman's ascetic practice as to that of men, whether conducted in a community or in the family household.[176]

Such singing represented the divine economy no less than an appropriate disciplining of the ascetic body in its subjectivity. The desert mother Synkletica admonished her nuns to avoid foolish speech: "For it is shameful for the organ [made for singing] hymns to utter shameful statements"; she further advised that the spirit of despair should be countered "by means of prayer and singing of psalms."[177] Sometimes, particular communities of nuns were well known for their singing, as seems to have been the case at Matrona of Perge's convent in Constantinople.[178]

While psalmody invariably held a uniquely hallowed place for late antique Christians,[179] scholars have often noted that the terminology of our ancient authors was notoriously inexact. The limitation of the term "psalmody" to the biblical Psalms is sometimes clear, and sometimes uncertain; it could indicate a variety of musical forms.[180] References to the singing of choirs of nuns or virgins do not always specify exactly *what* was sung.

Choirs of nuns are mentioned periodically in late antique texts describing civic as well as monastic liturgies. They were also visibly and audibly evident in the processions that went from city to shrine at the celebration of saints or martyrs' feasts.[181] When the emperor Julian traveled through Antioch around the year 362, a choir of strident nuns harassed and taunted him with their loud singing of Psalm verses chosen to mock his rule.[182] When Gregory of Nyssa returned to his city following an extended absence, a choir of virgins greeted his arrival at the church, processing with candles like "a stream of fire coursing into the church . . . kindling the whole to a splendor with their blaze."[183] The *Life of Rabbula* described eighteen choirs of deaconesses attending the bishop Rabbula's funeral in Edessa.[184] Perhaps such citations indicate special liturgical activity—an emperor's *adventus*, a bishop's arrival, the funeral of an important church leader—as opposed to the regular services of morning or evening prayers, or the Sunday liturgy, as assigned to the Syriac daughters of the covenant. Yet the frequency of such indications gives the impression that choirs of virgins or nuns represented a valued, even revered, adornment of worship ceremonial, especially in circumstances that warranted its more elaborate or fullest expression.

According to Egeria, during the late fourth century, male and female ascetics sang antiphonally at daily predawn services in Jerusalem.[185] Although Egeria mentions what appear to be these groups as choirs only at this one point in her text (chapter 24), the following detailed description of Jerusalem's liturgical customs (chapters 25–49) refers repeatedly to the singing of hymns and psalms by all liturgical participants, clergy, laity, baptized, and catechumens. The amount of singing she mentions required some kind of formal, organized direction, such as would have been provided by trained chanters and choirs. As so often in textual descriptions of religious ritual, Egeria omitted the logistical details, probably owing to the familiarity of the practices involved. But it seems likely that the singing *monazontes* (masc. pl.) and *parthenai* (fem. pl.) mentioned in chapter 24 would have continued to take a role of musical leadership in the other services mentioned.[186]

Choirs of nuns or consecrated virgins were part of the liturgical life at Hagia Sophia and other, smaller churches in Constantinople by the sixth century.[187] Various liturgical manuals, service books, and monastic rules indicate the assignment of *asketriai* and *kanonikai* (consecrated virgins) to chant psalms in morning and evening prayers.[188] The famous list of supported staff for the cathedral and its dependent churches from the emperor Justinian's Novel 3.1.1 includes forty deaconesses, who likely also served in this capacity.[189] Novel 59.2–4 mandates the payment by local churches of consecrated women's choirs—*asketriai* or *kanonikai*, in groups of eight, each forming an *asketerion*—to serve in funeral processions, and the provision of such choirs to sing psalms at the funerals of the poor. Safeguards are specified to protect the women in cases of delayed or

FIGURE 5. Children's choir. Mosaic, Temple of Diana Tifatina, near Capua (now the Basilica of Sant'Angelo in Formis), 2nd–3rd cent. CE. Capua Provincial Museum of Campania.

delinquent payments.[190] Romanos the Melodist appears to reference a women's choir in the likeness of the myrrh-bearing women who went to Christ's tomb in his kontakion "On the Resurrection (6)."[191] The significance of these choirs as trained liturgical specialists serving in an urban context is only now receiving scholarly investigation.[192]

Constantinople was also known for its choir of orphaned children, a tradition that apparently began in the fifth century and continued for centuries thereafter.[193] By the middle Byzantine period, women identified as Myrrophoroi sang in the Easter services in Jerusalem and Constantinople, attested in ecclesiastical typika as well as the witness of visitors.[194] Anna Komnena recounted that the emperor Alexios I established choirs of male and female singers "in the manner of Solomon" for the cathedral of St. Paul; these were also associated with the choir of orphans.[195] While references in Byzantine sources are rare, the twelfth-century account of the *Timarion* indicates that choirs of nuns and "righteous laywomen" sang in the cathedral of Thessaloniki for the festival of St. Demetrius.[196] Scholarship on Byzantine choirs has only recently begun to include such evidence for women's singing. Yet these occasional indications do not imply that women's liturgical choirs were something abnormal or problematic.[197] Rather, especially as choirs of nuns or deaconesses, they seem to have been part of the liturgical experience of Byzantine society.

We may set the emergence of the Syriac women's choirs within the historical trajectory here discussed. In the late fourth century, ecclesiastical synods in the larger Roman Empire produced the first official canons to address singers, and their rank and conduct, within the church hierarchy. The evidence appears to address male chanters and singers, without reference to women; female singers may or may not have been active. Christopher Page has argued that the office of singer (*psaltēs/cantor*) developed out of that of reader, since the Canons of Laodicea make deliberate connection between the two actions and functions.[198] He has further suggested that choirs emerged from groups of ascetics who gathered to sing psalms together in urban ascetic households and on liturgical occasions such as morning and evening prayer, such as described by Egeria in Jerusalem.[199] Kaija Ravolainen has presented a more detailed analysis of canonical legislation that pursues the development of this picture.[200] Both have argued that the fourth century was the turning point at which the circumstances of liturgical expansion created the need to clarify and cultivate the role of a trained soloist, as well as that of trained groups of singers.

The case of Ephrem the Syrian and the Syriac women's choirs reflects this larger social context. Ephrem and his successors composed hymns for performance in liturgical settings, often including repeated, simple refrains. We will look at this in detail in chapter 3, but can note here that different forms of hymns required different kinds of performance. Sometimes a soloist was needed, in addition to choral singing and/or congregational singing. The historical evidence indicates that a solo liturgical singer might also serve as musical director. Distinct again was the emergence of liturgical choirs, whether professionally trained or more informally gathered and rehearsed. These developments are only partially visible from the documentary sources, whether liturgical or legislative.

Fourth-century ecclesiastical rules in Greek and Latin were also translated into Syriac and transmitted in medieval Syriac canon collections. These included the often-bewildering array of rules from earlier church synods that treat lower clergy such as deacons, deaconesses, readers, and singers—bewildering because they are often inconsistent about these lower orders, and also insufficiently descriptive. The West Syriac *Synodicon* includes a ruling from Hippolytus (ostensibly third century) that states that deacons could excommunicate subdeacons, readers, singers, or deaconesses, if necessary, but that none of those were permitted to excommunicate others. A further ruling from the same source stated that *eulogiae* (consecrated bread remaining after the eucharist was served) was to be distributed "four parts to the bishop, three parts to the presbyter, two parts to the deacons, but one part to the others, [namely] sub-deacons or readers, psalmists or singers or deaconesses."[201] Were women's choirs included under the category "singers"? As discussed above, by the fifth century there is Syriac evidence that deaconesses served as choir directors for the daughters of the covenant. Should we then understand such rulings to be applicable in the situation of Syriac women's choirs? If so, the ruling indicates that choirs were included among lower clergy who had noteworthy but limited capacity to exercise institutional authority.[202] Such associations and privileges heightened their position in the liturgy as ritual agents.

Amid all the female song here considered, Syriac women's choirs nonetheless present a distinctive picture. I would argue they were distinctive on several counts. First and surely most importantly, Syriac women's choirs stand apart because they were canonically mandated and affirmed across a series of ecclesiastical councils convened in both Roman and Persian territory, in both West and East Syriac canon collections. The assignment of liturgical singing to the daughters of the covenant—or to consecrated virgins, "sisters," or deaconesses—granted them an established place in church ritual order, with an institutionally recognized and conferred religious authority. Their liturgical participation was not happenstance; it was deliberate, weighted, and valued.

Second, the assignment of the choirs to sing the madrashe was also distinctive and arguably unique. In the instances cited for Greek or Latin practices, the types of hymns sung by women's choirs are not specified apart from the Psalms. But the madrashe were a genre of Syriac poetry, of several types, which had a particular function; they were composed to instruct. Their subject matter in their liturgical forms was largely biblical.[203] Crucial to the doctrinal well-being of church congregations, madrashe provided a mode of sacred instruction distinct from, yet consonant with, that provided by bishops and clergy. It was different again, yet also compatible with, that offered in spiritual counsel by holy men and women who guided the faithful. In late antique Syriac ecclesiastical canons, the proper presentation of this instruction by means of madrashe was the purview of women's choirs. Greek and Latin hymns had different literary forms, and different performative requirements; we know of none assigned specifically to women's choirs apart from the Psalms.

Syriac women's choirs developed in institutional contexts that authorized and validated their work, and within social and cultural situations that fostered appreciation of that work. As the present chapter has argued, both social communities and ecclesiastical leaders saw these choirs as fitting and appropriate for proper liturgical practice: fitting and appropriate as expression of right human social order, and, further, in the enactment of right human-divine relation performed through sacred ritual.

A number of late antique Syriac texts offered reflection on how and why the women's choirs should matter for the larger Christian congregation. Although rare, these accounts addressed the theological significance of women's voices in the liturgical context, and especially the fact that they sang the madrashe. Poetic genre, liturgical performance, and biblical exegesis were tightly intertwined in these citations of women's liturgical singing. To these matters we now turn.

2

Singing Women

Portraits and Meanings

Extant evidence for Syriac women's liturgical singing in late antiquity is almost exclusively textual. Chapter 1 identified certain methodological considerations important for its assessment. In the case of documentary evidence such as synodical canons, for example, caution must be exercised regarding authority, distribution, compliance, and transmission. In the case of literary texts, moreover, I argued that ancient rhetorical conventions often inflected literary citations of women's singing, coding women's voices with binary qualities of vice or virtue through gendered tropes. Women's singing could represent moral and theological laxity, danger, or depravity; or it could represent utopian ideals, harmony, and perfection.[1]

Three literary accounts of Syriac women's choirs stand out for their presentation of how these choirs functioned and how they were perceived: (1) a composite picture drawn from the fourth-century hymns of Ephrem the Syrian; (2) the extensive description in Jacob of Sarug's homily "On Mar Ephrem," composed at some point prior to Jacob's death in 521; and (3) the short but detailed chapter 31 from the anonymous *Life of Ephrem* circulating by the mid-sixth century. All three carry important ramifications for understanding how the choirs performed, and how performance shaped and impacted reception of the hymns they sang. I will turn specifically to issues of performance in the next chapter. Here, first, we must consider these portraits as literarily crafted, each in turn.[2]

EPHREM: WOMEN'S VOICES AND BIBLICAL TYPOLOGY

In a hymn composed for Easter, Ephrem the Syrian highlighted the women's choir: "Our ears are filled with the musical strains of virgins."[3] In honor of the feast, he presented the image of the church in its gathered wholeness. To the liturgy,

44

he sang, all Christians brought a gift appropriate to their place; with these, the collective church wove a crown of beauties to offer to God in thanksgiving:

> Let us plait a magnificent crown for [God];
> . . . .
> The bishop weaves into it
>   his biblical exegesis as his flowers;
> the presbyters their martyr stories,
>   the deacons their lections,
> the young men their alleluias,
>   the boys their Psalms,
> the virgins their *madrashe,*
>   the rulers their achievements,
> And the lay people their virtues.
> Blessed be the One who has multiplied victories for us.[4]

Such was the clarity of place Ephrem identified for the women's choirs: a place defined amid the ranks of worshippers from their different life stations, their different genders, their different liturgical duties, their different roles. The instructional work of the madrashe belonged to the virgin choirs: a kind of teaching distinct from homily or sacred readings or songs of praise by others.

In some hymns, Ephrem speaks directly to a choir of women. When he does, he points to their singing as instructive not only for the (correct) teaching proclaimed through their voices, but, further, that declared by their example. To Ephrem, these women stand as illustrations and reminders of God's work in a human time that is also sacred time. Their place is typological. They are living icons of biblical figures, fulfilling particular roles from the biblical salvation drama, as God's work continues its course through the history of the church. In Ephrem's *Hymns on Virginity*, for example, the women's choir represents the type of the Wise Virgins from Matthew 25:1–13, whose lamps stayed lit to receive their Heavenly Bridegroom: "Since the time of the Bridegroom is not revealed to us, you virgins have become our Watchers / so that your lamps might gladden, and your hosannas might glorify."[5] Most often, however, Ephrem exalts the women's choir as consecrated virgins who stand as types of the Virgin Mary. Because of Mary, women's condition was transformed from the shame of Eve to a state of glory:

> Let chaste women [sing] praise [to] that pure Mary
> Since in their mother Eve their disgrace was great,
> behold in Mary their sister their triumph has been magnified.
> Blessed is He Who shone forth from them!
>   *Refrain:* Most blessed of all is He by His birth![6]

Ephrem presents a pattern of recapitulation for which women's work in the image of glorious Mary has undone that in the image of fallen Eve. Hence, in

Ephrem's hymns, the notion that women and music incited sinful actions can now be rectified. Women's voices are fitting for God because Mary's voice had been fitting. Sinful women had done Satan's work, and could still do so: Ephrem castigates the "heretical" Sabbateans for allowing a woman to teach from the bema of the church.[7] But faithful women now serve God rightly, he insists, as Mary had done. They sing words of truth, pleasing to God:

> The unchaste dance pleased the tyrant [cf. Mt 14:6].
> May the chant of chaste women please You, my Lord,
> May the chant of the chaste women dispose You, my Lord,
> to keep their bodies in chastity.[8]

In Ephrem's *Hymns on the Nativity*, in particular, this changed role for women's voices is set in high relief. Ephrem knew the feast as one celebrated on January 6 in commemoration of the Virgin Mary. Here, in the *Hymns on the Nativity*, the women's choir do more than stand in Mary's place; they also sing in Mary's voice.[9] In passages sometimes short and sometimes extended, Ephrem sets verses of direct speech in the first-person voice, imagining Mary's words at the birth of her divine Son.[10] He crafts Mary in wonder-struck prayer:

> . . . Am I having a dream
> or a vision that, behold, upon my lap
> is Emmanuel? I shall cease all [else]
> and give thanks to the Lord of the Universe each day.[11]

In these hymns, each verse proclaims Christ's divinity, yet Mary is every mother marveling at her baby: "Indeed, how much am I amazed . . . / The murmuring of His mouth—how it seems to me / as if His silence were speaking with God!"[12] Nor does Ephrem shirk from the human realities of childbirth, even while acclaiming the miracle of divine incarnation. Preparing to nurse, Mary sings to Christ:

> How shall I open the fount of milk
> for You, the Fount? How shall I give
> sustenance to You, the All-sustaining,
> from Your [own] table? How shall I approach
> with swaddling clothes the One arrayed in streams [of light]?[13]

In Ephrem's verses, Mary wrestles to grasp who she is and who is her son. In stanzas sung by and with women's choirs, Mary names her reversal of Eve's work: "In the place in which Eve succumbed, I shall glorify Him."[14] In these hymns, Mary sings in prophecy; she sees visions.[15] Her lullabies must become a new form of speech. She gives birth to new song:

> With You I shall begin, and I trust
> That with You I shall end. I shall open my mouth,

> And You fill my mouth. I am for You the earth
> and You are the farmer. Sow in me Your voice,
> You who are the sower of Himself in His mother's womb.
> . . . .
> . . . Blessed be the Babe
> Who made his mother the lyre of His melodies.
> And since the lyre looks toward its master,
> My mouth looks toward You. Let Your will arouse
> Your mother's tongue. Since I have learned by You
> A new way of conceiving, let my mouth learn by You
> A new [way of] giving birth to new glory.[16]

In her new lullabies, in her new song,[17] Mary's voice crosses from the biblical past into the historical present of the worshipping church. Addressing her son, Mary's imagined figure offers Ephrem's congregation instruction in right faith on the occasion of the feast celebrating the Nativity event of biblical—and present—time. Never spoken in reality, the words of Ephrem's Mary proclaim a reality unspeakable:

> . . . A new utterance
> of prophecy seethes in me.
> What shall I call You, a stranger to us,
> Who was from us? Shall I call You Son?
> Shall I call You Brother? Shall I call You Bridegroom?
> Shall I call You Lord, O [You] who brought forth His mother
> [in] another birth out of the water?[18]

Ephrem grants Mary a prophetic voice, one that declares God's intention in the presence of God's people. In his hymns, hers is not a hidden voice, spoken in the sheltered space of a household—the expected place for women's speech in the late antique social world. Rather, her words are prophecies of truth that ring out amid the gathered congregation of the believing community, including women. Their sung responses—including those of women and girls in the congregation—in turn affirm and acclaim her voice. Ephrem is both imagining the words Mary would have said, and proclaiming those words as a public presentation, sung in the presence of all. Hers is a living voice, ringing out in the worship gathering.

Ephrem's *Hymns on the Nativity* highlight Mary's voice by setting it in the first person, and by drawing attention to the qualities of Mary's words as song, as prophecy, and as praise. His verses highlight her voice further by their performance, when women's choirs gave song to her words. Perhaps his emphasis on Mary's "new song," her "new kind of utterance," also indicates appreciation for the heightened role his hymns allowed for women's voices in the liturgical celebrations of the local congregation. Certainly, the resonance between imagined words and voiced expression sounded in the ears of listeners, as Ephrem signaled them to attention.

But there is a poignancy in these hymns that adds a further dimension to his portrait, for Ephrem alludes frequently to the slandering of Mary by the women of her time—and to the slandering of the virgin choirs in his own. In various hymns, he presents Mary as scorned for her poverty, maligned for her lowly circumstances, and castigated for her misunderstood pregnancy.[19] She sings of these assaults with bluntness:

> Behold, I am slandered and oppressed,
> but I rejoice. My ears are full
> of scorn and disdain, but it is a small matter to me
> how much I shall endure, for a single [word of] consolation from You [O Lord]
> is able to chase away myriads of grief.[20]

In such verses, the line between Mary's voice and that of the virgin choir blurs. In *Hymns on the Nativity* 12, Ephrem describes the slandering not only of Mary, but of all women who have betrothed themselves to Christ in virginity.[21] These, too, he understands typologically as images of Mary. As Christ dwelt in the Virgin Mary's womb, so now he dwells within his consecrated virgins, who, as Mary had done, suffer abuse for their choice. When the women's choir sing in Mary's voice, "For Your sake, behold, I am hated,"[22] the women sing their own present circumstances as much as Mary's biblical ones.

Sung at the Nativity vigil, these hymns move delicately between the biblical narrative and the city beyond the church doors. Mary's vindication at the birth of the Savior becomes the vindication also of the virgins who sound her voice as choirs. So, too, did Ephrem evoke the church itself as a slandered virgin, one who kept herself pure, in "orthodox" teaching, in the midst of heretics, pagans, and Jews.[23] Furthermore, Mary's justification was also that of mothers—of the consecrated widows, faithful wives, and pious laywomen who joined the refrains to Ephrem's hymns. We hear all these "virginal" personae affirmed as Mary sings out, addressing each in turn, assuring them of Christ's steadfast defense:

> O chaste woman, eagerly await my Beloved [Christ]
> so that He may dwell in you, and unclean women, too,
> so that He may purify you; churches, too,
> so that He may adorn you. He is the Son of the Creator
> Who came to restore the whole creation.[24]

Ephrem's focus on the slandering of Mary by the Hebrew women no doubt refers to polemics between Christians, Jews, and pagans over the Christian claim of Mary's virginity, a frequent and heated point of dispute in early Christian religious debate and in Ephrem's own anti-Jewish disputation.[25] But Ephrem denounced the slandering of the virgin women's choirs in his contemporary society, a culture he shows to have been critical of their unmarried state just as he claims that society in

Mary's time had been of her illegitimate pregnancy. Ephrem comments with wry insight, addressing Christ:

> You [O Lord] dwelt in Mary, but the unclean said falsely
> that the fetus was not Yours. Since You dwell now
> within chaste women, behold they are slandered
> as [if they were] pregnant. They slander the pregnant one
> and those who are not pregnant—a great atrocity!
> . . . .
> Praise to You [Who] purify Your flock
> as Your mother, and Your chaste women
> as the one who bore You, and Your handmaids
> as the one who nursed You. From them and from her
> and from all of us glory be to Your name![26]

Ephrem trumpeted the valuation of consecrated virginity in the midst of a social order that, in the mid-fourth century, genuinely struggled to accommodate its consequences. Of course, men also participated in the emerging valuation of celibacy as a life choice. But in Christian discourse celibacy was most often articulated in gendered terms, with the female virginal body as its foundational image.[27] No doubt the slander Ephrem mentions refers to the criticism Jews and pagans alike heaped on Christians for a commitment—virginity—that their own traditions countenanced only under highly specific circumstances.[28] Such passages serve as a reminder that Ephrem wrote for a Christian population still very much in the minority in the cosmopolitan cities of Nisibis and Edessa during his lifetime.[29] Yet Ephrem's verses also signal the fact that Christians, too, were resistant to assimilating women's choice of virginity into a social order rooted in marriage and biological families. A vibrant culture of monasticism was not yet in place.[30]

The concern in Ephrem's hymns for the reputation or status of the women's choir, composed of consecrated virgins, contributes to the typological portrait of Mary that he offers. In Ephrem's hymns, women sing in the liturgy because God worked salvation through a woman's body and a woman's voice: Mary sang "a new song," one that heralded a new creation.[31] (Female) virginity marked its start, and its singularity as a historical moment in the created order. Women's voices biblical and liturgical sounded that new beginning.

Ephrem's alignment of the women's choirs with Mary's image or type is echoed repeatedly in Syriac hymns from late antiquity.[32] Mary's model was also sung in Jacob of Sarug's metrical homilies, as here:

> Let all the multitude of virgins praise Him with wonder,
> because the great Savior shines forth from them to the whole world.
> Let the voice of the young women be lifted up in praise,
> because by one of them, behold, hope is brought to the world.[33]

Other biblical women also provided typological models for women's singing, although without the explicit identification Ephrem and others drew between Mary and the choirs.[34] Such typological models demand further discussion in the context of performance and meaning I will take up in chapters 3 and 4. Here, we return to the matter of literary portraits of the choirs to ask how rhetorical strategies shaped presentation.

JACOB OF SARUG: TYPOLOGY AND SOTERIOLOGY

Ephrem made no claim to founding women's liturgical choirs. Rather, he addressed them as an active and vital part of liturgical worship. However, two sources unambiguously attributed the Syriac women's choirs to Ephrem's initiative: Jacob of Sarug in his homily "On Mar Ephrem,"[35] and the anonymous *Life of Ephrem*, chapter 31.[36] In this, the *Life of Ephrem* seems to follow Jacob's homily. The two texts display close parallels in language and imagery for this foundational story; possibly Jacob's homily was slightly earlier, or they may have shared a common source since lost to us.[37]

Composed in celebration of Ephrem, Jacob's homily does not offer a summary version of the saint's life.[38] Rather, it is a shining example of Jacob's own poetic prowess. The text is in the form of another favored genre of Syriac liturgical poetry, the memra (sing.; pl. *memre*), a metrical sermon composed and chanted or intoned in isosyllabic couplets.[39] Jacob's homily lauded Ephrem as a mighty fighter of heresy, a brilliant poet of the Syriac language, and a great protector of truth. Moreover, Jacob attended in some detail and at length to presenting Ephrem as the founder and leader of women's liturgical choirs.

Jacob provides no source for the story and appears to be its earliest witness, along with the anonymous *Life of Ephrem*. Subsequent references to Ephrem as founder of the choirs are based on these two accounts and most often on Jacob's homily.[40] In his exhaustive treatment of the historical sources for Ephrem's life, Bernard Outtier opined that while Jacob's homily lacks concrete historical details, at no point does he seem to counter what we can learn from Ephrem's authentic writings.[41] Certainly, the story is one that echoes Ephrem's affirmation of women's liturgical singing.[42] It remains a cherished tradition among Syriac Orthodox in the present day.[43]

Yet the record is puzzling. A sizable number of late antique and medieval sources contain biographical accounts of Ephrem; none but these two mention the choirs at all.[44] Kathleen McVey has argued that Jacob's account can (and no doubt should) be read as a defensive *apologia* for the choirs.[45] In this homily ostensibly devoted to celebration of Saint Ephrem, women's choirs comprise fully one-quarter of the text.[46] Perhaps such elaborate defense of these women indicates serious questioning of their validity at the time Jacob wrote. McVey suggests the vehemence of Christological controversy as the complicating circumstance that might have cast women's public profile in ecclesiastical settings in a vulnerable light.[47]

However, the story is not innocent. By appearing to set a specific start to the practice of women's choirs, it erases the memory of their prior presence. Furthermore, it marks off Syriac liturgical practice as distinctive and thereby different from that of others. It thus occludes the participation of choirs of nuns or consecrated virgins, which, as noted in chapter 1, appears to have been fairly common in Greek and Latin churches, although not confirmed or supported by late antique Greek or Latin synodical canons. The story acknowledges the practice of Syriac women's choirs, and it provides authentication for their presence. But because it represents their presence as dependent on a historical moment of change—the moment Ephrem decided to recruit consecrated virgins to sing his hymns—it renders their status unstable, the product of one person's effort in a particular situation. Both Jacob and the anonymous *Life* will offer further means of bolstering that status, but there is tension as well as affirmation in this story of origins.

Jacob begins his homily on Ephrem by praising the saint with a series of dramatic titles: Ephrem was the "great master of teaching," an "athlete who triumphed in doctrinal disputes," and a "valiant one who humbled all heresies," an incomparable champion of orthodoxy.[48] Jacob presents Ephrem first and foremost as a teacher, one who taught through the poetry of song performed in the liturgical assembly of the church. Imagery of physical prowess and martial strength also adorns Jacob's depiction of Ephrem throughout the homily. But his use of such images is always mediated through those of teaching and song. For Jacob, Ephrem's strength was his knowledge of truth; his weapons were hymns: powerful words of truth, heightened in might by his musical genius. This, indeed, is Jacob's portrait of Ephrem:

> This man's mouth was a bow, and his words were arrows,
> He forged songs like spearheads for the weapon which he fashioned.
> This man hurled wonderful melodies against the evil [ones];
> With his instruction, he eliminated stumbling blocks which had multiplied.[49]

In Jacob's depiction, Ephrem did not debate with heretics or argue for right belief. Rather, he taught people to understand truth by teaching them to sing—in Jacob's phrase, to drink a "new wine" (Acts 2:13). And, from the start, the whole church, men and women, were included in that instruction. With a "new wine whose color and fragrance are from Golgotha," Ephrem "intoxicated . . . men and women to give praise"; with "a fountain of melodies . . . he has intoxicated the earth."[50]

Jacob's account of Ephrem's founding of the choirs begins here. Composing hymns of truth, Ephrem began to train choirs to perform these hymns and themselves become teachers. Jacob notes that Ephrem's choice of women might appear surprising. Alluding to the famed Pauline passage in 1 Corinthians 14:34, where the apostle admonished women to be silent in the assemblies, Jacob depicts Ephrem's choral strategy as nothing short of revelatory. In his view, Ephrem perceived women's silence as a mark of the fallen dispensation; but, now, Christians live in the new order of salvation in Christ. Ephrem saw that it was time for women's voices to be heard. Addressing the saint directly, Jacob sang:

> Our sisters also were strengthened by you [O Ephrem] to give praise;
> for women were not allowed to speak in church.
> Your instruction opened the closed mouths of the daughters of Eve;
> and behold, the gatherings of the glorious (church) resound with their melodies.
> A new sight of women uttering the proclamation;
> and behold, they are called teachers among the congregations.
> Your teaching signifies an entirely new world;
> for yonder in the kingdom, men and women are equal.[51]

Jacob admits that the practice of women's choirs appears to differ from scriptural injunction, and gives the impression that it differed from earlier Christian custom as well. He notes that both the sight and sound of women's choirs were unnervingly bold. Rather than mitigate the implications of such liturgical prominence for women, however, Jacob highlights its force, its unlikeliness, even its ability to shock by seeming to break social conventions. Thus he claims that women sing the "proclamation"—here using the Syriac word *karuzutha*, which, like the Greek term *kerygma*, denoted preaching, and most often, the proclaiming of the gospel or of prayers or blessings in the liturgy.[52] Moreover, he names these women as "teachers," *malphanyatha*, the feminine plural form of the term often used for (male) teachers of exceptional learning and wisdom; *malphane* (masculine plural) often signified the great theologians of the church.[53] These were words of serious weight in Jacob's time, terms that engaged sources of social and ecclesiastical authority commonly revered and honored. Applied to women in the context of liturgical participation, such words commanded attention.

Women's choirs, Jacob argues, were crucial components of Ephrem's work against heresy. From Ephrem's perspective (as Jacob presents it), education was not only a matter of the content he taught or the proper understanding of doctrine. It also required that instruction be offered through *the manner of performance* of that teaching. Liturgy did more than offer words: it displayed truth. Liturgy was the occasion where the church gathered as a whole community. Ritual form, expression, and participation all served to articulate the deepest meaning of the truth being taught with words. A "new world" had come through Christ, a new dispensation. In response, Ephrem's hymns offered a "new sight" *and* a new sound. Because "men and women are equal" before the Lord, women, like men, must sing in the liturgy. While the analogy would also hold for congregational singing and is no doubt intended to do so, Jacob's choice of wording here, as well as explicit statements later, indicate that he has choirs especially in mind: "You [O Ephrem] labored to devise two harps for two groups (*tagme*); / you treated men and women as one to give praise."[54]

With great delight, Jacob takes up the typology of Moses leading the Hebrew women in song at the Red Sea in Exodus 15. In the biblical account, Moses first led the Israelites in a song of victory (Ex 15:1–18); then Miriam led the women "with timbrels and dancing" in song (Ex 15:20). Jacob bypasses Miriam's role, instead setting up a series of supersessionist parallels between Moses and Ephrem.[55] As Moses led the Hebrew people in song, so Ephrem led the Syrians and through them, all peoples. As Moses worked God's power through his staff, so Ephrem had the power of the cross. But Jacob focuses on the women in both instances:

> That wise Moses instructed the daughters of his nation
> not to refrain from the required praise.
> Likewise the blessed one [Ephrem], who became a second Moses for women,
> taught them sweet melodies to give praise.[56]

Jacob explains that Moses led the women to sing praise of their deliverance from Egypt, because women as well as men were led across the water to their freedom. With their brothers, fathers, and husbands they had passed through terrors and suffering, crossing the water unharmed. It was not seemly that the men, alone, should sing praise: "A single deliverance took place for both you and them from God; / Let a single song of praise rise from your mouth."[57]

What Ephrem did with his choirs, then, was to fulfill what typology revealed. As Moses had done, so, too, did Ephrem do when he turned to Syrian women to "sing praises with their hymns," "with sweet melodies" and "joyful sound," for the deliverance from sin and death through baptism and eucharist.[58] For here Jacob joins typology to sacrament and, further, to soteriology. By one baptism, from one font, were men and women baptized into Christ; from one chalice did they drink, from one loaf were they fed communion. One and the same salvation was worked for men and women alike: both alike must sing God's glory! To this resounding image, Jacob adds the typology of Mary as the Second Eve as he imagines Ephrem's mighty exhortation, summoning women to song:

> [O women,] Your silent mouth which your mother Eve closed,
> is now opened by Mary, your sister, to sing praise.
> . . . .
> Until now, your gender was brought low because of Eve;
> but from now on, it is restored by Mary to sing Alleluia!
> . . . .
> Uncover your faces to sing praise without shame,
> to the One who granted you freedom of speech by his birth.[59]

In each scene he offers of Ephrem with the women, Jacob presents Ephrem in the role of teacher and also of choir director, instructing the women and also training them. While his exhortation of women to song could well be a call for the full participation of the congregation, women as well as men, Jacob—and Ephrem in his depiction—appears to intend a more targeted formation.[60] He presents the women as a select group whom Ephrem coaches, drills, and cultivates. Toward this picture, Jacob treats Ephrem's establishment of women's choirs a second time in his homily, after again recalling the typology of Moses:

> Blessed (Ephrem) observed that women were silent from praise,
> and (this) wise man decided that it was right for them to sing praise.
> As Moses had given tambourines to the young girls,
> this discerning man composed hymns (*madrashe*), and gave them to virgins
>   (*btulatha*).[61]

According to Jacob, not only did Ephrem single out the women, but he trained them until they sang as a well-practiced choir. Jacob describes the scene, with verses matched closely by the account in the anonymous *Life of Ephrem*:

> It pleased [Ephrem] while standing among the sisters
> to stir the pure women with melodies of praise.
> He was like an eagle perched among doves,
> (as) he taught (them) a new song of praise with a serene sound.
> Flocks of humble partridges encircled him,
> learning from him a sweet song with a pure melody.
> He taught the swallows to chirp,
> and the church resounded with the pure voices of pious women (*knikatha*).[62]

Jacob's account presents Ephrem pursuing a deliberate sequence of actions. Providing hymns that taught truth, Ephrem trained the women to sing. Moreover, expounding the typology of Eve and Mary, he taught them the significance of their singing. In effect, Jacob describes a threefold curriculum for the choirs: what to sing, how to sing it, and why it mattered. By this means, Jacob intoned, Ephrem taught the women "to make their chants instructive melodies."[63] The sound of their voices no less than the words they sang declared that salvation had come for all people. And so it was that "[Ephrem's] hymns went forth like legions against falsehood."[64] Teaching, performance, and the holy war against heresy were tightly interwoven in this account.

In his homily on Ephrem, Jacob presumes that God had made divine will a clear and active force in human history. The faithful could discern this by observing typological models from scriptural stories. According to Jacob, two primary models guided Ephrem's work with women's choirs. One was the type of Ephrem as a new Moses, summoning women to sing the fullness of God's deliverance. The other was the type of women as daughters of Eve and sisters of Mary, dynamically transforming women's silence to women's speech in the new dispensation of Christ.

With characteristic drama, Jacob drove home his point with two lengthy imagined speeches, first of Moses to the Hebrew women and then of Ephrem to the Syrian women. Each speech stressed that women's voices should and must be heard, else the glory of deliverance and the God who worked it were diminished. Each summoned women to song as an act of mighty power. To these rousing scenes of majesty, Jacob added a fierce assault against social custom. Women's place as one of silence was a matter of the fallen order, of outdated custom, Jacob sang. New times and new challenges demanded its end. In the wake of heresy, misunderstanding, and injustice, women's voices were now necessary to bring the work of salvation to fullness.

Perhaps nowhere else in ancient Christian literature will one find such celebratory affirmation of the equality of women and men as in Jacob of Sarug's extraordinary metrical homily on Ephrem.[65] Yet, no less powerful is Jacob's insistence that this equality carries a necessary ethical mandate. Women must not only "sing praises" like the men. They must also "make their chants instructive melodies" (v. 114), that the battle against Satan's work might be won. Women's singing, Jacob implores, provides a teaching of God's truth—against heresy, but also about redemption, anthropology, and salvation—that cannot be taught in any other way.

THE *LIFE OF EPHREM*:
LITURGY AND SOCIAL MEMORY

By the middle of the sixth century, an anonymous hagiography of Ephrem was circulating in Syriac; three closely connected recensions remain extant. Numerous redactions followed, including translations into Arabic, Armenian, and Georgian. A patchwork of episodes largely cobbled together from fourth- and fifth-century Greek sources, the *Life of Ephrem* accomplished a surprising transformation of the saint.[66] Ephrem's own writings had shown him to be a teacher who diligently served the church under a series of bishops, first in Nisibis and then in Edessa.[67] As he himself indicated, many of his hymns guided civic flocks and were sung by women's choirs. Other madrashe he composed, along with his exegetical commentaries and metrical sermons, instructed students similarly devoted to ecclesiastical service, in some kind of school setting.[68] Ephrem's students probably included the consecrated virgins who sang his madrashe in liturgies, as Jacob of Sarug depicted.[69] However, in the anonymous *Life of Ephrem*, the saint appears as a monastic hermit of profoundly abstemious ascetic practice, avoiding civic life as far as possible and rather aggressively misogynistic in the (few) encounters with women that he was unable to avoid. There is little connection between these two depictions of Ephrem: his own presentation of a civic ecclesiastical teacher, and that in the anonymous *Life of Ephrem* of a solitary desert ascetic.[70] Yet, discordantly to the rest of the text, chapter 31 of the *Life of Ephrem* presents the story that Ephrem chose to combat heresies thriving in Edessa by composing orthodox hymns of different kinds, and training the daughters of the covenant to sing them at daily and weekly church services.[71]

According to the anonymous *Life*, Ephrem was prompted to write hymns when he observed the Bardaisanite heresy flourishing in the city of Edessa because of their popular hymns.[72] The account is striking for its use of rhetorical tropes presenting music first as dangerous (in the heretical hymns) and then as therapeutic (in Ephrem's hymns). Thus we are told that Ephrem recognized the "shallow" and "foul" teachings of the heretics, but worried that the populace would be captivated by their "alluring" and "ungodly" sounds. For Harmonios, the son of Bardaisan, had composed hymns "in which he mixed the ungodliness of his father with attractive melodies." By these "he lured and dragged [unsuspecting Christians] off to perdition."[73] In one version, Bardaisan had started this dangerous route by establishing choirs of children who "sang with stringed instruments according to various melodies" the "poison" that he taught them.[74]

To this dreadful state of affairs, Ephrem responded with a twofold attack: he composed hymns with peerless skill and beauty to counteract those of the heretics; and he recruited the daughters of the covenant to sing them in an array of liturgical services. With words as his weapons, he chose his army: "He prepared troops for battle against those heresies. . . . He appointed teachers (*malphanyatha*) among all the Daughters of the Covenant." Then he set about their training:

> All the Daughters of the Covenant would come down regularly to the church. He established instruction for them and taught them hymns as well. Evenings and mornings they would gather in church before the liturgy and in the martyrion and for funeral processions and they would sing.[75]

The anonymous *Life of Ephrem* in all its major recensions stresses three elements: Ephrem's compositions, the daughters of the covenant as his chosen choir, and the training the choir received for their mission. The contrast to the alleged choirs of children is especially sharp: Ephrem's are choirs of adults, who, with firm intellectual understanding, practiced disciplined and skilled presentation of orthodox teaching. Additionally, all recensions stress that form, content, and performance were the crucial qualities that made Ephrem's hymns effective weapons against falsehood. Like Jacob of Sarug, the *Life of Ephrem* identifies the form of hymn as itself significant. But here it is not only the notion of madrashe as instructional hymns (or teaching songs) that is highlighted, but an entire array of liturgical hymnography ascribed to Ephrem's prolific artistry:

> He assembled and organized the Daughters of the Covenant and taught them hymns (*madrashe*) and songs (*seblatha*) and antiphons (*'onyatha*) and intercessions (*ba'watha*). He arranged songs (*qinyatha*) and verses (*mushatha*) in rhythmic measures and transmitted his wisdom to all the learned and wise women. And he mixed in the hymns and chants sweet melodies which were pleasing and delightful to their hearers.[76]

The *Life of Ephrem* indicates not only the types of hymns, but, further, the teachings Ephrem provided:

> He put in the hymns (*madrashe*) words of subtle meaning and spiritual knowledge about the birth and baptism and fasting and the entire economy of Christ: the passion and resurrection and ascension; and about the martyrs and repentance and about the deceased. He composed (hymns) on all of these.[77]

We might note that this list of topics is reminiscent of the one in the *Didascalia Apostolorum*, chapter 15, where widows, laymen, and women in general are forbidden to teach on precisely these topics![78] Yet these are the topics addressed in Syriac liturgical hymnography, a primary means by which congregations received and learned instruction on doctrinal matters. And here, in the *Life of Ephrem* as in Jacob of Sarug's homily, the task of that instruction was assigned by Ephrem to choirs of women, in this case explicitly the daughters of the covenant.

The *Life of Ephrem* seems to follow Jacob most closely at the point where it describes Ephrem's rehearsals and performances with his choir:

> It suited him to stand among the sisters, alternating verses of hymns with them. . . . They would surround him like a flock of pure partridges and he resembled an eagle perched among doves being instructed by him, a sweet master with a pure melody. It was likewise fitting for the church which rang with the melodies of chaste women. . . . And he, like a father, would stand among them (as) a harpist of the Spirit, arranging various songs for them and demonstrating and teaching and alternating melodies until the entire city gathered around him.[79]

Finally, the account in the *Life* presents Ephrem in triumphant victory, "lead[ing] these women out to do battle against the strong one."[80] According to the *Life of Ephrem*, then, Ephrem's strategy against heresy was at once military, pedagogical, and therapeutic. His hymns "offered to hearers an antidote at once agreeable and wholesome." By such means, Ephrem instructed the city, its environs, and the hinterland beyond. Moreover, the victory was ongoing: "These hymns brighten the feasts of the triumphant martyrs even now." Repeatedly in its short but detailed account, the *Life* stresses not only the power of the hymns, but also the power of the women who sang them:

> My friends, who would not be astounded and filled with fervent faith to see the athlete of Christ [Ephrem] amid the ranks of the Daughters of the Covenant as they chanted songs, hymns, and melodies? Their songs resemble the songs and ethereal melodies of spiritual beings who chant to the spirits of humans with the sweetness of their songs.[81]

In addition to its shared themes with Jacob of Sarug's homily on Ephrem, the *Life of Ephrem* attends to ecclesiastical details in ways that Jacob did not. Here the women Ephrem recruits are specifically the daughters of the covenant, who are set to work in the liturgical cycle of the local church in terms strongly reminiscent of the Rabbula canons.[82] Moreover, the *Life of Ephrem* names a number of types of hymns, celebrating not only the madrashe but other hymnographic genres that form the scaffolding for the different church services of the daily, weekly, and festal calendars: *qinyatha, seblatha, 'onyatha,* and *ba'watha.* These appear to indicate the hand of a later scribe or editor, since a number of these forms do not appear until after Ephrem's lifetime, and some even later than Jacob's.[83] But these details of ecclesiastical office, hymnographic genre, and liturgical order succeed in anchoring the tradition of women's liturgical choirs to the institutional life of the church in explicit and normative terms. Jacob's homily had defended the practice of women's choirs by offering a majestic theological vision of the equality of men and women in the divine economy. The anonymous *Life*, instead, offers a thoughtful vindication of ordinary church life as people encountered it on a daily basis in their local communities. It is an account that stands on institutional authority, where Jacob drew on biblical authority through biblical typology. From this perspective, their strategies of defense are strikingly different, even though they overlap in depiction and imagery.

Nonetheless, both strategies effectively offer a buffer against the inherent instability of the foundation story attributing women's choirs to Ephrem's initiative. At base, such a story offered a narrative of contingency for women's choirs. But if the story of Ephrem as founder served to single out one man and one historical moment, both Jacob and the anonymous *Life* bolstered the validity of these choirs in larger terms. Jacob tied them inextricably to the typological and soteriological teachings of the church, while the *Life* grounded them in synodical canons and liturgical rubrics, the normative operations of ecclesiastical service. Either way, such justifications were formidable. They spoke to profound awareness that women's musical contributions to the ordinary functioning of the church were significant both theologically and practically.

IMAGERY AT WORK

The accounts by Jacob of Sarug and the anonymous *Life of Ephrem* engaged a number of literary tropes for music and gender. While their imagery is striking, it also drew on familiar patterns in the late antique eastern Mediterranean, demonstrating that Syriac literature was deeply embedded within Mediterranean literary currents, actively participating in a shared culture not accurately portrayed when divided between labels of "Greek," "Roman," or "Semitic."

The imagery of Ephrem's holy song as a strategy against heresy, for example, drew on the trope of music as a therapy (for good or for ill) in which words (true or false) are mixed with sweet melodies to delight the listener. It is present in the account of Ephrem reported in the ecclesiastical histories of Sozomen and

Theodoret, where the poisonous songs of Bardaisan and Harmonios are counteracted by the truthful songs of Ephrem.[84] It occurs in the anonymous fifth-century *Life of Rabbula*, in scenes where Bishop Rabbula also struggles against the Bardaisanites in Edessa.[85] It reappears in the ninth century in Barhadbeshabba's account of Narsai of Nisibis, where the East Syriac (dyophysite) Narsai is prompted to compose memre of high poetic art to fight the metrical homilies "eloquent for evil" of the West Syriac (miaphysite) Jacob of Sarug.[86] Ephrem himself had used this image in his own *Hymns against Heresies*.[87] A homily attributed to Jacob of Sarug, in a common trope, described the songs of the theater as dangerously seductive in exactly this imagery, and counterposed the mixture of truthful words and sweet melodies of hymns as the appropriate remedy.[88]

Consider again the same imagery to urge the use of biblical Psalms as therapeutic remedies for the conditions of the soul. Basil of Caesarea, for example, explained that the Holy Spirit had composed the Psalms in response to seeing the sorry condition of the human race, "mix[ing] sweetness of melody with doctrine so that inadvertently we would absorb the benefit of words through gentleness and ease of hearing."[89] John Chrysostom similarly expounded on the Psalms:

> When God saw that the majority of men were slothful, and that they approached spiritual reading with reluctance . . . he mixed melody with prophecy, so that enticed by the rhythm and melody, all might raise sacred hymns to him with great eagerness. For nothing so arouses the soul . . . as concordant melody and sacred song composed in rhythm.[90]

Hence composers divine, human, or demonic could mix words and melodies in powerful combinations, and Ephrem no less.

To this rich vein of therapeutic imagery, Jacob and the anonymous *Life of Ephrem* added the striking metaphors of archery: Ephrem's lips as a bow, his words like arrows. Here was a (nonmusical) pattern of images that recurred in contexts of exceptionally powerful speech: that of Rabbula confronting heretics; or in Isaac of Antioch, of a monk whose prayer wings heavenward with mighty strength.[91] It was used by John Chrysostom for the formidable words of the martyrs Juventius and Maximinus, and also the singular power of Chrysostom's own words in a funeral oration on his behalf.[92] The image has deep roots in Greek classical literature, but perhaps for Christian writers also draws from Psalm 11 (LXX 10):2, where real archers in real battle were evoked.[93] As poet and hymn writer, then, Ephrem is portrayed as a wise doctor who was also a mighty warrior, one whose medicines were also weapons.

What associations did the women's choirs add to the notion of Ephrem as teacher, doctor, and warrior? The imagery used by Jacob and the anonymous author of the *Life of Ephrem* renders these women as wise "teachers" whose "instructive songs" and "sweet sounds" soothe and heal the troubled or weary Christian. Moreover, and in briefer terms, they are troops in the battle for truth, marshaled by their heroic leader, Ephrem. Although we might expect teaching, medical, and battle imagery to be inflected in gendered terms in the masculine, the choirs are not presented in such terms. On the contrary, it is their female aspect that highlights Ephrem's military prowess in opposition to Satan and heretics, whose weaknesses are thereby revealed. So pathetic is the enemy that mere women, with their gentle tones, could prove triumphant with the right weapons:

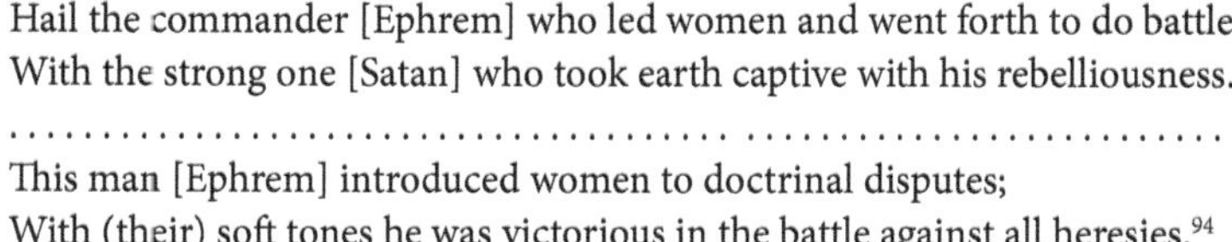

> Hail the commander [Ephrem] who led women and went forth to do battle
> With the strong one [Satan] who took earth captive with his rebelliousness.
> . . . .
> This man [Ephrem] introduced women to doctrinal disputes;
> With (their) soft tones he was victorious in the battle against all heresies.[94]

In Jacob's telling and that of the anonymous *Life of Ephrem*, the women's choirs are not rendered "female men of God," as hagiography sometimes termed women saints.[95] Nor do the texts utilize their virginity to cast them as something other than women—whether masculinized or a third gender. Rather, their virginity is presented in terms that enhance their nature *as women*. They are rhetorically gendered in wholly normative terms. They are not themselves leaders, but are rather led by Ephrem; the hymns they sing are not their own, but rather the compositions of their brilliant (male) director; they are chaste, disciplined, of modest decorum, and obedient to their ecclesiastical authorities.[96] The people they instruct and lead are the laity, who are ranked below them in the ecclesiastical hierarchy. Biological sex and rhetorical gender thus coincide in these presentations to correspond to normative late antique social expectations.[97]

In all three portraits of the choirs discussed above, virginity is the mark of purity, understood to be a state at once physical, moral, and theological.[98] In the *Life of Ephrem*, it signals a status distinct from the "secular" laity, a difference further emphasized by the designation of the office of daughter of the covenant for these choirs. In Ephrem's own hymns, as in Jacob of Sarug's homily "On Mar Ephrem," virginity is a condition that marks humanity's salvation in the new dispensation of Christ. It is the condition of the Virgin Mary after reversing the state of Eve; it is the status of the wise virgins who await their Bridegroom in Matthew 25:1–13; it is the eschatological condition of a humanity at the brink of eternal life and hence no longer in need of procreation. Ephrem himself occasionally highlighted the voices of the women who sang his hymns as noteworthy additions to liturgical participation. But Jacob's homily "On Mar Ephrem" and the anonymous *Life of Ephrem* seem to have added the virgin women's choirs to their portraits of the saint in order to enhance Ephrem's own sanctity—not (or not only) to defend the women.

Significantly, both Jacob's homily "On Mar Ephrem" and the anonymous *Life of Ephrem* were written during a period when Ephrem's own reputation was undergoing complex reevaluation.[99] The volatile Christological debates of the fifth and sixth centuries had grown increasingly venomous and destructive in consequence. Syriac Christians were among the hardest hit by the crisis, with the dyophysite Church of the East effectively forming an autonomous institution in Persia during the fifth century, and the miaphysites beginning the hard work of establishing their own separate hierarchy in eastern Roman and Persian regions during the sixth.[100] Ephrem's stature as saint was destabilized by his earlier historical moment. His use of imagery for theological and especially Christological discourse had grown quickly anachronistic and then problematic, even obsolete, as tensions escalated in the decades following his death.

By the late fifth and early sixth centuries, leading Syriac theologians such as Philoxenos of Mabbug were praising Ephrem's name but distancing themselves from his work.[101] Manuscripts, too, showed the intrusion of editorial efforts to reorganize, reframe, and even to delimit transmission of Ephrem's writings.[102] His hymns ceased to be used in entire versions; rather, verses were excerpted and rearranged in the liturgical books.[103] This became standard for his poetry in subsequent centuries as his hymnography was transmitted piecemeal, interspersed among hymn verses by later poets, sometimes with substantial changes in meaning or theological context.[104]

Hence the story that Ephrem championed orthodoxy by establishing virgin choirs was one that added a distinctly hallowed tone to Ephrem's own persona at a turbulent time for his memory. Choirs of pure, inviolate female voices performed his hymns of truth, like pure vessels giving voice to Ephrem's divine inspiration. How exactly did the notion of women's choirs do that?

EXALTED VISIONS

Several idyllic portraits of women's choirs from Greek and Latin authors are interesting to consider in comparison with those of Ephrem and the Syriac women's choirs. At issue in each case is not historicity—for they are not historical accounts—but rather a utopian ideal expressed through a literary representation of women's sacred singing. What did such representation convey?

Best known to modern scholars is Philo of Alexandria's description of the double choir of men and women in his account of the Egyptian Therapeutae and Therapeutrides.[105] A first-century Jewish philosopher, Philo presented this ascetic community in his work *On the Contemplative Life*, a text whose historicity continues to be the subject of scholarly debate and speculation.[106] Jacob of Sarug's typological casting of Ephrem and his choirs strongly echoes Philo's depiction. In Philo as later in Jacob, hymnography is described as intoxicating wine, and the shared liturgical song of male and female choirs is justified by extensive reference to Moses with the Hebrew women at the Red Sea in Exodus 15.[107]

Philo's account provides important evidence of continuity between early Jewish and Christian patterns of worship and prayer, even if—as many scholars think—its presentation is fictional.[108] But this work of Philo's, in particular, influenced early Christians through its transmission in Eusebios of Caesarea's *History of the Church*.[109] Eusebios was sure that Philo was reporting on an early Christian proto-monastic community, and presented the account as such. The timing of Eusebios's work is significant here. He researched and wrote his *History* over the course of the late third century and the first few decades of the fourth.[110] His interests in philosophical asceticism are apparent throughout his text.[111] His work coincided with the emergence of monastic communities in diverse forms throughout the eastern empire, especially in Egypt, Cappadocia, Mesopotamia, and Syria; it also contributed to the culture of religious competition over the philosophical life that characterized fourth- and fifth-century intellectual circles.[112] These were fertile conditions in which to have Philo's Therapeutae reintroduced into intellectual discourse. It is possible that Jacob knew the account via its Eusebian transmission, a work available in Syriac in Jacob's time.[113]

In his account, Philo presented the joyous song of combined male and female choirs enacting the ongoing fulfillment of God's redemptive work in the life of the worshipping community, a theme strongly echoed in Jacob of Sarug's homily on Ephrem. But Philo's account also differs in significant ways. Philo's setting for the choirs was a banquet, a kind of alternative symposium to that enshrined in philosophical memory by Plato, a comparison Philo sets up directly.[114] Each week, the Therapeutae and Therapeutrides gathered over an ascetic meal to join in prayer and holy instruction by their leader. An austerely disciplined community, the women as well as the men were celibates, all devoted to pursuit of holy wisdom. The community sat in gendered segregation, women on the left and men on the right, separated by a short wall.[115] Periodically, the gathering celebrated the Feast of Fifty, an occasion of heightened sanctity. The leader would expound his sacred teaching, culminating in a hymn. Then the congregation, too, offered their hymns in turn, and at the refrains "all lift up their voices, men and women alike."[116] A simple meal followed, after which a vigil service began.

In the vigil service, Philo describes the men and women standing as two separate choirs (*choroi*), each with its own director, for each "the most honoured amongst them and also the most musical (*emmelestatos*)."[117] The choirs sang separately and antiphonally, keeping time with hands and feet. In due course, in the ecstasy of worship, the choirs joined together. Their rapturous song replicated that of the Hebrews at the Red Sea, where Moses led the men and Miriam the women in hymns of thanksgiving. Philo continues:

> It is on this model [of Exodus 15] above all that the choir of the Therapeutae of either sex, note in response to note and voice to voice, the treble of the women blending with the bass of the men, create an harmonious concert, music in the truest sense (*enarmonion sumphōnian apotelei kai mousikēn ontōs*). Lovely are the thoughts, lovely the words and worthy of reverence the choristers (*oi choreutai*), and the end and aim of thoughts, words and choristers alike is piety.[118]

Philo's account emphasized different elements than that of Jacob for Ephrem. For Philo, the women are included in secondary terms, mentioned briefly, after the men, who are the primary focus of Philo's attention in this work. In turn, Philo gives a (literally) detailed report of the hymns studied and composed by the Therapeutae, and the music performed at the banquets and the vigil service: the types of hymns, the melodic and metrical patterns, and the musical sounds of the two choirs singing separately, responsorially, in octaval harmony, and in unison.[119] The memory of Exodus 15 is crucial for Philo. It is a scriptural passage he cites in other writings, referring each time to the singing of both the men and the women, led respectively by Moses and Miriam. Only in *On the Contemplative Life* does he present a contemporary fulfillment of that model, with the combined male and female choirs singing in unison.[120] Finally, the entire account is located in clear separation from the mundane life of Jews in the Roman Empire. The singing of the two choirs, separately, sequentially, and in unison, is a practice emblematic of their shared life of ascetic philosophical contemplation. It represents a utopian ideal, the power of which rests on its difference from the life of ordinary Jews in villages, towns, or cities. It may or may not matter that Philo at no point identifies the Therapeutae and Therapeutrides as Jewish; he presents them as ideal humanity.

Jacob of Sarug shared Philo's themes of divine intoxication and especially of Exodus 15 as a typological model. However, for Jacob in his homily on Ephrem, the women are the primary focus of his attention when describing liturgical song. He refers to the singing of the men, both at the Red Sea and in Ephrem's liturgy, but only as a backdrop to the exhortations that women should sing. He concentrates on the singing of the women's choir and the sounds that their voices contribute to the liturgical celebration. He is not attentive to musical technicalities, rather describing Ephrem's compositions in broadly general terms as "measured lines" (*bmushatha*) in "verses" (*pethghamaohi*) that "make a joyful sound" (*lmyabbu*);[121] "wonderful melodies" (*qalai tahra*) that were also "like spearheads for a weapon," with words measured, balanced, and arranged in order.[122] In different verses, he describes the women's singing as "joyful" (in the infinitive: *l-myabbu*) (v. 59) "serene" (*shaphya*), "sweet" (*halya*), "pure" (*dakya*) (vv. 99–101); "instructive melodies" (*qalai dmalphanutha*) (v. 114) sung in "soft tones" (*raphyatha*) (v. 152). Such descriptors, unlike Philo's, convey quality of sound rather than musical detail. Most striking in contrast—again a theme shared in the anonymous *Life of Ephrem*—is Jacob's setting of where and why the choirs sing: they sing in the liturgy, in the regular worship gatherings of the civic population. The narratives provide heroic imagery, but the real-life context is wholly that of the local church.

A different picture is offered in Methodios of Olympos's *Symposium*, an enigmatic text from the late third century.[123] The text purports to be a curiously inverted iteration of Plato's *Symposium*, with echoes also of Plato's *Phaedrus*. Rather than men, all the characters are women: from the two who recount and discuss the event, Eubulion and Gregorion, refracting the account of Theopatra, who was present at the occasion; to the ten virgins who meet in Arete's beautiful garden for philosophical debate. The topic of dialogue is not eros, but rather virginity. Drinking, slaves, musicians, and other luxurious pleasures of Greek sympotic events are absent. After each participant offers her speech, victory for the most persuasive oration goes to Thekla, identified by Arete as the legendary companion of the apostle Paul.[124] In honor of her splendid discourse, Arete invites Thekla to lead the virgins in a thanksgiving hymn to God.[125]

Methodios's *Symposium* has been the subject of recent scholarly discussion. Of primary interest has been its format as a work of sympotic literature, by which it seems a strongly antagonistic contribution to an otherwise concordant body of texts.[126] The figure of Thekla has drawn attention as evidence of her own cultic development, as well as the developing concepts of female sanctity.[127] Virginia Burrus has highlighted the extraordinary quality of female voice that the text presents. All the characters speak, at length and with keen distinction, a quality that appears in other late antique hagiographic accounts of female saints.[128] The issues are compelling: Why did Methodios choose to present his notions of virginity, virtue, ethics, apocalyptic, and eschatology—indeed, of Christian philosophical discourse in broad terms—through this wholly female cast of characters, and in a literary form that had represented a predominantly male, highly sexualized tradition of social and literary conventions? If the figure of Diotima created a profound puzzle in Plato's *Symposium*—a woman as the highest source of wisdom, whose teachings were reported through layers of male reminiscence[129]—do we have here an entire dialogue of Diotimas, each wiser than the one before?[130]

Rarely discussed is the role of song in Methodios's text, and the presentation of the hymn itself toward the end of the dialogue. Yet the text is not only about dialogue, philosophical debate, and agonistic (prose) contestation. The theme of holy song is suggested in brief glimpses prior to its celebratory culmination in the hymn that will end the event. In the first speech, for example, Marcella cites the eschatological vision from Revelation 14:1–5, pointing out that the passage shows "that the Lord is the leader of the choir of virgins."[131] When Thalia presents the third speech, she narrates a version of the creation account in which humans were created for the purpose of shared liturgy with the heavenly hosts, so that all might join "in a song which would be an antiphon to the angelic voices wafted from heaven."[132] The image prefigures the kind of exchange that will follow in the hymn at the dialogue's end, when Thecla will sing the verses and the virgins respond with the refrain.[133] In Logos 4, Theopatra describes their dialogic endeavor as "singing the praises"(*hymnēsomen*) of Christ's gift of virginity, "enhanc[ing] what is beautiful with grateful speech (*logois eucharistēriois*)."[134]

Thekla takes her turn in Logos 8, setting her words with an image of music: "I am like a cithara inwardly attuned (*harmozomenēn*) and prepared to speak with care and with grace and dignity."[135] She warns her companions to keep their sights on heaven, flying away from the "charm of [the] beautiful voices" (*thelgētra tēs kalliphōnias*) of Satan and his demons, more dangerous even than Homer's sirens.[136] When Arete declares Thekla the winner of the debate, she summons all the participants "to rise from table and, standing underneath the chaste-tree, to sing a becoming hymn of thanksgiving (*eucharistērion preponpontōs hymnon*) to the Lord; and she asked Thekla to begin and lead the way." Standing in the middle of the virgins with Arete on her right, Thekla took her place—just as Ephrem was pictured leading his flock of women in song: "She then began to sing beautifully (*kosmiōs psallein*); and the other maidens stood around her in a circle, thus forming a choir (*en chorou schēmati*), and joined her in the refrain."[137]

What follows is the full text of the imagined hymn that Thekla sang, an epithalamion, or wedding song, calling the virgins to meet their Heavenly Bridegroom and to escort as a glorious choir the Church as Bride to her bridal chamber. Each of the twenty-four verses ends with a refrain that casts the maidens in the image or type of the Wise Virgins from Matthew 25:1–13: "Chastely I live for Thee [O Christ], / And holding my lighted lamps, / My Spouse, I go forth to meet Thee."[138] As Herbert Musurillo notes, the hymn shows pronounced similarity to the poetic forms that would emerge in Syriac and Greek over the fourth and fifth centuries, characterized by the Syriac madrasha and the Greek kontakion.[139] Within the narrative fiction of the text, the hymn and its performance echo the memory of lyric victory hymns sung by girls' choirs in ancient Greece.

As in the instance of Philo's Therapeutae and Therapeutrides, Methodios presents a virgin choir in hymnodic splendor as the crowning vision of his idyllic portrait. Indeed, for both authors the sight reported is surpassed by the sound portrayed. In both texts, the musical culmination lends a sense that the rational limits of human speech must be transcended, a feat accomplished by moving from prose to poetry, from speech to song. With voices heightened beyond the measure of learned discourse, both communities stand in virginal choral formation, lending the power of melody, meter, and musical expression to their words of thanksgiving.

In both cases, the virginity of the participants signals a perfection of devotion, an unimpeachable purity of faith and single-hearted commitment to the divine. The virginal body is presented as a physical metaphor of such perfection, an inviolability that is theologically, ethically, and morally complete. For the ancient Jewish or Christian author, such notions were often cast through a gendered imagery of virginity: that of the female body. Hence Philo must include female as well as male ascetics to render his portrait of philosophically perfect devotion. Moreover, for Christian authors, virginity provided the ultimate image of redeemed humanity, when mortality would be replaced by eternal life, and procreation would no longer be necessary. The female body, as image, allowed virginity to function for ancient authors with singular power as a measure of absolute flawlessness; the virgin body was intact, impenetrable, and in these portraits of holy choirs, fulfilled.[140]

Philosophical ideals permeate these accounts of Philo and Methodios, and gendered rhetoric in the guise of female participants or characters serves to express a perfected human state both authors wish to capture in their portrayals. The addition of song to the performance of divinely inspired discourse carries further nuance. Philo's description of ecstatic worship recalls the divine inebriation of Plato's highest state of illumination, captured in both his *Symposium* and *Phaedrus*, where wisdom exceeds the bounds of human rationality.[141] In Methodios, the sense of philosophical ecstasy is joined by an intensity of eschatological wonder.[142]

A similar quality of eschatological fervor pervades another literary portrait of an imagined women's choir, that of the late fourth-/early fifth-century Latin ascetic, theologian, and biblical scholar Jerome of Stridon. In his well-known Letter 22, "To Eustochium", the daughter of his friend Paula, Jerome presents an impassioned call to virginity and ascetic devotion.[143] In masterful prose that moves seamlessly between persuasion and invective, with dazzling displays of classical and biblical learning, Jerome urges Eustochium to commit herself to lifelong virginity. His argument is highly eroticized both in rhetorical imagery and in narrative content.[144] But at the culminating moment, Jerome, too, portrays devotional fulfillment with the image of a women's choir in sublime hymnody. In the final sentences of his letter, he exhorts Eustochium to envision what will await her if she can preserve her vow of virginity unsullied to her death, when she will meet Christ her Bridegroom in heavenly joy:

> Go forth, I beg you, for a little while from your body and picture before your eyes the reward of your present toil. . . . What will be the glory of that day when Mary, the mother of the Lord, will come to meet you, accompanied by choirs of virgins (*choris occurret comitata Virgineis*); when Miriam, after the passage through the Red Sea and the drowning of Pharaoh with his army, holding her tambourine, will chant to the answering women, "Sing to the Lord, for he has triumphed gloriously . . . [Ex 15:20–21]." Then shall Thekla fly with joy to embrace you. Then shall your Spouse himself come forward to meet you. . . . Then yet another chorus of chaste women (*alius castitatet chorus*) shall come to meet you: Sarah will come with the matrons and Anna, the daughter of Phanuel, with the widows [Gen 17–24, Lk 2:36]. There, as in different groups, will be your physical mother [Paula] and your spiritual mother [the widow Marcella]. The one will rejoice because she bore you; the other will exult because she taught you.[145]

Jerome's heavenly choir of women is an arresting vision. In fact, the figure of Christ as Bridegroom is barely visible amid the hosts of women's choirs assembled in their gathered ranks. The choir directors are biblical women: the Virgin Mary, Miriam at the Red Sea, Sarah the wife of Abraham, the prophetess Anna. They include a legendary saint: Thekla, the companion of the apostle Paul. Moreover, they include the women of Eustochium's own circles: her mother, Paula, and their dear friend the widow Marcella. Thus the notion of female sanctity for Jerome in this letter surpasses the precision of lifelong virginity to include, in separate yet exalted ranks, the chaste wife and pious widow, represented here by the flocks of women who accompany Miriam, Sarah, Anna, Paula, and Marcella. All, in this joyous gathering, will sing forth their celebration as they welcome Eustochium to their heavenly abode.

Jerome's depiction shares a number of figures and images with the accounts of Philo (via Eusebios), Methodios, Ephrem himself, Jacob of Sarug, and the anonymous *Life of Ephrem*. There were a limited number of biblical texts on which to draw, and they recur across these texts. Exodus 15 was the favored model. It is worth recalling that for Christian authors the character of Miriam at the Red Sea was invoked not only for her model of singing, but also as a type foreshadowing the Christian ideal of lifelong virginity.[146] The Virgin Mary recurs, although interestingly not with reference to her singing of the Magnificat in Luke 1:46–55, but rather as virgin and mother, or the Second Eve. Echoing in several of these depictions is the passage from Revelation 14:1–5, where the eschatological choir of 144,000 (male) virgins sings "a new song" at the heavenly throne. Both Methodios and Jerome cite the passage explicitly.[147] Moreover, Thekla appears in Methodios and Jerome. The theme of women as teachers recurs; so, too, does a shared tone of eschatological expectation. Methodios, like Jerome, envisioned that an angelic choral escort would greet the souls of faithful virgins upon their deaths, guiding their entrance into heaven's splendors.[148] Interestingly, the scenes in the anonymous *Life of Ephrem* are the outliers: the least biblical or typological, and decidedly utopian rather than eschatological. However, in each of these accounts, human perfection is imaged as embodied and celebrated by choirs of female virgins.

These figures and themes carried a resonance across the late antique Mediterranean, for authors Greek, Latin, and Syriac. In combined configuration, they supported a gendered rhetoric whereby the notion of a virginal women's choir could be used to represent perfection of devotion (by liturgical song), and fulfillment of salvation in a perfected human body (by virginity). The image of women's singing could perform such perfections, and the contributing women's stories—whether biblical or hagiographic—provided justification.

As a utopian or eschatological image, then, women's choirs might provide an ancient author a powerful trope with which to work. The qualities noted above permeate the hagiographic depictions of Ephrem as saint that Jacob of Sarug's homily "On Mar Ephrem" and chapter 31 of the anonymous *Life of Ephrem* sought to present. But the clearest aspect of these comparisons is the simple fact that differentiates Jacob's homily and the anonymous *Life of Ephrem* from the utopian portrayals by Philo, Methodios, and Jerome: the Syriac women's choirs were described in local, civic church settings. The idealized portraits of hagiographic texts and the imperfections that attend lived religious practice may well have offered stark contrast. Nonetheless, women's choirs were a basic part of ordinary Syriac liturgical life, and these accounts place them there.

From this perspective, the use of women's choirs as idyllic image by the likes of Philo, Methodios, and Jerome may offer further indication of a common practice of women's liturgical singing more broadly across late antique congregations, in choirs of nuns or consecrated virgins and widows such as noted in chapter 1. Jerome, for one, surely heard choirs of nuns in the Holy Land liturgies, as reported by the pilgrim Egeria in the early 380s, roughly contemporary with Jerome's travels in the same region.[149] Methodios most probably heard the practice of psalmody by household ascetics or consecrated virgins.[150] Philo's account, the earliest of the lot, shows familiarity with the common Mediterranean practice of mixed choirs, and gives no indication that a mixed choir for sacred song was unseemly.[151] Their literary portraits may have resonated with the lived experience of their readers, rendering each a more powerful encounter. Such, it would seem, is how we should read the literary portraits presented in Ephrem's hymns, Jacob of Sarug's homily "On Mar Ephrem," and the anonymous *Life of Ephrem*.

MODES OF INSTRUCTION

The portraits of women's choirs presented by Ephrem, Jacob of Sarug, and the anonymous *Life of Ephrem* demand consideration of their literary forms and techniques in order to grasp their full content. But how were they disseminated? Who heard or read these portraits? Also crucial for understanding the import of the choirs are the factors of performance, audience, and reception. Chapter 3 will address these issues in some detail, but some observations should be made here. In Ephrem's case, he himself along with the women's choir sang his portrait of the choirs in the presence of the congregation who gathered for the festal vigils to which their composition was directed. His presentation performed its work with and through women's own voices: performance was enactment, in the presence of the gathered church. During Ephrem's career, this would have been a powerful cultivation of women's liturgical song. While his hymns were not continued in their original form in later generations, similar voices addressing and evoking women's singing cast in imagined first-person (female) speech continued to appear in later Syriac hymns over centuries. Such verses continued to nourish an appreciation of women's voices in liturgical contexts.[152]

In Jacob of Sarug's case, his homilies were intoned in the presence of the entire church, as they came together—whether to celebrate Ephrem's feast day or, in the instance of other homilies where he discusses the choirs, as they came together for ordinary Sunday eucharistic worship. Jacob chanted his homilies in the first part of the service, the Liturgy of the Word, when a full congregation including catechumens was present. In one instance, he indicates his homilies followed the scripture readings and were immediately preceded and again immediately followed by the singing of the women's choir.[153] Hence his preaching about the choirs provided a commentary accompanying their performance. Jacob's homilies would have continued their instruction long after the specific occasions on which they were delivered. His homilies were collected and circulated widely through Syriac communities. They were read and chanted through subsequent centuries in vigil services and in monastic services, a practice that continues in some monastic communities today.[154] His teachings, then, had the potential to be ongoing in their impact.

In the case of the anonymous *Life of Ephrem*, the text might have had a less extensive exposure than would have been available in the worship cycles of civic communities where Ephrem's hymns and Jacob's preaching took place. Given its heavily monastic content, it is most likely that the *Life of Ephrem* was intended for monastic communities. In such settings it would have been read for Ephrem's feast day but also at other times in contexts of individual or group meditative study.[155] It may also have been read on his feast day in civic churches. Whether or not chapter 31, the sole place where the choirs are treated, would have been included in such reading or study is impossible to know.

Shared across these three portraits is the palpable tension of late antique religious competition. Christians worshipped in a social context rife with disputes, contestation, and competing claims to truth. These tensions played out internally among Christians as different groups struggled to define the terms of orthodox belief and practice, and used powerful social and political channels to press their positions. These tensions also played out externally, in a society composed of diverse religions not easily coexistent in a culture of intense rivalries and political antagonisms.[156] Ephrem, Jacob, and the anonymous *Life of Ephrem* all cast their portraits of Syriac women's choirs within such contexts. They depict the choirs as active and potent participants in the effort to establish true faith, worship, and practice. Fittingly, in a homily on the prophet Elisha, when Jacob of Sarug lauded the Syriac women's choirs for their role in bringing victory to God's faithful, he did so through an image of choral competition:

> The sound of Your praise [O Lord] thunders awesomely among the congregations,
> And through it the impudent song of idolatry was silenced.
> . . . .
> By the sweet voices of the young women who sing Your praise
> You have captured the World so that all of it would be moved to Your praise.
> The World had been lost to the music of Idolatry
> Through the songs of the virgin daughters of the pagans.
> The captivity that You have returned from the stumbling blocks has applauded.
> All of the nations have gathered and assembled for Your song of praise.[157]

Through women's sacred song, Jacob exulted, God's truth prevailed.

The ancient Syriac women's choirs are anonymous in our sources. No singer is named, no choir specifically identified.[158] Nor do any Syriac sources survive to us written by women until modern times (at least, none of which we can be certain). Thus there is no evidence for women's perspectives on these or any other matters. The evidence was produced exclusively by men. Ephrem, Jacob of Sarug, the anonymous author of the *Life of Ephrem*, and others who wrote about the choirs were church leaders or monastic writers. They had clear agendas regarding the appropriate place of women in their patriarchal social order. Yet they were also men who served with and heard these choirs. Their portraits provide insightful reflection on the functions, roles, and significance these choirs provided, with striking implications in ecclesiastical and theological terms—perhaps even in terms of social meanings.

In the next chapter, I turn to issues of ritual context, space, and presentation. I will ask how the evidence for liturgical celebration contributes to and inflects the performance of these choirs. In turn, I will consider the differently gendered forms of liturgical song within which the choirs did their work.

3

Singing Voices, Voices Sung

Performance, Genre, Biblical Models

Syriac women's choirs performed a ministry of teaching in which poetic form, musical expression, and biblical and theological content all contributed to the instruction provided. Ritual context and ritual presentation shaped how the material was offered and received. Liturgy was an ordered act of worship, the purpose and goal of which depended on a distinct sequence of ritual declarations and actions. Order granted each act its particular meaning and efficacy but depended above all on performance: who did what, when, and for what purpose.[1] Explanatory commentary within the liturgical setting itself directed participants—not only the congregation, but also the clergy, other ritual assistants, and the choirs themselves—as to how one ought to understand and value what the choirs provided.

Singing the instructional hymns of the church was, to be sure, a matter of performing and expressing "Truth." But female vocal performance in liturgical settings of any kind intrinsically raises issues of gender, ritual authority, and ecclesiastical order. The teaching ministry of women's choirs involved more than the words they sang, and was greater than the verbal content of their hymns. All these aspects contributed to the message(s) the women's choirs conveyed, and, indeed, to how their sound was heard, whether in the liturgical assembly or in the civic, public community.

WHAT, WHERE, WHEN, AND HOW?

Little information on the actual performances of Syriac women's choirs survives. Nonetheless, we can try to reconstruct the picture, taking account of the logistics involved and their social and cultural implications. What did people see and hear when these women's choirs sang?

71

As Françoise Briquel Chatonnet has pointed out, late antique Syriac literary sources present the church as the center of daily life for any given community.[2] Church buildings—cathedrals, small chapels, martyria, shrines—demarcated different types of spaces for worshippers in an array of architectural designs (basilicas with or without domes, aisled tetraconch, octagon). At the same time, ecclesiastical operations provided a scaffolding for people's lives, individually and in their families or communities, monastic and civic, anchoring and framing the days and seasons.[3] There were the daily offices: relatively short morning and evening prayer services with psalms and prayers. Deacons or priests led litanies of responsorial supplications for the health and well-being of religious and political leaders, church, community, families, and the world. Small choirs chanted the Psalms, setting the familiar patterns of daily life into a larger frame of sacred memory and divine-human relation.[4] Evening vigil services were especially important on the eve of feast days or other special occasions. Ephrem's hymns, often composed for these vigils, referenced a context of candle light, incense, and evening quiet amid a rhythm of scripture readings and prayers interspersed with hymnody.[5] In *Hymns on the Nativity* 1.63–83, he contrasted the congregation keeping faithful vigil in the dark church with the unfaithful in the city, who, under cover of night, kept a vigil of immoral and unethical conduct.[6]

On such occasions, hymns were important for the nature of the service and also a good way to fill the time constructively. Hymns provided a means for teaching and reflecting on the readings, or the purpose of the occasion itself, whether a special feast day, a "regular" gathering, or a special moment of crisis or celebration. Hymns enabled congregational participation (which helped to keep people engaged), or provided variety through different kinds of performance, as when female and male choirs sang antiphonally. Hymns in the form of dialogue between biblical characters (discussed below) were especially popular, and added a sense of liturgical drama.[7] Hymnography provided variation and color for the services, important especially for those lasting through the night. Church leaders regularly mentioned problems of sleepy, bored, or distracted worshippers.[8]

Sunday liturgies were more elaborately structured, although a detailed picture emerges only slowly.[9] The evidence internal to Ephrem's fourth-century hymns signals liturgical differences to what is described in the late fifth- and early sixth-century homilies of Jacob of Sarug: variance in practices, calendars, lectionary sequences, and theological language. It is tempting to supply missing information by standardizing from the liturgical patterns of Jerusalem, Antioch, or Constantinople, where greater evidence survives. But, again, the Syriac evidence often differs, and sometimes substantially.[10] There is further temptation to standardize across Syriac texts, harmonizing across different locales; or to read anachronistically, supplying information from later centuries.

Late antiquity was a time of extensive liturgical experimentation and expansion throughout the Roman Empire. Regional distinctions could be considerable. Local contexts were always subject to local variations and habits.

Still, as an example we might take the picture offered by Jacob of Sarug in his memra "On the Partaking of the Holy Mysteries," which accords with other evidence at the turn of the sixth century and later.[11] The general template is as follows. The first part of the liturgy, commonly called the Liturgy of the Word, was devoted to the proclamation and interpretation of scripture. Sung invocations and prayers ritually guided a series of readings from the Old and New Testaments, interspersed with alleluias and short hymns. Syriac lectionary lists provide surprisingly numerous scriptural passages for each Sunday, and the West Syriac rite, in particular, evidenced wide variation in its lectionary offerings.[12] These lists date from as early as the fifth and sixth centuries, and may indicate traditions already long in use.[13] As many as fifteen different passages for one service were identified in the earliest list; but, as Gerard Rouwhorst has argued, these may represent options from which the local clergy or bishop might choose a selection.[14] Nonetheless, the large number of readings helps to contextualize the enormous range of scriptural citations and allusions we find throughout late antique Syriac liturgical poetry. The homily followed the readings, with explication, interpretation, and application of biblical stories to Christian life of the present.[15]

The Liturgy of the Word was open to any and every one; catechumens (those people preparing for baptism) or other noninitiates were expected to be present. At its conclusion the unbaptized were required to leave; supervising their orderly exit was one of the duties of deacons and deaconesses. The remainder of the service was exclusively for the baptized, devoted to the ritual preparation for and reception of the eucharist (in Syriac, the *qurbana*).[16] Jacob of Sarug complained that sometimes restless or disinterested baptized participants discreetly (or not so discreetly!) left the service early, along with the catechumens, a behavior sorely rankling the clergy.[17]

Other services adorned late antique civic life: for visitation by distinguished government officials or church leaders; special ecclesial occasions such as feast days, or the arrival of relics or the consecration of shrines or other buildings; funerals; exceptional services for intercession in times of hardship, or thanksgiving in times of abundance or help received.[18] Liturgical occasions, with their structured yet flexible components, provided visual and audible expressions of order to the social structure of a community. They articulated meaning and purpose for daily life, both its mundane cycles and unexpected changes.

Archaeological remains for late antique Syriac churches are scant, owing to a volatile history marked by the tragedies of war, political instability, and natural disasters.[19] These circumstances are somewhat mitigated by literary sources, occasionally providing precious glimpses. An anonymous sixth-century memra on the cathedral dedicated to Holy Wisdom in Edessa likens the structure of the building to the temple of heaven: a wondrously gleaming expanse of pillars, arches, and vaults supporting an exquisite dome.[20] The beautifully rendered edifice is described as radiant with light from windows, gleaming surfaces, and the glow of chandeliers

FIGURE 6. Silver liturgical instruments with gold trim. Attarouthi Treasure, Syria, 500–650 CE. Metropolitan Museum: Purchase, Rogers Fund and Henry J. and Drue E. Heinz Foundation, Norbert Schimmel and Lila Acheson Wallace Gifts, 1986.

and candles. Intricate columns and furniture articulated the interior space with biblical symbolism.[21] John of Ephesos mentions embroidered tapestries covering the altar and other furniture even in small home chapels, as well as holy paintings and images for the walls.[22] Jacob of Sarug, along with various church canons, mentions the need to clean, repair, and renew liturgical accessories.[23] Syriac artisans were especially known for their fine skills with silver and gold. Archaeological finds have recovered liturgical instruments and lectionary covers on a spectrum from simpler to the more elaborate wealth of major urban churches.[24]

But Syriac literary sources rarely trumpet churches as places of material beauty. Rather, they stress the splendor of liturgy *as performed ritual*: of orderly movement, of inclusive collective presence, and above all, as beautified by the adornment of song.[25] If I am repeatedly emphasizing the importance of voices, it is because the sources themselves celebrate enhancement by song above all else. In a memra celebrating the annual autumn Feast of the Sanctification of the Church, Narsai of Nisibis depicted the liturgy as a glorious wedding feast between Christ the Bridegroom and the Church as Bride.[26] He extolled the occasion as one of gifts sung by every guest: scripture readings as the sung offerings of prophets, apostles, priests, kings, and martyrs, while angelic and human throngs offered their intermingled melodies, singing their joy.[27] In services short or long, the beauty of sacred song was enriched by the attendant sounds of swinging censers and liturgical fans, of swishing vestments, of prostrations and processions. Repeatedly, Syriac hymns mention the *sounds* of joining heaven and earth in worship, and celebrate the highest form of worship as that of holy song.[28]

Sources offer only partial indications of where the choirs stood for their performance within church buildings. In Ephrem's hymns from the fourth century, the poet tells us that madrashe were sung from the bema, a raised, horseshoe-shaped platform usually in the center of the nave, the place from which the lections were also read and the homily delivered. Ephrem referred to himself singing from the bema, leading the choir, who stood close by, and the congregation in the refrains, evoking a give-and-take, responsorial pattern of exchange.[29] The description is one of effective teaching and lively liturgy. Elsewhere, he refers to the women's choir standing by or at the bema, implying a ritual significance to the location, where they could be audible and visible to all.[30]

The bema was also a feature in synagogues and Manichaean churches of the same period. Approximately forty-five such arrangements are extant in Syrian churches built between the second half of the fourth century and the early seventh century.[31] Their liturgical use differed somewhat between the West and East Syrian liturgies, and there is variation in the surviving plans as to their design, material (stone or wood), and location within the nave (in the center or at the back). However, the bema churches are extant only in a relatively small area of the region in which Syriac liturgies were served. Other church remains indicate an ambo or smaller platform more like a pulpit. In either case, a walkway extended out from the altar in the sanctuary to the platform in the nave.[32]

Church canons restricted access to the bema or ambo. The Syriac version of the Canons of Laodicea (late fourth century) included this rule: "Regarding those who are entitled to recite on the ambo. It is unlawful for others to sing in the church, except only the *benai qyama*, the chanters (*psaltes*), those who ascend the ambo and recite the (sacred) books."[33] Did this rule include the bnat qyama as well—the daughters of the covenant as well as the sons of the covenant, for the masculine plural form might be used generically? Does it signal the possibility that women's choirs stood on the ambo or bema for certain hymns? Or was it only the soloist or leader (for example, Ephrem, or the deaconess choir director) who stood on the elevation? Some archaeological findings indicate these platforms were large enough to provide a raised step for the choir as well as the soloist, and scholars such as Pauline Donceel-Voûte and Robert Taft have presumed choral performance from these steps or platforms.[34]

Readings, sermons, and singing from the bema or ambo carried enhanced authority compared with locutions from other areas of the nave. Linked architecturally and choreographically to the altar at which the sacramental offering took place, these raised platforms served to differentiate, arrange, and order proceedings and persons.[35]

Such evidence as we have most often set the women's choir at the front of the women's section of the congregation, next to the bema or ambo.[36] There may also have been instances when they performed from the bema or ambo, with increased authoritative presence. In one hymn, Ephrem denounced the heretical liturgies of the Sabbateans, scornful that they allowed a woman to teach from the bema.[37] The visible, elevated authority of the bema, then, was most often gendered: men sang, read, and taught from its platform. Women might gain a proximate, shared authority for the teaching their singing provided from their stance nearby.

Local practices clearly varied. But, however choreographed, the women's choir had a designated space that accorded them distinct if limited ritual authority. Standing between congregation and clergy, with gendered inflection (standing on the women's side), the choir's instruction was meaningfully located ritually as well as spatially, their authority limited yet nonetheless affirmed.[38]

What did the choirs wear? If they were composed of daughters of the covenant, as seems most frequently the case by the fifth century, then we may expect that they wore the simple black robe of these covenanters, including the black headscarf.[39] Such apparel was common for late antique female ascetics in general, including consecrated virgins, widows, and nuns. The sixth-century Canons of John of Tella (Johannan bar Qursos) addressed families with children tonsured as sons and daughters of the covenant. Canon 27 required them to provide these covenanters with "a decent garment" from their childhood onward, in contrast to the "luxury of white linen garments," that is, the fine clothing of local notables.[40] Clothing of suitable quality was important for proper liturgical decorum. Canon 26 of the same collection admonished the clergy, "A beautiful appearance [using the Greek word, *skhēma*] and order must always be found among you in chaste dress and sober walking."[41]

The Syriac version of the Canons of Laodicea transmitted in the West Syriac *Synodicon* stated that readers and chanters should not wear liturgical stoles when they read or sang.[42] Did the rule indicate desire or need to lessen the liturgical prominence, and thereby the institutional authority, of singers, including women's choirs? Does it suggest that at some point some kind of liturgical adornment may sometimes have been added to the basic garb of the daughters of the covenant? Or was it only the soloist (musical leader) or deaconess choir director who might have sought or been awarded adornment with a stole? We do not know. The mention of such details may have been prescriptive rather than descriptive: imagining or anticipating a problem, rather than reacting to an existing one. Either way, such a rule signals a late antique cultural milieu in which there were social reverberations to such basic components of liturgical performance. Comportment contributed to liturgical authority as well as social status, in a cultural climate that valued external appearance, sartorial definition, and adornment.[43]

Most often, as noted in earlier chapters, references to the women's choirs describe their singing as "loud," "bold," or "with a loud voice." Other common descriptors include "sweet," "pure," "soft," and "instructive." The constant emphasis on loud volume may be simply a reminder that these choirs operated in a premodern society without microphones: their singing needed to be loud to be effective. The acoustics of late antique churches presented challenges to preachers as well as choirs, although the buildings were often designed with sophisticated acoustical engineering.[44]

However, a great deal of worship in late antiquity took place outdoors, in public shrines and civic processions, and on occasions of public religious ceremony. Numerous Syriac sources refer to women's choirs singing in such outdoor liturgical gatherings. In these instances, participants are described in their ranks. The order of procession, or the order of stance in public gathering, followed that in the liturgy: bishops, priests, deacons, sons of the covenant, daughters of the covenant, widows, ascetics, laity. As in church, the daughters of the covenant—the women's choir—stood in a specific location, between (ordained) clergy and (nonordained) monastics and laity.[45] But, outdoors, loud singing was even more important than inside a church building, for the acoustical issues were heightened by the heated social climate of religious competition.[46] Jews, pagans, Christians, and the diverse groupings of each, all performed religious activities in outdoor, public locations. Processions were a major part of civic life, and songs were invariably involved.[47] Choirs had to sing loudly to be heard, and to outsing their rivals. When Jacob of Sarug claimed that the thundering voices of Syriac women's choirs had silenced those of pagan women's choirs, it was this context that provoked his exultation.[48] We will return to the tumultuous civic milieu in subsequent chapters. But, for the moment, it is worth remembering that women's choirs had to "thunder" their songs "with loud voice" in order to be effective performers in these circumstances.

There was direct correlation between these outdoor performances—whether in the civic square, streets, or shrines—and those that took place in church buildings, whether local churches or cathedrals. Liturgical protocol pertained in all settings of Christian ritual, and thereby liturgical authority and significance as well. Formal liturgical practices and ecclesiastical rulings demarcated the nature and qualities of religious authority granted to each participant. But the ritual body defined in such formal settings continued to operate as such in other locations.[49] Insofar as women's choirs received designated authority by virtue of their office, their place, their garb, and their liturgical responsibility to sing the madrashe, that authority attended their singing in all contexts. When historical chronicles mention the public singing of women's choirs in instances of crisis, public mourning, or celebration, such accounts affirm their ritual significance and also their ecclesiastical authority as teachers of right belief.

Amid all this ritual framing, what did the women sing? From their earliest attestation, Syriac women's choirs were identified as singing a specific type of Syriac hymn, the madrasha, in a variety of liturgical contexts. As a literary form, the madrasha was a flexible genre that may originally have been spoken rather than sung.[50] Scholars dispute whether "hymn" is the proper designation for the form, preferring the term "teaching song" as more accurate and appropriate to the types of content.[51] For the texts relevant to our study here, madrashe (plural) were sung poems—hymns—of varied isosyllabic meters, arranged in stanzas or sometimes in couplets. Sometimes they were written in acrostics to mark the verses, using the name of the poet or the letters of the alphabet. Stanzas were generally followed by a short, repeated refrain. There were different types of madrashe, but, as their name suggests (from the root *daleth-resh-shin*, to practice, train, or instruct), their form signaled instructional content. The use of verses with refrains created a dialogic quality that echoed common schoolroom practices of the time, with melodic recitation and response as a learning mechanism.[52] Such refrains also resonated with a civic culture wherein repeated acclamations characterized public participation at games, the theater, political events, and other forms of civic activity.[53]

In late antiquity, the period with our most abundant evidence for Syriac women's choirs, madrashe were used liturgically and also in school settings. Their content for both was devoted to biblical instruction through the retelling of biblical stories, while also addressing major feasts or liturgical seasons and primary ecclesiastical teachings of the church.[54] I refer to madrashe as "teaching hymns" because all such content was used for doctrinal purposes in ancient Syriac liturgical contexts. The goal was proper understanding of Christianity and its teachings, in a historical context riddled with religious and theological disputes.

Liturgical madrashe took various forms, with an array of performative arrangements by choirs male and female, the congregation, and chanters and clergy, in different patterns of vocal interaction. The chanter or soloist might sing the stanzas and the choir the refrain; or choirs might sing antiphonally; or the choir(s) might sing the stanzas and the congregation the refrain. Meter allowed great variety in the presentation of material, while melody cast it in memorable form. Refrains contributed to the didactic quality: their brevity and repetition underscored key themes or ideas, drilling their import into the mind.[55] Refrains also engaged the congregation as participants, making the hymns an interactive component of worship rather than a concert-like presentation. Hymns engaged the liturgical gathering as a whole into dialogic encounter.

The melodies of late antique Syriac hymns have been lost, although as is the case for the biblical Psalms, titles are indicated in the manuscripts, where each hymn is prefaced by a *qala* or melody title that indicates its meter.[56] These *qale* appear in the manuscripts of the earliest Syriac hymnography collections, dating from the sixth century, and continue thereafter. However, present Syriac sacred music derives from substantially later historical circumstances and cannot be imposed back onto the texts of late antiquity.[57] Sometimes stray verses of Ephrem, Jacob of Sarug, or other ancient poets are still sung in contemporary liturgies; these, however, are removed from their original literary and musical settings, even when melodies are indicated by the same title.[58]

The performed offering of the choirs was framed and enhanced by its interaction with the broader ritual setting of physical space, arrangement, decor, and choreography.[59] Amid these factors, liturgy provided a sonic feast. In late antiquity, its entire presentation was done through forms of heightened speech: whether the melodies of song in hymns, alleluias, or responses; or the more contained patterns of intonation or cantillation that inflected readings, sermons, litanies, supplications, and prayers. The singing of the women's choirs interacted with songs, melodies, and chants voiced by others.[60]

In the remainder of this chapter and throughout the rest of the book, I pursue a different route toward understanding the Syriac women's choirs. I suggest that we may hear resonance between the *sounded content* of the liturgical poetry they sang—or the content of that intoned or chanted by male liturgical participants in sequence with the women—and the *sounding presence* of the choirs themselves. In that resonance, I will argue, we may grasp something of the vitality of ancient Syriac liturgical practice. Moreover, we may hear something more substantive: a powerful weight and meaning of women's voices, both real and imagined, for late antique Syriac society and culture.

For the present chapter, I turn to the specific example of the Virgin Mary. Mary's voice entered Syriac liturgy in three basic ways: voiced in Ephrem's hymns and others along his model as lullabies imaginatively added to the gospel accounts; in dialogue hymns of Mary's battles with other figures from her gospel story; and in narrative metrical homilies such as those preached by Jacob of Sarug, expanding and expounding the biblical accounts. Mary's distinctive case, then, will also introduce the primary poetic genres of late antique Syriac liturgy, each with different performing voices.[61]

EPHREM'S MARY: SINGING THE PROPHETESS

Ephrem's madrashe introduced a robust presence of women's choirs in Syriac services, but we have no direct evidence of how the singing was arranged. Ephrem mentions in several texts that women's choirs sang the madrashe, without further detail. From the varied hymnic structures his madrashe present, we can—and should—picture a variety of styles, as I have noted. In some instances Ephrem (or a soloist) will have sung the verses while the choir led the refrains; in others, the choir sang the verses. In hymns where he placed Mary's words as direct first-person speech, women's voices would have highlighted the affect, adding an evocative quality to the imagined scene. In all cases, the women's singing was a constant reminder that a woman played a major role in God's redemptive work. We should keep these possible variations in mind as we consider the content Ephrem offered.

In chapter 2, I discussed Ephrem's presentation of Mary as a typological figure for the women's choirs. In his Nativity hymns, Ephrem depicts Mary as the object of liturgical and devotional attention for her role in salvation. But he presents her further as a subject who participates in the larger task to which these madrashe contribute: collective worship. In these hymns, Ephrem represents Mary as one who offers her own voice as a vehicle for teaching, proclaiming, and revealing the fullness of divine dispensation—the very work the women's choirs enacted.

Interestingly, Ephrem does not set Mary in the context of a musically drama-tized narrative, as other Syriac writers did, to retell the gospel stories. Nor does he set her in an active dialogue with other characters from her story. Instead, Ephrem locates Mary both within and outside of time; she speaks from the world of the biblical past, and at the same time somehow together with the gathered faithful of the church community in the present. Sung by women's choirs, the performance of these hymns would have heightened their rhetorical content: women's voices would have raised Ephrem's words, fashioned as Mary's song.

In his *Hymns on the Nativity*, Ephrem most often addresses Mary's song to Christ, her newborn son:

> My mouth knows not how to address You,
> O Son of the Living One. I tremble
> To dare to address You as son of Joseph,
> For You are not his seed. Yet I shrink
> From denying the name of him to whom I have been betrothed.
> > *Refrain*: Praise to You, Son of the Most High, Who put on our body.
>
> . . . .
>
> Although You are the Son of the One, I shall call You henceforth
> Son of many, for myriads of names
> Do not suffice for You, for You are Son of God
> And Son of Man and Son of Joseph
> And Son of David and Lord of Mary.[62]

Again, and after each verse, the congregation sounded the refrain. Directed to her child, Mary's voice sang out from within the community, leading the task of praise. Even so, as mother hers was a voice distinct from all others.

Ephrem's Mary reiterates themes that Ephrem delighted to highlight else-where.[63] Voiced from her perspective, these themes become embodied rather than observed. The paradoxical wonder of the human mother who bore, suckled, and nurtured the divine Creator was a favorite theme across patristic authors of the time.[64] In *Hymns on the Nativity* 4, Ephrem offers his own voice with a cascade of images, including startling play with gender when he follows a Syriac tradi-tion that sometimes granted feminine characteristics to a creator God most often portrayed in masculine terms.[65] In this hymn the very Word of God drinks the mother's milk he himself created; he who suckles all creation to give it life nurses at the breast of Mary. He whose own womb contains the universe, who himself burst forth from the womb of Sheol, yet confined himself to Mary's womb, allowing his greatness to be carried and cradled by her smallness.[66]

Images of wealth and poverty, honor and shame, could provide further impetus for the wonder of divine glory rendered in the humbleness of human life. Ephrem underscores the imagery by grafting its literal example onto the Mary he pres-ents in song. Strikingly, he portrays her as materially poor, vulnerably young, and

FIGURE 7. Nativity scene. Fresco, Northern conch, Church of al-'Adra, Deir al-Surian (Monastery of the Syrians), Wadi Natrun, Egypt, 10th cent. Mat Immerzeel/Paul van Moorsel Centre, Vrije Universiteit Amsterdam.

scandalously female. Such presentation raises sharp critique of class, gender, and other social markers: how could such a figure be God's choice? With this depiction, Ephrem displays the dazzling power evoked by the notion of universal salvation. This he demonstrates in hymns without Mary's voice:

> Women heard that behold a virgin indeed
> would conceive and bring forth. Well-born women hoped
> that He would shine forth from them, and elegant women
> that He would appear from them. Blessed is Your height
> that bent down and shone forth from the poor.
>
> Even little girls taken by Him [as brides]
> spoke prophetically, "Yours, Lord, let me be,
> for I am ugly, to You I am fair,
> and if I am lowly, to You I am noble."[67]

The congregation's response affirmed Ephrem's declaration: "Glory to Your dawn, divine and human."[68]

When Ephrem gives Mary voice from the social location of poverty, she is presented through her words as the sudden instance of paradox and inversion. There are real-world implications to this perspective. The marginalized stand at the center, the voiceless become heard, eloquent and clear, as the social world beyond the church doors looms into view. The congregation's refrains caused each verse to stand, poised, its words momentarily paused in a shimmer of song. Mary sings:

> All the chaste daughters of the Hebrews
> And virgin daughters of rulers
> Are amazed at me. Because of You, a daughter of the poor
> Is envied. Because of You, a daughter of the weak
> Is an object of jealousy. Who gave You to me?
>> *Refrain*: Glory be to You, My Lord, and through You to the Father,
>> on the day of Your Nativity.
>
> Son of the Rich One, Who despised the womb
> Of rich women, what drew You
> Towards the poor? For Joseph is needy,
> And I am impoverished.[69]

In his construction of Mary, then, Ephrem takes theological themes of grave philosophical weight and reifies them into the specific, and literal, person of the young unwed mother. Casting Mary as Daughter of the Poor, Ephrem set theological discourse as a social reality. Familiar doctrinal teachings were shown to be concrete in their instantiation. As we saw in chapter 2, Ephrem's Mary was a scorned, maligned figure, suffering willingly for her Lord's sake.[70] The image of Mary as Daughter of the Poor would continue in Syriac tradition. Its contrast to the triumphal, imperial, and royal depictions of Mary in Byzantine tradition, starting in the early fifth century, and subsequently in medieval European expressions, remains stark.[71] The contrast underscores the distance Syriac Christianity remained from structures of political dominance through its long history.

A certain temporal permeability pervades Ephrem's hymns. What time and location frame Mary's character: When and where does she speak? Where is the surrounding moral order?[72] Her representation in Ephrem's verses implicates the contemporary Christian community. Her character challenges worldly order. In *Hymns on the Nativity* 17, Mary is borne on divine pinions in a heavenly ascent. From the heights, she sees a new order in which slave and free, male and female, will be able to attain perfect freedom for devotion to Christ; in like manner, the sick will find their health, the lepers their cleanliness. Mary sings:

> O chaste woman, eagerly await my Beloved,
> so that He might dwell in you, and unclean women, too,
> so that He may purify you; churches, too,
> so that He may adorn you. He is the Son of the Creator
> Who came to restore the whole creation.
>> *Refrain*: Praise to You, Son of the Creator, Who loves all![73]

Ephrem's *Hymns on the Nativity* include no historical narrative frame, presuming the familiar story of the gospel Nativity accounts. Yet they do not follow those accounts, rather locating Mary's speech in unidentified moments of the larger story. Their content does not contribute to the narrative lacunae of gospels, canonical or otherwise. Instead, these verses engage the work of interweaving Old and New Testaments and biblical with historical time, providing an exegesis that sets the Nativity and its characters typologically within scripture as a whole. Performed as the worshipping song of the gathered church, their content is also contextualized in the present life of the civic Christian community. Mary's voice—sounded by women's choirs, echoed by the congregation—wove together with Ephrem's own voice an understanding of the biblical narrative as the emergence of Christian history.

Yet even in these hymns where Mary's voice is proclaimed and celebrated, Ephrem curtails its effect. For the voice he grants her remains safely within the ritual structure of the church—a structure that supported and sustained the Christian community as a viably constituted social body. Within the sphere of sacred ritual, the constraints of civic order could be challenged, negotiated, and upheld through redefinition as the instrument of divine dispensation.[74] Hence Ephrem reminds his congregation that Mary's voice could be active, outspoken, and yet obediently deferential. She might challenge a fallen world order, but she would not question divine initiative. For that would be speech of a truly dangerous kind: the heretic's hubristic inquiry into matters beyond human ken. Ephrem's celebration lays the boundaries for Mary's words:

> Blessed are you also, Mary, whose name
> Is great and exalted because of your Child.
> Indeed you were able to say how much and how
> And where the Great One, Who became small, dwelt in you.
> Blessed is your mouth that gave thanks but did not inquire,
> And your tongue that praised but did not investigate.
> Since His mother was awed by Him, although she bore Him,
> Who is sufficient [to know] Him?[75]

To this the congregation sang their assent with the refrain, "Glory to the One Who sent Him!"[76]

DIALOGUE IN SONG: THE CONSTRAINTS OF STORY

Apart from Ephrem's towering genius, late antiquity was a fertile period for Syriac composers. A vibrant diversity of liturgical poets and forms flourished long after him. Among these there survives a large body of anonymous hymnography in the form of dialogue poems (sing. *sughitha*, pl. *sughyatha*), many composed in the late antique period. These were a subgenre of madrashe, with simply metered stanzas separated by a short, repeated refrain. A literary genre of verbal contest, the sughitha has roots deep in the ancient Near East. In Syriac and in Christianized form, it was a favored mode of liturgical poetry.[77] The sughitha presented a dialogue between two characters, set between a short narrative frame at the beginning and a closing doxology at the end. Sung antiphonally by two choirs in alternating verses—identified as such in the manuscript transmission—it set up a conflict or contest of competing positions. Each character required the same number of verses to voice their role; usually, this meant a verse for each letter of the alphabet. The argument moved back and forth until one side finally prevailed through persuasion (sometimes aided by divine inspiration on the losing side).[78] As madrashe, these hymns would have been assigned to the women's choirs. Although the manuscripts indicate two choirs, they do not specify gender. Perhaps, given their form as a dramatic dialogue, a male choir of sons of the covenant or deacons would have sung the opposing voice.

Not all sughyatha treated biblical stories, and not all of the biblical sughyatha offered a male/female exchange. But when women were one of the speaking characters, the performative alternation between male and female voices again raised the prominence of the female choirs. That prominence would have been further underscored by the literary structure requiring an equal number of verses for each of the characters, whether or not the biblical account granted such ample exchange—and in the case of women, the Bible rarely presented their speech. The Virgin Mary was one of several biblical women whose stories were presented in this form. In her case, the dialogue poems provided generous opportunity for imagining Mary's voice as an active agent in God's salvific plan. At the same time, the requirements of the literary form, as well as what emerged as the conventions of the liturgical presentation of Mary, combined to shape a highly stylized construction for her voice.[79]

The Syriac dialogue poems about Mary were set in specific gospel scenes:[80] the exchange between Mary and the archangel Gabriel at the Annunciation, the (imagined) argument between Joseph and Mary when he learned of her pregnancy, the inquiries between Mary and the Magi at the Nativity, and the exchange between Mary and the Gardener in the resurrection narrative of John 20 (in Syriac tradition, it was the Virgin Mary and not Mary Magdalene who was the recipient of this first resurrection appearance).[81] In related anonymous madrashe, Mary sings lullabies to the newborn Christ child and also engages in a shorter dialogue with the prophet Simeon the Righteous at the presentation of Christ.[82] Each of these dialogues has a biblical basis in the gospel texts, whether explicitly, as with the Annunciation (Lk 1:26–38), or implicitly, as with Joseph's doubts (Mt 1:18–24). The scene and its place in the gospel narrative were familiar to the congregation. But apart from Mary's brief response to the archangel in Luke 1:38 ("Let it be to me according to your word") and her Magnificat sung to her cousin Elizabeth in Luke 1:46–55, none of these biblical accounts included words spoken by Mary.

Straightforward and unadorned, the sughyatha effectively presented the major themes of Marian doctrine. This they did in the form of a basic argument between faith and reason, each side personified by a biblical character offering conventional objections and rebuttals. The antiphonal format expressed the conflict and its resolution in stately simplicity. But if the verses of these hymns present standard formulae, Mary's voice is nonetheless striking—and problematic. Although the sughyatha lack the sharp-edged social critique of Ephrem's *Hymns on the Nativity*, Mary's character cannot be voiced in these exchanges without gender and class status as complicating factors. Hence these hymns repeatedly express puzzlement, frustration, and even dismay that Mary speaks in opposition to the male partner in the dialogue. The complication adds dramatic friction to the familiar narrative context.

In the sughitha on the Annunciation, Mary stands against the archangel Gabriel. She refuses to accept his greeting, asking, "Who are you, sir? And what is this that you utter?"[83] The angel's replies do not convince the wary virgin, whose suspicious hesitation elicits the angel's astonishment: "It would be amazing in you if you were to answer back, / annulling the message which I have brought to you."[84] But Mary holds her ground. Citing the disastrous model of Eve, who received the words of the serpent without question, Mary refuses to accept from Gabriel a pronouncement she cannot understand. As the verses alternate, the angel's exasperation mounts. He sings:

> The angelic hosts quake at His word:
> The moment He has commanded, they do not answer back;
> How is it then that you are not afraid
> To query the thing which the Father has willed?[85]

"I too quake, sir, and am terrified," Mary sings in reply, but still she questions.[86] The constraints of metered verse do not diminish Gabriel's annoyance: "It is appropriate you should keep silence, and have faith too."[87] A further eleven verses of argument ensue before Mary's mind turns, and the dialogue changes to one of shared praise for the wonder of divine activity.

Throughout this entire hymn of fifty-four verses, the congregation sings its response: "Praise to You, O Lord, / whom heaven and earth worship as they rejoice." These are words of shared witness to the momentous events set in motion by this imagined exchange. The final four verses call for all of heaven and earth to join their voices and give thanks, that from every mouth, visible and invisible, praise should sing forth.[88]

In the sughitha with Joseph, Mary insists on her virgin conception in the face of her husband's anguished disbelief. The exchange carries a harshness ill concealed by the dignity of antiphonal singing between two choirs:

> JOSEPH These words are inappropriate,
> Mary, for a virgin; keep silent,
> For falsehood will not stand up.
> Speak the truth, if you are willing.
>
> MARY I repeat the very same words—
> I have no others to say.
> I remain sealed, as the seals of my virginity,
> Which have not been loosed, will testify.
>
> JOSEPH You should not contradict,
> But confess that you have been seduced.
> Now you have fallen into two wrongs:
> After getting pregnant, now you tell lies.
>
> MARY You should believe my words,
> For you have never seen any falsehood in me:
> My chaste and truthful life bear me witness
> That I am a virgin and have not lied.
>
> JOSEPH I am astonished at what you say:
> How can I listen to your words?[89]

Demure as this representation of Mary may be, her voice grates against social convention. Expectations of socially correct speech are violated not only by the content of her words, but also by her act of opposition to her husband. Instead of the humorous frustration of the archangel Gabriel, we are here given Joseph's anger. Their message is the same: "Woman, be silent; do not contradict."[90] Still the exchange continues: Mary is not silent; she does contradict.

Here again, a generic refrain punctuates the verses of the dialogue between Mary and Joseph. In this case:

> Praise to You, Lord, for at Your coming
> sinners turned from their wickedness
> and entered into the protection of Eden's Garden,
> which is the holy church.[91]

Through forty-five verses of tense exchange, the congregation repeats its witness, allowing all participants to linger on each moment of this encounter. Voices perform; voices bear witness; voices participate.

In the sughitha of Mary and the Magi, issues of status further complicate the problem of Mary's voice. Trying to protect her son from his enemies, Mary flaunts her poverty to conceal his identity, asking defiantly, "When has it ever happened / that a poor girl has given birth to a king? / I am destitute and needy."[92] The Magi, mistaking her ruse for lack of comprehension, patiently and condescendingly attempt to instruct her on the nature of her child; repeatedly, they call her "young

FIGURE 8. Nativity scene. Manuscript illumination, Berlin Sachau 220, fol. 3r, 11th cent. Staatsbibliothek zu Berlin.

girl," speaking as if she were naive. But it is she who is wise, knowing, and rightly concerned about persecution: words are her only weapons, and she uses them well. As if to sum up the cultural discordance of granting such importance to a woman's speech, the sughitha of Mary and the Gardener has Christ in the guise of the Gardener attempting vainly to fend off Mary's persistent inquiries about her son. He exclaims, "How you weary me with your talk / how you vex me with what you say!"[93] Yet Mary prevails: the truth is revealed because she will not be silenced.

Because of their rhetorical form, the dialogue poems set the significance of Mary's speech in high relief. In each sughitha, an equal number of stanzas must be sung in her voice as in that of her male opponent—stanzas intoned by women's choirs, in a performative voice that enhanced their sung content. Moreover, Mary's words are the point. The opening and closing frames to the hymns do little more than identify the narrative context; they do not describe or fashion a character for her. Instead, whatever sense of character she is given derives from the dialogic exchange: the words she speaks, those spoken in return, the engagement of verbal contest, and its resolution by spoken reconciliation. In these hymns, speech is the action that defines Mary. Indeed, as action, her speech is extraordinary in its power: it can stem God's salvific plan or bring it to effect.

Nonetheless, at the same time that these hymns highlight the import of Mary's words, they constrain them to a far greater degree than was evident in Ephrem's hymns. Though presented and performed as dialogue—as liturgical drama—these words are rigidly embedded in a narrative of defined temporal and spatial location.[94] They are located in the time and place of the biblical account. Ephrem's hymns had crossed the entire spectrum of biblical time, across Old and New Testaments, and also traversed the spectrum of historical time, past, present, and future. The presentation of Mary's voice as prophetic contributed to this dynamic of open temporality. In the dialogue hymns, by contrast, Mary speaks not as prophetess, but as a character in a given moment. The salvific consequences were surely understood to be eternal (if not timeless), but the moment was precisely demarcated, without possibility of slippage.

JACOB OF SARUG AND METRICAL NARRATIVE

A third poetic form beloved in Syriac tradition was the metrical homily (sing. *memra*, pl. *memre*). Unlike the madrashe, these were not sung by choirs, female or male, but rather chanted by the (male) homilist in a simple pattern of isosyllabic couplets.[95] The great Syriac poets of late antiquity produced these lyrically vibrant homilies: Ephrem the Syrian, Jacob of Sarug, Narsai of Nisibis, the Isaacs of Antioch, and others, each with a favored meter. For Jacob of Sarug, the choice was equal syllables in patterns of 12 + 12; other poets composed in 5 + 5 or 7 + 7. Shorter metrical units, often comprised of standard poetic formulae, comprised the building blocks for each line. The effect was not unlike that of ancient epic poetry.[96] Occasionally in the manuscripts, memre, rather like madrashe, were punctuated by refrains from choir and congregation. Both poetic forms treated a wide variety of subjects on the life of faith, biblical stories, exegesis, and basic doctrinal instruction. Like the madrashe, memre were described as "sweet" and "pleasant" in their melodies.[97] Simple repetitive patterns helped to make content accessible. Rhythm, meter, and melody (or chant) were useful to aid memory. Sung poetry was effective as a teaching tool, as we have seen, and also as a learning tool. For Syriac poets, the memra as much as the madrasha served this purpose.

The memre of Jacob of Sarug provide another important instance of Mary's voice within Syriac tradition.[98] The performative quality of these homilies is immediately different from that of the hymns we have considered thus far: the male preacher chanted these verses. On the other hand, Jacob's homilies on Mary are presented in long, even leisurely retellings of the gospel stories with excurses on major doctrinal issues. They focus on the same scenes already noted above, with the addition of Mary's visit with her cousin Elizabeth. Into his narrative accounts, Jacob adds substantial blocks of dialogue at the expected interludes: between Mary and Gabriel at the Annunciation, between Mary and her cousin Elizabeth at the Visitation, Mary and Joseph upon her return from her cousin's home, the lullabies of Mary to her newborn son, and the exchange between Mary and Simeon at the presentation in the Temple.[99]

In different homilies for different liturgical occasions, and particularly for the feast days associated with these episodes, Jacob recalls the same events, each time with different points of emphasis, imagery, or doctrinal instruction. As is characteristic of his writings in general, these homilies follow familiar, standardized presentations of theological and doctrinal positions. If Ephrem's artistry dazzles as much by his peerless originality in imagery as by poetic technique, Jacob's prominence in the Syriac literary memory rests on the genius of presenting traditional materials in familiar yet well-crafted form, often polished with strokes of lyrical beauty.

In comparison with the hymns we have considered thus far, Jacob's literary form allows him the fullest construction of Mary's character and voice. Long narrative passages recount the story, following and embellishing the gospel accounts. Hefty chunks of imagined speech, whether monologue or dialogue, are embedded as the narrative both encloses and also laces through the encounters. The homilist tells his congregation *what* to hear (the imagined words of Mary), and, further, *how* to hear—for her words are surrounded by accompanying comment. In some respects, Jacob's homilies control Mary's presentation as a speaker far more tightly than any other text here considered. On the other hand, Mary's voice remains a volatile entity, even in Jacob's homilies. Jacob makes this point by offering much discussion *about* Mary's speech, in addition to crafting its expression; he refers to her words and describes them more often than he presents them. Ephrem had represented Mary as subject: designated subject of devotion, and participatory subject as speaker. Jacob, by contrast, firmly locates Mary as object: she is the object of his text as she is the object of the congregation's devotional piety.

In his homily "On the Partaking of the Holy Mysteries," Jacob tells us that women's choirs sang immediately before and after he intoned his homily.[100] But whatever the exact liturgical arrangement, their voices would have lingered in the air—and in the ears of the worshipping community—providing a particular sonic frame to Jacob's words. The close correspondence between some of Jacob's dialogues and the dialogues from the same scenes in the sughyatha is also noteworthy.[101] It was perhaps a good preacher's trick to incorporate passages from familiar hymns into his sermon: something to catch the ear of listeners and draw them in through their own recognition of the imagined dialogue. But it would also mean that Jacob's voice carried further resonance with that of the choir, as the homilist chanted words sung by the choir on other occasions.[102] The dynamic was subtle but concrete: voices interlaced in the listeners' memories through words echoed in complementary but distinct performances.

In his treatment of the Annunciation, Jacob presents the paradox of Mary's position by stressing the frailty of her human stance in contrast to Gabriel's celestial splendor. In Jacob's reckoning, the cosmic order itself hinged on this exchange:

> That moment was full of wonder when Mary was standing conversing
>   in argument with Gabriel.
> One humble daughter of poor folk and one angel met each other
>   and spoke of a wonderful tale.
> A pure virgin and a fiery Watcher spoke with wonder: a discourse
>   which reconciled dwellers of earth and heaven.
> One woman and the prince of all the hosts had made an argument for the
>   reconciliation of the whole world.[103]

In Jacob's telling, the moment echoed an earlier encounter, when a woman's voice had first set things awry while carrying the weight of all humankind. In that first exchange, when the serpent had spoken in Eden, Eve had listened and kept silent.[104] Now, Jacob stressed, Mary chose differently. Faced with a strange, nonhuman messenger, she was not swayed as her foremother had been. Instead she questioned and queried; she badgered, she tested. (Jacob's account sings on at length!) Not until she had received answers sufficient to her understanding would she grant her consent—and her consent, the human action necessary for God's redemptive plan, would come only as an act of her own choice. For Jacob, Mary's voice was proof that humanity had not lost its free will. Alone, with no assistance, encouragement, or guidance from others, Mary made her decision, and made it well. If Ephrem had crafted Mary's character as the paradoxical extreme of human insignificance—female, poor, young, of no account—Jacob took these attributes and emphasized two further elements discordant with the ancient social order: Mary as a sharp-minded intellectual, and Mary as the exemplar of human autonomy; "She rose up to this measure on her own."[105]

Jacob's Mary thus spoke a voice that raised tension with the late antique social order. But laying open that tension, Jacob would also immediately curb its impact. For no sooner had Mary spoken her great feat of consent, he claimed, than she turned to a more seemly stance: "She inquired, sought, investigated, learned and then kept silence."[106] It was in fact the measure of her contrast to Eve that Mary knew when to speak and when to be silent. In that difference lay the fate of the human condition:

> As reprehensible as Eve was by her deed, so Mary was glorious,
> And as the folly of this one, so that one's wisdom is shown up.
>
> . . . .
>
> By Eve's silence, guilt and the fouling of a name;
> By Mary's discourse, life and light with victory.[107]

Elsewhere, Jacob sets up Mary and her cousin Elizabeth as the conduits of divine inspiration and revelation—women who spoke a new teaching. They, too, must act on their own: their men are speechless, silent, uncomprehending, just as Luke's Gospel had explained in its first chapter. Joseph was absent, while Elizabeth greeted Mary in the presence of her mute husband, Zechariah, and the voiceless infant John in her womb. The women themselves carried the language of truth in their pregnancies, Jacob declares, for Elizabeth carried the Voice, the Forerunner who would cry in the wilderness, while Mary carried the Word, the divine Son. Elizabeth spoke first, mirroring the role of her menfolk, had they the power to speak:

> And she [Elizabeth] became a mouth for her husband who was not speaking,
> And a harp for the sounds of her baby who was making merry.
> . . . .
> She was explaining what Zechariah was seeking to do;
> She was expressing what the lad was eager to say.[108]

Emboldened by their circumstances and filled with divine inspiration, Mary and Elizabeth spend the time of their visitation engaged in speech. "For three months," Jacob intones, "the sublime and divine story / was being told in the house of the priest on account of Mary."[109] Together, Jacob proclaims, the women read the scriptures and interpreted their readings; together they encouraged, narrated, meditated on the prophets, explained, showed, and discussed. Together they spoke. What contrast, Jacob marvels, when Mary returns to her husband to be greeted by his scandalized disbelief. "Secretly" Joseph attempted to speak with Mary about her pregnancy. But Mary had gained words of power:

> The Virgin also, with loud voice and uncovered face,
> Spoke with him, without a bride's veil.
> And with the revelations and interpretations of the prophecy,
> She was urging him not to doubt on account of her conception.
> . . . .
> She was telling him the words which she learned from the angel,
> And she was narrating to him how the priests in Judea had received it.
> She was also reminding him what the prophets spoke.[110]

By her speech with Gabriel, Mary had acted to effect the divine incarnation; by her speech with Elizabeth, she acted to place that event rightly in the sacred history of scripture, to understand its biblical foretelling and its historical consequences. By her speech with Joseph, Mary acted to bring biblical witness into living history. Elsewhere Jacob would marvel that "by the mouth of Mary" Christ reached out into human encounter, and "with Mary's voice" the Holy Spirit stretched forth into human experience.[111] Indeed, Jacob's Mary rejoices that her words will become the source of new speech by others, even calling forth the women's choirs who would continue the exaltation and praise begun at the Visitation when the two women spoke:

> [Mary speaks:] In the world I will be a great parable full of wonder;
> All mouths will speak of me, profusely.
> . . . .
> Let all the multitudes of virgins praise Him with wonder.
> Because the great Savior shines forth from them to the whole world.
> Let the voice of the young women be lifted up in praise,
> Because by one of them, behold, hope is brought to the world.[112]

In this passage, Jacob's Mary summons the women's choirs who would come to sing the hymns and dialogue poems we considered earlier, and others like them. It is, moreover, from Jacob that we have much of our information about these choirs, as we have already seen. Among the themes in his homily on Ephrem is the notion that Eve had closed the mouths of women in shame, but Mary had opened them in glory.[113] The passage quoted above forges an explicit link between the voice of Mary as chanted by the women's choirs and as intoned in Jacob's own verse homilies, a link earlier enacted in Ephrem's hymns. Ironically, although Jacob controls Mary's speech far more carefully than Ephrem had done, he, too, will use Mary's voice to justify the liturgical practices of his church in terms that recognize their tension with normative social reality beyond the church doors. When he speaks of men and women standing equal before the Lord, he also states that such standing lay "yonder in the Kingdom"—not here in the present world.[114] There are spaces and times appropriate for women's words in Jacob's view; within the church (building and community), and within its historical memory of the biblical past, Mary's character as Jacob represented her could provide the proper voice for those words.

The Syriac texts discussed here differ in literary form and in liturgical presentation. Ephrem's hymns would have been sung, perhaps by choirs together with the congregation, or by the male soloist and the women's choirs. The dialogue hymns would have been sung antiphonally with women's choirs, perhaps alternating the verse dialogue with the male choirs of sons of the covenant or deacons. Jacob's verse homilies were intoned by the preacher, and perhaps framed before and after by the singing of women's choirs. In performance, then, these texts differed in the degree to which they were inclusive of women's voices in their ritual presentation.

In content, these texts also differed in how they located the temporality of Mary's voice. Ephrem's fashioning of Mary's voice as that of prophetess caused an elision between biblical past and historical present, locating her speech in the midst of the gathered congregation in its present worship. The dialogue hymns performed Mary's voice as liturgical drama, yet placed the exchange within specific narrative moments of the church's salvation story. Jacob of Sarug enclosed

Mary's voice within the clear boundaries of narrated account; within that narration, he constructed the social spaces of her speech as decidedly domestic rather than public. While in performance her words were intoned in the space of public ritual, they were mediated by the voice of the male priest, echoed by the ritually contained voices of the women's choirs.

SOUNDING VOICES: SENSING THE ISSUES

The example of Mary's voice opens the rich panoply of voices real and imagined that sounded forth in late antique Syriac liturgies. The voices of the women's choir interwove those of male readers, singers, and clergy; the voices of the laity, male and female, to whom we will soon turn, replied. We can imagine the sounding presence of each of these participants in sequenced interplay of solo, choral, and collective song, with different liturgical moments highlighting the audibility as well as the visibility of each. In turn, every voice in its highlighted moment received a ritual authority and a communal import that carried well beyond its designated turn.

The imagined voices of biblical women also sounded forth: bold, assertive, discomfiting, instructive. The diverse narrative patterns of Syriac poetic forms provided means to constrain or restrict these mythic voices, to be sure. Yet, as we will see, Syriac poets did not often choose to craft their biblical women as paragons of deferential, unobtrusive, socially prescribed behaviors. Strong discordances with cultural norms repeatedly ring out: archangel and husband alike scold and hush an unapologetically vocal Mary who refuses to be silenced. Mary and Elizabeth study, interpret, analyze, and expound the sacred scriptures in the place of their silenced menfolk. Mary's words—imagined, fictive, mythic—sing out beyond the confines of socially limiting spaces, into a public domain that could not be wholly enclosed within church buildings or behind ecclesiastical walls. They were certainly not restrained by restriction to the voices of male performers.

Ironically, these powerful portraits of Mary and others, repeatedly shot through with unsettling social tensions, were the product of male poets.[115] And yet I suggest a complexity of voices even here. The notion of authorship is an especially unstable entity in the context of ancient liturgical texts, as it was for the stories of biblical characters whose narratives spread far beyond their scriptural versions. In the case of exceptional poets like Ephrem or Jacob, an individual's work is clearly evident; but only in part. For liturgical poets incorporated familiar phrases from other hymns or prayers, and above all followed the narratives of scriptural stories. Scripture, in turn, even if somewhat standardized in a recognized canonical version, was itself the product of multiple tellings and retellings; its borders were fluid. These were stories with neither texts nor authors, as Christine Thomas has pointed out so perceptively.[116] No single version belonged to particular writers or poets. Indeed, the religious authority of sacred stories lay in their capacity to navigate multiple views of history, memory, and experience. Women as well as men contributed to the transmission and retelling of these stories. Would they not also have contributed to the hymns?

In the case of anonymous hymns like the sughyatha, the question of "authorship" is particularly precarious. The stanzas are short, and generally in simple meters. In those (admittedly few) cases where a sughitha survives in more than one manuscript, there can be variations within the verses, and sometimes different stanzas.[117] In such instances, we see local variations, unidentified. Did the local choir, or its director, add or exchange a verse? Or pen a fresh version of a familiar gospel scene, already well-known from hymns and homilies sung and heard again and again? Like folk songs, the songs of sacred stories and religious feast days contained well-known characters and episodes, often told with familiar phrases.[118] Their performance was dynamic over time—constantly adjusted, reset, revitalized, even within canonical familiarity. There is no reason to think that women contributed only their singing voices to Syriac hymns over the centuries. They could well have scripted verses to be sung or even entire hymns.

Among the vast corpus of Syriac hymnography—a copious literature of dynamic vitality, produced over centuries—much of the extant material is anonymous.[119] Feminist historians have long questioned the possibilities behind texts of unidentified authorship.[120] "Anonymous" is a capacious term. It may have enabled compositions by women to become part of liturgical collections, transmitted over centuries, precisely by concealing their authorship in times when women's writings were not valued.[121]

I suggest that the sound of women's voices, real and imagined, in ancient Syriac liturgies widens considerably the perspectives by which we should consider late antique societies and, indeed, late antique Christianity. In the annals of ecclesiastical offices, liturgical rubrics, and historical records, as in the Bible itself, women were most often placed at the margins, if not altogether obscured from view. What the Syriac women's choirs teach us, I suggest, is that there is more to be heard and more to be seen. If we shine the spotlight solely on the bishop or priest, or other male ritual agents, we miss a great deal of what took place. The bishop was not the only teacher, whether of Bible or of doctrine. Nor was the message, apart from its teacher, the only piece of the liturgical event that mattered. The evidence discussed thus far shows us that Syriac women's choirs were canonically, spatially, literarily, and ritually subordinated to the male clerical and social hierarchy. Yet this same evidence also shows their presence to have been important—even crucial—to the purpose and meaning of liturgical celebration. Their contributions were substantial, whether in performance or content. This is something scholars have missed. At the least, the Syriac record requires a redistribution of how we understand the forms of authority operating in ancient Christianity as interacting and intersecting forces. Further, it requires us to rethink the social and cultural spaces available to women, and the kinds of agency that resulted. Social and cultural power dynamics were constantly at play, as the liturgical process allowed its participants to challenge, negotiate, and reinscribe a normative social order—a process we will see more fully in the chapters to follow.

In the next chapter, I present the poetic portraits of other biblical women, apart from the Virgin Mary, whose sung voices cast the women's choirs in high relief. In portraits from both the Old and New Testaments, I will argue that the liturgical performance of women's voices—by women, and also with and by men— demands that we reconsider how scholars (and practitioners) have understood women's place and roles within the ancient Christian community. Their contribution was different from that of the men, but no less essential. Women's stories highlighted women's liturgical service as carrying meanings that resonated well beyond the ritual confines of space or rank.

4

Voices Sung

Women's Voices in Contextual Narratives

In ancient Syriac Christianity, liturgical poetry was the primary medium for formative religious teaching, especially teaching the Bible. Genre, expression, and context were significant elements here: *poetry* was a different mode of articulation than prose; *singing* was not the same manner of expression as speaking; and *collective, structured worship* was different than private study or individual reading. How did literary form, oral performance, and liturgical context affect meaning? What did sung liturgical poetry as a mode of biblical teaching accomplish? How did the presence and participation of women's choirs contribute to the process?

In this chapter, I argue that understanding the performance of Syriac women's choirs requires consideration of (1) the social context of biblical needs and interests that gave rise to the liturgical poetry in which the choirs participated; and (2) the biblical stories explored in that poetry, both the hymns and the sermons that occasionally provided commentary on their singing.

ANCIENT LITURGY AND BIBLICAL WOMEN

Between the fourth and sixth centuries, a striking prominence was granted to biblical stories in Christian teaching, including those of women. This attention was often expressed in the poetry of liturgy: in the hymns people sang and in poetic sermons chanted and intoned by priests or bishops. Among others, the interest seemed to flourish especially in the hands—and voices!—of Syriac Christians.[1]

Late antique Syriac homilies and hymns present a number of biblical women as favored exemplars of faith. From the Hebrew Bible came the stories of Sarah the wife of Abraham, Tamar the daughter-in-law of Judah, Rahab the prostitute

96

of Jericho, Jephthah's Daughter, Ruth the Moabite, the Widow of Sarepta, the Shunammite Woman; and from the New Testament, the Virgin Mary, the Sinful Woman of Luke 7, the Canaanite Woman, the Hemorrhaging Woman, the Samaritan Woman, Mary and Martha of Bethany, and others. These and many more were explored in Syriac liturgical poetry through a variety of exegetical techniques, elaborated in hymns and sermons. Clergy, deacons, male and female choirs, and congregations all intoned, chanted, or sang in praise of women of the Bible to the larger Christian community.

Several things make this occurrence important for the history of Christianity and, in turn, of biblical interpretation. First, in the Bible itself women are generally minor characters. Often they are unnamed. Yet in late antique Syriac hymns and homilies, these same women were sometimes set at center stage. Their stories were sometimes told as if from their perspective, and even offered in their (imagined) voices. This attention to biblical women was shared by the larger Jewish and Christian world of the time.[2] A number of biblical women would eventually gain hallowed places in liturgical calendars as well as other devotional traditions throughout Christian communities.[3] In late antiquity, however, such institutional developments were very much at their inception. These liturgical texts helped to pave the way toward those later expansions.

At the same time, the literary forms and performative requirements of these stories in liturgical contexts were not arbitrary. In Syriac tradition, poetry did this work. How it was presented, when, and by whom were matters that informed its task of biblical teaching and interpretation. Offering women's stories through such presentation cast them in a particular light. By the heightened sound of poetry, and in the ritual space of worship or prayer, women's stories were rendered sacred: infused with divine source, even revelatory purpose. Removed from the ordinary words and places of people's daily lives, they were altered toward a timeless, ahistorical, even mythical domain. What meanings did such performance add to the stories of these women?

The interest in biblical characters of all sorts as subjects for liturgical focus occurred at a particular historical moment for Christianity, during the liturgical expansion of the fourth century as Christianity gained prominence. Large numbers of converts arrived at churches, many unfamiliar with the Bible or related matters of doctrine or practice. Liturgy, as we have seen, was a prime place to address this challenge.

Since few people could read, and fewer still could or would have owned a Bible, liturgy was the place where most people gained their biblical knowledge. Scripture readings were laced through the services.[4] Biblical imagery filled hymns and prayers, while biblical characters and stories were displayed throughout church buildings in frescoes, mosaics, and icons. Preachers used their homilies to explicate these images, to retell the stories, and to explain the readings. The very structure of liturgical ritual was used to instill biblical awareness. Rarely was the Bible itself, as a text, the object of study or even scrutiny for most Christians. Instead, homilists and hymn writers cultivated a sense of "biblical memory," whereby people learned their Bible as the Christian story of salvation told in and through liturgical acts. Hence people learned the Bible in an interpreted form.

While storytelling was a fundamental priority, Syriac liturgical poetry also used biblical characters as symbols whose citation provided another means of exegesis.[5] Citations might be as simple as the mention of their names in prayers or litanies; or they might comprise the imaginative retelling or re-presentation of their stories with much dramatic elaboration. The result was a constantly renewed sense of presence for these beloved figures of the sacred past. The attention given to biblical women was part and parcel of this larger, educational enterprise.

LITURGICAL POETRY IN CONTEXT

We have seen that late antique Syriac writers crafted their liturgical poetry in two basic forms: madrashe (hymns) and memre (metrical homilies). The madrashe took various forms, including the sughyatha or dialogue poems, in a variety of isosyllabic meters, and an array of performative arrangements by choirs, congregation, and chanters in different patterns of vocal exchange. The memra was a more narrative presentation, intoned in rhythmically metered isosyllabic couplets. Chanted or sung by its presenter (bishop, priest, or deacon) to the congregation as audience, it offered a different dynamic than that of hymnographic participation or dialogue. As we saw in chapter 3, these differences in literary type and ritual performance affected how these texts did their work.

One of the favorite types of teaching employed by Syriac homilists and hymn writers was the presentation of biblical stories in imaginatively elaborated form, starting from the base of a biblical text and retelling the story through the eyes— and especially the imagined words—of its characters.[6] The rhetorical technique of imagined speech, sometimes in the form of soliloquies and sometimes in dialogue with other characters, was an often-used and brilliantly engaged aspect of Syriac poetic instruction.[7] In the case of biblical women, this meant composing long and sometimes elaborate speeches and dialogues for female characters whose presence in the Bible made them important, but who, in their scriptural texts, were silent or barely granted brief comment. Major theological themes, as well as matters of social and religious tension, were addressed through these means. We have seen the example of the Virgin Mary in this regard above in chapter 3.

Oftentimes, Syriac poets employed narrative or dramatic techniques similar to explorations of biblical characters also current in rabbinic exegesis, particularly as found in haggadah and midrash. Indeed, the term "midrash" derives from the same root as "madrasha"—*daleth-resh-shin*, "to tread out or thresh out," as on a threshing floor. This was not only a matter of exegetical technique. Syriac elaborations of biblical stories often show close interaction with Jewish discussions of the same characters and stories.[8] Often, the source of a Syriac interpretation may be found in Jewish texts, to a degree far more common than in Greek or Latin Christian authors. Moreover, like their Jewish counterparts, Syriac writers sometimes produced compelling dramatic versions of biblical stories that were not, apparently, intended for liturgical presentation. Some of the most powerful Syriac literature—such as the dramatic memre of Sarah at the binding of Isaac (Gen 22) or the saga of Joseph, including a courageously repentant Potiphar's Wife (Gen 39)—was the product of brilliant poets, largely unnamed, whose texts contain no indication of liturgical usage but nonetheless show significant interaction with liturgical content on the same biblical figures.[9] As with their Jewish counterparts, such texts demonstrate a vibrant literary culture connected to, but separate from, scholarly practices of biblical study or its more accessible liturgical presentation.

Ephrem's *Commentary on Genesis* is an example of a scholarly work that proved influential among generations of ancient and medieval students, poets, and theologians. It shows scrupulous care in its treatment of the biblical text, but also offers narrative elaborations that, however brief, provided the kernels for further imaginative exploration of the characters in other works, whether by Ephrem or other authors.[10] Some of the most striking hymnographic or homiletic portrayals of stories from Genesis can be traced back to a remark in Ephrem's *Commentary on Genesis*, as we will see shortly in the case of Tamar, the daughter-in-law of Judah. The same can be said of Ephrem's other commentaries on both Old and New Testament writings.[11]

The narrative traditions that late antique Syriac scholars produced and circulated were not only grist for the consideration of educated intelligentsia. They also found expression in the hymns and homilies brought to liturgical presentation. From this perspective, they had a social history as well as a scholarly lineage. The laity who heard the stories expressed in the poetry of song and sermon were unlikely to have known the exegetical routes by which a story gained its expanded telling. They heard the results: a compelling portrait, an affective account that roused their interest, their emotions, their devotional convictions, their religious sensibilities. In liturgy, the stories were granted a social location and a social purpose: the cultivation of a Christian subjectivity, a moral and ethical character, and a citizenry who would conduct their lives domestically and civically according to the teachings of their church.

In each case, performance inflected presentation. What was said in an imagined dialogue, in the retelling of a biblical story, was qualitatively changed by who said it, from what narrative perspective, in what ritual context, and with what performative features. Further, the authority—religious, moral, ethical—of the interpretation given could be heightened or diminished depending on whose voice presented it: that of the biblical character, male or female; that of the narrator, whether literary or performative; or that of the office through which it was sounded: by bishop, priest, chanter, choir male or female, or congregation. These were more than multiple voices. They carried multiple religious authorities, distinct yet overlapping, of different registers yet mutually constitutive, offering the teachings to be learned.

Particular stories highlighted the singing of the women's choirs. Sometimes this was by direct means through their own singing, as in the case of hymns cast in the voice of the Virgin Mary. Other times, the highlighting occurred through the imagery of imagined sound and voice recited by male singer or priest in ritual proximity to the women's choirs. In what follows, I suggest two overarching biblical narratives that seem to have provided ongoing contextual frames for the singing of the women's choirs. From the Old Testament, I take the example of the scandalous foremothers of the messianic lineage fulfilled in the birth of Jesus. From the New Testament, I take the examples of the bold witness offered by the women Jesus met. I look first at how Ephrem presented these women in his madrashe, and then their homiletic presentation by Jacob of Sarug, a century and more later.

CONTEXTUAL NARRATIVES 1:
HOLY FOREMOTHERS, SACRED SCANDAL

We have already considered Ephrem's *Hymns on the Nativity* with respect to his construction of voice for the Virgin Mary.[12] But the hymns he composed for the Nativity feast ranged across a much larger biblical landscape. Ephrem knew this feast in its earliest eastern form, celebrated on January 6.[13] A recent addition to the Christian liturgical calendar in his day, Ephrem found the Nativity an occasion and a means to champion various causes that were particularly inflammatory at the time. Primary among these were a biblical canon that included both the Old and New Testaments (as he called them); the theology of the Nicene Creed, with an emphasis on Jesus's full humanity as well as his fully divine nature; and the defense of the Virgin Mary against slanderous questioning of her virginity. In his historical context, Ephrem's Nativity hymns were polemical weapons, in a controversially heated climate.

Ephrem's Nativity hymns offer clues to the scripture readings that would have been part of the Nativity season, and were perhaps included in the vigil service at which the hymns were sung.[14] These hymns are dominated by references to the Hebrew Bible, often to the great patriarchs and prophets, but often, also, to those figures, men and women, cited in the genealogy of Jesus from Matthew 1:1–16 and Luke 3:23–38. By such references, Ephrem's *Hymns on the Nativity* retell the broad sweep of the salvation drama, from the fall of Adam and Eve through the vicissitudes of Abraham and his descendants, the great prophets, and the trials and tribulations of the ancient Israelites: all in lyrical cascades of names in typological array.

In these hymns with their dizzying rosters of biblical persons, Ephrem does not assume that his congregation have detailed knowledge of these figures. Rather, he wants the congregation to understand how these figures should be recalled, in what groups and in what relations. What were the key characteristics or qualities that should be associated with these names? What virtues or vices should the names represent? As the congregation sang the refrains to the hymns, not only were the patterns of the refrains imprinted in their minds, but the congregation also took their own place in the hallowed history unfurled before them.

At the same time, Ephrem's insistence on reciting these formidable lists of names was a polemical tactic. Such a historical sweep required a biblical canon in which the Hebrew Bible was joined to the New Testament. It presented a claim—driven home to the congregation by their repeated refrains—that the stories, generations, prophecies, triumphs, and sufferings of the Hebrew Bible could be rightly understood only in and through the birth of Christ, the Messiah. Moreover, the Messiah could be rightly understood only in and through these inherited biblical histories. Here and elsewhere, Ephrem explicitly castigated Jews, Marcionites, Manichaeans, Valentinians, and others: those who touted other Bibles with other scriptures, or who interpreted the same writings differently.[15] All these groups flourished in the cities of Nisibis and Edessa, where Ephrem lived and taught. By Ephrem's count, the Nicene orthodox of his community were a small minority of the Christian population. It was crucial that they should understand the sacred narrative of the biblical canon as a whole as *their own* story and history.

With exuberant splendor, Ephrem's *Hymns on the Nativity* glide through the generations of sacred history that led to the moment of Christ's holy birth. In his poet's voice, Ephrem rejoices at the fulfillment of God's plan in the incarnation, delighting in God's victory over Satan's wiles and the folly of human weakness. Celebrating Mary, he extols the earlier mothers of the salvation drama. His highest praise is for those who bore their children of seemingly unholy alliances. Like Mary, they had suffered calumny and scandal for their acts of faith; like her, they were vindicated by the event of Christ's birth.

Repeatedly, these hymns reference the women named in the messianic lineage of Matthew 1:1–17: Tamar, Rahab, Ruth, Bathsheba, and Mary.[16] Their names were troubling to Ephrem, as they were for the Gospel writers (and, apparently, Jewish commentators before them); in the lineage recalled in Luke 3:23–38, women were omitted altogether.[17] In the Bible, Tamar, Rahab, Ruth, and Bathsheba acted in ways crucial to God's purpose for his chosen people. Yet these four also blatantly transgressed the sexual mores of their times. The widowed Tamar (Gen 38) disguised herself as a prostitute and seduced her father-in-law, Judah, to conceive an heir. Ruth, another widow, climbed into the bed of her cousin Boaz, seeking shelter (Ruth 3–4). Bethsheba, the wife of Uriah the Hittite, committed adultery with King David (2 Sam 11–12). Rahab was a prostitute who helped the Hebrews to victory at the battle of Jericho (Josh 2:1–21, 6:17–25). Each of these women had conceived and borne sons who were critical links in the genealogy of the Messiah. Each had done so in a sexually transgressive manner. In Matthew's genealogy, the inclusion of these four women with the Virgin Mary as the only named women of the messianic lineage is frankly disquieting. Was Mary to be grouped with the other four as an adulteress among adulteresses or promiscuous woman among harlots? Surely not!

Yet how should these matters be understood? How, indeed, should the scripture reading of Matthew 2, with Joseph's doubts about Mary's pregnancy, following the recitation of this genealogy and its women, be explained? In his hymns, Ephrem does not—and *cannot*, in this literary form—reprise the scripture readings, or expound on them in order to explicate. Instead, he and his choir sang stanzas with short, lively images attached to each name: each story in a nutshell, so to speak.[18]

In his Nativity hymns, Ephrem imaged the divine nature that would become incarnate in Jesus as a "holy seed," a "fiery coal" hidden in the Davidic line that would become the "medicine of life" for all people. Since "fiery coal" and "medicine of life" were terms also used for the communion bread, Ephrem built an intimate connection between this story of genealogy and the individual Christian's own liturgical life. The scandalous women of the messianic lineage were those who hungered for that seed with singular longing, pursuing it by every and any means. Thus, Ephrem sings, Tamar stole it from Judah; Ruth lay with Boaz in order to seize it; Rahab beheld it and chose her salvation.[19] "Theft," "deceit," and "shamelessness" are the terms Ephrem repeatedly employs for these women.[20] Heedless of consequence, relentless in their quest, they had no patience for social conventions. Ephrem marveled, "Because of You [O Christ], women pursued men!"[21] The wonder, Ephrem sings, was that good could be worked through such impudence:

> . . . by filth
> [Tamar] stole chastity, and by nakedness
> she entered furtively to You, the Honorable One,
> Who produces chaste [people] from the licentious.
> . . . .
> For the adultery of Tamar was chaste
> because of You. . . .
> She desired You, pursued You, and even
> became a harlot for Your sake.
> For You she longed, You she kept [in memory], and she became
> a chaste woman. She loved You.[22]

In extraordinary images of paradox—indeed, with a rhetoric of paradox par excellence[23]—Ephrem sings of carnal acts with the language of ascetic perfection. Reversing every order, respectable women degraded themselves for the glory of God—and behold, Ephrem sings in astonishment, they were justified! "May Ruth receive good tidings. . . . Let Tamar rejoice," for

> By You honorable women made themselves contemptible,
> [You] the One Who made all chaste.
> . . . .
> Ruth lay down with a man on the threshing floor
> for Your sake. Her love was bold
> for Your sake. She teaches boldness
> to all penitents. Her ears held in contempt
> all [other] voices for the sake of Your voice.[24]

Rather than folly, their acts had been prophetic, enabling the singular moment of God's incarnation to come about. On the one hand, Ephrem proclaims their acts to have been justified, and therefore redeemed by Christ: "You repaid [Ruth] quickly / the wage of her humiliation: instead of ears [of wheat], / the Root of kings, and instead of straw, / the Sheaf of Life that descends from her."[25] On the other, he presents these women in the mode of holy fools, whose apparent folly is revealed to be surpassing holiness. At the same time, in his lyrical sleight of hand, all become types for the impossible yet true revelation of the Nativity: a virgin bears a child; a newborn babe is God without age; the poverty of the manger enthrones the Almighty. The women of Matthew's genealogy are shown to be types of concealed sanctity, whose paradoxical witness anticipates the impossible contradiction of God-become-human.

When he turns to the righteous foremothers, those whose sons were legitimate heirs of their fathers, Ephrem celebrates in more subdued tone. These mothers were bare shadows of Mary in her perfection. They had begged for children without trusting in God's purpose:

> Rachel cried out to her husband; she said,
> "Give me sons!" Blessed is Mary
> for, without her asking, You dwelt in her womb
> chastely, O Gift
> who pours Himself upon His recipients.
>
> Anna with bitter sobs
> asked for a child; Sarah and Rebekah
> with vows and words, and even Elizabeth,
> again, with her prayer [asked] for a long time.
> Although they suffered, afterward they were consoled.
>
> Blessed is Mary, who without vows
> and without prayer, in her virginity
> conceived and brought forth the Lord of all.[26]

Bound by convention, these righteous mothers had not perceived the truth unfolding through their very bodies. All the more was Mary blessed, for "without vows /

and without prayer, in her virginity / [she] conceived and brought forth the Lord of all."[27] In her lullabies, Ephrem chanted triumphantly, "a new song" was born.[28]

But what Matthew's grouping of women implied, Ephrem's hymns spelled out: the Virgin Mary was maligned and scorned in her own day, just as Tamar, Ruth, and Rahab had been in theirs. The Nativity proved not only her innocence, but also the justification of the women before her who had chosen scorn over propriety in order to fulfill God's purpose. Hence Ephrem's Mary rejoices, "I who am slandered / have conceived and given birth to the True Judge / who will vindicate me. For if Tamar / was acquitted by Judah, how much more will I be acquitted by You [O Christ]!"[29]

Moreover, as we saw in chapter 2, the vindication of Mary—and Tamar, Rahab, and Ruth—by the Nativity event also effects the vindication and justification of the consecrated women of Ephrem's day—including his choirs who sang these hymns.[30] When Mary's voice sings out for Christ to vindicate her blackened reputation, the women's choirs who sang these hymns became themselves the objects of divine advocacy and protection.

How might we account for Ephrem's exuberant praise for the illegitimate mothers of the messianic line, in contrast to his more sober (albeit lyrical) praise for the righteous wives who also bore sons for that lineage? And how can we reconcile his advocacy for virginity in the very hymns where he has lauded the actions of Tamar, Ruth, and Rahab in a divine pursuit sexually enacted? For there are broadly two problems here, even as Ephrem was fighting two main battles with these hymns.

One was the battle for Nicene orthodoxy in a city rent by numerous Christian factions, and in which the Nicenes (as Ephrem complained bitterly) were the poor minority. A tireless champion on behalf of the Nicene church, Ephrem wrote at length—in hymns, prose refutations, and verse homilies—against those Christian groups he deemed heretical.[31] Certainly, Ephrem wrote his hymns as polemical statements: not only to instruct right doctrine, but explicitly to refute false teachings.[32] Celebration of the Nativity allowed a Nicene theology that affirmed the genuine reality of Christ's human nature, contraposed to an (alleged) Arian understanding that subordinated the Son to the Father. At the same time, it provided an occasion to glorify Christ's divinity. The Nativity further affirmed the reality of full humanity and full divinity against groups like Manichaeans, Marcionites, or Valentinians. All these, according to Ephrem, taught that divine and human natures could not mix and derided the idea that the physical could be a vehicle of divine saving action. Repeatedly in the Nativity hymns, Ephrem emphasizes the humiliating reality of Jesus's human person, dwelling on the sweat, spittle, blood, dung, and poverty that were necessarily part of his incarnate experience.[33] This motif, in addition to Ephrem's continual stress on the reality of Mary's birth giving and motherhood, were polemically charged theological teachings.

The fourth century also brought the rise of asceticism as a distinct form of Christian life. Throughout the Christian communities of the Roman Empire and

Persia, considerable anxiety accompanied that rise. Where should asceticism be located in the social order? How would the ecclesiastical structure order it? Where would authority lie? What were the implications for normative civic life? These questions were particularly challenging when it came to women's ascetic practices. Ephrem lived and worked in cities (Nisibis and Edessa) all his life. He knew ascetics within the life of the city, and he knew what scholars sometimes call "proto-monasticism," since organized monasteries or convents would not become common until after his death. His *Hymns on the Nativity* provided a forum—one of many, for him—in which to advocate the superiority of the consecrated life within the civic Christian community.[34] Not only did the figure of the Virgin Mary provide a justification for women's ascetic vows. Further, the figures of Tamar, Rahab, and Ruth provided models for devotion to God that were wholly physical, indeed even wholly sexual. To be devoted to God was to be wholly given, body and soul, to the Heavenly Bridegroom. In early Syriac tradition, betrothal imagery drenched the languages of baptism, worship, and piety. In Ephrem's hymns, the holy desire of Tamar, Rahab, and Ruth had enacted that devotion just as surely as the consecrated virgins of his congregation now embodied it within the Christian community. Again, a polemical social context appears to lie behind the hymnographic presentation.

A century and more later, Jacob of Sarug also treated the scandalous foremothers of the messianic lineage, in an exceptionally beautiful verse homily that retold the story of Tamar and Judah from Genesis 38 in the form of narrative drama.[35] The scriptural choice is puzzling, since Genesis 38 as a reading appears in no known Syriac lectionary list, including those before Jacob's career.[36] But Jacob's homily "On Tamar" includes a number of important motifs from Ephrem's references to her in his Nativity hymns, and further includes consideration of other women of the messianic line: Leah, Rachel, and Ruth. In fact, Jacob begins the narrative portion of his homily by expressly stating the importance of the genealogy by which the divine image "travelled down all the generations / transmitted mysteriously over the lineages, / So that God Himself might be mingled amongst humanity."[37] Because this clear genealogical context frames the entire homily, it seems plausible that, like Ephrem, Jacob preached this homily during the Nativity season and in response to lectionary readings that included the genealogical passages from the Gospels of Matthew and Luke.[38]

Jacob takes up his narrative by recalling the generations from the beginning that led to the messianic line, from Adam to Seth to Noah to Abraham, stating that God's revelation to Abraham of his "elect seed" established an expectation and a desire for the incarnation. Women were especially enamored with this holy hope: "In various places women were yearning for the choice seed— / that from them He who was expected to come to earth might shine forth." This holy thirst included the "straightforward women of integrity," Leah and Rachel, sisters who competed to bear sons to the Hebrew patriarch Jacob in Genesis 30. Inflamed with the "fire" of divine love, these two had acted shamefully, "impudently," in ways "most hateful to chaste women," as if they loved lust, when in fact it was the divine lineage for which they longed:

> They acted without restraint, showing no shame, because they were aware
> of what wealth was concealed in the godly man [Jacob].
> Rachel, importunate and like a prostitute, demanded of him,
> saying, "Give me children, otherwise I will die."
> Leah, like someone infatuated and loving adultery, hired him,
> and she was not ashamed to plunder the wealth that she so desired.
> It was not with the lust of adulterous women that they were fired,
> but it was for the seed of their weighty man [Jacob] that they longed.[39]

So, too, Jacob recalled, had Ruth appeared to act "in the outward guise of wanton women" when she crawled under Boaz's cloak. "She was not ashamed, chaste woman that she was, to seize hold of his legs," Jacob insists. Rather, determined to seize the holy seed, "in her vigilance she stole it, just as she had wanted, in an impudent way." What a history, Jacob marvels!

> When and how have women so run after men
> as these women who contended over the Medicine of Life?
> . . . incited . . .
> with love of the Only-Begotten before He had ever come.
> It was because of Him that they acted without restraint and schemed,
> putting on the outward guise of wanton women,
> despising female modesty and nobility,
> not being ashamed as they panted for men.[40]

How should the congregation understand this sacred story of scripture? Jacob crafted his lyrics carefully: "It was not harlotry in the case of these sincere women, but love for the blessed seed that incited them." Despite their carnal acts, Jacob intoned, these women "remained chaste," since it was they who ensured that God's plan was fulfilled in human destiny.[41] Indeed, it was that fulfillment in the incarnation for which they truly longed, the source and focus of their otherwise scandalous desires.

Turning to Tamar, Jacob admits that the story defies every moral code: she acted as a prostitute, and with her own father-in-law! Yet, Jacob exhorts, the faithful will find another meaning in the text if only they will approach it with the right disposition:

> In the case of the story of Tamar, unless a mind that has faith
> Listens to it, the discerning woman will seem worthy of reproach,
> Whereas if an intellect that loves to listen to the mysteries
> Should hear this tale, it will render back in return for it praise.
> All the words that the Spirit of God has placed in Scripture

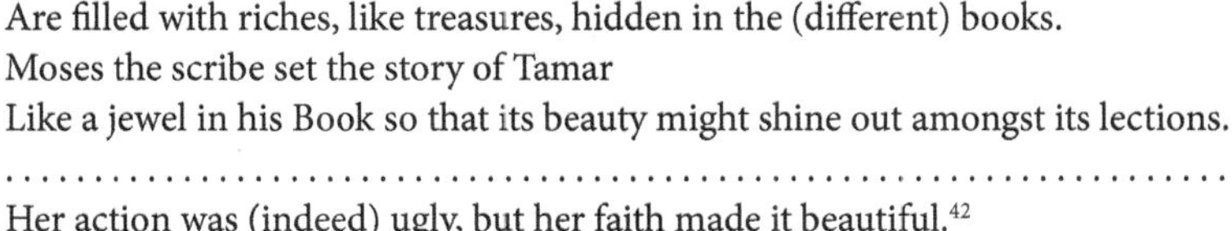

> Are filled with riches, like treasures, hidden in the (different) books.
> Moses the scribe set the story of Tamar
> Like a jewel in his Book so that its beauty might shine out amongst its lections.
> . . . .
> Her action was (indeed) ugly, but her faith made it beautiful.[42]

By this narrative strategy, Jacob will go on to present Tamar as the image of the church, betrothed to Christ her Heavenly Bridegroom. In the process of this explication, he depicts Tamar, her shocking plan for conception, and her shrewd escape from the death penalty through images and vocabulary that evoke in turn the Suffering Servant of Isaiah 53; the Virgin Mary, unjustly doubted by Joseph and maligned by the townspeople; and the righteous Susannah of Daniel 12 (LXX), wrongly condemned to stoning for adultery, only to be rescued just as the crowd descends.

Thus Jacob tells us that Tamar came to her marriage with the expectation of joining the messianic line, but found herself widowed. "Trembling," "diminished," with her heart "shattered," the faithful Tamar waited for her husband's family to fulfill their duty. Instead, "she was treated unjustly, humiliated and put to shame, / she was pained, broken and afflicted."[43] In desperation, she resolved "to steal the blessed seed," planning to "set a trap to enmesh Judah himself." Alight with fervent prayer, determined to succeed, Tamar then strips off the respectable garments of widowhood and clothes herself "like a prostitute" in the "clothes of flighty women."[44] Jacob lingers on this paradoxical image of concealed sanctity:

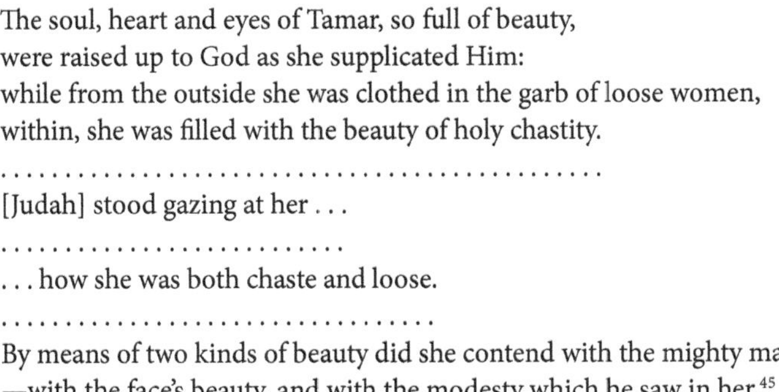

> The soul, heart and eyes of Tamar, so full of beauty,
> were raised up to God as she supplicated Him:
> while from the outside she was clothed in the garb of loose women,
> within, she was filled with the beauty of holy chastity.
> . . . .
> [Judah] stood gazing at her . . .
> . . . .
> . . . how she was both chaste and loose.
> . . . .
> By means of two kinds of beauty did she contend with the mighty man
> —with the face's beauty, and with the modesty which he saw in her.[45]

Strangely moved by the uncanny beauty Tamar exudes in the fervor of her prayer, Judah falls into the trap. Soon, "robbed and plundered," yet wholly unawares, he departs, "faith having accomplished the affair." Tamar, "rejoicing" and "exultant," returns to her widow's withdrawal. Yet shortly her pregnancy is apparent:

> Judah's whole household bristled with threats and denouncements,
> along with numerous insults to the outcast woman.
> But Tamar sat there, serene and silent, unperturbed,
> for she was confident, feeling no shame over the matter.[46]

Describing Judah's explosion of anger at the news, Jacob reflects on the Mosaic law that condemned adulterers to death—a law that ought to have condemned Judah no less than Tamar. But Tamar rises up at the last moment, brandishing the tokens of staff, ring, and scarf to prove the paternity of her child, and speaking with boldness, "My lord judge, I have witnesses. . . . Son of Israel, judge a bereaved woman justly."[47] Abashed and mollified, Judah pronounces her innocence. Thus, Jacob sings, "like an athlete who had won in the arena, she received a crown." At this he launches into an extended hymn of glory, addressing first a lyrical celebration to Tamar, "filled with the beauty of righteousness"; and then an earnest charge to his congregation to take Tamar as the perfect image or type of the church. Like Tamar, the church must hold fast to the holy yearning that binds her to her Heavenly Bridegroom; like Tamar, the church must guard steadfast the tokens her Lord has given for her protection—faith, baptism, and the cross of light. By these, the church as "Bride of Light" will arrive safely at judgment day. Urging that Tamar "serve as a mirror for the entire world," Jacob draws his homily to a close.[48]

As with Ephrem, Jacob presents his account of Tamar in response to differing religious controversies. For Jacob, late in the fifth and early in the sixth centuries, the theological battle was against Chalcedonian (dyophysite) Christology. His celebration of Tamar and the scandalous women of the messianic genealogy allows him to counteract the dyophysite charge that the (miaphysite) dissenters damaged the full humanity of Christ, absorbing his human nature into his divinity.[49] At the same time, Jacob, too, faced controversy over the role of holy women in the church. Unlike Ephrem, he need not defend women's monastic vocations—a battle resolved by his time. However, the stabilization of women's monasticism and the prominent role given to women's civic ministries in Syriac Christianity particularly in the fifth and sixth centuries made possible strong leadership roles for holy women in the public, civic sphere of Christian activities.[50] At times, that public role could be abrasive to the social order. By Jacob's own presentation, the women's choirs apparently shared this sense of contested propriety in their public role.[51] Jacob's portrait of Tamar provides justifying models by which to negotiate such tensions.

The presentations Ephrem and Jacob provide of Tamar and other women of the messianic lineage offer a jolting contrast to standard late antique models of female piety, and to the normative homiletic exhortations addressed to late antique women by church leaders.[52] Most often, the touted models—whether biblical figures, martyrs, saints, or exemplary women of the community—were presented in terms conforming them to familiar stock types: the pious widow, faithful virgin, steadfast, morally impeccable martyr, and any number of variants. By these familiar types, women were exhorted to follow a life of faith. Moreover, as types, the roles of these figures were identified and reinforced through performative features.[53] For example, in most instances, female nakedness would be deplored as immoral. But in the female martyr—stripped naked in the stadium before the entire city and subjected to heinous torture—nakedness was invariably a mark and measure of her virtue; rather than evoking lust in the onlookers, it revealed the martyr's glory and innocence.[54]

This kind of paradoxical inversion of social codes is evident in Ephrem and Jacob on Tamar and her associates. Where impudence, boldness, and above all sexual transgression would otherwise be unthinkable as female virtues, in the context of God's salvific plan for incarnation—a plan requiring the messianic lineage—such traits were necessary. And they were necessary above all for women to display, since, as Ephrem, Jacob, and others often recalled, it was by a woman's misplaced boldness that humanity first fell, when Eve chose to act with impudent desire for her own ends. Thus by the very means humanity was led astray in the first place (Eve's ill-chosen disobedience), women could return humankind to its rightful course, with boldness and yearning for God's own body. That body, incarnate, would return everyone and everything to their rightful order.

Such theological schemes were not the stuff of rarified scholarly biblical commentaries in late antiquity.[55] Ephrem and Jacob presented their accounts of these biblical women in the most public, accessible, and inclusive location of Christian teaching available in their times: the liturgy. In hymns and verse homilies composed expressly for the purpose of public teaching, their presentation of the biblical past through figures like Tamar carried powerful resonance for the congregation's contemporary times. In these instances, the voices of women's choirs singing these hymns, leading their refrains, and framing the homily before and after its recitation were set in high relief. Women's voices sang and attended these stories, reminding the congregation at every turn that the scandal of women's participation was the very measure of God's intention.

CONTEXTUAL NARRATIVES 2: BOLD VOICES BEARING WITNESS

Ephrem's common theme for biblical women is that they stood as figures faithfully devoted to God in the face of grave social opposition.[56] Above all, they bore witness to Christ as the incarnate Son of God. Ephrem's *Hymns on the Nativity* accentuated the humanity of Christ by their stress on the physicality of his human lineage, underscored in Ephrem's hymns by the history of sexual misconduct and scandal that brought it to fulfillment. At the same time, Mary's virginal conception and birth giving attest to Jesus's uncompromised divinity.

In his *Hymns on Virginity*, by contrast, Ephrem puts forth New Testament women apart from the Virgin Mary as a twofold model of witness and proclamation. They are the ones who realized, acknowledged, and bore witness, without compromise or denial, to Christ as the divine Son fully human. Unlike the male disciples, they did not misunderstand or fail or deny their Lord. Rather, they proclaimed the gospel—God's truth revealed through his Son—with bold, commanding, public declaration.[57]

In *Hymns on Virginity* 26, Ephrem addresses an array of New Testament women in turn, directly, personally, with joyous acclamation. To Martha (Lk 10:38–42) he sings, "Blessed are you, Martha, to whom love gave / the confidence to open your mouth. . . . / . . . Blessed is your mouth that sounded forth with love."[58] To the woman who called a blessing to Christ from the crowd in Luke 11:27, he offers thanks for her "voice that became a trumpet . . . among the silent."[59] To the Canaanite Woman who dared to approach Jesus despite her heathen status, and who refused his rebuke in her insistence that he heal her daughter (Mt 15:21–28), he sings salutation for her boldness (*hutspa*) that "conquered the Unconquerable One": "Blessed are you who broke through the obstacle fearlessly."[60] In this one hymn of sixteen strophes, Ephrem names and addresses the Virgin Mary, Martha and Mary of Bethany, the Sinful Woman, the woman who called out a blessing from the crowd, the Hemorrhaging Woman, the widow who gave two mites, the Canaanite Woman, the Widow of Nain, the mother of James, and the wife of Pilate. Each he praises for her wondrous devotion, exhibited despite obstacles or reproach—and in several of these gospel episodes, the reproach had come from Jesus himself.

In *Hymns on Virginity* 34, Ephrem praises the Hemorrhaging Woman, the daughter of Jairus, the Samaritan Woman, and the Canaanite Woman, "whose love bellowed out" in her approach to Christ.[61] The clustering of biblical exemplars is characteristic of these hymns, as is Ephrem's emphasis on faith given voice, loud and bold. By their forthrightness, he sings, their witness vindicates but also exceeds that of Old Testament women. Thus in *Hymns on Virginity* 26, Martha's complaint to Jesus amid her harried service to him and his disciples is cause for Ephrem's praise. He contrasts her with Eve, whose silent acceptance of the fruit in Eden caused the downfall of humanity—and also the silencing of all women thereafter, in their shame. Moreover, Martha's witness was greater than that of the Old Testament women, for she did not speak to angels, as had Sarah when the heavenly messengers visited Abraham in Genesis 18, but with divinity itself:

> Blessed are you, Martha, to whom love gave
> the confidence that opened your mouth.
> By the fruit Eve's mouth was closed
> while she was hidden among the trees.
> Blessed is your mouth that sounded forth with love
> at the table at which God reclined.
> You are greater than Sarah who served the servants,
> for you served the Lord of all.[62]

But Ephrem grants special regard to the Samaritan Woman of John 4, who met Jesus at the well and returned to her city to proclaim that the Messiah had come. Ephrem praises her as the enlightener of her people—for Ephrem, like other church fathers, treats the Samaritans as Gentiles who, in contrast to the Jews, were willing to receive Christ as the Messiah. In *Hymns on Virginity* 22, he praises the Samaritan

Woman's openness to Christ and also her generosity, as one who did not keep her discovery to herself: "You left behind your pitcher, but you filled understanding / and gave your people to drink."[63] Although maligned and slandered as a barren widow of dubious reputation, she spoke up "with perception,"[64] "as a learned one, as a disputant, yet modestly."[65] "Modest," yet with "head high," "her voice was authoritative" as she exchanged conversation with Jesus, who led her progressively to understand him first as a Jew, then as a prophet, then as Messiah, and finally as God.[66]

Ephrem joins the Samaritan Woman to other biblical women who were reproached or slandered by their people but eventually vindicated by God: Elizabeth the mother of John the Baptist (Lk 1:25), and Hannah the mother of the prophet Samuel (1 Sam 1:1–2:11). He names others who, like the Samaritan Woman, devised deceits to protect their integrity: Sarah in her disguise as Abraham's sister (Gen 12), and Tamar the daughter-in-law of Judah disguised as a prostitute (Gen 38). Like these, the Samaritan Woman was a marvel of faith, one whose hope of salvation was not in vain. Indeed, "She is the type of humanity / [whom God] leads step by step" in knowledge.[67]

In *Hymns on Virginity* 23, Ephrem's praise for the Samaritan Woman rises to exalted heights. Her public preaching of Christ to her people is a wonder as great as the virgin birth. Ephrem sings:

> For [Mary] from within her womb
> in Bethlehem brought forth [Christ's] body as a child,
> but you [Samaritan Woman] by your mouth made Him manifest
> as an adult in Shechem, the town of His father's household.
> Blessed are you, woman, who brought forth by your mouth
> light for those in darkness.[68]

While the congregation chanted the refrain—"Glory to the Discoverer of All!"—Ephrem continued to contrast Mary's physical conception with the Samaritan Woman's spiritual one. Both received God's revelation by word, and both brought that Word forth:

> Mary, the thirsty land in Nazareth,
> conceived our Lord by her ear.
> You, too, O woman thirsting for water,
> conceived the Son by your hearing.
> Blessed are your ears that drank the source
> that gave drink to the world.
> Mary planted Him in a manger,
> but you [planted Him] in the ears of His hearers.[69]

As the hymn continues, Ephrem repeatedly praises her word and her voice. She is a prophet whose prophecy was fulfilled; and an apostle *before* the apostles, for she preached before they did, bringing life to a city that was spiritually dead.

In this hymn, as so often, Ephrem moves back and forth between third-person description and second-person direct address, blurring the line between the Samaritan Woman of New Testament times, the women's choir who sing her voice, and the congregation in whose midst he sings. Praising her glory, he joins the biblical past to the present moment: "Your love was zealous / to share your treasure with your city."[70] Rendering her musically present, he holds her as a living exemplar for choir and congregation both, women and men who themselves join his song with zealous love, sharing through their hymns their treasure with their city.

The emphasis on bold speech is one he offers at other times for New Testament men as well. To the blind man who approached Jesus in Mark 10:46–52, he sings in similar terms:

> For if you had been silent as you were admonished,
> silence would have kept you in darkness.
> Blessed is your boldness, for in it you also offer a type
> that the sinner, if he be bold, will obtain mercy.[71]

The bold and loud voices of the New Testament faithful hence provide the model for the voices of the women's choirs that sing forth Ephrem's hymns, and for the congregation who join their voices for the refrain. Their "joyful shouts" should reach the ears of the unbelievers with powerful effect.[72] On Easter morning, Ephrem exults with the refrain: "Blessed is He for whom the silent have thundered out!"[73]

Jacob of Sarug followed Ephrem in portraying New Testament women as bold witnesses to God's salvific plan. Following Ephrem but with sharper emphasis, Jacob places their stories in civic rather than domestic domains. His homilies on the Samaritan Woman, the Canaanite Woman, and the Hemorrhaging Woman stand out in these terms.[74] In Jacob's memre, these female characters boldly approach Jesus directly, in public, face-to-face, without intermediaries. In all of these cases, Jacob's rhetorical habits lead him to grant these women long, forceful speeches, powerfully forensic, with arguments suited for prosecution in courts of law, irrefutably magisterial in their moral and ethical power.

Needless to say, the biblical texts provided far simpler dialogic exchange between these female figures and Jesus. Speech-in-character was, however, a favorite ploy of Jacob's. To employ it as extensively as he did for these women is an interesting feature of his homilies. In part, these speeches are the rhetorical vehicle that enable him to present the women as generic models of virtue: that is, these speeches transgress the social boundaries of household piety and exemplify virtues applicable to men as well as women, in narratively identified public and civic locations and contexts. The biblical women then become not so much "women," but rather "faithful Christians," and thereby models for all.

A brief glance at Jacob's presentation of the Samaritan Woman makes the point.[75] As Ephrem had done before him, Jacob presents the Samaritan Woman as an intellectual. He refers to her as "wise," "perceptive," "learned," "enviable," "rational," "discerning," "blessed," and "wondrous in [her] words." While other kinds of imagery weave in and out of the homily, Jacob returns often to the imagery of education. Jesus "teaches";[76] the Woman is a "perceptive woman disciple" who is "wise (*hakimtha*) and learned (*mdarshtha*) / and enlightened by the learning of the house of God (*beth Alaha*)."[77] She thirsts not simply for knowledge, but for truth. She pursues it cautiously at first, with decorum, but with increasing urgency as her dialogue with Christ proceeds:

> The Woman had a great desire for whatever was true;
> the Instructor [Jesus] met her and she was burning to ask,
> "My Lord, I desire to learn true things from you;
> be for me a schoolmaster and make me wise in hidden things."[78]

Her dialogue with Christ moves in even exchange, as in the ancient classroom where dialogue and disputation were basic pedagogical patterns. At one point, Jacob pauses to marvel at her astute, profound love for God. The homilist addresses her directly, asking her, "Who showed you [to know these things about God and the Messiah]? . . . Who revealed to you? . . . Who announced to you? . . . Tell me, O Woman, who told you that the Messiah is coming?"[79] And he imagines her reply, in which she describes at length the biblical accounts, of Moses and the Law, of Jacob and the patriarchs, and of the prophets, all foretelling the coming of the Messiah. She is a scholar, an exegete, an interpreter. When she runs to proclaim the good tidings to her city, she does so "burning with zeal," "with a loud voice." She is teacher and proclaimer to her own people. Thus far, Jacob's portrait is similar to Ephrem's in *Hymns on Virginity* 22 and 23.

At this point, however, Jacob seems to recoil at his own presentation. For as the woman runs, exulting in her task, her zeal grows rash. She becomes "pompous," "puffed up," proclaiming hubristically, "This good thing is from me!"[80] And the speech of her boasting follows. In the end, her townspeople must rise up to shut her down, rebuking her into silence and dismissing her words as no longer relevant now that they have seen the Messiah themselves in person. She vanishes from the page, like a popped bubble.

In these final scorching lines of Jacob's homily, it is hard not to see a heavy agenda of social control: the hand of patriarchal authority asserting itself to make sure that every woman in the congregation understands her place. Despite or perhaps because of the women's choir, whose loud voices framed his homily, it is almost as if encountering too many strong biblical women threatened to provide dangerous models for real women, who might mistake their proper role and place in the Christian community. Perhaps. To be fair, Jacob's final section in this instance does show a close, midrashic-style reading of the ending of the pericope in John 4, the wording of which could suggest such an outcome. Nonetheless, the contrast to his presentation of other biblical women is striking.

Over and over again in his homilies, Jacob of Sarug presents female characters drawn from biblical narratives. With his long, fictive, first-person speeches, Jacob presents biblical women as articulate, eloquent, persuasive, determined, faithful, wise, and very much able to speak and act for themselves. Their imagined voices are strong and clear, even when stereotypical or socially normative. They sound forth, repeatedly. And what, we should ask, was their sound?

As was the case for Ephrem, Jacob of Sarug's presentations were colored by their ritual context. His homilies, intoned and chanted as they were, were ritually embedded among singing female voices—whether the women's choir or the responses of the congregation, including its female members. This ritual context provided added dimension to gendered rhetoric as a tool of moral suasion within homiletic discourse. In his homily "On Mar Ephrem," Jacob exhorts the women's choir to sing "with loud voice," "without shame," "with faces uncovered." In the same homily, Jacob refers to the singing of the women's choirs as "instructive," naming them "teachers" (*malphanyatha*) of the "proclamation" (*karazutha*), the good news of salvation.[81] Such terms and imagery were mentioned and echoed occasionally in Jacob's presentation of biblical women and their voices. Do the loud, insistent voices of Jacob's female biblical characters provide an echo—or paradigm or model—for the voices of the women's choirs?

Consider Jacob's homily on the Canaanite Woman, recounting the episode of Matthew 15:21–28 and Mark 7:24–30 (where she is called the Syro-Phoenician Woman).[82] In the biblical story, the Canaanite Woman's daughter was sorely afflicted by a demon. The woman approached Jesus, begging for his intervention. Because she was of the Gentiles ("Canaanite"), he dismissed her with disdain. She retorted, argued with him, and won his favor. Jesus granted her request.

Persistently, if only occasionally, Jacob's homily stresses the sound of the Canaanite Woman's voice. Her voice, as we would expect from other examples cited here, is "loud." She "shouts out" "with mournful cries," "with groans,"[83] and "with her loud voice," she calls out to Jesus.[84] But now and again, her loud voice "sings." Faith in Christ "was sung" by the Canaanite (*mezdamar (h)wat*), it "was proclaimed" (*methkarza*) by her.[85] Again, "by the Canaanite woman . . . faith was sung to all peoples."[86] Petitioning on behalf of her daughter, the Canaanite Woman proclaimed Jesus as the Messiah among her peoples, "singing out" and "pronouncing" the new gospel.[87] Among the peoples of many gods (pagans), "she became a harp for the undivided faith."[88] "With her loud voice she disturbed the apostles," Jacob exclaims.[89] And with her loud voice, "she shouted her need."[90] Jacob exalts her "boldness."[91]

Like the other women discussed in this chapter, the Canaanite Woman offered a powerful portrait of a woman compelled by unwavering faith in Christ and resolute devotion to her daughter. She refused to be deterred even when scandalizing others. No men acted with her or for her. Her agency was immediate and unmediated. Jacob presented her in vibrant colors and ringing tones as a paradigm for every Christian. Thus he ends the memra with resounding admonition: just as this Woman fought for the sake of her daughter and refused discouragement, so, too, should one fight for one's own soul, even when it seems God does not respond, even when it seems Christ does not answer. "[Christ] revealed [the Canaanite Woman] to the assembly so that everyone might be bold and imitate her. / Her boldness, full of wonder, take for yourself, O Man, / and with it you will be able to cast out suffering if it enters you."[92]

Jacob did not mention the women's choirs in his homilies on the Samaritan Woman, or the Canaanite Woman, nor in the many other sermons he intoned on other biblical women. Yet we know from various sources, including others of his own memre, that their voices framed his preaching, inflecting his chanted performance and enfolding it in their echoing song. How should we not hear their voices—the voices of these women's choirs—in that of the Canaanite Woman, whom Jacob evoked as "singing," "with a loud voice"? Jacob's intoned descriptions rang with the voices of women ritually present and ritually active. His performance interlinked with theirs. Nor should we doubt such resonances of the voices sung and voices heard by the late antique Syriac congregations. In late antiquity, at least, the voices of women rang forth in Syriac liturgies. And in hymns and homilies, biblical women, however slender their stories, helped to model their way.

COMPETING VOICES: DAUGHTERS OF EVE

Like broader cultural attitudes, however, liturgical voices were not always positive when it came to women. What were the female voices that competed with Syriac women's choirs in their liturgical performance? What counternarratives were presented, and through whose voices were they told?

If a long list of positive biblical women can be found for Syriac liturgical poetry, including women of scandal who are nevertheless presented as exemplars of faith, the list of negative biblical women is short. Moreover, it is ambiguous. Some biblical characters are notable for beginning as negative models, then changing to wholly positive ones, like the Sinful Woman who washed the feet of Jesus with her tears of repentance (Lk 7:36–50).[93] Even Potiphar's Wife (Gen 39), in some instances, repents and leads her husband to seek mercy and reconciliation.[94] Most importantly, the figure of Eve in Syriac liturgy was more often portrayed as redeemed from tragedy rather than condemned as evil; she, like Adam, is comforted and reconciled to God through Christ.[95] As Jacob of Sarug had sung at the Feast of the Nativity, "Let Eve, whom the great serpent had smitten in Eden, rejoice, / because the Son of her daughter has stood up and crushed the Asp that had mocked her."[96] On the negative side, Delilah (Jd 16), Jezebel (1 Kg 19:1–3, 21:5–25; 2 Kg 9:30–37), and Salome the daughter of Herodias (Mk 6:21–29) are the female villains most often cited. Interestingly, their characters are not accorded the attention, nor the complexity, of the positive models we have been considering.[97]

FIGURE 9. Adam and Eve in garden with Greek inscription. Floor mosaic, Maaut el-Na'aman, northern Syria, 5th cent. CE. Cleveland Art Museum, 1969.115.

Still, it is worth pausing on the question of countervoices in the liturgy. Scholars are familiar with early Christian diatribes that castigated Eve as the cause of the Fall, and identified women, as a category, with Eve's disastrous work. Tertullian's famous denouncement of every woman as Eve is often taken as representative of the general view:

Do you not believe that you are [each] an Eve? The sentence of God on this sex of yours lives on even in our times and so it is necessary that the guilt should live on, also. You are the one who opened the door to the Devil, you are the one who first picked the fruit of the forbidden tree, you are the one who persuaded him whom the Devil was not strong enough to attack. All too easily you destroyed the image of God, man. Because of your desert, that is, death, even the Son of God had to die.[98]

In Syriac, the notorious counterparts to Tertullian's venom might be seen in the work of two authors, Aphrahat and Narsai of Nisibis. Both authors raise the questions of when, where, and how such views were propagated.

Aphrahat has often been cited for a well-known passage from his *Demonstration* 6, "On Covenanters," a text we considered in chapter 1 for its depiction of the sons and daughters of the covenant in their social and ecclesiastical contexts.[99] At one point, Aphrahat presents a summary of biblical history from Adam through John the Baptist—a history, he claims, of Satan defeating men through the wiles of evil women. His culminating statement appears to evoke the sound of women's singing:

> Brothers, we know and have seen that from the beginning women have been a way for the Adversary to gain access to people, and until the end he will [continue to] accomplish this. For [women] are the weapons of Satan, and through them he fights against the [spiritual] athletes. Through them he plays music at all times, for they have been like a harp for him from the first day. It was because of her that the curse of the Law was established, and it was because of her that the promise of death came. With pain she brings forth children and delivers [them] to death. Because of her the earth was cursed, so that it would bring forth thorns and thistles.[100]

We have no information about Aphrahat's location other than generally, "in Persia"; nor about his audience in this instance, other than that he specifically addresses sons and daughters of the covenant as a select inner circle within a larger Christian community. Written in the form of a letter, there is no indication that the text had a liturgical or public use. Given Aphrahat's slender manuscript tradition and lack of citation by other writers, it would be difficult to claim the text as one of wide circulation.[101] Still, as with the general Christian evidence for late antiquity, such sentiments recur especially in ascetic, monastic, and scholarly discourse, for Syriac authors as for others.[102]

But one must also remember that Aphrahat himself, as noted in chapter 1, liked to think in binaries of virtues and vices. He was fond of lists to illustrate both. Robert Murray speculated that "no other patristic author has more" lists of biblical exempla than Aphrahat.[103] In *Demonstration* 6.3, Aphrahat presented a list of biblical female villains: Eve; Potiphar's Wife; Delilah; Bilhah, Jacob's concubine, who slept with his son Reuven (Gen 35:21–22, 49:3–4); Miriam, who incited Aaron's jealousy against Moses (Num 12:1–2); Zipporah, Moses's wife, whom Aphrahat calls a "wicked counselor" (with reference to Ex 4:24–26); Bathsheba, whom Aphrahat claims led King David into temptation (2 Sam 11); Tamar the sister of Amnon (2 Sam 13); the foreign wives of King Solomon (1 Kg 11:1–13); Jezebel (1 Kg 21:25); Job's Wife (Job 1–2), Maakah the mother of King Asa, who made an idol (1 Kg 15:13); Salome the daughter of Herodias, who asked for the head of John the Baptist (Mt 14:6–8, Mk 6:21–28); and Haman's wife, Zeresh (Est 5:9–14). A careful reader might note that some of these women suffered as victims in the incidents cited, rather than as perpetrators of wrongdoing; but Aphrahat made no such distinction. Elsewhere, he included women among his lists of biblical exemplars of virtue. He includes Hannah, the mother of Samuel, and Esther among those whose prayers were powerful.[104] In a list of Gentiles justified by their faith, he includes Rahab and Ruth.[105] In *Demonstration* 14, "An Argument in Response to Dissension," he cites women in several lists:[106] the Woman of Tekoa (2 Sam 14); the "wise woman" of 2 Samuel 20; Deborah, Jael, and Rebekah among those who brought peace (14.11); Rahab and Esther among those who loved abundantly (14.14); Sarah, Rachel, Hannah, and Esther among those whom God raised up; and Miriam, Hannah, Huldah, Elizabeth, Mary, and Deborah among the prophets honored by God (14.33). In this same *Demonstration* 14, Aphrahat provides many other lists of biblical *men* who did evil, led others astray, or deliberately opposed the will of God, from the time of Adam until the present. In other words, the passage from *Demonstration* 6.3 citing women as Satan's accomplices since the time of Eve forms part of Aphrahat's habitual binary remembrances of biblical stories. He often made didactic use of biblical lists; he included both men and women in lists both negative and positive.[107]

As noted above, there is no evidence of Aphrahat's use in liturgical contexts where the broader civic community would have gathered. Rather, for liturgical evidence consonant with Ephrem, Jacob of Sarug, or the anonymous poets we have been considering, the East Syriac poet Narsai of Nisibis might be the best comparison. An elder contemporary of Jacob of Sarug, Narsai was a shining light at the School of Edessa in his early career. At some point he relocated to Nisibis, founding a new school there that he led until his death around the year 500.[108] The years Narsai and Jacob overlapped in their ministries were times of bitter rivalry between the dyophysite and miaphysite Syriac churches.[109] According to the historian Barhadbeshabba, writing a century after the events described, it was Jacob's exceptional prowess as liturgical poet and preacher that prompted Narsai to take up the same effort on behalf of the dyophysites. The passage is notably similar to those describing Ephrem's turn to hymnography in response to heretics in Nisibis and Edessa:

> One of the [sons of error] whose name was Jacob of Sarug, who was eloquent for evil and closely joined to heresy, began to compose his heresy and error hypocritically by the way of the *memre*, which he composed, since through the pleasant composition of enticing sounds he drew the bulk of the people from the glorious one. What then did the elect of God [Narsai] do? . . . He set down the true opinion of orthodoxy in the manner of *memre*, fitted upon sweet tones. He combined the meaning of the scriptures according to the opinion of the holy fathers in pleasant antiphons in the likeness of the blessed David.[110]

Often compared with Ephrem and Jacob for his skill in the craft of memre, in his homilies Narsai also drew frequently on biblical stories as he sought to instruct his students in exegesis, liturgical tradition, and theological exposition.[111] Yet, unlike Ephrem or Jacob of Sarug, Narsai rarely preached on biblical women. Moreover, he seems to have made no reference of any kind to women's choirs. It may be that his silence was a function of his context: Narsai spent his career in an exclusively male school environment. Perhaps his lack of attention to biblical women betrays an audience for whom they would have seemed less relevant than that in the civic church settings where Ephrem's hymns and Jacob's homilies were often offered. Both Ephrem and Jacob refer to the mixed population of their congregations, to the presence of women and children along with their menfolk; and, as we have seen, both also refer to the participation of women's choirs. It is difficult to know who attended the liturgical services at the schools in Edessa and Nisibis, although it seems that sometimes laity were present, apart from the students. We cannot be sure that Narsai's audience was wholly male. But the contrast in the content of his preaching to that of Ephrem or Jacob is considerable.

Nonetheless, in three notable homilies, Narsai drew attention to biblical women. The Virgin Mary figures prominently in his "Homily on Our Lord's Birth from the Holy Virgin," which covers episodes from the Gospel of Luke, from the Annunciation through to the circumcision of Jesus.[112] Narsai's treatment of Mary in this memra is reserved, showing none of the exuberance characterizing presentations by Ephrem, Jacob, or other Syriac hymnographers.[113] The tactic was surely deliberate, as Narsai sought to protect a Christology he perceived to be damaged when Mary's role was elevated excessively, a danger he found lurking in the burgeoning Marian devotion of the fifth century.[114] This homily takes an aggressively didactic tone, presenting narrative elaboration of the biblical text generously interspersed with theological and doctrinal commentary. Narsai makes little use here of fictive speeches. In this long homily of 508 lines, Narsai has Mary speak three lines of text only: an immediate acceptance of the archangel Gabriel's announcement of her divinely instigated pregnancy! Intriguingly, Narsai casts the encounter and ensuing conception as a musical interlude:

> The pure virgin carried the fruit which the (angel's) voice had sowed:
>> and the Spirit sounded on the harp of her soul a hymn of praise.
> A hymn of confession she offered as a requital for her new conception, (saying:)
>> "Blessed is He Who chose a dwelling place for His love within my limbs!
> Worthy of praise from all mouths is the Fashioner of the universe,
>> because by my humility He has willed to exalt the dust of Adam!"[115]

For the remainder of the memra, Mary is depicted moving through the Nativity events in silence. Narsai portrays her very much in the background of the events discussed. In an extended concluding section, he provides a Christological analysis that sets her, to his mind, in her proper theological position.[116] Equal to all other women in her humanity, Mary is exalted because she is the mother of the second Adam.[117] Her son is like all other humans, but "holier and more glorious" because his humanity is the dwelling place of the Divine Son.[118] By Mary, God reverses the work of Eve from the Fall, commencing our ability to confess God rightly and in truth.[119]

In much closer keeping with the texts of Ephrem and Jacob of Sarug is Narsai's homily on the Canaanite Woman.[120] Here Narsai, like Jacob, attributes abundant speech to the woman as she battles her way through obstruction by the disciples and rejection by Jesus to make her case on behalf of her daughter. While differing in emphases, themes, and details, the similarities between Narsai's and Jacob's homilies are still strong.[121] Might one have heard the other preach on this biblical story? It is possible, given their overlapping dates and the possibility of common location in Edessa during the same years. More likely is that both knew Ephrem's discussion of the gospel passage in his *Commentary on the Diatessaron*, while also following common exegetical patterns for the gospel pericope recurring in Greek and Latin sermons of the same era.[122]

In this homily, Narsai like Jacob presents the Canaanite Woman with distinct emphasis on her voice. Differently than for Jacob, for Narsai the woman's voice is virtually a separate character within the narrative, with agency and deeply interior motivation of its own. It rises out of the woman's senses and emotions; it calls out from mouth and mind alike; it wails.[123] "Upon the harp of the mouth," the woman's voice became herald and guide.[124] It spoke her love.[125] Ceding to its power, Christ commanded her: "Behold, I am opening the door of your voice!"[126] And he instructed her, "Go and show . . . Go and tell . . . Go and inform . . . Go and bring . . . Go and explain . . . Go and tell . . . Go and test."[127]

For Narsai, too, the woman's voice "sings."[128] Moreover, her voice signals Satan's downfall. Indeed, Satan's humiliation is worsened because his demise is wrought by a mere woman, a "feeble rib."[129] His attempt to conquer humanity is sounded in oscillating melodies of seduction and lament:

> Upon the harp of Eve [Satan] played his tunes of deathly bitterness,
> and in the daughter of Eve he heard the tidings of the amulet of death.
> In Eden he composed joyful tunes as one victorious,
> and here he lamented in a voice of groans as one condemned.[130]

For Narsai, Satan "heard the voice of the woman," at once "seemly" and "very hateful."[131] Wondrously, the two voices became a battle, as the voice of Satan disturbed and distressed the woman's daughter with its "chanting" while the woman herself mourned, wept, lamented, and wailed.[132] By her voice, Satan's work began to come undone.[133] Just so did the woman become inspiration and model for all to take up their own battle against the Evil One: combat to be fought within the interior mind, intellect, thoughts, and impulses of the heart, guarded by God's continuing presence.[134]

While Narsai's characteristic themes and imagery abound in his memra on the Canaanite Woman, the text appears to be singular in his extant corpus for featuring a female character as hero. As a rhetorical portrait, his presentation is not unproblematic: he elevates her triumph by accentuating the inferiority of her ethnicity and gender. Yet the portrait is intriguing. Where Jacob emphasizes the woman's speech as a means to highlight the power of her agency and actions, Narsai focuses on her voice to allow his distinctive exploration of interiority—of motivation, inclination, and internal impulse.

Narsai is also known for a third memra relevant here: his homily "On the Reproof of Eve's Daughters and the 'Tricks and Devices' They Perform."[135] Not unlike the passage from Aphrahat's *Demonstration* 6.3, but here crafted in homiletic form, Narsai's text is an acerbic attack on "women's wiles," cast against a biblical backdrop stretching from Genesis 3 through biblical history into the present time. According to Barhadbeshabba, the memra was prompted by Narsai's poisonous relationship with Mamai, the wife of the bishop Barsauma of Nisibis.[136] Corrie Molenberg has argued that there was a larger context eliciting Narsai's venom: the legislation of Bishop Barsauma allowed the marriage of priests for the dyophysite Christians of Persia, within a culture heavily dominated by Zoroastrian opposition to celibacy and high valuation of marriage and family.[137] Within that setting, Molenberg posits, Narsai's homily provides an account of ascetic virtues and their fragility in the face of insufficient care. Worldly women, wicked "daughters of Eve," endangered men who pursued ascetic lives in service to the church.[138] But in fact there is no indication of the audience or occasion for the memra.[139] Was it preached in a public liturgy? Or at an occasion at the School of Nisibis—and if so, did the congregation include women as well as men?

The memra is a nearly relentless offensive against women. Narsai begins with an account of Eve as devious and destructive almost from the moment of her birth, profoundly damaged by Satan but also soon rivaling him in her thirst for destruction. In turn, Narsai chronicles the boundless wickedness of the daughters of Eve, their innumerable vices, their nets and traps. He cites the examples of Bathsheba, Jezebel, Potiphar's Wife, and Delilah, each of whom brought Eve's "stupendous deeds" of evil into their own generations. Repeatedly, he returns to Eve as the paradigm: "The Evil One [Satan] is not as evil as her evil, however evil he may be."[140] In between, Narsai offers extended ruminations on the dangerous ways of corrupt women. He is particularly vexed by what he sees as Eve's desire to overreach Adam, and her daughters' subsequent continuation of that effort:

> Her mother's habit accompanies her in all generations and just as she embraces the
> sinner she embraces the loathsome sin.
> Superior to a man she desires to be, just as the one who gave birth to her
> And if it were possible she would desire to become a man.
> She boldly wants to seize power over men and to disturb the vast order of the
> creation.[141]

Yet, despite his venom, Narsai's homily is not without its moments of grace—as, indeed, befit his understanding of divine providence and human freedom. Early in the homily, he recounts the angels' grief upon witnessing Eve's fall with Satan. God heard their mourning, and acted upon another "daughter of Eve," sending her a different "fruit": that of his incarnate Son, carrying the gift of immortal life. One woman began the human history of evil, and one woman would end it. "Out of a daughter of man death began to destroy and / out of a daughter of man life began to renew."[142]

Toward the end of the homily, Narsai takes up an imagined dialogue with the "daughters of Eve" within his own time and place. Despite his fierce admonishment of their vices, he also believes their human nature exceeds their gendered inclinations. For Narsai, the essence of humanity lies in the capacity for free will, the ability to choose good over evil, God over Satan. That capacity is strong, as strong as the power to work destruction. He addresses Eve's daughters directly:

> I am intensely amazed about the fight against you [women], how strong it is, and therefore I make an appeal to you, the cause of all evil.
> The evil propensity in you is not in (your) nature; your will it is which commits sin and it leads (you) into sin in conformity with your will.
> All good and evil done by you is yours, and you, being a free woman, have dominion over both of them.[143]

Urging women to exercise their free will and choose the better path, Narsai offers to serve as their guide. Once again, biblical stories provide his models. Women were not only purveyors of evil. On the contrary, the biblical record also shows them to have been exemplars of faith, paragons of virtue, and sources of salvation:

> Hear, if you want, (my) account of the history of some of your sex, who endured passions and did not become weak before trials.
> Form a picture of their way of life in your mind, and purge away the dirt of your thoughts with their purity.
> See and observe Sarah and Rebecca particularly because they bore the pains of barrenness without becoming depressed.
> Let Hannah be a mirror for the eyes of your soul and gain perseverance through her perseverance at the day of trial.
> You are of the same kind as these women, oh daughter of men. Proceed on the path of their perseverance and desist from fear.
> And why do I say that you are from the lineage of these reverend women?
> Behold, one of you was the woman, who bore life for men.
> From one of your sex endless life sprang up for us.[144]

Sternly admonishing that the better way lies before them if only they will choose it, Narsai ends his exhortation to women on this gleaming note of hope. He concludes with remembrance that women, too, can occupy their lives with praise for the Maker of All.

Scathing though the homily is, Narsai's sermon yet affirms the (public?) community as one in which men and women can—and must—seek a life of faith

FIGURE 10. Last Judgment scene. The ranks of saints and sinners are split by a central panel where Adam and Eve wait before the Throne of the Second Coming while archangels summon the living and dead to account. Fresco, church interior, western wall, Mar Musa Monastery, Nebek, Syria, 12th–13th cent. Mat Immerzeel/Paul van Moorsel Centre, Vrije Universiteit Amsterdam.

together, in common devotion to their Lord. The Bible provided a remembrance of human folly through women's failures, but also a commemoration of human strength through women's greatness and, indeed, their essential role in God's salvific plan for humankind. Liturgy was a shared space in which biblical history was recalled and retold. As such, it provided constant reinforcement of the notion that Christian history was a record, biblical and historical both, necessarily inclusive of women as well as men in its defeats and triumphs. As even Narsai had to point out, women were important exemplars in that picture from both directions.[145]

In fact, both East and West Syriac liturgies are notable for containing lists of righteous biblical women that remain part of Syriac liturgical practice for these churches to the present day. Included above all in the marriage rites, these lists are found also in services for the consecration of female monastics, services for women saints, services in commemoration of the Virgin Mary, and at certain other services of the ecclesiastical calendar.[146] The most outstanding example is the lengthy East Syriac "Hymn on the Holy Women," dating back as far as the eighth century, naming at least thirty-nine biblical women, in addition to a roughly equal number of women saints and martyrs.[147] Such lists are included in the practice maintained in some West Syriac churches of reading the names of the biblical

FIGURE 11. Last Judgment scene, detail: Adam and Eve in supplication before the Throne of the Second Coming. Fresco, church interior, western wall, Mar Musa Monastery, Nebek, Syria, 12th–13th cent. Mat Immerzeel/Paul van Moorsel Centre, Vrije Universiteit Amsterdam.

righteous, saints, martyrs, and local holy men and women from a tome called the *Book of Life*.[148] Again, the number of biblical women named in the different surviving examples is noteworthy.

Eve is often included in these liturgical lists of saintly women, as a singular measure of the human capacity for change.[149] She is recalled in hymns and liturgical prayers, both ancient and still in use, as the one whose own daughter Mary paid her debt, healed her remorse, comforted her sorrow, and restored her life.[150] Eve is found among the righteous ones named on particular occasions, but also in the lists of those saints through whose intercession the liturgy is offered, in the closing prayers of the weekly Eucharist, for example, in the Anaphora of St. James.[151] She was painted with Adam in church frescoes depicting the resurrection, and at the throne of the second coming.[152] From this perspective, Eve, like Adam, provided the paradigm for both fall and redemption, and continues to do so.

Lists of worthy women abound in Syriac liturgical tradition. As such, they were in the past and are now a part of the public, general, and inclusive work of liturgical practice. Women's witness, women's models, women's stories, and women's voices have been integrally woven into the practice of worship for the Syriac churches since their early centuries.

REMEMBRANCE AND PRESENCE:
WHY THESE MATTER

Such remembrance is a major omission when historians do not take account of liturgical practices as central to the social and institutional histories of religion. Focus on bishops or priests, as is common in scholarship, occludes the multiple authorities at work during liturgical events. Other ritual agents—including choirs, including laity—provided actions, gestures, and voices necessary to the efficacy of the whole. Similarly, focus on episcopal preaching or teaching without consideration of the larger ritual event in which it took place—including the other voices by which it was framed, encased, received, and responded to—misses contextual elements that impinged on and to some extent mitigated the generally patriarchal discourses of Christian history.

A further issue arises from the biblical women highlighted in this chapter. As we have seen, both the scandalously impudent messianic foremothers in the Old Testament and the outspoken women who approached Jesus in his ministry in the New were presented by Ephrem and Jacob of Sarug as bold, loud, and persistent. They were also shown to be autonomous in their acts: not helped or supported by male kin, partners, or onlookers, nor divinely assisted by celestial or saintly agents. In her recent discussion of female saints in late antique hagiography, Maria Munkholt Christensen presents the paradigm of "holy women as humble teachers."[153] Drawing on Latin, Greek, and Syriac examples, Christensen argues that these women were defined by their (male) hagiographers as teachers of humility, specifically, not only in their discourse but also in their behavior and self-regard. The contrast to the presentation of Syriac women's choirs as teachers, and to Ephrem and Jacob's portrayal of biblical women as models of faith, is striking.

There may be more at work here than matters of gender. The great female saints of late antiquity were largely from elite families. Their hagiographic depictions negotiated cultural contestation around class, ethics, and religious claims to the values of simplicity, humility, and renunciation in an elite culture.[154] They spoke in a philosophical discourse to and within ascetic and monastic contexts. Liturgy, as I am suggesting, presents a different setting and speaks to a broader social landscape.

Historians of late antique Christianity are all too familiar with the kinds of negative rhetoric often directed toward women, and by which women were often characterized in early Christianity, as in the broader Greek and Roman ethos.[155] Highlighting ancient Syriac women's choirs and the presentation of biblical women in Syriac liturgical poetry as an alternative focus raises important issues in this regard. It suggests other avenues of exploration.

First, performative context is crucial when looking at gendered discourse in antiquity. I am drawing attention to depictions and performances that took place in public liturgical occasions, open to and inclusive of the entire worshipping community. Negative discourses were strongest, I suggest, in other contexts: in texts that targeted monastic communities, or those intended for highly gendered presentation, for example, in (male) scholarly or intellectual circles. It is notable, and not surprising, that the most vitriolic rhetoric about women is located in texts utilized in such settings, where women would not have been present. While there are consistent tropes and conventions across the whole of early Christian literature, these distinctions are nevertheless important.

Second, liturgy—as a broad umbrella of occasions, and in all its forms—was the primary location in which women participated in Christianity in a public context. They did so on a frequent and even daily basis in late antiquity. Liturgy was the space where Syriac women encountered the larger church community. It was also where they encountered women's choirs and a heavily positive roster of biblical female models and female saints. Fundamental themes presented in liturgical contexts often *did not* include the negative tropes scholars have emphasized from theological, monastic, or other elite literature, or at the least were not the only message women heard. This does not diminish the negative effects of such discourse in undergirding a patriarchal society and culture. I have already detailed ways in which institutional structuring contained and restrained the authoritative impact of the women's choirs or the stories sung about biblical women. The omnipresence of the male hierarchy was indisputable. But it is important to see who was saying what, where, and how; and to consider what women heard when they attended and participated in these shared events.[156] The following two chapters will explore these questions, asking how liturgy opened possibilities for cultural negotiation over gender and religious authority, or may have differentiated individual over collective reception.

Syriac women heard women's voices and women's stories as an integral part of their community's ritual practice, in ordinary, daily life. When historians consider the foundational, formative discourses enveloping ancient women, they need to remember that liturgy was one context—and a major one—that provided tools by which to negotiate and define how one understood one's own self and place, whether in the local community or in society more broadly.

In the remainder of this book, I turn to the voices of laity, the other liturgical identity through which women's voices sounded and were heard in public Christian ritual. For laity, and in the context of the civic community, a different roster of biblical women can be seen as key models for devotional attention and ethical formation than those highlighted in these first chapters for the women's choirs. Agency, boldness, and loud voice will again be advocated, but in changed or contrasting contexts. To these differences and their implications, we now turn.

5

___

Singing Voices

Women Among the Assembly

From Ephrem and Jacob of Sarug, we know that ancient Syriac Christians heard their women's choirs sing with loud, bold, instructive voices. But the choirs were not the only source of women's contributions to liturgical celebration. Women featured also and prominently among the congregation, another group whose voices were central—indeed, crucial—to liturgy in all its permutations. Among the congregation, women were present as widows, consecrated virgins, nuns, and ascetic solitaries; and as laity, married and unmarried: young girls, grown women, and elders. Female slaves came in attendance with their mistresses, or sometimes in the stead of their owners.[1] Within this diversity, women were singing constantly throughout the different services: providing the required responses of "Lord have mercy," "Amen," "Alleluia"; joining the refrains; reciting the creed and Lord's Prayer; singing the collective hymns, such as the Trisagion and the Sanctus; voicing their confession, supplications, and acclamations. Women's voices from the choir led the congregation to sing their own participation; women's voices from the congregation responded in turn, sounded from among the assembly. Throughout the liturgy's progression, women's voices wove in and out of the sequenced actions, inflecting its sounds and enhancing its harmonies.

To locate women among the laity, we must identify their place and their tasks. In this chapter I will first approach laity as a status or "office"—that is, as a place in relation to others and specifically to the clerical hierarchy. I will then consider the laity's most fundamental tasks: singing and listening. Both were actions liturgically performed. In both cases, moreover, they were actions with individual and collective impact for reception, interaction, and response. Women were integral to the laity and their work.

FIGURE 12. Syriac family portrait with names inscribed in Edessan Aramaic. Moqimu, funeral mosaic, Edessa, 3rd cent. CE. World History Archive/Alamy Stock Photo.

THE PARTICIPATION OF LAYWOMEN

Liturgy was a composite event, bringing together the church as a gathered community. A complex collection of worshippers was present, each a ritual agent in their own right. These are often grouped in both ancient and modern treatments according to institutionally designated ranks: ordained (bishops, priests, diaconate); consecrated (so-called minor orders: subdeacons, readers, chanters, singers, widows, consecrated virgins); monastics (monks, nuns, and solitaries); and laity (in church canons often distinguished by gender, age, marital status, and sometimes social rank). All these different persons participated at different points of a given service. Sometimes a particular role or office was required;[2] at multiple points, the entire assembly joined their voices together. These multiple voices, from their varied social locations and designated roles, were each necessary to liturgy's proper exercise and function. Hence each carried a degree of religious authority, just as each carried significance within the larger constitution of the church body. Attention to women's participation reminds us that no simple division between ordained and nonordained captures the full picture of what took place. A mosaic of voices, just as a variety of ritual roles, was at work.[3] Laity, too, had their ministry to offer: a ministry of presence, participation, and partaking. Women joined that ministry.

Such examination, then, decenters the authority and activity of bishop or clergy; it recalibrates the patriarchal ecclesiastical structure amid a broader, more richly textured communal body. Various levels or modes of religious authority were recognized and exercised. These were not rival authorities, nor interchangeable. Rather, they were complementary, mutually constitutive, and even mutually necessary. Clergy, consecrated, monastics, and laity were functions existing in relation to one another.[4] In Syriac tradition, these groupings interacted with a capacious sense of shared vocation. Each included more than the term generally signals in our scholarship. The dividing lines were fluid and ill defined; the roles of each drew often upon imagery of the others. "Priesthood" might characterize any of them in particular contexts or moments. Certainly, each had its ministry.

When Ephrem the Syrian praised the liturgy as a woven crown to which each rank and member contributed, he named these: bishops, presbyters, deacons, chanters, choirs male and female, rulers, and laypeople.[5] In a pattern familiar to premodern societies, there are multiple levels of order to be gleaned from such a delineation of ranks and purposes. Ancient Christians understood the church's hierarchical ordering to mirror a parallel hierarchy of social order, including the order of households no less than political structure. Class, gender, and race or ethnicity were all assumed to be rightly defined within these structures. Further, these nested layers of hierarchical order were, to Ephrem's mind as to others, divinely ordained. There were cosmological ramifications to this order: from the microcosm to the macrocosm, the rightly ordered "self" enabled a rightly ordered civic community and a rightly governed ecclesiastical community. And when all was in order in the earthly community—as it should be in God's providential plan— then all was in order within the cosmos at large. Peace, prosperity, and joy would result: the true fruits offered in the liturgy that Ephrem and others extolled. Jacob of Sarug has a number of such descriptions in his memre, offered as prayers at a sermon's end. Here is an excerpt from a much longer such passage:

> Let the prophets glorify your name [O Lord] by the beauty of their revelations,
> Let the apostles and martyrs by the immolation of their persons.
> Let the pontiffs profess you by the complete sacrifices of their ideas,
> And let all priests by their dress and appearance.
> Let the nations and generations glorify you, my Lord, with their shouts of Hosanna,
> And all the uttermost ends of the earth and its four corners with their inhabitants.

The sea with its waves, the abyss with its fish, and the height with its torrents,
The depth with its classes, the dome with its light, the earth with its children.
The sky with the angels, the winds with their breeze, and the clouds with lightning,
The thunder by clamors, the mouth by speech, the mind by marvel.
Intellects by love, the cherubim by trembling, the seraphim by sanctity,
The fire by fervor, wind by its force, altogether.[6]

In this worldview, no individual acted without ramifications for the whole. There was an intimate cosmological connection throughout the entire created order. In the late fourth century, the anonymous homilist of the Syriac *Book of Steps* addressed an ascetic community wherein some, apparently, chafed at the obligation to attend liturgy with the larger congregation—ordinary people in secular society. But the homilist insisted that liturgy was properly and truly served only in the context of the gathered congregation of the whole. He described the "true church" as threefold. First, there was the hidden church of the heart, wherein the body served as temple and the heart the altar upon which the individual offered fitting sacrifice of prayer. Second was the visible church, with its public temple and its public altar, the only means by which the Christian might find the true place of worship. Finally, there was the invisible church, the heavenly glory wherein worship was offered in the very presence of God, "face-to-face": "When a person is diligent in this visible church, he is living in that church of the heart and in that higher church [in heaven]."[7] The visible church—public, and physically rendered—was necessary for worship to be rightly performed, whether in one's own heart or in the celestial heights; and the congregation was necessary for that to happen.

Already we have seen that the voices of the women's choir carried a particular importance for Syriac Christians, an authority of teaching enhanced by the sound of their singing within the order of a given service. Laity, too, had their religious authority. In a civic context, laity probably comprised the majority of the people assembled for worship, whether inside the church building or outdoors in liturgical or paraliturgical processions. Laity often participated additionally in monastic liturgies, celebrated at male or female monasteries or at other locations of religious assembly such as shrines, pilgrimage sites, stylite columns, and cemeteries. Such liturgical celebrations were part of religious travel, and also part of local devotional piety.[8] Laity also contributed to liturgical piety through their religious practices in domestic contexts, at home. Syriac sources emphasize that liturgies of all kinds generally included mixed populations of clergy, monastics, consecrated, and laity. While I will occasionally draw attention to the congregational participation of ascetic and monastic women, in this portion of the book I focus on laywomen who were members of families and households.

Turning from women's choirs to female voices amid the laity raises a new set of questions in the effort to hear women's presence in ancient Syriac Christianity. What was the significance of their contribution? How and why did it matter, to whom, and when? How were laity encouraged to understand their contributions, and by whom? How were their voices cultivated?

Women were active liturgical agents with their voices. Like the rest of the congregation, they also participated with their bodies through posture and gesture as the liturgy worked its course: standing, processing, bowing, kneeling, making the sign of the cross; kissing liturgical instruments, or their neighbors at the Kiss of Peace, or the communion bread before its consumption; touching to venerate sacred spaces, decor, and objects; breathing the sweet scents of incense, holy oil, fragrant lamps and candles; seeing and hearing, watching and receiving the actions, gestures, and teachings of other ritual agents, whether ordained, monastic, or lay. Liturgical participation was a fully embodied experience, without question. But given the nature and purpose of liturgy—the offering of human worship to the divine, and the offering of (divine) instruction to the (human) faithful—its embodied aspects all served in one way or another to heighten the importance of words: words offered by voice, and words heard in reception. To these words, voiced and received, laywomen contributed through their ministry of participation.

LAITY IN THE LITURGY

As Christianity's fortunes rose during the fourth century, Christian liturgy gained complexity as well as beauty, professionalization as well as grandeur. In the midst of this growing magnificence, the laity both faced and presented a challenge. What was the contribution of ordinary people to be? How could they contribute to the offering of worship, in ways that could be seen, heard, and experienced as vital and significant for Christian faith? With what authority might they do so?

The collections of ecclesiastical rules (the so-called church orders) of late antiquity provided basic paradigms for church offices, including the laity understood as such: as an "office" with its own responsibilities. However, these rule collections are deeply problematic as historical sources.[9] Ascribed pseudepigraphically to apostolic authors, and surviving in a welter of manuscripts, these texts circulated widely and in a variety of languages. The Syriac versions are among the oldest in their textual witnesses. We cannot know their origins, nor the extent to which they were actually employed as authoritative guidelines at the time of production or for some time thereafter.[10] Yet these texts represented views commonly expressed in other kinds of ecclesiastical sources (episcopal letters, sermons, church canons) on the roles and functions of the laity within the liturgical assembly, as well as disciplinary instructions for their moral and ethical conduct in the larger community. Prescriptive rather than descriptive, they provide a sense of the ideals church officials imagined, and the types of instruction they would have offered their communities as a result.

In the Syriac *Didascalia*, for example, two lengthy chapters are devoted to the laity.[11] The bulk of chapter 9, "An Exhortation to the People, That They Should Honor the Bishop," is devoted to defining the bishop and other clergy over and in relation to the laity. It exhorts that laity should understand that the bishop is teacher, father, chief, leader, and king over them. The relationships of the church body should be patterned on the cosmic structure God himself defined:

> But let [the bishop] be honored by you as God (is), because the bishop sits for you in the place of God Almighty. But the deacon stands in the place of Christ, and you should love him. The deaconess, however, shall be honored by you in the place of the Holy Spirit. But the presbyters shall be to you in the likeness of the apostles, and the orphans and the widows shall be reckoned by you in the likeness of the altar.[12]

In relation to this ostensibly divinely constituted constellation, the *Didascalia* defines the task of the laity as twofold. First and foremost, laity are to honor the bishop and clergy: "To every position, therefore, let each of the laity pay the honor which is right to him, by gifts and honors and with earthly reverence."[13] The chapter stresses the absolute primacy of the bishop at length, while the other offices are affirmed as authoritative by and through the bishop's establishment. Then, as their second task, the laity are admonished to provide the offerings by which the bishop sustained the church: "On this account be constant in doing work, and be laboring and bringing an offering."[14] The bishop would distribute due portions to all the offices noted. Moreover, it was incumbent on the laity to trust that he would do so fairly; they were fiercely admonished neither to question nor to judge his distributions, but rather to tend to their business of providing the means: "But work and labor simply in the house of God."[15]

Chapter 13 of the *Didascalia*, "Concerning the People," speaks to the responsibility of the laity for liturgical attendance.[16] They must attend the services in their entirety, never missing them, whether for work or worldly obligations, and certainly never for the theater, pagan assemblies, or the services of heretics. The chapter admonishes that pagans and Jews are faithfully observant of their own worship obligations; how, then, could Christians be otherwise for theirs? Like chapter 9, chapter 13 stresses the need for laity to work hard to support the church financially. But that work should never be done in place of attendance at the services.

If the *Didascalia* sets the hierarchical order firmly in place, other passages from the church orders preserved in the West Syriac *Synodicon* attest directly to the liturgical functions of the laity. The "Testament of Our Lord," for example, in prescribing the ordination service for the bishop, concludes the service in this way: "All the people shall say: 'Amen.' And then let them cry out, 'He is worthy, he is worthy, he is worthy.'"[17] So, too, for the presbyters, deacons, and widows, the people must give their "Amen."[18] For subdeacons and readers, the bishop's consecration must be given in the presence of the people, "when all the people (are present) to hear," and "in the sight of the people."[19] In other words, the laity *must* affirm and complete the consecrations of the offices, in order for the ritual process to be fulfilled. The laity are necessary to the institutional establishment of the offices, and their participation ensures the ongoing functioning of the whole. Further guidance is provided for the reception of catechumens and the preparations for and administration of baptism.[20]

Included here are instructions to designate the seating of the women so that they are on the left side of the church with men on the right, with female catechumens separated from female baptized, girls from (married) women, consecrated virgins and those preparing for such a vow, all in separated ranks. The Kiss of Peace was to be exchanged only within these designated ranks, and not across the congregation as a whole. Guidelines for women's comportment, manner of dress, and behavior within the assembly are given, to be overseen by the widows.[21]

Subsequent canons addressed liturgical participation in greater elaboration. The hierarchical ordering of the community is repeatedly reinscribed and reinforced, above all by the order for reception of communion: first the bishops, next presbyters, deacons, widows, readers, subdeacons, those with charismatic gifts, newly baptized babies, then old men, virgins, "and then the rest."[22] The canons specify roles, actions, statements, gestures, timing, prayers; they suggest regulations for fasting, eating, order of services, prayer schedules. They address excommunication; they elaborate strict codes of moral conduct, within the ranks of the church body and also in the social order beyond; they apply guidelines for each of the ranks of clergy, monastics, and laity.

Amid the proliferation of canons, the liturgical voices of the laity flicker in and out. "All the people shall respond, 'Hallelujah,' to the psalm and to the chant with voices in harmony, sung together with one accord."[23] "The [Nicene] creed must be recited with a loud voice by the whole assembly every Sunday at the moment when the priests ascend to offer the oblation after the doors are closed."[24] In every such statement, women's voices were included. The presence of the laity—including the presence of women—was not passive. Every admonition regarding their ordered conduct, their obedience, their appropriate arrival or departure, attests to the absolute necessity of the laity's participation in, and affirmation of, the church as a gathered body, whether in relation to its human, social ordering or to the human-divine relationship that it sought to enact. Women's voices sounded in that work.

The church orders and canon collections provide a bewildering array of directives. We know little about training or compliance, especially at the local level. Some scholars argue that most laity—and most local clergy, especially in the villages—would have had an unsophisticated understanding of roles and practices. Habituated through generations of traditional religious behaviors, they would not necessarily have been attuned to the particular nuances of Christian formation or responsibility.[25]

More immediate is the picture we can draw from texts that engaged the laity face-to-face, in the midst of their liturgical tasks: the hymns and homilies that involved their participation. Here the tasks of lay education and formation were direct, albeit dependent on who listened, and how. Active reception was clearly the hope.[26]

LAITY IN THE LITURGY AND LAITY IN THE WORLD

Ephrem the Syrian composed his madrashe, as we have seen, with pedagogical intention: to teach the church as a community the right understanding of the Bible, doctrine, and devotional practice. Additionally, his hymns served a formative purpose: by their liturgical presentation, Ephrem sought to form particular notions of Christian subjectivity.[27] As chanters and choirs sang his verses, and laity responded with refrains, Ephrem's madrashe instilled through words and sung dialogue various patterns of faith. Within the ordered sequence of liturgy, laity both heard and contributed to the sung content of sacred teaching. At the same time, by their manner of sung contribution—orderly, sequentially, responsively, and in harmony—they learned how to "perform" liturgically as Christians in the world.

Notably, Ephrem used his hymns to cultivate an awareness in the laity that their place and role in the liturgy provided the map for their place and role in the world.[28] For the laity came to worship, just as people had approached Jesus in his ministry, in their worldly condition: often sick, distressed, impoverished. Sickness was a bodily condition, to be sure. Christ had come to heal the blind, the lame, the deaf, the leper; he had come to heal mortality itself. But sickness was also a moral state, the suffering of which provided a mirror for the larger collective life of the community. Vices—fear, envy, greed—were illnesses of the soul. Such moral illness produced misery no less physically experienced than that of fever or wound. Moral illness yielded dissension and falsehood as well as injustice, oppression, and war. Christ had also addressed these illnesses, teaching virtues—love, compassion, justice, truth—as medicines that could heal the wounds of vice. Where harmony reigned, Ephrem exulted, Satan could not live but rather flickered and died.[29]

Ephrem here follows imagery deeply embedded in Syriac Christianity from its earliest moments: of Christ as the Good Physician and the eucharist as the Medicine of Life.[30] Such imagery allowed Ephrem to interweave individual and collective, physical and moral conditions. He used it to instruct his congregation that liturgy was the place to encounter Christ and his healing, and also the place to learn how to become the healing work of Christ in the world.

Ephrem rejoiced in his Nativity hymns that the birth of Christ was the occasion of every kind of healing, from mortality to hunger to need. All human suffering was illness, and for all illness Christ's birth provided the cure. In *Hymns on the Nativity* 3, he sang:

> Blessed be the Child . . .
> . . . Who today made humanity young again.
> Blessed be the Fruit Who bowed himself down for our hunger,
> Blessed be the Gracious One who suddenly enriched
> all of our poverty and filled our need.
> Blessed be He Whose mercy inclined Him to heal our sickness.
> > *Refrain*: My Lord, blessed be Your Child, Who raised to
> > honor our hardness of heart.[31]

The hymn continues: "Glory to God the Healer of human nature."[32]

Ephrem emphasized that the incarnation brought Christ's work of healing at the most basic level of human physicality. Christ would heal the sick with his own "sweat and spit and tears and even blood."[33] But equally powerful were the social dimensions of his birth. Ephrem's Nativity hymns addressed the newborn Christ as the "Son of the Poor," born to Mary, "a daughter of the poor," and Joseph "a needy one," in the bare dirt of a cave, in a town of no account.[34] Again, Mary's identification away from political power compelled a quality of social critique to Ephrem's words. Empowering the weak and powerless when he "bent down [from his height] and shone forth from the poor,"[35] Christ healed unjust social order by divine favor.

Ephrem sang the gospel stories as events of personal, direct, transformative encounter between the incarnate Lord and every individual he met. In turn, Ephrem's hymns instructed the congregation that this, precisely, was the work of the liturgy: personal, direct, transformative encounter with God's own self that healed every ill through the "medicines" of the sacraments.[36]

As Ephrem sang his hymns, the congregation sang their refrains in response. This was part of their liturgical role. But how did that role provide a model for their contributions in the world? What should be their response to liturgy itself, to the healing it offered through its divine medicine? In Ephrem's hymns, the healed body was not only one where sickness was turned to health, but furthermore one where vices were turned to virtues. Physical and moral transformation in the liturgy must become social and ethical transformation in the civic community.

In *Hymns on the Nativity* 1, Ephrem called for the faithful to approach their vigil service in preparation for the great feast of Christ's birth in terms that would transform the civic community.[37] The physical discipline of participating in the night service offered a direct foil to the state of the city outside the church doors. While the faithful fasted and kept vigil, Ephrem sang, the unfaithful, too, were busy: the greedy worked at extorting interest, the thief at stealing, the glutton at excess; the merchant kept vigil to plan his profits, the rich man to gain more wealth, the worrier to tend his anxieties. For these, Satan taught a vigil that strengthened the vices: a vigil of unchastity, jealousy, anger.[38] Instead, Ephrem exhorted, the faithful must keep their vigil of the Nativity "as bright ones on this bright night . . . wrapped in hidden brilliance in the midst of this visible darkness."[39] The work of liturgy healed the faithful, yielding serenity of heart, a body attuned to divine presence, and actions that performed true worship.[40] That healing must be offered, in turn, to heal the work of Satan's vices:

> On this day on which the Lord of all came among servants
> Let the lords also bow down to their servants lovingly.
> On this day when the Rich One was made poor for our sake,
> Let the rich man also make the poor man a sharer at his table.
> On this day a gift came out to us without our asking for it;
> Let us then give alms to those who cry out and beg from us.[41]

For Ephrem, liturgy yielded healing that must radiate beyond the church's door. And this was the ministry for the laity, especially, to address. For if liturgy was the place where virtues were *formed* in the service of worship, then the civic community was the place where virtues were *performed* in a further service of worship, the offering of Christ's work in the world.[42] Elsewhere, in another Nativity hymn, he prayed, "May our prayer in words be in deeds."[43] To the laity belonged the liturgy of the streets—itself a ministry of participation that extended sacred action beyond the specific spaces of ecclesiastical worship and into a community larger than the confines of Christian membership.

Like Ephrem before him, Jacob of Sarug praised the church rightly ordered in worship as a reflection of divine purpose. But where Ephrem's verses often moved pragmatically between liturgy and society, as mutually formative moral and ethical locations, Jacob's chanted couplets worked to instill a liturgical sense of order that yielded a particular aesthetics of community.[44] Time and again, he preached that worship was the purpose for which God intended all creation from the beginning. Jacob envisioned worship most importantly as ceaseless adoration, following the imagery from Isaiah 6:1–4. In various memre, he taught that at the first moment of creation, God had filled the heavens with angelic hosts, "choirs of ministers" to sing and offer worship with glory, splendor, and honor.[45] By their example, "thundering forth," "with loud voices," all creation in turn came into being, joining the wondrous song.[46]

Jacob used this powerful imagery to instruct his congregations on how they should worship: what, exactly, they should do when they came to church for the liturgy. More than exhortation, he offered this vision as a prayer:

> [O Lord,] Let the earth thunder with the assemblies of those who glorify you,
> As heaven throngs with the companies of those who serve You.
>
> . . . .
> Let people praise as also the angels praise.
> Just as the [angelic] ranks of the house of Gabriel serve,
> So let also the churches serve without contention.
> Just as these [angelic] companies of Michael shout for joy,
> Let your exaltation among our assemblies move with pure love.
> As that pure assembly of Seraphim cry "holy,"
> Let the order of humanity declare You holy in all the earth.[47]

In Jacob's rendering, God had made earthly creation like that of heaven, able to exist in a state of ceaseless, joyful wonder. Nature, too, offered humanity a model of proper worship. By virtue of marking time's progression, morning and evening, "like deacons reverend, vigilant and undefiled," instruct humankind "like mellifluous choirs" in the wonders of God's works, providing the occasions and inciting the singing of praise as appropriate response. "The morning and the evening endure unchanging, like luminous signs, / and from them, the world learns to give glory."[48] Moreover, Jacob exulted, every form of nature, and every kind of being—on land, sea, or in the air—contributed their own song of worship.[49] He sang:

> Heaven and earth are filled with His glory as it is written
> And whatsoever is created whispers praise to its creator.
> All His creations with their tongues sing the glory
> But in what manner and how much, you can never hear.[50]

Like the heavenly hosts, and like the world of nature, society presented a diversity of voices by which to express the wonder of devotion. For Jacob (as for Ephrem), liturgy took its models from scripture. Different biblical characters provided types for how and why the different segments of the human community could and should join together in glorious song. Because a virgin conceived Christ, Jacob extolled, the choir of virgins sings praise. Because Christ was a baby in the arms of his parents, babies in the arms of their parents are anointed and baptized in his name. Because Mary was chosen from human women to be his mother, mothers and husbands join in the festal songs. As Joseph, Mary, and the whole of creation sing because of the Christ child, so, too, all children, all pregnant mothers, all parents, all unmarried young virgins rejoice in song. Adam, Eve, and all the elderly rejoice; pastors and flocks, the church, the gatherings of peoples and congregations all sing together.[51] Jacob's festal homilies often conclude with cascading lists of all who sing forth God's glory, on earth, in the natural world, and in heaven. Jacob delighted in singing these lists.[52]

In such passages, Jacob identified every member of the gathered church as crucial to, and fully participant in, the activity of liturgical celebration.[53] By naming each group by gender, age, ethnicity (the "Peoples"/ the "Nations"), social location, and ecclesiastical rank, Jacob effectively cast the liturgical body—the worshipping congregation as a whole—not in terms of hierarchical divisions, but rather as an entirety of multiple yet distinct parts. This, too, was a beloved literary trope among ancient Christian authors. Narsai had praised the mystical wedding of Christ to the Church as a liturgy to which everyone flocked: "Men and women, the old and the young and all statures (*mushatha*), moved to present to [the Bride] hymns of glory as a gift."[54]

A consequence of such naming was the vision of inclusion it enabled. Only the laity could provide a presence that completely and fully represented the human community before God. At the same time, whatever their rank, people came with their needs. Mindful of the needs and desolation of many, Jacob offered thanksgiving on their behalf for the blessings of divine compassion:

> The scattered whom you [O Lord] gathered, the defeated whom you established, the
>   broken whom you healed,
> The servants whom you freed, the expelled whom you returned, the little ones
>   whom you magnified.
> The sick whom you visited, the ill whom you cured, the captives whom you saved,
> The weary to whom you gave rest, the angry whom you appeased, the impure
>   whom you purified.
> The imprisoned whom you released, the confined whom you brought out, the dead
>   to whom you gave life,
> May they profess your love, without repaying you. Praise to you.[55]

Jacob's insistence on the congregation's all-inclusive constitution was a statement on the laity's role and purpose. Only when liturgy comprised the complete human community, their conditions named with the promise of redemptive healing, could liturgy express divine order, on earth as in heaven. Hence Jacob, like Ephrem, presented a notion of worship fulfilled by justice, healing, and mercy.

Such naming of rank and difference carried further resonance. Jacob emphasized the sound of liturgy as intermingled song: unified, yet not undifferentiated. In his descriptions of creation's worship, Jacob exults that multitudes sing. He delighted in naming legions, hosts, every created being or thing, each in its own form, and, in his words, each with "its own mouth." The music was textured, variegated, multifaceted. Jacob, like Ephrem before him, presented an aesthetics of glory, in which the qualities of abundance and multiplicity were essential for beauty. Each difference was a delight when the whole was harmonious rather than discordant. Difference was included, not erased. Voices intermingled, but unity in no way obscured or hid or diminished diversity.

For Jacob, singing as an act of worship was the right response to God's grace, whether in heaven or on earth. Such singing was purposeful: not only as a response to God, but also as a means of uniting a divided creation. God's act of incarnation had joined together divine and human; in response, singing joined together the whole of creation, earthly and heavenly. God joined the natures; singing joined the entire fabric, literally echoing the divine action. Ephrem had described the night when Christ was born: "All creation became mouths . . . above and below."[56] Jacob, in turn, presented creation as an act of song: for Jacob, musical harmony is the fundamental ontology of existence, the basic mode of being.

Jacob characterized the liturgical significance of the laity as twofold. On the one hand, the laity were crucial for *how* they participated in the liturgy: with orderly, loud, attentive song. Even more fundamentally, Jacob argued, the laity were crucial to liturgical order *by their presence*. The laity stood—and sang!—as living icons of salvific grace. They were not a passive audience, but active participants who served, no less than ordained clergy or consecrated choirs, to proclaim divine truth mercifully fulfilled in a universal salvation.

Laity were hence presented by Syriac theologians with a place of profound worth within the ordered ranks of the liturgical community. By formation and performance (Ephrem), by presence and participation (Jacob), laity—including women—served within the "priesthood of all believers" (1 Pet 2:9).[57]

LITURGY IN THE CIVIC COMMUNITY

Liturgy taught more than doctrine or the Bible. It also taught habits of collective behavior. Shared ritual activity habituated people to routine practices by which to respond to events that disrupted or disturbed their local community. The liturgical voices of laity were needed beyond church walls, in the very streets of their lives. Several passages from the sixth-century *Chronicle of Pseudo-Joshua the Stylite* will lay the scene.

The *Chronicle* recalls a number of significant (even traumatic) events just before and after the year 500 CE in the regions around the city of Edessa. In 497/8, the emperor Anastasios I remitted a steeply burdensome tax that had sorely tried the tradespeople of the region. In celebration, the Edessans rejoiced:

> The whole city . . . dressed up in white, from the greatest to the least, and carrying lighted candles and burning censers, to the accompaniment of psalms and hymns they went out to the martyrion of Mar Sergios and Mar Simon, thanking God and praising the emperor. There they held a eucharist, and on coming back into the city they extended the feast of joy and pleasure for a whole week, and declared that they would celebrate this feast every year.[58]

The following year, an annual saint's festival at a martyrion in Arsamosata brought together a great crowd "of men, women, and children, and of all ages and ranks."[59] Alas, their celebrations were disrupted by an earthquake, the more tragic for the array of people exposed without shelter.

Tragedy continued. At one point the next year, the bishop Peter summoned a public liturgy of supplication in Edessa:

> He took charge of all his clergy and the whole Covenant (community), men and women, and all the (lay) members of the church, both rich and poor, men, women, and children. They went through all the streets of the city, bearing crosses (and singing) psalms and hymns, (dressed) in black garments of penitence, while all the monasteries in our country also kept up their services with great diligence. By the prayers of all . . . we received a little consolation.[60]

When severe famine subsequently struck, the people of Edessa tended the starving. Still, many died. The bishop rallied the city for the necessary burials:

The whole city took care collectively to accompany those who were taken out of the *xenodocheion* (hospice for the poor) [for burial], with psalms, praises, hymns, and songs full of the hope of the resurrection. Women also (took part) with mournful lamentation and emotional cries. At their head went Mar Peter, the worthy pastor, and with him was the governor and all the free-born.[61]

This wretched time of suffering came to a head with a war between Rome and Persia fought in Edessa's territory. At last, in 506/7, the Romans prevailed, and peace returned to the region. The Edessenes again poured out to celebrate, this time to honor the victorious *magistros* and his army:

All the Edessenes, from the greatest to the least, came out to receive him with great joy, carrying wax candles. All the clergy, the children of the covenant, and the monks also came out.... Rejoicing in the peace that had been made ... exulting in the hope of blessings expected in the future, and praising God ... the citizens sent [the *magistros*] on his way with songs fitting for him and for (the emperor) who had sent him.[62]

Such passages abound in Syriac historical writings to mark occasions of public crisis or celebration. They punctuate hagiographies and martyr texts similarly. The literary tropes for every major event, or sorrow, need, or joy, portray public scenes in which the entire civic community was present. The formulaic accounts identify the participants according to age, gender, and rank, just as the passages from Pseudo-Joshua the Stylite cited above. Sometimes religious identity was included: Jews, for example, were said to have joined their song to the mourning crowds on the death of Bishop Rabbula of Edessa.[63] Invariably, these crowds of the full population sang psalms, hymns, and songs, whether of supplication, lament, or celebration.

An example of the scripted rubrics that underlay such actual events is presented by Syriac codex Rahmani Syr. 33, which preserves the opening portion of a sixth-century service for the entrance of a bishop into a provincial town.[64] The elaborate processional service moved from the city gates through the streets to the main church. Worshippers were to carry crosses and torches. The rubrics instructed the celebrants to pause repeatedly for incensations and diaconal litanies. Each litany, at every pause, was to be punctuated by the congregation singing *kyrie eleison* (Lord, have mercy) ten times. Laity including women—prominently cited—were to accompany the clergy, as the procession in ordered ranks finally arrived at the church and escorted the visiting bishop inside. The ritual actions and sounds of such processions inscribed liturgical order, meaning, and purpose into the very streets of a city. In turn, the ritual patterns of movement, pause, call, response, and extensive repetition, inscribed liturgical process and authority into the bodies of the participants.[65] In such processions, the singing participation of the laity was as crucial for the occasion's success as that of clergy or bishop.[66]

Church leaders emphasized that these sung prayers were powerful in their impact. They were mighty weapons against Satan, powerful supplications for divine mercy, and life-giving in their encouragement to the faithful. Martial language was used not only for the hymns of Ephrem or the sung preaching of Rabbula; hymns were also armaments of the laity. Cyrillona at the turn of the fifth century captured this sense when preaching amid an assault of locusts, drought, and foreign invasion by Huns:

> O chosen people,
>   lift up your heart;
> clasp hands
>   and raise up a hymn of praise (*shubha*).
> Stomp upon the Evil One
>   with the heels of your voice,
> and trample upon error
>   with the soles of your breath.
> Let each one fill
>   the slings of his mouth
> with the solid stones
>   of all hymns (*hullale*).
> Let each draw up a company (*gude*, lit. choirs)
>   within his thoughts,
> and marshall hosts (*haile*)
>   in the hosts of the heart.[67]

Further in the same text Cyrillona makes clear that the entire populace is involved: "See the song in the mouths of babes / and your psalms (*zmirathak*) among women."[68]

Other evidence supports the picture. Recall Ephrem's second madrasha for the Feast of the Resurrection, where he ennumerated the sung offerings of each group of the ecclesiastical community.[69] Several verses of this same hymn specifically exalt the contributions of children, as distinctively sounded amid the larger rejoicing:

> This joyful festival is entirely made of tongues and voices:
> Innocent young women and men sounding like trumpets and horns,
> While infant girls and boys resemble harps and lyres;
> Their voices intertwine as they reach up together towards heaven,
> Giving Glory to the Lord of glory.
>   *Refrain*: Blessed is He for whom the silent have thundered out![70]

Ephrem then cites Noah's Ark as a type for these singing children. Inside the ark, Ephrem recalled,

> . . . all voices cried out:
> . . . lovely voices;
> tongues, all in pairs, utter together in chaste fashion,
> thus serving as a type of our festival [of the Resurrection] now
>   when unmarried girls and boys
> together in innocence sing praise to the Lord of that Ark.[71]

Ephrem goes on to recall the children of Palm Sunday who had "scattered praises like flowers, their songs [of joy] like lilies" as the Lord had entered Jerusalem. Just so, he sings, "Now too at this festival does the crowd of children scatter for You, Lord, halleluiahs like blossoms. / *Refrain*: Blessed is He who was acclaimed by young children."[72] In turn, Ephrem summons all to gather and fill their minds and ears with the songs of the women's choir, exulting, "Blessed is He who is garlanded with His handmaids!"[73]

Scenes of liturgical celebration that included the entire civic community abound in the prose and poetry of late antique Syriac authors. Formulaic and conventional in their literary expressions, they nonetheless convey the significance of events that involved or bore upon or affected or impacted their local communities. In every such description, singing is mentioned, and the singing is described as involving the full civic community.

These texts are more than clichés. They marked actual moments of collective process and meaning, whether in joy or need. Liturgy marked civic life in these ways, beyond the regular liturgical cycles within church buildings. Embodied and sensorily palpable—audible, visible, adorned with incense, ritual clothing, and defined ritual ranks—these processions brought the voices of the entire community into public sound. As such, these formulaic tropes provide us access to the public presence and participation of members of society who are generally not visible to us as historical actors in daily life. Women, children, "uneducated" laity, the socially dependent, the poor, and sometimes the enslaved are mentioned in our sources as present and singing in events of the civic life of late antique communities, in a variety of social locations. We lack their personal voices in the vast majority of our extant evidence. Yet here, in such literary passages, we are reminded that these voices sounded, present and active, in their contributions to these important community events.

Such witness appears not only in literary descriptions or lists of participants. The poetry itself offers us important historical witness. One example is the following portion of an anonymous Syriac Nativity hymn, a hymnographic counterpart to the passages from Pseudo-Joshua the Stylite quoted above. Probably written in the fifth or early sixth century, it is one of dozens of such sung exclamations:

> Today let all creation thunder out in praise,
> Let each mouth give a shout of "glory,"
> Let tongues be stirred with a song of praise.
> Let all the peoples cry out together in song.
> In heaven, praise to the Lord,
> And on earth, peace to all flesh,
> For a Savior has shone forth for all the world.
>> *Refrain*: In both height and depth have You resided, Lord:
>> In the womb of Your Begetter, in hidden fashion,
>> And [in] Mary's bosom, made manifest.[74]

This kind of verse ("Let all creation thunder out in praise") with its responsive refrain provides a brief glimpse into areas of the social world of late antique Syriac Christians we rarely otherwise see. These hymns were performed publicly, often outdoors, through village, town, or city streets. The processions were sometimes liturgical, sometimes paraliturgical. They were not simply gatherings of people. Under the aegis of a widely acknowledged, shared common culture, familiar religious ritual patterns—whether "ordinary" (as part of the regular liturgical cycle) or "extraordinary" (in times of crisis)—were followed with an ethos of divine approval and authorization. Indeed, hymns often referenced the participation of the angelic hosts, as did the verse just quoted. These were publicly significant occasions on which the voices of women, children, the poor, and the enslaved were heard publicly, and heard to carry meaningful religious authority.

The institutional grounding of religious offices extended authority to ritual practitioners in domestic settings as well. Consider John of Ephesos's account of an ascetic household in the countryside of Melitene, belonging to the two brothers Elijah and Theodore, laymen who had been traders. According to John, this household resounded morning and night with the psalmody and services chanted by everyone who lived there. These, John enumerates, included the poor and sick of every age who came for succor, the freed men and women who were attached to the patronage of Elijah and Theodore, the household slaves, and the children born to Elijah and his wife, Maria.[75] Liturgical singing, then, whether in formal liturgical contexts or in paraliturgical gatherings, brought into public view and public hearing the presence of social demographics generally ignored, occluded, or hidden in historical sources. Remember Ephrem's refrain: "Blessed is He for whom the silent have thundered out!"[76] In public religious processions or in domestic gatherings, in the context of ritually expressed sacred song, *these voices mattered.*

Like the entries in the *Chronicle of Pseudo-Joshua the Stylite,* John of Ephesos's account of Elijah and Theodore's household provides a list of ritual participants similar to those celebrated in liturgical poetry. These lists could serve different agendas, and despite their similarities might also indicate different social contexts. In a monastic or ascetic context such as John of Ephesos presented, listing by gender, age, and social status might indicate a functional and inclusive equality between the participants, across social and economic categories: the participants sang as equals. By contrast, in a civic context such as that portrayed by Pseudo-Joshua the Stylite, the same listings could reinscribe the categories of social hierarchy that indicated a well-functioning and ordered civic community. As such, they reinforced a patriarchal hierarchy that fixed people in prescribed and contained sociopolitical and economic roles. People sang in their ranks.

But, again, there were further possibilities. In the liturgical poetry of Ephrem or Jacob of Sarug—or any such celebrant—such listings also evoked an ideal civic or worshipping community. In all these instances, considerable slippage between these effects could take place. Liturgy (formal or informal) offered a place for everyone. It also sustained and reinscribed the patriarchal social order of the late antique Roman Empire. Ironically, the ritual processes that upheld that social order also provided means for its critique and even its disruption. Women, children, the poor, the enslaved—all could sing with voices that were, at least at times, religiously, socially, and even civically valued and authoritative, even within the unyielding restraints of socially defined categories.

JACOB OF SARUG ON LISTENING: THE EXPERIENCE OF SOUND

Singing was a primary task of the laity. So, too, was listening. Among other foci, Jacob's homilies attended to the liturgical participant *as listener*, a role Jacob saw as one of active contribution. Jacob was particularly attuned to hearing as a sensory experience, one with primary import for moral formation and condition.[77] He shared a cultural sensibility of sound as something that literally struck the listener: the impact was tactile, physical. Sounds drew attention: they might distract or they might enable concentration.[78] "Give ear, O prudent one," Jacob sang, "and lucidly focus your mind."[79] Sound connected words, persons, events, and experiences separated by space or time; it could sunder harmony or stillness, or weave together coherence or concord.[80]

In Jacob's rendering, the listener not only received the words and teachings and sounds of liturgy. Listeners also interacted and reverberated within these encounters, granting affective meaning, allowing dispositional impact, and within that process formulating their own response, to be enacted and voiced in turn.[81] The memra—the homily Jacob chanted to instruct the faithful—was the liturgy's fulcrum. It taught doctrine, explicated scripture, illuminated the liturgy's ritual patterns; it prepared the congregation for the sacrament to follow. The congregation had to actively receive this preaching and then respond, bringing the words of the preacher to fulfillment. In his homily "On the Tower of Babel" Jacob exhorted the faithful:

> Therefore, prepare to listen sincerely, O discerning ones,
> to this *memra*, which is full of every profit for the one who gives heed to it.
> Both the speaker and the listeners are co-workers;
> the word of the one who speaks and of the one who gives heed is the same.
> From the speaker and the listeners, one eulogy goes up
> to the One who fashioned for us a mouth and ears in his wisdom.[82]

Listening required attention, discernment, and a conjoining of purpose to that of the homilist, so that both preaching and listening became one and the same act of offering thanksgiving to God: "*Both the speaker and the listeners are co-workers . . .* [from whom] *one eulogy goes up.*" While Jacob presented this picture

in Christianized terms, he was also drawing on an inherited philosophy of pedagogy explored at length by the likes of Plutarch and cultivated in Christian circles
by Augustine of Hippo and other influential preachers.[83]

In Jacob's view the congregation's task of listening was a sacred one. It was worthy of divine assistance, and even required it. Hence, at the start of a homily on
the prophet Elisha, he paused to pray for both himself as the one who must preach
fittingly on the topic at hand, and for his congregation as those who must respond:
"[O Lord] awaken my word, and awaken them [the congregation] to sing praise."[84]
Preaching on the ascension of the prophet Elijah, he prayed with images of labor
pangs and birth giving:

> May my tongue, [O Lord] with pangs of Your love, bear You for listening,
> while You cause my lips to give birth to You for those who listen.
> You are the speech full of splendors for the one who hears it.
> You are the voice full of Life for the one who attends to it.[85]

Such invocational prayers are a hallmark of Jacob's memre, distinctive to his poetry
and basically unique in the Syriac corpus.[86] As a rhetorical device, these prayers
assuredly enhanced the beauty of the text. But they also served a functional purpose: demarcating the constituents of preaching as an event, so that preaching
became an activity of performance and participation for everyone involved. The
opening lines of his homily "On Pentecost" establish this construction:

> O Lord, kindly open to me the door of Your treasury,
> So that I may carry along and bring forth all kinds of advantages.
> Grant me the word by which I may recite Your grandeur,
> and an exalted voice that proclaims Your glory all day.
> Let a homily [*memra*] of wonder be impelled within me by Your gift,
> And in the hearers, wonder and love regarding Your story.[87]

The prayer names each role present: Lord, speaker, memra, and hearer. Further,
it sets them in the mode Jacob desires. The Lord is summoned to presence by
means of petition, not only the governing presence but also the source of enable-
ment for the other three constituents of the performance. The speaker—the poet
preacher—requests words and voice for the task at hand. Hence these will be not
his own, but divinely provided. The memra itself receives constitution and agency:
it becomes both an act and its content. It will come forth itself by the Lord's gift.
Finally, the congregation—the hearers—will be imbued, "impelled," by wonder
and love to receive the memra in full awareness of its divine source.

Delineating these four roles is a practical performative move. On the one hand,
it prepares the congregation for the sermon they are about to hear. But a more
important goal is at work. Jacob's verses here comprise stage directions, so to
speak, guiding the participants to their proper roles in the human-divine interaction that liturgy enacts.

Jacob performed his invocational prayers as petitions, offered in the second-person form of direct address to the Lord. Who was listening? Why? And to what? Sure enough, in due course Jacob must turn his prayer to the congregation, who otherwise have been eavesdropping on an ostensibly "private" (or personal?) supplication offered by Jacob to his Lord. In his homily "On the Fashioning of Creation," at the start of the first day of creation, for example, Jacob's invocational prayer addressed God as Creator, himself as creature, and the memra as God's creation or sown Word. Next, Jacob summoned the congregation: "O lovers of life, come be refreshed by [God's] teaching. / Gold is pleasing to the one who loves to buy gold, / But it is not so pleasing as teaching for one who meditates."[88]

At once the listener has a designated identity: not simply one who hears, but a "lover of life" for whom these words will be a source of life, a treasure more pleasing than gold. As such, the listener is also constructed as one who understands the preacher to be God's inspired poet, and to know the words that are preached, the memra's content, as God's own. Jacob's invocational prayers often continue at length. Only when he has set the four constituents into right relation—Lord, listener, memra, and speaker—can the work of preaching begin.

In this instance ("On the Fashioning of Creation"), Jacob turns to the beginning of the narrative that the memra will tell, the story of the first day of creation. Now he presents the situation of preaching as an exchange between speaker and listener, with the memra itself as the agent that binds their relationship. He begins, "A homily [memra] stirred within me that is full of wonder about creation, / and now it throbs within me to unveil itself to its hearers."[89] With this poetic turn, God has stepped out of the spotlight, no longer the person of direct address. Rather, it is God's account—the memra stirring within Jacob—that comes to articulation, through Jacob's voice and into the listener's hearing. The memra itself holds center stage.

When Jacob offers such markers of the homiletic process, he summons the listeners to their own work. For these prayers also establish those who hear—the members of the congregation, both lay and consecrated—as themselves ritually essential and ritually distinct in the role they fulfilled for the memra's liturgical task.[90] Jacob will sometimes cue behavioral responses at this point, as well as dispositional recognition. In his first homily on the prophet Elisha, for example, Jacob provides instructions first to himself as the homilist, still in the form of petition to God: "The mouth should speak Your praise out of the fullness of the heart. / It should not proclaim Your word to listeners out of habit."[91] Jacob's job is to provide speech worthy of God and worth hearing by listeners, not the rote teaching of routine. In turn, he cues the congregation:

> Wonder prompted me to speak about Elisha.
> [O] Discerning [listener], you shall not grow weary when you hear
> about the disciple rich in blessings and full of beauty. . . .
> The birth pangs of his story [memra] are attacking and motivating me
> So that it may be born, for it is also a wonder to the one who hears it.[92]

It is all very well for Jacob to promise his congregation, "You shall not grow weary when you hear." In fact, he often peppered his homilies with the exhortation to be attentive: "Look, O discerning one (*porusha*)," or "Note, discerning ones," or "Understand, O discerning ones." He rouses them up when their attention flags: "Discerning one, you shall not grow weary when you hear [my sermon]!"[93] He scolds those who misbehave, lest they become a distraction to others: "For there is another who is anxious to listen carefully."[94] Sure enough, we can hear his frustration close at hand. He complains, "In the world you are awake, but [here] in the house of God, behold, you are asleep!"[95] He prays, "[O Lord], silence our improper, tumultuous talking, / so that Your word alone resounds in our assemblies."[96]

Writing at the turn of the sixth century, in a now-dominantly Christian civic culture, Jacob worried about complacency in the Christian populace.[97] He recognized that poor or inattentive preaching could be a contributing factor. But so, too, could listening if it was reduced to habit: "Routine damages the Word and makes it grow cold, / so that if you listen to it by habit it becomes commonplace. / . . . It will give you no advantage."[98] The congregation's (occasional? frequent?) restlessness vexed him. In his long homily on Ephrem the Syrian, he wrestled for their attention:

> Rebellious children, do not grow weary with lengthy accounts;
> (rather) love instruction, for it is a great treasure for the one who possesses it.
> Be students of learning without growing bored;
> with sincere hearing which does not find fault with straightforward accounts.
> . . . .
> Why do you patiently occupy yourself with providing drink for your body,
> But when you hear the Word of Life, you grow weary?
> You are anxious enough for the food which turns to waste,
> while teaching, which is pure gold, is burdensome for you.
> . . . .
> Chosen Ephrem did not grown bored when he taught;
> you should not be bored when you hear the story about him.[99]

Nonetheless, there was a further element the congregation needed to add: the listener must hear with love. This was crucial for the deeper resonances of meaning. The Lord's Prayer, for example, taught by Jesus to his disciples (Mt 6:9–11), "becomes clear to you when you listen affectionately."[100] For the delicate task of understanding difficult or contested biblical stories, the situation required careful generosity on all sides. Preaching on the conversion of the apostle Paul on the road to Damascus, Jacob exhorted:

> Love requires that this story be told by love:
> Listening, however intently, without love has no effect.
> You and I will not be wearied by its length!
> Come and rejoice! Every little detail is filled with love![101]

In Jacob's view, the congregation had a holy purpose, a sacred vocation in their listening.[102] It was their responsibility to rise to that task: "If ephemeral affairs are dear to you, / it is difficult for Scripture to speak to you concerning the hidden things."[103] This required their active participation throughout the liturgy, and not only during his sermon.

In his homily "On the Partaking of the Holy Mysteries," Jacob walked his listeners through the entire service, identifying and naming their role at each point. To each component, Jacob intoned, the believer must "be patient and listen," "pay heed," "turn your ear and receive," "learn and believe," "listen and pay heed."[104] The reason for such strict attention, he instructs, is that listening affects the soul's disposition. "The human soul is open to influence; / the more she [the soul] reflects on something, the more she absorbs to become similar (to that thing)."[105]

This was precisely why the sounds or singing or performances of the city outside the liturgy posed such danger, Jacob warned. "The lamenting voice of wailing women," the "singing and playing of the actors [in the theater]," "bad news," or "good reports"—all that one hears penetrates the soul's disposition, and causes it to respond in kind, with weeping, laughter, fear, or happy mood. One is pulled in every direction, fragmented. Here, then, is the importance of listening in the liturgy. For, by contrast, "when [the soul] hears the voice of the service of God's house, / she is moved spiritually with the love of God."[106] Listening in liturgy united the self that the sounds of the world outside literally pulled to pieces.

In Jacob's view, listening required openness to the various dimensions of liturgical sound. Not only should one listen to the words, but also to the "tunes" and "melodies": the music itself worked upon the soul, penetrating beyond cognitive recognition to the inner quality of disposition. Jacob stresses here the accruing force of beauty as well as sequence and repetition: "[The Soul] takes delight in the holy hymns. . . . The more she hears these hymns that are sung for her, / the more she becomes pure, modest, and full of hope and discernment."[107] As Jacob noted elsewhere, the music of these hymns was offered by the singing of the women's choirs with their "instructive melodies"; their "soft tones" were a victorious weapon in the battle against heresy.[108]

Still, the work of the laity did not stop with listening, however intentional and discerning their listening might be. Liturgical listening bore its fruit in the fullness of liturgical song, unfolding with heightened power as the service turned to the eucharistic sequence. As Jacob instructed, together the congregation sounded forth their prayers, their confessions, their praise. Together with the priest they petitioned the Lord to send the Son and cause the Holy Spirit to enter the bread and wine. Together they prayed the "Our Father"; together they sang the Sanctus. Together they prayed for forgiveness, together they received communion. Again, he emphasizes the progressive force of the ritual pressing upon its participants as the sequence of actions moved toward culmination amid the layered sounds of words and music, sung by each contributor in their different roles.

The accumulating force of the ritual affected not only the believer, Jacob insisted, but also Satan himself. For it was Satan who nudged the congregation to restlessness, who prompted the complacent or distracted to leave early. "Satan is annoyed by these holy hymns," Jacob assured his flock—the "truthful songs" sung daily by the "chaste congregation."[109]

Repeatedly Jacob stresses that one must be present at the liturgy, be attentive, and *be heard* to call out in song, in prayer, and in supplication. He exhorts the congregation, time and again, to stand, listen, hear, attend, receive, sing, cry out. Listening yielded song.

In Jacob's verses, both the civic and liturgical domains were locations of orchestrated collective interaction: locations of collective performance. Both involved sustained dialogic exchange, often of crafted vocal genres. In his stress on volume, Jacob points to the diverse competitions intrinsic to late antique civic life. Faithful believers competed with heretics, religions with one another; monasteries competed with cities, households with shrines. Truth competed with falsehood. As Jacob had observed about Ephrem, music was a primary tool in these battles. Hence he admonished that one must do more than sing truth; one must outsing falsehood. And one must be heard to do so.

For Jacob, the (loud) singing of sacred song—the singing of praise and thanksgiving—was the full realization of worship. In this, Jacob admonished, humanity had a unique role. The natural world offers its praise merely by virtue of its functioning. Of all creation, he insisted, humankind alone can sing praise of God of its own free will.[110] Thus he summons the congregation's voice: "Be awakened O Church, with your beautiful chants / and offer to the Son gifts of praise."[111]

Here, for Jacob, was perfect liturgy. In this description, the term I translate as "voices," *qale*, could equally well be translated as "melodies":

> And voices upon voices crowd around [Christ] from every side,
>
> . . . .
>
> The voices of the nations who clap their hands to give praise,
> and the voice of handmaids grouped in choirs to make a joyful noise.
> The voice of churches who sing praise with their harps,
> and the voice of monasteries who make a joyful noise to him with their alleluias.
> The voice of priests who consecrate him with the gentle waving of their hands,
> and the voice of saints who bless him in every place.
> The voice of men who sing praise with their tongues,
> The voice of women who exalt him with their *madrashe.*
> The voice of children who repeat before him. . . .
> The voice of teachers who set their knowledge in array before him.
> For praise of the Father, the Son wakens all creation.[112]

For Jacob, liturgy, properly served, worked through its sounds: the hearing and voicing of scripture, prayers, instruction, and praise; in songs heard and songs sung. In the tasks of listening and of singing, the laity, including women, per-formed their ministry of presence and participation.

AN IMAGE FOR THE LAITY: WOMAN AS PRIEST

The pedagogical impact of Syriac liturgical poetry was a combination of content, performance, and participation by all who were present in the worship event. As was the case for the women's choirs, so, too, for the laity stories about biblical women might highlight their voices, suggesting multiple levels of meaning. The intersections could be surprising. The occasional depictions of biblical women as priestly figures provide examples. These passages stand in contrast to the real-ity of an exclusively male, ordained Christian clergy, to be sure. But their play on gendered authority in the church was by no means an ancient advocacy for female priesthood within Christianity. Rather, the image suggests that laypeople, too, were significant actors in Christian worship, and, further, that lay piety was a form of ministry.

Within the early Christian notion of the priesthood of all believers, grounded in the New Testament instruction of 1 Peter 2:9, stood a point of intersection for the roles of layperson and priest.[113] It was the point at which the actions of the layperson transformed into more than acts of personal devotion. They became, instead, gestures or practices that participated in the ritualized life of the worship-ping community, liturgy in its broadest sense. When the actions of the layperson could be seen as analogous to the actions of the priest, both the person and the deed were transformed. The person gained heightened religious authority, and the deed gained heightened potency. The shift in perspective from lay to priestly affected the representation of both the human domain in which the layperson's act was performed, and the divine realm from which and by which both person and act took their meaning.

For the ancient church, liturgy worked as the conduit of human-divine interac-tion and exchange. Certainly, liturgy was not the only way, nor the only means, by which the human-divine relationship was expressed or explored. But its ritually articulated roles, actions, and performances provided a template that shifted the meaning of any person or act within its purview. Ritual agent, ritual space, and ritual instruments were key elements marking the shift from mundane to sacred.

Take the example of the Sinful Woman who came to the house of Simon the Pharisee to wash the feet of Christ with her tears, wipe them with her hair, and anoint them with fine oil (Lk 7:36–50).[114] In Ephrem's *Hymns on Virginity*, this woman was set before the faithful as a compelling model of faith, one who showed *what* faith is—the recognition of God's capacity to redeem—and *how* to be faithful.

So, in *Hymns on Virginity* 35, Ephrem called on the congregation to recognize their condition as sinners and to give thanks for the Sinful Woman, who, "unclean . . . was not ashamed / to enter the banquet of the pure and holy."[115] Further, they should consider her "boldness" as well as her self-abasement, wiping the sweat of Christ's feet with her hair, adorning them with kisses and tears. Wondrously, Ephrem marveled, the woman whose body had once offered a model for how to sin, now offered her body as the model for how to worship:

> By that thing by which she was lost, she was found, since she believed,
> so that triumphant was the oil that had condemned her,
> and sanctified was her mouth that had defiled her,
> and purified was her beauty that had debased her.[116]

Here and elsewhere, Ephrem exhorted his congregation to imitate this woman: "Without embarrassment let us approach the fearful one [Christ] without fear."[117] But Ephrem praised more than her disposition. He also praised her postures, gestures, and actions. By this woman, he sang in another hymn, "[Christ] taught His church to kiss in purity / [His] all-sanctifying body."[118]

In literal terms, Ephrem presented the woman's actions as the model for how the believer should approach the communion chalice in the eucharistic liturgy: as a sinner, yet unafraid; receiving God's body in one's own hands, reverencing it with kisses; offering worship both physical and spiritual, intimate, direct, and whole. Yet, even as Ephrem presented the woman as a model for lay piety, his imagery highlighted the ritual elements of her actions: there was holy anointing; there was cleansing of body and soul. Was the woman also a model for priesthood?

In Ephrem's "Homily on Our Lord," the Sinful Woman's actions were a witness, a confession, a proclamation that Jesus was more than a prophet. Rather, her actions proclaimed him to be the Lord, the Treasury of Healing:

> Streaming tears immediately announced that they were being shed as in the presence of God. Plaintive kisses testified that they were coaxing the master of the debt to tear up the bill. The precious oil of the sinful woman proclaimed that it was a "bribe" for her repentance. These were the medications the sinful woman offered her Physician, so that He could whiten the stains of her sins with her tears, and heal her wounds with her kisses, and make her bad name as sweet as the fragrance of her oil. This is the physician who heals a person with the medicine that that person brings to Him![119]

Ephrem named the components of her devotion—tears, kisses, perfumed oil—in terms that granted the woman's behavior a ritual signification. With sensory elements evoking baptism and eucharist, Ephrem mingles terms of redemption and salvation. The encounter between the woman and Christ gained liturgical tones. Yet, Ephrem marveled, the woman exceeded liturgy: "That sinful woman . . . came to God, not to priests, to forgive her debts."[120]

For Jacob of Sarug, the Sinful Woman imaged humanity's condition of moral sickness, at the same time that she performed the work of priesthood.[121] Just as a church sanctuary is perfumed with the mingled scents of incense and holy oil (chrism), so did the woman transform the space of Simon's banquet from mundane to sacred by the aroma of perfume compounded by fervent intent: "With the fire of her love she kindled her tears like ointment / and the fragrance of her repentance was increasingly sweet."[122] To the scent of oil rendered holy by the very feet it would anoint, the woman added the fragrance of a love that burned so fiercely she herself was transformed, at once sacrificer and sacrificed:

> Weeping was for her a pure censer, and she brought it with her,
> and with groans she kindled it to smoke in the Holy of Holies.
> She was for herself a priest who made petition for forgiveness,
> and willingly with contrition she made sacrifice for reconciliation.[123]

Jacob continued: as she washed Christ's feet, the woman's tears became baptismal waters consecrated with her perfumed oil. Washing and anointing, she entered into the "second womb of the place of atonement," finding herself baptized in the sea of Christ's love as he cleansed and purified her so that she might rise up pure and reborn.[124] Baptism and eucharistic sacrifice converge in Jacob's telling:

> Before the great flood of holiness she offered herself,
> and He poured upon her waves of His love that she would be absolved by Him.
> Her soul offered to the living fire the evilest body
> and it kindled in the thicket of her soul and all of it was consumed.[125]

Weeping, washing, kissing, anointing, offering: by her priestly actions the woman rendered Simon's house a sanctuary, wherein she entered as into the Holy of Holies, into the presence of the Lord.

So, too, in Jacob's hands, did the Virgin Mary become a priest as she prepared herself to receive the incarnation of the Lord. In his first homily on the Nativity, Jacob imagined the Virgin Mary in the moment after the archangel Gabriel had delivered the news of the incarnation. How should she prepare herself to receive this event—the arrival of the person of God into her womb? Jacob imagined her preparing her body as a housekeeper would prepare a dwelling for a royal visitor. Hence, he intoned, she cleaned and swept out from her mind any unworthy thoughts or emotions; she repaired, tidied, freshened, refurbished, turning the "house" of her body into "a pure temple" worthy of its guest. She adorned and embellished, decorating with "all kinds (of acts) of reverence," "with blossoms of all manners of modesty," with ornaments of virtues; she laced together good works, embroidering with devotion, beautifying with her prayers. She poured out good deeds like oil into her lamp, illuminating "the temple of her body." As she worked she sang, until, filled with fragrance and light, all was made ready:

> She burned the fragrance of her prayers warmly
> So that the pure fire of her faith should serve as incense.
> She threw, as sweet spices, the sounds of praise into the fire of her love
> And from her thanksgiving breathed the fragrance of choice incense.
> . . . .
> And while the house was made radiant by these things in a holy manner,
> The Son of the King entered and dwelt in the shrine of virginity.[126]

Here is Mary, perhaps the faithful housewife, or bride. But surely Jacob is also describing the priest who must prepare his church building for the services he celebrates. I have often wondered if Jacob speaks here of his own labor as itinerant priest through the towns and villages of the Syrian hinterland, preparing each nave and sanctuary before services began.

Elsewhere, Jacob used similar imagery to instruct his congregation on how to pray the Lord's Prayer. Guiding their recitation, he paused on the phrase "May Thy kingdom come" to urge them, "Behold, you summon the Kingdom to come. Prepare a place, / a house pure and completely filled with holiness." First, the door of the house, the mouth, should be set right and adorned. Then,

> Inside the house, which is the heart, sprinkle purity,
> all the thoughts which love beautiful things every day.
> In the soul, which is the court of the house of the king to come,
> cense sweet fragrances, good works, on all sides.
> On the floor of the house set a rug of pure love,
> For He examines to see where love dwells.

Clearing away any unworthy thoughts or emotions, any unpleasant odors of impure deeds, any vices that diminish the beauty, one renders the self a fitting place: "Let your soul become a place worthy of the king's encampment. / He will come to dwell."[27]

In each case, the purity of prayer, the fervor of the offering, the ritual language of liturgy all inflected the narrative with clear sacramental, sacerdotal tones.

Ephrem and Jacob of Sarug presented the Sinful Woman and the Virgin Mary in mythic terms in these texts. The actions they imagined in these scenes stood outside historical events, outside the gospel narratives, within the sacred time of the biblical past. Yet in each instance, they presented these women as models for the laity. In these models, ordinary acts of piety—approaching the chalice for communion, performing domestic piety, saying the Lord's Prayer—were transformed by the qualities of ritual conduct and sensory affect that expressed their purpose. They took on sacerdotal authority and sacerdotal power.

What happened when priesthood was cast in such strongly gendered imagery? The rhetorical use of "female" qualities in these texts highlighted priesthood in specific ways. With the Sinful Woman, priesthood was represented as servitude of a particular kind, a bodily ministry requiring bodily devotion. In ancient rhetorical conventions, Syriac as well as Greek, the bodily was invariably cast as "female." In the case of the Sinful Woman, an erotic tone tinged that devotion, accentuated by self-abasement. Her physicality engaged the kind of mystical love the church recognized in texts such as the biblical Song of Songs. By contrast, with the Virgin Mary and her housework, we are given something more humble: the good housewife (perhaps echoing Proverbs 31:10–31, although the sacerdotal context is missing from the Proverbs passage), a variation on the believer as Bride of Christ.

Other biblical women are presented in Syriac tradition with different imagery, as apostles, disciples, even teachers.[128] The binary of sexuality represented by the Sinful Woman and the Virgin Mary—harlot and virgin—adds a certain tension to the notion of priesthood. The priest is shown *not* in the image of Christ, but rather in the image of *relationship to* Christ, a relationship requiring one's entire being, very much grounded in bodily existence and practice.

These images of "woman" as "priest" provided recognition that acts of devotion intrinsically participated in liturgical order, even outside the formal boundaries of ecclesial activity—an instructive idea to offer the laity. Applying such imagery to women, whether biblical characters or not, lifted the practices of lay piety to heightened dimensions of efficacy. It granted laity a distinctive sacred authority, not conferred by the ecclesiastical hierarchy but rather bestowed directly by the Lord, to whom such acts of devotion were offered, and whose gracious reception of these offerings was thereby promised.

These passages speak to the tradition of the priesthood of all believers in arresting terms. Just as Ephrem and Jacob had extolled a liturgy to which every participant—identified by rank, gender, age, and location—was crucial, so, too, did Syriac poets understand that every believer, male and female, had a priesthood to fulfill. Whether in the liturgy, in the civic community, or in the prayer of the heart, theirs was holy work.

Ancient Christians told the story of Saint Eugenia, an adventurous saint from Egypt martyred in the city of Rome. According to the Greeks, Eugenia converted to Christianity when she heard a group of "numerous and virtuous" monks "chanting [Psalms] in a quite orderly fashion (*lian eutaktos*)."[129] In Syriac, however, the story was told differently. Eugenia did not hear monks. She heard *Christians* singing the Psalms; and "the fear of Christ entered into her heart when she heard this singing."[130] Stealing away in disguise, she and her eunuchs encountered the bishop Helenos "with a great multitude who were with him, praising and singing and saying together: 'The paths of the righteous are straight, and the paths of the holy are ordered.'"[131] Perceiving a divine call, Eugenia said to her companions, "Let us go in with a good will and mingle with this crowd of singers, and let us be of them and be numbered in their ranks."[132] In the Greek story, it was the exceptional singing of monks that caught Eugenia's attention—the singing of an elite group, set apart. In the Syriac story, it was the collective voice of the Christian community that galvanized her: "Let us mingle with this crowd of singers, and let us be of them and be numbered in their ranks." As so often, the Syriac telling emphasized the singing of all.

In this chapter, I have considered the laity's liturgical participation not only as singers but also as listeners. Both were forms of active, constructive contribution to the event of liturgy, its meaning, impact, and authority within the local community (both religious and civic) and within a larger conceptual sense of the church as an institution. As we have seen, liturgy was the school wherein laity received instruction on the Bible, doctrine, and devotional practice. It was also the place where they received their formation as Christian subjects, learning their proper roles, functions, and ministries. And it was the place where laity performed their work: not only receiving but also displaying their learning, witnessing to their knowledge, honoring their right location amid a liturgically ordered world. Event, school, place, stage: liturgy engaged, enacted, and instantiated the religious community in its fullness. Each role was essential to the whole; each voice mattered.

In the next chapter, I will ask what possibilities the tasks of singing and listening opened for laypeople, including women. I will argue that the ritual circumstances we have considered thus far opened avenues for distinct forms of agency in the liturgical encounter with women's choirs and with biblical women. Performed stories opened more than their narrative content; they opened multiple narratives. This allowed a listener the capacity for choice on what to hear, and even, how to use it. Although we lack evidence for individual women's responses, close literary analysis within ritual context can indicate significant opportunities beyond what scholars have allowed to ancient women.

6

—

Models for Laity, Models for Faith

In this study I have highlighted the interactive exchange of liturgical voices: those of choirs, clergy, and congregations. Interwoven through the entire discussion have been further voices: those imagined by Syriac liturgical poets, ascribed to the persons and beings of Christian existence. These included voices from the biblical past, the created world with all its inhabitants and forms of being, the celestial realm, and the social and political world outside the church's door. From all these domains—each a context of human-divine relationship—voices sang forth in the hymns, sermons, prayers, and responses of the liturgy. These imagined voices included those of women, especially in the lively expansions of biblical stories that characterized late antique devotion. As listeners, laity received these imagined voices as vehicles of their religious instruction and formation; sometimes, their own voices were the sounding instruments for those imagined. Now we must ask, What was the ministry of these imagined voices? What did their sound contribute to the combined song of the liturgy's celebration, not only by their content but further by their robust performance—whether by choir, preacher, or responding congregation?

The issue of imagined voices is closely tied to that of the figures they expressed and the stories they represented. Reference to a particular character—saint, martyr, or biblical figure—was the first step toward hearing the imagined voice. At first sight (or sound), these familiar characters represented basic, well-known narratives. But ancient authors often rendered these stories in flexible terms: a saint could embody or exemplify more than one story. Adding voice, imagined or performing, to the narrative could raise further possibilities. Listeners contributed

157

more than dutiful attention. It was theirs to decide which story to hear, with what qualities of voice.

LITURGICAL LISTENING: HEARING STORIES

The Syriac version of the *Life of St. Pelagia* begins with a spectacular, albeit indirect, encounter between Pelagia, notorious courtesan and actress of Antioch, and Nonnos, charismatic and wise bishop visiting the city.[1] Soon afterward, both attended the Sunday liturgy: Nonnos as a distinguished guest among the clergy and Pelagia, on an uncharacteristic whim, among the women of the congregation. Following the scripture readings, the archbishop handed the gospel book to Nonnos as an invitation to preach. A mighty sermon followed.

> Fervent in the Holy Spirit, he gave his homily . . . with the result that the entire people were moved to contrition in their emotion as they listened. Now the subject of his homily was the judgment in store for the wicked and the good hope stored up for the righteous. The whole congregation was reduced to weeping at his words, and the floor of the church became soaked with tears.[2]

Among those stricken with compunction was Pelagia, whose groans, tears, and anguished sobs caused many in the congregation to recall the biblical figure of the Sinful Woman.[3] Departing with the catechumens before the Eucharist, Pelagia, "stirred with contrition," quickly sent a letter to Nonnos requesting a meeting so that she might undertake a new and changed way of life. Her letter begged his merciful attention, citing weighty scriptural example—although not, in this early exchange, the story of the penitent harlot:

> '[Jesus] spoke with the Samaritan woman at the water well, with the Canaanite woman who cried out after him, with the woman who was smitten with illness, whom he healed, with Martha and Mary whose brother he raised. He did all this, as I have heard from the Christians, and now, my lord, if you are the disciple of this God who has done all this, do not reject me or turn me away.'[4]

I draw attention to this portion of Pelagia's Syriac *vita* to point out the multivalent nature of biblical stories encountered in a liturgical context.[5] In the Syriac version of Pelagia's story, the liturgy is described with some care; it is a place of dramatic exchange and transformation, both for the collective community and for the individual. According to the text, biblical readings and their explication are the fulcrum of these interactions.

Yet everyone appears to have heard something different. The story's (fictional) narrator, Deacon Jacob, heard Nonnos preach about divine judgment: damnation for the wicked, hope for the righteous. Many of the congregation, hearing the readings and homily and seeing Pelagia's response, recalled the story of the Sinful Woman of Luke 7:36–50, understood to be one of sexual sin and repentance. They interpreted Pelagia's persona and her responsive penitential actions accordingly, inscribing that character and story onto hers.

Pelagia herself, a character in the text representing every extreme of wanton depravity, heard a different narrative still. She cites a wide array of New Testament women who represented marginalized outcasts owing to ethnicity or illness (the Samaritan Woman, the Canaanite Woman, the Hemorrhaging Woman), who yet reached out to Jesus and received his healing ministry; or who were devoted disciples (Mary and Martha of Bethany) to whose needs Jesus responded belatedly but miraculously with the raising of Lazarus. All of these New Testament stories featured women initially hindered by men in their approach for divine mercy, but whose bold determination in each instance brought compassionate resolution of their need. When Pelagia later in the narrative adds the Sinful Woman to her list of biblical exemplars, she appears to stay with the script of obstructed but ultimately victorious female devotion—a more generous narrative arc than the congregation's initial reductive response of penitent harlotry. Speaking to the deaconess Romana, Pelagia cites the Sinful Woman together with the Canaanite Woman and the Samaritan Woman as women whose efforts to approach Jesus were repeatedly blocked by men, but who persevered and prevailed.[6] In Pelagia's citation, these were stories of female ostracism and female agency, of human weakness paired with the great strength of true faith.

The deacon, the congregation, and Pelagia are all depicted as hearing the same readings and the same homily. And, indeed, they all recall a basic story of sin and repentance. Yet they are portrayed as hearing different versions, even within this one literary narrative. In those differences lie important lessons. Listening in the liturgy was not a simple act; various factors contributed. Ritual space, adornments, and sequence framed the voiced presentations; ritual agents in diverse roles contributed to and received the teachings. Melodic performance heightened significance; lections and preaching followed canonically prescribed lectionary choices, the ecclesiastical calendar, and mandated rubrics.[7] Liturgical listening was ritually, musically, and rhetorically guided. Yet its messages were multivalent. They were differently textured depending on the listeners and their circumstances, and differently received. Moreover, gender was a factor across this spectrum: the gender of the liturgical agent, the biblical character, or the listener. Each had an impact on what was heard, and how.

In the broader Christian tradition, Pelagia was one of a number of so-called penitent- harlot saints, generally presented as variations on the gospel narrative of the Sinful Woman of Luke 7:36–50.[8] Still, when Jacob of Sarug chanted a homily on the Sinful Woman,[9] he, like Pelagia's Syriac hagiographer, drew the narrative in a different direction. At one point, Jacob used the same set of predatory descriptors for the Sinful Woman's life as prostitute as Pelagia's Syriac hagiographer used for her: she was "a vulture," "a stone" on which others stumbled, and "a she-wolf."[10] But these brief descriptors of the stereotypical harlot are not Jacob's focus, nor where he sets his congregation's eyes in this long and splendid memra. Instead, he sings a story of confidence that one will receive divine mercy if one persists in asking. Jacob badgers his listeners from the moment he starts: Have they become complacent in their prayers? Have they forgotten that repentance is hard work?

> Do not be wearied by making a petition [for mercy], no matter how much you have sinned.
> It does not weary the Compassionate One when he forgives you.
> . . . .
> Has habit led you to come and pray, but you fail to receive?
> It is because only by [true] suffering are the ulcers of iniquity healed.
> Even the prostitute really wept when she was healed.
> For the pain of iniquity was swelling in her, [wanting] to leave.
> . . . .
> Jesus drinks in the melodies of suffering that are sung unto him.[11]

Jacob's homily explores the woman's story from multiple directions, while also reminding the congregation of the importance of their own singing voices, especially in repentance: "Jesus drinks in the melodies of suffering that are sung unto him" (l. 302). Here is the call to their own voiced offerings. Jacob's overall narrative moves from the self-recognition of repentance to the persistence of faith that God will forgive. This is the conviction necessary to change one's own life. It echoes the continual supplications of liturgical participation, with their continually repeated refrain, sung countless times by every liturgical participant: "Lord, have mercy."

The themes of repentance for sin (or "harlotry," or unworthiness of any kind) and persistent supplication as actions of faith are vividly conveyed in an anonymous Syriac dialogue hymn (sughitha) that presents an extended exchange between the Sinful Woman of Luke 7 and Satan. The hymn, some sixty verses, survives in multiple Syriac manuscripts but probably dates to the fifth or sixth century in its earliest form, and hence is roughly contemporary with Pelagia's story and Jacob's preaching.[12] The dialogue imagines a scene outside the gospel account: an interlude in which Satan voices all the reasons why the woman should not approach Jesus at the house of Simon the Pharisee. His voice represents her inner turmoil as she struggles to turn away from her former life. In Satan's words, sung by the first choir, she is beyond forgiveness in the depth of her pollution; she would only incite revulsion, mockery, and even violent disdain if she attempted to enter Simon's house. By contrast, in the matching verses sung by the second choir, the woman firmly rebuffs each objection. And with each response, she voices her conviction that Christ will receive her with grace, that God is merciful, that salvation will be hers.

The hymn had begun by recalling Jesus's healing forgiveness for many: the blind, the paralytic, the lame; Zacchaeus the tax collector, the sons of Zebedee (Simon Peter and Andrew), the Samaritan Woman, and, finally, the Sinful Woman (vv. 4–5). The list of figures once again mixes types, refusing to reduce the woman to a single kind of sin or need, and crossing and combining differently gendered portraits. Choir A sings the voice of Satan as one of inner doubts and fears. Choir B sings the voice of the woman with hope, penitence, humility, and unbending certitude. At one point, there is a contrast between the feckless singing of her sinful life, and the worshipful song of her new one:

> [Satan] Your tongue used to sing every day
> And people would admire in the streets;
> Now I see it is full of suffering
> And it resounds with prayers.

> [Woman] It is right that the mouth which sang every day
> Should now be filled with lament:
> instead of its former laughter,
> it should sing praise to God Most High.[13]

This narrative of confident faith in the face of grueling obstructions is one that Jacob of Sarug will also tell in his homily on the Canaanite Woman, another figure cited in Pelagia's Syriac hagiography. In Jacob's telling, the Canaanite Woman was repeatedly rebuked and turned away—by the disciples, by the crowd, by Jesus himself; yet she persisted in her appeal to Christ. Boldly she declared his divine identity and boldly she demanded that he heal her daughter in an act worthy of his divinity. So, too, Jacob exhorted his congregation, must they also persist in their petitions for mercy: "Do not be silent from your petitioning . . . do not weary of supplication." Rather, he continued, "her boldness, full of wonder, take for yourself!"[14] This narrative turns a gendered story—a woman dismissed by men as unworthy, even foolhardy—into an address to the men of the congregation. These, Jacob scolds, may be mired in the complacency of self-satisfaction, of habit, of their own self-importance. Or they may be lost in a complacency of despair that change is not possible or God will not be merciful.[15] The Canaanite Woman in the bold faith of her persistent effort is a model for all, not for some.

For Syriac authors, the Sinful Woman as a type, or even a label (as for Saint Pelagia), signified agency and faith: the ability to act toward change, and the conviction that God will accept that change. So, too, did the Canaanite Woman and others signify this hope for change and the agency to make it happen. The story of the Sinful Woman appears to be a narrative especially suitable for liturgy in the civic sphere.[16] Such a narrative was not bound to gender as an embodied category, although gendered stories could effectively convey its message. Male versions of this type would be the Publican (in contrast to the Pharisee, in the parable in Luke 18:9–14) or the Prodigal Son (from Jesus's parable in Luke 15:11–32) or Peter following his denial of Christ after the arrest or the Penitent Thief on the cross. Here, for example, is a verse from a hymn ascribed to Jacob of Sarug and sung in the voice of Peter after his betrayal:

> O my tongue, sculpt the sounds and sighs that are needed for grief,
> For it was with you that I once sang, (and with you I uttered) the words of denial.
> With you may I strike out and utter words of confession,
> For it was your looseness that broke me down: let it in turn bring me healing,
> For your Lord is merciful.[17]

Such a narrative, whether with female or male protagonist, encouraged individual action: neither the collective church nor its institutional hierarchy was a required source for change. The only requirement was an individual's decision to turn to God.

Each name or title of a biblical character carried meaning for ancient Christians. Their basic narratives were told and retold, in various combinations, each combination carrying a different resonance. Consider this short concluding hymn attributed to Bishop Rabbula of Edessa:

> Like the publican and the thief and the sinful woman I cry out, our Savior, and like Simeon the Pharisee and the Samaritan woman I ask your forgiveness. Open to me your gates of mercy, and accept the tears that I cry. Forgive my debts and my sins, my failings and my transgressions, by your grace. You who receive those who repent, Lord of all, glory to you.[18]

Such constant referencing across and through different media and events meant that key figures were readily familiar. Often they were stock types encountered in folk traditions and also in popular culture: at the theater, in folk songs, in games, in oratory. The reformed prostitute was one such.[19] Yet these were capacious characters. Certain key figures, like the Sinful Woman, often appear to modern readers as essentializing and reductive stereotypes. But in liturgical poetry—and beyond, as Pelagia's story, Jacob's memre, or the anonymous dialogue hymns indicate— they could in fact signal a variety of narratives, of different qualities and possibilities, applicable across gendered and social categories.

LITURGICAL LISTENING:
HEARING TITLES, HEARING SCRIPTS

A further example of liturgical listening comes not from a literary account referencing specific biblical stories, but rather from what we can see of such an event as it happened in performance. Toward the end of a long, majestic verse homily on the feast of the Nativity, Jacob of Sarug offered an unusual twenty-line interlude.[20] Jacob's homily had ranged widely from humanity's need for salvation to the Virgin Mary's miraculous conception, pregnancy, and birth-giving. As the homily soared to its peak, Jacob paused to interpose a short alternative account of humanity's redemption. In this interlude, Jacob suddenly speaks of the Nativity feast as "a new creation," one beginning with the Redeemer's invitation to an unnamed "Despised Woman" to enter his celebration.[21] A series of startling images follow, as one by one Christ takes and lifts up the Barren Woman, the Humiliated Woman, the Sorrowful Woman, the Lamenting Woman, the Enslaved Woman, the Persecuted Woman, and the Imprisoned Woman, each now freed of her suffering and each graciously led to the festal celebration. Then, as quickly as it began, the interlude passes. Jacob returns to a rousing and triumphant final call to the congregation. Ninety lines later, the homily ends.

Removed from its literary and liturgical context, the passage at first glance appears to be an affirmation of universal salvation. The parade of beleaguered women presents images that heighten humanity's pathos and promise poignant inclusivity for even society's most marginalized. On closer inspection, the passage offers an imposing example of early Byzantine typology. Jacob evokes Isaiah 54 (God's redemption of the barren and repudiated wife), Ezekiel 16 (God's rescue of Israel, the disobedient harlot), and Galatians 4:22–31 (the allegory of Hagar and Sarah as enslaved and free, foreshadowing Christian notions of synagogue and church). The list of titled but unnamed women offers a powerful typological cluster of female figures who, in other Christian contexts, were identified with the church, imaged as the disgraced and then redeemed Bride of Christ.[22] In fact, the passage references a complex and sophisticated supersessionist anti-Jewish exegesis, predating Jacob and well known to Ephrem and other early Syriac authors.[23]

But this homily was not preached to a learned audience of biblical scholars. It was preached to a festal audience: the civic community. This was largely a congregation of laity, and largely inclusive of women. The passage occurs late in an otherwise lengthy homily, with no discernible cues to set it off from its surrounding verses. A jeweled piece among numerous jeweled pieces—twenty lines amid nearly twelve hundred, preached during a lengthy festal liturgy adorned with pomp and splendor, perhaps after an all-night vigil—its startling imagery would have shimmered for the listening congregation, who would not have had the means to grasp or hold it still. Yet its memory might have lingered: Who was the Despised Woman? Who were these suffering women?

What did the laity hear? They were not trained, in the sense of formal schooling, in the Bible, exegesis, or doctrine. They did not know the rigorous intellectual tradition on which Jacob drew and which added meaningful exegetical authority to the passage and to the homily as a whole. Rather, they were trained in all those areas *in and through liturgical formation.* As such, the congregation heard the titles of these despised women according to narrative models they often encountered: narratives and models familiar from liturgy and named in hymns, prayers, supplications or retold in biblical stories preached in lyrical homilies like this one. Like Nonnos's congregation in Antioch or the character of Pelagia herself, they recognized familiar figures by name or title, recognizing also the accompanying types or scripts they carried.

Hearing stories through the abbreviated form of a biblical character's symbolic title (name excluded) was a common experience for any ancient congregation.[24]

Indeed, in the same homily on the Nativity, Jacob of Sarug had referred to the Virgin Mary as "the Believing Woman" (ll. 30, 153, 429, 461, 569, 763), "the Destitute Woman" (ll. 305, 668), "the Blessed Woman" (ll. 154, 383, 513). She is "the Daughter of David" (ll. 40, 110) and "the Daughter of the Poor" (l. 142), "the Pure Woman" (l. 433) and "the Powerful Woman" (l. 539). When accused about her pregnancy by doubting Joseph, Mary becomes "the Solitary Woman" (l. 774) and "the Falsely Accused Woman" (l. 959). Similarly, Mary's kinswoman Elizabeth is called "the Sterile Woman" (ll. 493, 504, 533, 536), "the Barren Woman" (l. 487), and "the Old Woman" (l. 534). These titles are not unlike those appearing in Jacob's series on the Despised Woman. The sleepy or distracted listener (Jacob complains of both) might well not have realized that Jacob's homily had moved from its primary story about Mary on to a different "woman" altogether—the allegorical figure of the Church as Bride—if she or he were not paying attention.

On the other hand, a listener might have recognized the narrative of the Church as Bride as one familiar from other festal homilies by Jacob. On the Feast of Christ's Baptism, for example, Jacob referred to the Church, personified, as the "Afflicted Woman" and the "Persecuted Woman" whom Christ purified and then betrothed.[25] Elsewhere again, in his homily "On the Ascension," the allegory of the Church follows reference to Eve as a woman who, because of the feast, could raise "her head that was bent" by the bond of shame.[26] Here, the personified Church appears "poor, barren, and smitten." Christ arranged for her release, then "gave gifts to the weary woman [the Church] who was needy. / She turned away from captivity and became an apostle."[27] The alternative, allegorical narrative of the Church as (rescued) Bride was one Jacob carried at the ready, especially for major festal celebrations. His congregation knew these narrative descriptors well.

Jacob complained vociferously about distracted listeners. But he may have underestimated their concentration, for the wandering mind need not have gone off to the marketplace or the theater (as he feared),[28] but rather to thoughts of other biblical women, who were sometimes referred to by the same descriptors as the Despised Woman in his Nativity homily, and in various liturgical texts.

Here the issue of poetic technique becomes especially important. Syriac liturgical poets were trained not only in rhetoric, but also in adroit deployment of metrical phrases. They commanded a vast store of familiar word patterns grouped by syllables in metrical units for use in constructing correctly metered lines. In Jacob's case, these were units of four syllables; three such units comprised one line of a couplet in Jacob's favorite twelve-syllable meter. The skills were analogous to those of an epic singer, and required an equally well-practiced mode of presentation.[29] Thus one often finds recurring patterns in different homilies by Jacob; many were perhaps habitually favored words or themes, but also served metrical needs.

Nonetheless, at times it seems that Jacob utilized certain word units, associations, or themes because he wanted his congregation to make connections between different biblical stories.[30] The word units suggested an expansion of typologies, enabling his listeners to bring together diverse biblical figures, perhaps even understanding their base narratives differently, as we saw above for the Sinful Woman. He was not alone in raising these possibilities. For example, Sarah the wife of Abraham is occasionally styled "Daughter of the Poor" in Syriac poetry, a title often attributed to the Virgin Mary in Syriac literature.[31] The double usage sparks the listener to make the comparison and connect the stories, even when the homilist or hymnographer does not explicitly do so.

The titles in Jacob's list for the Despised Woman, in turn, appear attached to other biblical women elsewhere, whether in Jacob's homilies or other Syriac liturgical poetry. Eve is often depicted as the woman whose bent or bowed head is raised up with joy at the Nativity.[32] The title of Barren Woman is often applied to Elizabeth, Mary's kinswoman, and also to Sarah, Rachel, Rebekah, and Hannah, the Old Testament mothers within the messianic lineage.[33] Jacob of Sarug spoke of Tamar, the daughter-in-law of Judah (Gen 38), as a "humiliated woman."[34]

Similarly, Susannah (Dan 13 LXX) is often the "Persecuted Woman";[35] or she, like Sarah when she and Abraham were in Egypt (Gen 12), may also be the "humiliated one."[36] New Testament women also carried these titles: the Sinful Woman of Luke 7, as we just saw, is poetically styled the "unclean woman" or the "defiled one," and also as the woman "enslaved" to Satan, rescued by her Bridegroom.[37] The Samaritan Woman of John 4 is the "reviled woman,"[38] or, with the Canaanite Woman (Mt 15:21–28, Mk 7:24–30), one "imprisoned" amid the idolatry of the heathen.[39] The Hemorrhaging Woman (Mk 5:25–34 and parallels) is also termed the Despised One or the Wretched One.[40]

For such biblical women, these titles carried a narrative different from that of the allegorical Church as Bride, despised and then redeemed. They are for the most part examples of the innocent and faithful woman, wrongly accused, who suffers heroically yet unjustly—biblical women as types of Christ himself, variations on the Suffering Servant of Isaiah 53.[41] Or, again, they can fit the paradigm of the Sinful Woman or the Samaritan Woman, as women whose redemption from their witting life of sin provides the most powerful measure of the redeeming love of Christ.[42] These biblical figures are staples of late antique Syriac liturgical poetry in all its literary forms. Their titles and their stories were familiar to the late antique churchgoer not only from sermon, prayer, or hymn. They were also depicted in the visual art adorning the walls of the churches in which their stories were heard, or in the devotional objects that laity might have had at home.[43]

A passage such as that on the Despised Woman in Jacob's homily on the Nativity might have instructed the congregation in multiple ways, for it represents multiple typologies. It expands the immediate narrative of the Nativity events with the further, typologically related anti-Jewish narrative of the election of the Church and the willful turning away of the Synagogue from the Heavenly Bridegroom. At the same time, it casts into the ears of the congregation other typological clusters—other biblical memories[44]—which served to reinforce other paradigmatic patterns important for them to remember. Moreover, it also referenced real persons in their local community: the poor, the despised, the marginalized. It taught multiple stories, by means of poetically employed titles, attached to but not exclusively owned by various biblical figures. In the work of a liturgical poet as skilled as Jacob, poetic technique combined with biblical instruction, with typological possibilities, and with a listener's sometimes uneven attention. Familiar stories or figures glistened with multiple narratives. This was not narrative instability. It was an opportunity for capaciousness, potential, and promise.

LITURGICAL LISTENING
IN PERFORMATIVE CONTEXT

The biblical figures and titles named above evoked for the ancient listener a diversity of narrative possibilities. Judgment, repentance, and forgiveness were the shared themes, represented with seemingly endless variety through the treasure of biblical stories on which ancient Christians drew, many with notable female characters.[45] My goal in the present chapter is not to add further examples, but rather to ask how these portraits, often conveyed through imagined voices, might contribute to our understanding of women's liturgical participation and devotional piety in ancient Christianity.

Scholars have focused for some time now on the rhetorical training and tools by which ancient authors constructed fictive speech for women in literary portraits of different genres: historiography, hagiography, hymnography, and homiletics all contain many instances. Imagining what women might have said or could have said or ought to have said in various famed events or sacred stories filled the school exercises of the late ancient classroom, spilling out into the exuberance of Greek and Roman oratory, novels, Jewish and Christian extracanonical literature, and the comedies and tragedies of the theater, as well as liturgical literature, as we have seen.[46]

In Syriac homilies, as in these other instances, the imagined speech of biblical women worked within existing social and cultural worlds. It affirmed and sustained social norms, presenting women in secondary and subordinate positions, and generally in domestic contexts, even while presenting them as heroically standing against men driven by devious motives, blinded by habit, or afraid when the requirements of faith appear to challenge social convention. Such stories were not offered to change the living social situation. They acknowledged discordant realities by acknowledging that women could and did offer powerful models of faith, while disallowing any consequence for ecclesiastical, political, or social order.

Syriac liturgical poetry and narrative literature have received particular notice for their powerful portraits of biblical women, often more positive than analogous depictions in Greek, for example.[47] It is difficult to know how to account for this difference. These portraits are not "historical," either in the sense of representing the real lives of women of their day, or in the sense of seeking historical accuracy for the biblical presentation (whatever that could have meant to an ancient author).[48] As ancient presentations of women, however, they are fascinating.

Some features distinctive to the Syriac liturgical context are suggestive when we think from the listener's side. Formal aspects of Syriac poetic composition sometimes set the significance of women's imagined personae in high relief. The techniques of metrical composition, as we have just seen, enabled figures to conjoin or interact across narratives, allowing the listener greater capacity for imaginative expansion of their own. Such intersections invited the listener to develop or extend a story beyond its bare scriptural outlines.

Furthermore, the requirements of Syriac poetic forms could highlight the importance of women as fictive speakers. In the case of the dialogue hymns, both the nature of the dialogue and its literary form were significant for the portrayal of women. The sughitha, as discussed above, was basically a dispute: a contest in which two characters argued opposing positions.[49] The poetic form required an equal number of verses for each character. Hence the demands of the literary genre required the valuation of women's voices when they were characters in the story, even when that went well beyond what the biblical text suggested.

The sughyatha also required a particular narrative pattern: the dispute had to have a theologically instructive purpose. Most often the basic dispute was "faith vs. reason" or "faith vs. temptation." Interestingly, in the surviving Syriac corpus, in most instances where the dialogue includes a female character, she is given the heroic role over and against a male opponent.[50] This is the case for dialogues between Sarah and Abraham, the Virgin Mary and various (male) interlocutors, the Sinful Woman and Satan, and Saint Marina and Satan. The exception appears to be two sughyatha on Potiphar's Wife and Joseph, based on Genesis 39, where the wife attempts to seduce Joseph, her husband's slave, while he argues for fidelity to God.[51] But, in this case, Joseph is a slave: the precarious power dynamics between enslaved man and master's wife represent the same kind of dangerous status differential as denoted by female characters in opposition to authoritarian men. Such fraught power dynamics added suspense, drama, and pathos to the portrayed dispute.

Indeed, the pedagogical goals and theological message of these hymns required the women speakers (or the enslaved Joseph) to be powerful, eloquent, compelling, and true in their words. Mary *must* out-argue her betrothed husband Joseph despite his anger at her pregnancy; the Sinful Woman *must* out-argue Satan when he tries to stop her approach to Christ. Both must demonstrate that the faithful Christian can persevere. The storyline was enhanced by strong, articulate female characters, since—literarily, at least—women generally represented weaker, more vulnerable characters than men. Gender enhanced the suspense of the encounter. Could a woman (or a slave) prevail? Could she be effective in her argument, stalwart in her faith?

The precarity of the innocent woman wrongly attacked heightened the pathos of her imagined situation. In an anonymous dialogue hymn between Saint Marina and Satan, Marina hauntingly maintains her faith, dooming herself to a life of disgraced punishment, despite Satan's barbed cajoling and harsh insults.[52] As Marina remains steadfast, Satan grows more strident: "I know that women don't have much intelligence or brain, / for they don't know what they are saying. . . . / . . . Check your words, stupid woman, and shut up." Marina perseveres: "Accursed are your words, Satan, and accursed is the instruction which you teach."[53]

The sughitha was a poetic form with strict requirements: a dramatic exchange expressed through antiphonal verses, narratively confined to two characters, agonistic in setup, and ultimately resolved through the triumph of faith.[54] Gendered characters enhanced the dramatic possibilities; gendered performance by women's choirs, with refrains sung by female laity, underscored the message.

The madrasha as a broad literary genre even beyond the subgenre of dialogue poems was unquestionably significant for the portrayal of holy women. In some instances, madrashe were composed in a single, first-person voice. Although rare for female characters, such madrashe set a woman's voice in dramatic spotlight. Ephrem's casting of Mary's lullabies for the newborn Christ child are the earliest examples.[55] But so, too, the poignant lament of Mary the niece of Abraham of Qidun: twenty-two verses of lyrical confession, repentance, and stalwart faith through the voice of a penitent harlot, each verse punctuated by the congregation's responsive refrain.[56] Mary of Qidun's lament underscores the performative aspects that added impact to this imagined voice: women sang these verses as choirs, and women in the congregation sang the refrains. Women's imagined voices were embedded within and sounded forth by women's participating voices. Such performance highlighted a gendered significance for the imagined as well as the actual voices. Male choirs and male laity also sang these verses and responses, inhabiting these voices and roles. Gender moved within these performances, illuminating different aspects of character, action, and consequence. Such possibilities did not reduce gender to flattened binaries; rather, again, gender enhanced possibilities. The different performative instances could invite reflection on gender and subjectivity in instructive fashion, allowing for the listener's own active deliberation.[57]

The liturgical performance of narrative memre could offer a similar dynamic. Jacob of Sarug is especially intriguing in this respect since his metrical homilies are notable for their generous inclusion of strong biblical women, with markedly lengthy fictive speeches. Further, Jacob comments that women's choirs sang before and after his homilies; and he stressed the importance of congregational singing. His memre suggest that the gendered dynamics of Syriac liturgical performance might have contributed to the listener's experience of the expressed content— biblical, doctrinal, ecclesiastical.

Perhaps most fundamentally, liturgy provided a context in which women's imagined voices, like women's participating voices, were presented in public.

Because liturgy is often not included in social analyses, this ironic aspect is often overlooked. A recurring theme in the rhetorical training of the late antique author was the social location for "proper" women's speech.[58] Invariably, this was domestic: women should speak at home, within their households—a sentiment echoed in the New Testament epistles.[59] Under special conditions, particular women might represent proper or acceptable speech; or specific circumstances might allow women's speech to be appropriate. As wholly exceptional, imperial women might speak publicly; but they rarely did so.[60] Women philosophers spoke, and fictive women presented as "avatars" of wisdom. But almost invariably these portraits, too, were presented as domestic in context.[61] Only in cases of extremity—severe political crises or tragedy—might women be allowed a literary presentation that included public speech. Christian authors tended to follow these normative models. The depicted speech of women saints was like that of philosophers: offered to their community and disciples, effectively their households.[62] Women martyrs were sometimes portrayed as having spoken publicly, in measure of their extreme circumstances.[63] The depiction of women's voices hence generally represented a traditional view of women's roles and the locations wherein those roles could be appropriately enacted.[64]

In the case of liturgical presentation, however, even a narrative context that upheld the normative domestic, philosophical, or heroic context for women's speech was destabilized by the performative setting. Liturgy was public, albeit ritually constrained. Its congregation was the civic, political community; it included the participation of local women, of different classes, ages, identities, and relationships. In Syriac liturgies with women's choirs, and with hymnographic forms that emphasized congregational refrains, multiple voices contributed. The public qualities were visible, audible, and constant. Within these performative elements, we must set the liturgical listener and wonder at the impact of imagined women's speech.

It is noteworthy that ancient Syriac literature produced strong portrayals of biblical women in other contexts. Such portraits were part of Syriac literary culture during late antiquity. A number of elegant memre present dramatic narratives of biblical stories dominated by strong and admirable female protagonists. These memre were not transmitted in liturgical manuscripts, and have no indicators of liturgical performance (for example, address to the listeners, or invocations or prayers on the part of the speaker). As such, these texts present a puzzle: For whom were they written? By whom? And for what contexts? Literarily beautiful yet without historical setting, these memre are nonetheless inflected with the kinds of narrative qualities of speech and character that appear in Syriac liturgical madrashe and memre. Stellar examples would be the portrayals of Sarah in expanded narratives from Genesis 12 and Genesis 22, a redeemed rendition of Potiphar's Wife for the story in Genesis 39, the faithful Widow of Sarepta in 1 Kings 17, and in a different literary genre, the figure of the Queen of Sheba from 1 Kings 10 as a wise and wily questioner.[65] Perhaps these texts indicate that within the world of Syriac literature, Syriac liturgical poetry had an impact on its listeners. Certainly, there is much evidence of intertextuality between and across these texts and genres.

STOCK CHARACTERS AND MORAL EXEMPLARITY

Often, the positive depictions of biblical women in Syriac madrashe and memre can be traced back to a point of origin in the writings of Ephrem. While his liturgical poetry was important in this regard, Ephrem's biblical commentaries were perhaps even more important for long-term influence.[66] Still, while Ephrem's ideas are evident throughout Syriac liturgical history, it was often Jacob of Sarug whose memre drew the women into prominence as imagined characters since he presented long, developed narratives with space for complex portrayals. And it is Jacob's memre that raise interesting hints about the intersection of imagined, performing, and participating women's voices.

As discussed above, Jacob's homilies occasionally provided models and paradigms for women's piety in general terms, as these might have applied to the villages or towns where he preached.[67] He did so with portraits aligned with stock character types familiar in ancient Mediterranean cultures. He added elements of humor, delight, pathos, suspense, or tragedy; and wove these into verses radiant with lyrical splendor.[68] A consummate storyteller, Jacob presented his biblical figures memorably—partly by their familiarity, partly by his exceptional poetic skill, and partly by an oral performance of intoned metrical recitation that encouraged remembrance in the listeners.

For Jacob's purposes, the heroic spectacles of martyrs and saints, including those from the Bible, were not the only sources of inspiration.[69] Religion was grounded in daily life and its realities. A skilled preacher like Jacob of Sarug could find rich material for a congregation, for example, in the ostensibly humble accounts of wives and widows that recurred in biblical narratives. These allowed for something so ordinary as motherhood to be a site for fierce spiritual testing and courageous triumph.

Such was the case for the unnamed widow in 2 Kings 4:1–7, who approached the prophet Elisha when her debtors threatened to enslave her sons.[70] In Jacob's telling, she went to Elisha with "an offering of tears due to her need," asking him "to fulfill the role of her husband in her needfulness" for "the Lord is the husband of a widow" and Elisha was the Lord's steward.[71] Jacob describes her supplication with teasing notes of humor:

> So, with a loud voice, she cried out thunderously before [Elisha]
> For him to pay off her debt and free her children from servitude:
> "Your servant, my husband, has died," the sensible woman said to him,
> "And the owner of the debt has now taken away the orphans to enslave them.
> You, yourself know that your servant was a worshipper of the Lord.
> Take his place for me, for the sake of the Lord whom he worshipped."[72]

Jacob characterizes the widow as demonstrating solid reasoning regarding God's patronage for widows and orphans. The moral mandate was incontrovertible: "The sensible woman presented her case wisely / So that the Prophet would be forced to take care of her affair. . . . / She forced him to take the place of a husband for the widow."[73] Here are the terms Jacob uses to characterize this widow: she "cries out," "with a loud voice," "thunderously" (l. 511). She is "sensible" (*ta'manitha*, ll. 513, 517) and speaks "wisely" (*hakimaith*, l. 517). She "forces" the prophet to take just action.[74] In turn, the prophet dutifully complies, performing the miracle of multiplying her oil so that she can sell the abundance, pay off the debt, and save her children. For Jacob, this is a simple paradigm of righteous behavior, boldly performed—a favorite model in his homilies (as in Ephrem's hymns).

But there is more. This Widow also becomes an important typological model for divine dispensation, and, indeed, the occasion for Jacob to marvel on the "wonders" and "splendors" of scripture, for "with that widow who was complaining to Elisha / a symbol was clearly drawn for one who studies it."[75] Jacob presents the widow as a type: first of the church and then of the sacraments. She signified the church because she closed her doors in order to enact the miracle in secret, just as the transformation of the eucharist takes place at the altar behind closed doors. Moreover, she signified the eucharist because just as the eucharist pays off the debts of the faithful, so, too, did the oil pay off the debts of the woman. Further, Jacob presents the incident as a type for the Trinity:

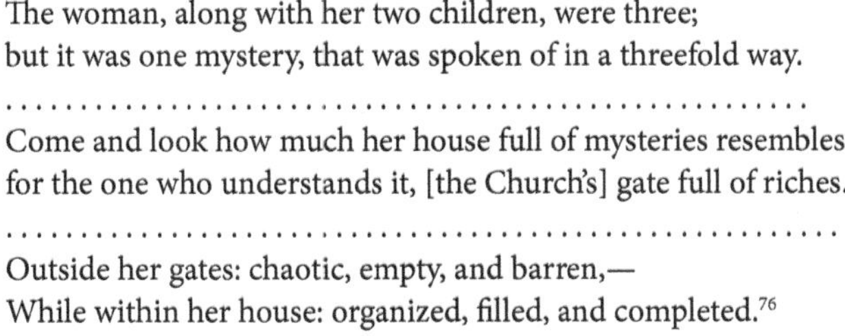

> The woman, along with her two children, were three;
> but it was one mystery, that was spoken of in a threefold way.
> . . . .
> Come and look how much her house full of mysteries resembles,
> for the one who understands it, [the Church's] gate full of riches.
> . . . .
> Outside her gates: chaotic, empty, and barren,—
> While within her house: organized, filled, and completed.[76]

In this fashion, Jacob sang that the moral virtues of the biblical figure provide typological teaching about church and sacraments. Moreover, they do so in contrast, he claims, to the confusion of life beyond church doors.

Nothing here requires Jacob's presentation to privilege women. The widow's gender adds to the story elements of drama, pathos, and humor. Gender heightens the story's narrative power, but does not present an exclusive model of virtues. Anyone, of any gender or status, would do well to follow the paradigm.

The story of a biblical woman did not necessitate the presence of women in the congregation. But it is worth considering the composition of congregations Jacob addressed. Some of Jacob's homilies without question addressed monastic gatherings, which, for the most part, were probably male.[77] Others, such as his festal homilies and those on liturgical participation, clearly presume a fully present civic community. In such instances, as we have seen, he delights in mentioning all the social ranks and types who are present: male and female, young and old, rich and poor, ordained, monastic, and lay. Remembering the mixed congregation, it becomes easier to appreciate how a figure like the Indebted Widow could serve as exemplar for both male and female worshippers, and why such a character might be acceptable to the men who were present. Such figures did not undo social stereotypes, but rather could be accommodated within them. A number of biblical women share the literary or rhetorical features of the Indebted Widow and fit her model of bold, outspoken faith: perhaps most prominently the Widow of Sarepta (1 Kgs 17:1–24), the harlot mother who went to Solomon on behalf of her baby (1 Kgs 3:16–28), the Widow of Nain (Lk 7:11–17), and the Canaanite Woman (Mt 15:21–28).[78] These stories often featured in late antique hymns and homilies generally, not only in Syriac. Such stock characters were much enjoyed by late antique civic communities. What might these social stereotypes tell us?

Sometimes, Jacob seems to be thinking about real-life social problems, including those that confronted women specifically. In the account of the Indebted Widow, for example, he gives special attention to the plight of widows and the hazards of having no husband: "She latched on to [Elisha] in God's stead to fulfill for her / The role of husband. . . . For whom can a widow go to when she is in trouble / If not to God alone, who is her husband."[79] Here he acknowledges a common stereotype (the complaining widow), presents her humorously badgering a beleaguered male protector, while yet underscoring the very real precarity of such a plight. Jacob used such stories to reflect on the familiar stations of women's lives: not only the widow, but also the wife, the mother, the daughter, the sister. It is often in these terms that he presents his female characters, with life stations almost like offices, rather than women as individuals. While this does not open the "real life" of late antique Christians to our eyes, it invites our reflection on their circumstances—as it did for his congregation.

Consider the wife and mother Jacob calls the Shilumite, who is the Shunammite Woman portrayed in 2 Kings 4:8–37. In another homily on the prophet Elisha, Jacob foregrounds this woman throughout as a paragon of virtue.[80] She is "wise," "discerning," "intelligent," and "worthy to receive [the prophet Elisha] through the Love of her faith."[81] But he also presents her quite directly as a model for married women. She keeps a holy house, a household "filled with distinction," and in "the beauty of her faith," Jacob sings, "she depicted a beloved image full of splendors for women / to look upon and to emulate with their husbands."[82] Here, according to Jacob, is the model of the good Christian wife:

> It is easy for a wife to instruct her husband about splendid things
> And to be a cause of Good for her house through her faith.
> Women's nature is not lacking in knowledge,
> And if they wish, they are very wise in their activities.

> Lax habits and the love of the World of vanity
> Brought women down from godly knowledge.
> But as created, the nature of a man and a woman are equal
> In knowledge, thought, discernment, and all kinds of intelligence.
> So if habit does not lower her to laxness
> It should be easy for a woman to understand everything clearly.
> Note how when she tends to love something she cannot be stopped,
> And her entire being takes hold of it acutely because of her love,
> And that she is very insightful about those matters that are hers,
> And that when it is necessary for her to do something, she does it with gusto.
> Where she loves something, she is extremely skillful with curses.
> When she insults her neighbor, her insult is smart and abrasive,
> And when she lies, she knows how to deny things skillfully.
> So if she wishes, she is quick-witted this way in all things,
> And is enlightened by divine instruction.[83]

A string of platitudes, as condescending as they are complimentary! Jacob includes a number of unflattering stereotypes about women: they are lax in their habits, prone to concern about worldly vanities, and skilled in cursing, insults, and lies. At the same time, Jacob presents women as capable of being wise teachers for their households, able to love forcefully and insightfully. They are in no way inferior to men as created beings: "equal in knowledge, thought, discernment, and all kinds of intelligence."[84] It is in fact *because* women are strong and effective in their abilities and understanding that they can be sources of good as well as bad. The determining factors are habit, will, and disposition. But these characteristics are a matter of choice. One can choose the virtuous model over others.

The portrait Jacob draws is distinctive from other such gendered models of antiquity. Plutarch's presentation of the "virtuous woman," for one, praises those who were silent in public, and spoke only at home and only if philosophically useful or in the instance of political extremity.[85] In turn, Proverbs 31:10–31, often cited by Jews and Christians both, presents the good wife as economically skillful, pragmatically astute, effective in household management and in the marketplace, and a wise exemplar of virtue: "She opens her mouth with wisdom, and the teaching of kindness is on her tongue."[86] Similarly, Sirach 26:1–27 praises the good wife as one who makes her husband happy: "Happy is the husband of a good wife; the number of his days will be doubled. / . . . A wife's charm delights her husband and her skill puts fat on his bones. / A silent wife is a gift from the Lord, and nothing is so precious as her self-discipline."[87] Jacob's Shilumite is humble, shrewd, and domestic in orientation, to be sure, though he does not mention anything pragmatic like food, clothing, or the marketplace. But she is also a teacher "of divine instruction" (*yulphana alahaya*, l. 74), something Jacob explicitly emphasizes for both women and men in the congregation:

> See the Shilumite's prudence and learn from her—
> For it would be proper for all women to take note of her—
> So that they would regularly practice righteous instruction,
> And be bound to the idea of holiness,
> And prove to be a good impetus for their husbands,
> And be seen to be teachers for their households,
> That good advice be spoken by their mouths
> To both their husbands and themselves within their homes—
> Like that [Shilumite] woman, who was the cause of all advantages
> Through her good advice, so that her entire household was blessed.[88]

Stereotypical start to finish, this diversion in Jacob's text speaks to the ordinariness of daily life and the inclusive population who attended his liturgies: not necessarily elites, not necessarily sophisticated, or cosmopolitan, but ordinary folk. For here is Jacob's ideal: the good wife is one who blesses her family with discerning and faithful teaching. Unlike church leaders such as John Chrysostom, Jacob did not often address matters of family life in his vast corpus of surviving memre. When he does, he provides glimpses of a pragmatically normative social world. Yet perhaps we might see that he does more. He reconfigures familiar social patterns and gender roles into mirrors for a liturgically rendered devotional life, resonant across domestic, monastic, and ecclesiastical contexts. The Shilumite as model echoes Jacob's descriptions of the work of women's liturgical choirs: women could be teachers of divine knowledge for all.

Jacob's account of the Shilumite Woman does not stop with praise for her womanly virtues. His narrative continues with actions wholly and impressively performed by her own agency. When her child—a gift from the prophet for her exemplary faith—suddenly dies, the woman does not hesitate. In a dazzling sequence of couplets, Jacob conveys her swift, strong response, confident in word and deed.[89] Finally confronting the diffident prophet, the Shilumite poured forth a speech of mighty moral force and ethical suasion, verbally battering the prophet into compliance with her need. And, sure enough, the deed of resurrection was performed. "In the Woman who came up pleading for [Elisha] to revive her child, / Grace itself was clearly drawn."[90]

Hence the Shilumite is both the clichéd "good wife" and also the paradigm of bold and faithful action. In this instance, Jacob stresses her capacity as teacher within the household and to her husband, the presentation of a normative social location and acceptable social terms. In other homilies, Jacob presents virtuous biblical women in similar terms but in the civic rather than domestic domain.

An especially poignant instance is Jacob's homily on the Hemorrhaging Woman, addressing the incident in Mark 5:25–34.[91] Here Jacob presents the woman herself as source and initiator not only of her own saving actions, but also of his homily:

> Now this Woman, full of faith
> Has summoned me today to relate her story, as I wonder.
> She became a teacher to herself
> And she knew how to bind up her great sore so that it was healed.
> In her Jesus depicted a type for His own teaching:
> How the unclean, if they call upon Him, will be cleansed by Him.[92]

Jacob elaborates the gospel narrative, presenting the woman's failed efforts to obtain effective treatment for her illness over many years. Driven to bankruptcy and desperation, she sings a series of interior monologues as Jacob imagines her excoriating her illness directly and with vivid anger. She debates internally whether to approach Jesus, and how; she is concerned with the ritual impurity of her condition. Finally, she decides to approach him secretly and silently in the midst of a crowd, there to touch the hem of his garment. In Jacob's telling, Christ realizes her dilemma and enables her action. But Christ also wants to instruct the people about the power of belief and trust in God. He pretends outrage that someone has touched him without permission, and he rebukes his disciples, especially Simon Peter, for their laxity in guarding his treasure. The woman is fraught with fear: Was she too bold in her action? Will her illness return? But she is unable to bear the injustice of the charges against Peter and the others. She claims her responsibility in the midst of the crowd:

> Bravely she raised her voice and spoke,
> "It is I who touched and stole strength from You;
> I touched (You) because I was in need of healing:
> . . . .
> The illness forced me to act boldly and touch You. I beg you, Lord,
> Don't blame the disciples instead of me, for I am the one who has done wrong."[93]

The woman presents herself in a series of agonized self-accusations: "'I, the downcast, came close to You,' . . . 'I, a sick woman,' 'I, a woman in need,' 'I, all befouled,' 'I, the woman with an affliction,' 'I, a dead corpse,' . . . 'I was in need, and I approached, and was healed in You.'"[94] Jesus's response, of course, was to praise the woman's action, upholding her as a paragon of faith: "In this way the people would learn that everyone who has faith / is close to God, and he cherishes them."[95] So, too, Jacob admonished, does the Lord wish everyone to approach and find their salvation.

With this homily, Jacob acknowledges familiar trappings of daily life: gendered rules of propriety, distrust of women's actions or speech, the inappropriateness of women's speech in public spaces, fear of women's physical bodies, the fear and isolation of lingering disease. But the woman is shown to be discerning, disciplined in thought, and assertive in action. Moreover, she takes responsibility for her action, holding herself publicly accountable without equivocation. She instructs by word and deed. She is worthy of imitation by the entire Christian community.

One could argue that the "public" aspect of liturgy was heavily qualified. As sacred ritual, liturgy was not the context of ordinary discourse in civic contexts. Words could be spoken there that would not be heard in the marketplace or in civic gatherings. Liturgical words would not be expected to carry the same political weight as words in the senate, for example. The words of biblical figures, however exemplary, were not the words of people in the present moment.

But such speech was not devoid of social meaning. The bold, confident speech of biblical women could be echoed in the confident public ministries of local holy women recorded in hagiography or chronicles, such as the widow and mother Euphemia of Amida, or Shirin the solitary in the village of Halmon in the district of Beth Nuhadre.[96] Wise and forceful speech was part of their ministry, declared across social, political, and religious ranks. John of Ephesos reports that Euphemia "was known to great and small alike in the city, and even at a distance everyone recognized the sight of her by her vigorous and swift gait" as she strode through Amida caring for the poor, sick, and needy. During the civic turmoil over the imposition of Chalcedonian orthodoxy, public officials complained that "the citizens revere and honor [Euphemia and her daughter Maria] more than the bishops!"[97] In the case of Shirin, her admirer Sahdona recalled that monastic abbots treated her "like eager disciples," while monks and ascetics "used to visit her from all over the place . . . as children coming for lessons in sanctity with her." He stressed, too, the frequency with which local women visited, including mothers with their children—as his own mother had often brought him.[98] The work of these women does not appear to have scandalized their communities; on the contrary, their followings were devoted. Liturgical listeners could make the connection.

Jacob of Sarug's presentations were colored by their ritual context, for his homilies were embedded among singing female voices, choir and lay. This ritual context provided added dimension to gendered rhetoric as a tool of moral suasion within homiletic discourse. Recall the Indebted Widow of 2 Kings 4, with whom we began. Remember Jacob's characterization of her speech: she "cries out," "with a loud voice," "thunderously." Her loud "complaints" are "sensible" and "wise." Such terms often characterize the speech of Jacob's women characters. What shall we make of this?

Loud and thundering voices are favorite images of Jacob. He uses them often, especially to describe the singing of praise and thanksgiving by beings celestial and terrestrial, angelic, human, and natural. Such loud, thundering song characterizes his descriptions of creation, and also of the new creation at the Nativity, and again the Apocalypse. He follows biblical models in such renderings, especially from Isaiah 6:1–5. Almost invariably in his festal homilies, he enfolds the loud-sounding voices of the liturgical assembly into the image of the whole of the cosmos, on earth and in heaven, joined in song. That song is always "loud" and "thunderous" in his descriptions.

Jacob does not mention the women's choirs in most of his homilies, including those discussed in this chapter. Nor does he describe his congregations, although he addresses them periodically ("O discerning listener!"). With the Shilumite Woman and his excursus on the Good Wife, we might well picture a civic congregation, and perhaps, too, with the Indebted Widow, whose household so closely resembles the church and its sacraments. But others are less clearly located. Gendered portraits, yes. But exclusive in the piety they model? No. As Jacob proclaimed at the end of his homily on the Hemorrhaging Woman, every Christian must seek to emulate her.

Yet Jacob's homilies were often preached in civic liturgies that included women's choirs. How should we not hear their voices in that of the Indebted Widow, whose loud voice thundered her supplication? Jacob's intoned descriptions ring with the voices of women ritually present and ritually participating. His performance interlinks with theirs. Nor should we doubt such resonances to the voices sung and heard by late antique Syriac congregations.

Let there be no mistake: in late antiquity, at least, the voices of women thundered forth in Syriac liturgies. And in the homilies of Jacob of Sarug, biblical women, however slender their stories, helped to model their way.

THE LAMENTING WOMAN:
A TYPE TOWARD RESTORATION

One category of women's public voices was omnipresent in the ancient world, in every context and domain: that of the lamenting woman. The death of a child, of a monastic, of a family member; the loss of a beloved spiritual leader; the mass destruction of earthquake, epidemic, or war—in all instances, we find grief brought into focus through images of sung lamentation, often led by women. As Jacob of Sarug intoned,

> Because the Creator had put deep feelings in their wombs,
> Women also raise up lamentations for the dead with deep feelings.
> Out of the depths of their innermost feelings suffering enters in
> And makes them much more fervent than men in weeping for the dead.[99]

The gendered nature of lamentation for the dead had been long and deeply incised into the religious traditions of the ancient Mediterranean.[100] It was women's work, always, to mourn with evident, loud, and dramatic weeping and wailing; to display outwardly the inward anguish of loss felt by the entire community.

In the course of late antiquity, Christian bishops struggled to recast the inherited piety of death and to "Christianize" the practices of mourning, whether male or female.[101] They called for the widowed and grieving to behave in a seemly manner. Mourners should quell their sorrow and remember the good hope to which the faithful Christian looked: the promise of eternal life in a redeemed existence the glory of which surpassed understanding.[102] They should deliver into the church's care the traditional practices, whether domestic or civic, by which the dead were honored, buried, and remembered. They should attend to the sacramental requirements.[103] With liturgically defined sequences of commemoration, and with ritually articulated stages of emotional progression, Christian leaders sought to constrain, control, and redirect the Christian negotiation of life and death.[104]

The difficulty of the effort is apparent from glimpses in the standardized rhetoric that attended bereavement practices. Syriac liturgical collections preserve a lament, "*ber(y) habibo*," attributed to Jacob of Sarug; the entire madrasha is cast in the voice of a mother for her departed child. Poignantly, even within the same manuscript text the child is referenced with differently gendered pronouns: the hymn could be sung at the death of son or daughter, available for any and every such tragedy.[105] Each verse begins with a statement of anguished love and loss; each ends with acquiescence that the Lord has chosen this child for reasons of divine purpose, however inscrutable. While formulaic, the images are sharp: "O my beloved son. . . . The sound of your cries shatters and dismays me as it echoes in my ears . . . crazed (mother) that I am. . . . The home that has lost you lies desolate. . . . My breasts and my bowels burn to weep for you bitterly."[106] In turn, with each such line the voice moves on to exalt the child's new home: "The Royal Son has taken you off to His luminous abode. . . . The fiery beings on high [cry out] 'Hosanna' at your wedding feast. . . . It is the worlds of light that you are inheriting."[107] The hymn ends with the mourner's fear, as God declares his divine sovereignty, bidding an end to her cries: "O unfortunate women, do not be upset by your strong emotion."[108]

In another homily, "On Women," also attributed to Jacob of Sarug, the homilist begins with invective as he recalls the fall of Adam and Eve in Eden, laying the entire blame on Eve for the bitter inheritance of death left for all.[109] Dramatically, the memra turns suddenly to present a short, intimate snapshot of a mother on her deathbed, grieving together with her children, who are gathered at her bedside. The homilist chants the sorrow of each in turn. First, the mother sings her lament with bitter tears, "the sounds [*qalai* = 'melodies'] of suffering on my tongue as on a harp."[110] In turn, the children's cries respond with touching images of their loss:

> Dear mother, whither do you hasten to depart?
> A small dove who raised and carried all her chicks,
> Now what hope do we have after your death?
> A dear sheep to which her sweet lambs clung,
> Why did you bitterly abandon your offspring in desolation?
> A fair bird who within her nest reared her offspring,
> Why did you remove that shelter in which (the offspring) dwelt?
> A hen who enshrouded her chicks with her wings,
> Why did you take your wings away from us, for behold, we are miserable![111]

The children's voices continue: the home itself mourns, its stones weeping, its walls lamenting, its roof covered with groans, its inner rooms wafting mourning like incense as house, family, and friends all weep. In her final prayer, the mother begs for the comfort of their tears amid the inevitability of death and ends with closing praise for God.

Such verses attest to the familiarity of the scene and its stylized expressions. In no way do they diminish the push and pull of painful loss, faithful devotion, the bitterness and the solace of mourning practices. As in other narrative contexts, the poignancy is heightened by the voices of women, epitomized in the grieving mother and her children.[112]

Laments marked the immediate grief of loss, while liturgical memorials continued its remembrance. Just as the mother's voice could mark an entire community's loss, so, too, could women's voices sound its recollection. Jacob of Sarug bemoaned two polarized problems in death's aftermath. The first was lax attention to the proper liturgical care of departed loved ones, after the immediate trauma had passed. The carelessness was rampant, he complained.[113] Men were inattentive, even indifferent to the church's requirements in these matters. Rather than bring the canonically prescribed bread and wine to the church in person for the offering of a eucharistic liturgy on behalf of their family dead, they preferred to go about their business. Some had stopped bothering with such memorials altogether. Others sent a slave in their place, or, worse yet, showed disdain to the point of sending only "such despised servants of the house as are put to the basest task."[114]

Women, however, presented a different problem. They bypassed the church's memorial services altogether, going instead to the cemeteries, where they mourned their beloved dead with their own disordered, even "violent" grief, like "mad women."[115] Jacob described them:

> Behold how [the women] surround the dead in the graves, to weep over them,
> And with wailings they show their love for their departed.
> They forsake the Church, her service and her oblations,
> And go weeping to their loved ones amidst the graves.
> O believing woman, seek your beloved [here] in the holy temple
> In the presence of God, in Whose hands resides all spirits.
> Do not cry out to the dead in the grave; he does not hear you;
> He is not there; seek him here, in the sanctuary.[116]

For Jacob, the problem was not only one of attitudes toward death, whether inappropriately dismissive or excessively fearful. There was also the matter of how the public display of mourning affected others. "When [the soul] hears the lamenting voice of wailing women," he warned elsewhere, "she moves in grief and sheds abundant tears for the dead."[117] Such encounters were distressing: proximate mourning inevitably opened one's own wounds of loss. If disinterested men threatened to loosen or disregard the devotional bonds of families and religious communities, the unchecked grieving practices of female voices could unmoor even the faithful from their local liturgical ties, enclosing them in their own isolating grief.

Death in the ancient world was very much a communal matter. In a world chronically underpopulated and constantly at the mercy of natural, social, or political disasters, every life was crucial to the well-being of the entire community. In turn, every death diminished the health of the whole. The conventions and tropes of ancient bereavement practices make clear that every loss merited shared sorrow, first with the tears and articulated bewilderment of lamentation, and then in the common practices of consolation that rewove families and communities into wholeness.[118] Recognition of these interconnections was evident in the poignant commemorations of the unnamed poor and strangers.[119] These included the remembrance of solitary ascetics whose deaths passed otherwise unmarked.[120] In hymns, homilies, and hagiographies, unknown deaths were periodically claimed as the responsibility of the living faithful.[121]

Another way to mark the universality of loss, as well as to honor the communal resources of solace, was the telling of biblical stories of death. These stories were far from the immediacy of daily life. Yet they could speak to it.[122]

Jacob of Sarug's ecclesiastical concerns about late antique bereavement contrasted sharply with homilies where he portrayed grieving and lamenting biblical figures, especially women. In this regard his homilies fit closely with a number of anonymous Syriac narrative poems, which also provide memorable portraits of biblical women in lamentation. These poetic portraits by Jacob and others are noteworthy, too, for the way they elaborate biblical accounts. For although the Hebrew Bible as well as the New Testament refer occasionally to lamenting women, no accounts of women's laments are included in any biblical book, unlike, for example, the lament of David for Saul and Jonathan in 2 Samuel 1:17–27.[123] Yet Syriac poets did not hesitate to imagine the grief that women must have voiced in response to biblical tragedy. Their accounts give us, among others, Eve mourning for both her sons, with Abel's murder and Cain's demise (elaborating on Genesis 4); Sarah's lament for Isaac when Abraham took him to Mt. Moriah for sacrifice (expanding Genesis 22); Dinah the sister of Joseph, when Joseph's brothers feigned his death (adding to Genesis 46); Jephthah and his daughter as they face her sacrifice by her father's hand (enhancing the account in Judges 11); and more.[124]

Syriac poets cast these lamentations, as we would expect, to honor beloved characters who died tragically. But they also used lament to account for human life tragically lived, above all in recognition of human sin and folly. Thus we find lament with a wider application than mourning for the dead. Speeches of supplication for mercy or speeches of penitential grief in verse homilies and poems take similar form, structure, and cadence to lamentation for the dead. Poignant examples are Sarah's lament for her marriage when Abraham presents her to Pharoah as his sister (Gen 12); or, above all for Syriac homilists, the Sinful Woman (Lk 7:36–50), who washes Christ's feet with her tears, an ever-available paradigm of one who laments without ceasing, in this case for her own sins.[125] In an anonymous acrostic hymn about the saint

Mary of Qidun, chanted during Lent, the entire hymn is presented in the voice of her penance.[126] To each verse of her sorrow, the choir led the congregation in their refrain: "Alas for me, my brethren, what has happened to me? Again alas for what the Evil One has wrought in me." Over the hymn's course, every voice has become hers: "Answer me, my Savior, as you did that Sinful Woman; / receive my tears as you did hers, O Lord." The concluding voice joins past and present in the final prayer, "From all who have lived and are living be praise to you, Lord."[127]

Through the imagined voices of biblical women, Syriac poets presented an arc of lamentation from mourning to supplication to penance: from grief at the finality of death's loss to fearful sorrow at life's tragedies to sad yet fervent hope that there can be a changed outcome within life still to be lived.

The portrayal of mourning within liturgical homilies evoked a haunting intersection between narrative imagination and established social customs. But imagined lamentation as part of a homily was also a performance, and often one of intense emotion deliberately engaged by the homilist. Moreover, it was a performance within the liturgy as a ritual process. As such, imagined lamentation was far more than an oratorical or literary adornment within homiletic instruction. It contributed to the work accomplished through liturgical ritual, work that invariably carried social and civic implications. These fictive laments stood in flagrant contradiction to the stern admonitions against mourning that filled late antique sermons. What, then, did imagined homiletic lamentation do, embedded within and framed by the course of a liturgy?

An anonymous late antique Syriac narrative poem portrayed lamentation in terms that acknowledged mourning as an experience that bound the people of ancient communities together. The poem depicts Joseph's reunion with his father Jacob and his sister Dinah, following the long years of his slavery, imprisonment, and rise to greatness in Egypt (the account is in Genesis 47, although the episode of this poem is wholly imagined).[128] In the poem, Dinah narrates to Joseph the grief of those who loved him and believed he had died. She became the lamenting woman who mourned without ceasing the loss of her brother through the many years of his absence. In her own sorrow during that long time, she became the sorrow of all who grieved. She describes her communal role to her brother, telling how she shunned every wedding; instead, she said,

> I would go to the graveyard and weep for you there, my brother.
> There was no newly departed in the vale of Hebron whose bier I did not escort
> As I lamented and wept because of you.
> At the beginning of all my laments, it was your person I would recall, Joseph.
> There was no limit to the way the Hittite women loved me,
> Thinking that it was for their departed that I was weeping, my brother.
> They would thank me—when it was for you I wept!
> And they said to our father, "Dinah, your daughter, Jacob, should be remembered
> For how much she weeps and laments together with us over our dead.
> Great is her love as she pours out her compassion: blessed is her father!"[129]

In the depiction of Dinah's grief and its communal role, we see something of civic life in antiquity. While Dinah insists her mourning was singular, yet the listener—like Dinah's neighbors in the story—recognized the universal dimension of sorrow and loss. In liturgy, that grief could be affirmed as cosmic. Just as the sun had darkened at the crucifixion of Jesus,[130] so, too, in an anonymous dialogue hymn on Cain and Abel did the natural world lament the death of Abel: the heights wailed, the depths wept, the hills lamented, the heavenly ranks grieved, the mountains wailed, the rocks sounded their suffering, the earth cried out and shook, the elements quaked in terror.[131] Such cosmic affirmation of loss often characterized the devotional piety that accompanied the death of saints in hagiography or hagiographic sermons.[132]

Jacob of Sarug also excelled at the presentation of grief as a universal emotion collectively owned. This was nowhere more powerful than in his depiction of Eve's visceral anguish at the murder of Abel by Cain.[133] In her mouth, Jacob places a lament for both her sons, "as a dove mourns with suffering for her nestling."[134] She grieves in bitter sorrow: "O Cain, you have broken me from the beginning to the end, / and you have made me suffer all the sorrows of married women."[135] For indeed from Cain, she weeps, she had learned the pains of childbirth, and now from him for the first time also the pain of death. She sings a double lamentation: "For the slayer and the slain one I will weep equally."[136] She sings in familiar images of fragile youth senselessly crushed: her sons are saplings beaten down by winds that uprooted one and tore the other; young trees assaulted by an axe that cut one down and left the other mangled. They are lambs attacked by a wolf, one butchered, the other lacerated but not killed; they are fledgling partridges, assailed by a hawk, who killed one and ripped the other; lovely blossoms afflicted by blight, leaving one plucked and the other withered. Her sorrow encompasses the whole of mortal tragedy. She addresses Cain, now trembling in terror at his own guilt:

> For whom shall I mourn, for the dead one or the living?
> For Abel shall I grieve, or for you, Cain, shall I make my mourning?
> There is no consolation for me for the dead man who was killed and thrown away,
> And there is no comfort [for me] from that one still living who endures terrors.
> The death of Abel and your terror, Cain, see how they besiege me!
> By the blood of the dead one and the quaking of the living one I am shattered.[137]

Jacob's Eve does not here weep for her past folly as the one who lost paradise. Instead, as Eve the Mother of Life, she sees the sorrow of all mortal beings in the face of death's now constant presence. Elsewhere, Jacob takes up the story of how the suffering house of Adam will find comfort with a new son, Seth. But first he highlights Eve's grief in the absence of others to share her sorrow:

> [Eve] had no sister to say: "Let your mourning pass!"
> And no relative so that she might be comforted about her beloved.
> She had no mother and no neighbor to come to her,

No one close to her and no one advising her to let her suffering go.
. . . .
[Adam and Eve] raised sounds of groaning on the earth, but no one was listening,
They raised up a song of suffering to one another.[138]

The isolation of Eve's grief, with only Adam to share it, points to the need for communal comfort. Sure enough, in Jacob's account of Jephthah's Daughter (Judges 11), lamentation pours out from multiple figures in the story.[139] Jacob portrays Jephthah as a priest who offers sacrifice in perfect image of God's own salvific action, as a father who will sacrifice his only begotten child on behalf of all his people. To accomplish this course, Jacob portrays Jephthah as one whose internal battle is far more brutal than the war he fought for the Hebrews with the Amorites; internally, his love for God must war with his love for his daughter. Jacob voices his anguish in sharp, bitter fragments: a grief so deep Jephthah cannot speak without moans and cries of anguish slashing Jacob's metered verses. "Prostrate with mourning," he awaits the event.[140]

By contrast, in Jacob's telling as in the biblical account, Jephthah's daughter accepts her course with loving devotion for the God they both serve. Instead, she laments the loss of life she did not have: for a spouse unwed, for her unborn children whom she even imagines and names, that she might grieve them, each one. She laments family, lineage, marriage, companionship. Around her she gathers her maidens, like a brood of moaning doves, who weep piteously, tearfully, sorrowfully, like partridges, like harps, in the beauty of their sad song.[141] When Jephthah and his daughter, their lamentation performed, turn themselves to the deed, Jacob pauses in his homily to address the congregation: "The story of Jephthah draws me to proceed with it; / [now you] accompany me, with voices of suffering, that we may journey with him."[142] With the skill of a consummate storyteller, he lingers (for thirty-seven lines!) on the impossibility of the task before him: how to portray adequately the dreadful deed of Jephthah's sacrifice. Yet sing the deed he does, sparing his congregation no horror as he brings his homily to its conclusion, Jephthah silent and blood-drenched while the Hebrew maidens and daughters sang their community's grief in the midst of human and divine presence.[143]

Jacob does not only present lamentation for the dead. In a homily on King Solomon, he includes the story of the two harlots who bring their babies, one dead and one still living, before Solomon for judgment. With compassion and drama, Jacob sings the horror of the mother who awakens to find the dead child in her arms and her own son claimed by another. When Solomon orders that both babies be cut in two and distributed to the two women, Jacob again draws in his congregation:

> Who of those in the middle of the crowd could watch what was happening:
> the sword drawn to cut up the babies without pity?

> Who had a heart of stone that could not feel pain,
> When hearing the weeping sounds of the baby and his mother?
> Sounds of grief were swirling all around; tears poured out of eyes,
> And she gave out cries that broke the hearts of those who heard them.[144]

Inflecting her speech with graphic anguish, Jacob chants the mother's impassioned plea, at once a cry for mercy and a lament for loss, as she begs that her child be given to the impostor rather than killed. Her lament is lurid with images of streaming tears and milk, as every part of her weeps for her child still living whom she will lose either to the executioner or to her rival. When Solomon in his wisdom judges her to be the true mother, the crowd sings out with joy, praising God who raises up the wise to judge and who himself will judge (wisely, we must presume) at the last judgment. So, too, at the homily's end, would Jacob's congregation have begun to sing the prayers for mercy that followed next in the liturgy's course.

In each of these homilies, and in others, Jacob presented a biblical tragedy of epic proportions, narrated in highly emotive, even visceral, terms. Despite the constraints of isosyllabic meter, his verses are rife with drama and pathos as he draws on the tools of the ancient rhetorician's trade. Following paradigms well known from declamations and progymnasmata, Jacob allows imagined women's voices to articulate extreme pathos within a mythic imagination.[145] Applying such strategies to biblical stories in the context of liturgy, Jacob acknowledges that death brings a grief at once singular and universal. Everyone's story is a biblical story; every biblical story can become one's own. At the same time, he performs these lamentations in his office as priest and bishop, in a ritual setting of liturgy that conjoined civic and ecclesiastical communities. He thereby employs strongly affective means to reeducate and reorient his congregations regarding the meaning of death in Christian terms. Its proper place, process, representation, and resolution all belong inside the church's walls.[146]

Although Jacob's metrical homilies and other Syriac narrative poems portray a number of biblical women with generous attention to their grief, one figure seems surprisingly absent: What of the Virgin Mary, who must behold her Son's death upon the cross? Syriac poets preferred to write about Mary in other contexts, above all at the Nativity. Both Greek and Latin tradition would develop extensive hymnography that voiced Mary's lamentation for the dead Christ. In Greek, the tradition begins in the sixth century with the powerful kontakion by Romanos, depicting Mary's dialogue with her Son as he walks to his death: she pleads for him to live instead, and he responds, "Mourn not for me, mother."[147] By the ninth century, Romanos's verses would be woven together with inherited folk traditions of Greek lamentation (the *threnos*), producing the piercing verses of the *stavrotheoto-kia*, sung to this day in Holy Friday liturgies of the Byzantine tradition.[148] In Syriac, such Marian laments are rare and of a different ethos, starting from bitter (anti-Jewish) invective before moving to triumphant—even vengeful—hope of resurrection.[149] Although Romanos was a poet deeply influenced by Syriac tradition, no counterpart to his kontakion of Mary on the way to Calvary is to be found in Syriac poetry.[150]

But think again about the examples of lamentation just mentioned. To the discerning listener (as Jacob names the well-behaved layperson), a haunting refrain lies behind all these laments. For the harlot mother witnesses the rescue of her child from the executioner's sword to her own arms, just as Dinah witnesses the return of the brother whose death she had mourned for many years. Sarah will witness not only the preservation of her rightful marriage (with its fruit, her son Isaac), but also the return of Isaac unharmed from Mt. Moriah. Even Eve: for in Syriac liturgy we have a different Eve than she of the theologian's denunciations.[151] In Syriac liturgy, Eve is recalled as a tragic figure whose redemption is the deed of her daughter Mary. She is the one whose debt Mary repays; the one bowed down whom Mary raises up. Like Adam, she waits among the dead to be restored to life.

In an anonymous Syriac hymn, the intimacy between Eve and Mary is extolled: "The Daughter gave support to her mother who had fallen, / and because she had clothed herself in fig leaves of shame / her daughter wove and gave her a garment of glory."[152] And in another, both foreparents are summoned with compassion:

> The Virgin Vine gave forth the Cluster of Grapes whose wine is sweet.
> Both Adam and Eve who were mourning
> received comfort in their grief,
> having tasted of that Medicine of Life,
> they received comfort in their grief.[153]

By such imagery, Eve (like Adam) remains part of the human community, both in the grief of loss and death, and in the hope of joy to come. In medieval Syriac wall paintings, Eve stands beside Abel at the resurrection.[154] And if Jephthah's Daughter fulfilled the perfect image of Christ in her sacrifice, so, too, would she fulfill it again in the resurrection to come.

Each of these laments, sung in the cadenced dignity of the liturgical cycle, held the promise of life restored. Each of these biblical women, then, became types of Mary: their anguished laments a foretaste of her own at the cross, their joyous resolutions anticipating her reunion with her risen Son—and in early Syriac tradition, it was Mary the Mother, not Mary Magdalene, who first met the risen Lord in the garden at the tomb, in the Gospel of John, chapter 20.[155] It is as if Jacob of Sarug and other Syriac poets imprinted Mary's image over that of every lamenting woman of the Bible.

The typology of the Lamenting Woman as Mary at the cross was, I suggest, a function of the liturgy itself, as a sequential process. For the homily was not an independent, freestanding component of the liturgy. As the culmination of the "teaching" portion of the service, it drew together the lessons of the readings and hymns that preceded it. It was the bridge to what followed, the entry into the eucharistic liturgy proper, where the congregation's work of active listening

FIGURE 13. Resurrection scene, detail: Adam and Eve. Fresco, Mart Shmuni Church, Hadchit, Lebanon, 1070–1129. Erica Cruikshank Dodd, *Medieval Painting in Lebanon* (Wiesbaden: Reichert Verlag, 2004), p. 132, pl. XLVb.

to scriptures and homily bore fruit in their active preparation for and reception of communion. Jacob of Sarug exhorted his congregation, "Stand, O sinner, at the moment of the [eucharist], beg for mercy, receive forgiveness, and then go out."[156]

By this structure, Jacob's memre that narrated biblical tragedies with suffering loss and fervent lamentation mirrored the process of the liturgy itself. With the homily as his vehicle, he guided his congregation through the sequence of humanity's larger narrative: love, loss, restoration; or creation, fall, redemption. His vividly rendered biblical stories led his listeners into the abyss of the human heart, a guided emotional journey, in which he took them into the depths of sorrow and brought them back out again. To understand the lamentation of biblical women in the typology of Mary was to anticipate the salvation every believer would be ritually offered in the eucharist. In this way, liturgical fulfillment joyfully completed every homiletic story, no matter how abrupt or tragic its ending. Indeed, liturgy thereby continued and completed what scripture itself had left unresolved.

No matter where the story ended, in lection or homily, the liturgy continued each time, with its comforting sequence of prayers for forgiveness, consecration of the offering, reception of the eucharist, and return to the world in transformed state. In every completed liturgical cycle, resolution was offered and received, ritually anticipating the final redemption yet to come. It was a promise Jacob of Sarug evoked in the voice he granted to Eve at the birth of her third son, Seth:

> The woman who was mourning for her sons became radiant through the noble Seth,
> and she began singing a song that reveals joy.
> . . . .
> Her mouth was full of radiant songs for her fruit,
> and through the chants she let go of the lamentations for Abel and his brother.[157]

Recall Jacob of Sarug's complaint about inappropriate commemoration of the dead, whether cavalier or overwrought. Just as he chose to portray the depths of human loss through the imagined voices of lamenting biblical women, so too did he portray the true piety of Christian sorrow through an idealized female figure:

> Blessed is the widow that bears her sacrifice in her own hands,
> . . . .
> She does not, like the rich man, send her loaf to the Lord [by the hands of others];
> She herself offers it to Him, imploring with grief to accept it from her.
> Like a priest, she brings her vow in to the Lord,
> As with pain she commemorates her dead over her oblation.
> . . . .
> Beloved is the widow's oblation when offered,
> For tears, love, and faith are intermingled with it.
> The prosphora [consecrated bread] is in her hands, tears are in her eyes, and praise
>   in her mouth,
> And the excellency of her faith, like her oblation, is great.[158]

Once more, it seems, Jacob plays with the gendered roles of his poetic subjects. Here is the irony of his depiction of grief for the dead, whether imagined in story or idealized as ecclesiastical practice: the male bishop chanted the lament of women's voices, while the pious widow performed the sacerdotal offering of the male priest. Even as his own ordained office reinscribed the gendered norms of civic and ecclesiastical order, Jacob's homiletic performance and his articulated ideals destabilize the expectations of custom. A larger, more inclusive human community flits (briefly) into view. Men, too, weep in anguish; women, too, make their offerings directly to God. Separate roles might yet become inclusive of the entire human community, male and female, in the shared recognition of grief, even as a higher resolution awaits.

The pious widow is Jacob's model for the right relation between the living and the dead. That relation is characterized by location, agency, and performance. In contrast to the (sometimes) misbehaving men and women of Jacob's wayward congregation, the pious widow is in the right place, doing the right thing, at the right time: she is in church, performing the proper liturgical order. Included in the "right doing" is right speech: "Praise is in her mouth," even with tears in her eyes. She is herself the type of Mary—at the tomb, and in anticipation of joy to come. Jacob does not tell us what she says (or sings). Narratively imposed silence replaces the wailing of real women in streets or cemeteries, just as the imagined laments Jacob narratively ascribed to biblical women replaced the words of grieving communities. Yet the sounds of women's voices were heard nonetheless, through the women's choirs of Syriac liturgies—which Jacob termed "a gift from God"—and in the voices of the girls and women who joined the congregation daily and weekly in prayer and song.

How might we characterize the work of imagined liturgical lamentation? I suggest it lay in sounding the depths of liturgy as ritual process. Through the homiletic mourning of biblical women, resolution of narrative tragedy and consolation in actual loss became one and the same act. Through sequenced progression, dramatic poetry, affective preaching, and collective participation, Jacob of Sarug could meet his congregation in full acknowledgment of their sorrow, even as he attempted to bring order to their liturgical lives. He did so with and through the voices of women, real, imagined, and remembered.

EPILOGUE: THE GOOD WIFE

Unlike other well-known preachers such as John Chrysostom or Augustine of Hippo, Jacob of Sarug is not familiar to scholars as a source for late antique family life. Yet he does provide occasional glimpses, as seen in the discussion above, and his perspective is interesting. He is worth a further look.

Jacob of Sarug describes weddings, wedding banquets, and wedding biers fairly often. The majority of the time, his intention is that shared by other Syriac authors: to extol the relationship between the Church as Bride and Christ the Heavenly Bridegroom, or to extol the relationship between the faithful believer and Christ as one in which death brings fulfillment of their long-awaited wedding. Jacob's homily "On Epiphany"—the occasion of the baptism of Christ in the Jordan—provides a sumptuous example of the first, in its depiction of the wedding between the Church and Christ.[159] His funeral memre—such as that for a daughter of the covenant[160]—provide poignant examples of the second, as they evoke the departed now at joyous nuptial celebration with their Beloved. Jacob's wedding references generally image the human-divine relationship either collectively or individually.

A number of "table homilies" survive from Jacob's pen. These were short poetic homilies presented at Christian gatherings over a meal rather than in liturgy. Fittingly for their settings, they offer glimpses of family life.[161] "Praise at Table 2," for example, provides a vivid wedding description to explain how wheat becomes communion bread:

> The spikes [of wheat] are adorned like brides in their bridal chambers,
> And the grains of wheat resemble the betrothed in their veils.
> Each grain of wheat is veiled, allowing no one to see her face,
> Until she reaches the threshing floor, her bridal chamber, along with the farmer.

> Then her betrothed, the farmer, reveals her face,
> Stripping her of her veil and gazing on her loveliness.
> He embraces her in a great heap and rejoices with her,
> Making her wedding banquet with the first fruits and the offerings.
> He summons the priest, who blesses the bride (the farmer) has brought,
> So that she becomes the wafer, returning praise to her Creator.[162]

Recently, Jeff Childers has argued that uniquely in Jacob's corpus one of these table homilies was designed for an actual wedding banquet, to be preached in the presence of the couple and their families.[163] Here, Jacob praises marriage and the marriage bed as divinely valued, without his habitual qualification that celibacy is better. The nuptial motifs in this instance, Childers observes, "serve the purpose of upholding the sanctity and intent of human marriage as created and blessed by God," quoting Jacob: "The bridegroom and bride portray a beautiful image of the Son of God and the Daughter of the Peoples, his betrothed (PT 9.1)."[164]

Such unmitigated praise for marriage does not characterize Jacob's preaching generally. Still, in "Praise at Table 1," he marvels at the abundant benevolence by which God nourishes babies within their mothers' wombs and at their breast.[165] In "Praise at Table 6," he speaks of divine grace as like the compassion of a wet nurse for a baby, or a mother for her son.[166]

Jacob's memre presume time and again that children are cherished and beloved. In festal celebrations, he delights in the presence of "babes in the arms" of faithful parents, children "yearn[ing] to sing many praises to you [O Lord] with their hosannas," and "mothers thronged together with their husbands to give praise to your name [O Lord]."[167] Moreover, whenever sacred narrative allows, Jacob is quick to elicit parental love. In his memra "On the Judgment of Solomon," Jacob's opening invocation alludes to a doting father:

> A child speaks to his parent with love
> While his father listens affectionately to all that he says to him.
> And when he hears the questions that are posed to him,
> He accepts them just as if someone were speaking of serious things.
> Even when [the child] chatters a lot without making clear what he is saying,
> [the Father] is happier with his speech than he would be with the speech of
>   philosophers.[168]

But for Jacob's paradigmatic marriage and family, one must turn to his homiletic presentations of Adam and Eve. In his magisterial homily, "On the Fashioning of Creation," Jacob presents the created universe on the sixth day as a sumptuous wedding feast, wherein Paradise opened her splendidly adorned house for the newlyweds, complete with exquisitely fashioned marital bed. The happy scene gives Jacob pause for further reflection. Adam and Eve, Jacob sings, were created as one inseparable being, for Eve was fashioned from within Adam's own body. The image becomes a marriage prayer: "And let no dispute nor deception nor contention / Perturb those two, who had been one in the beginning. / Rather, let them be of one will and of one thought."[169] Jacob pauses here:

> Why do husbands now disregard that union,
> And women disregard that clear path full of beautiful things.
> A husband prostitutes himself with other women and loses his path,
> While a wife is deceitful for she too corrupts her great image.
> . . . .
> The Creator fashioned them well, and made them equally beautiful;
> He formed the two of them beautiful that He might unite them together.
> But they quarrel, they dispute, and they prostitute themselves,
> And for this reason they are not one as they were constituted.[170]

Jacob's sadness for the state of marriage in real life echoes prayers he offers elsewhere on behalf of families and on behalf of the church. Here again is Jacob's favorite analogy, for the bond between clergy and their flocks is another marriage, just as that between the Church and Christ, or the believer and God. In one of his homilies on the resurrection, for example, Jacob concludes with a mighty and eloquent supplication on behalf of all:

> On your great day gladden your Church, O Son of God,
> And sign her children who are placed in your possession with the Cross of Light.
> . . . .
> Keep in harmony the shepherds and their chief shepherds
> And equally the innocent flocks of their assemblies.
> Keep your covenant from the railings that surround it;
> And may the choirs in the assemblies stand firm in splendour.
> May the great road of communion rejoice in your day,
> Since you are guarding peace for men with their wives.
> May the mothers together with their offsprings be glad in you,
> And to the barren (ones) grant the petitions of their supplications.
> Support the aged and give to the infants upbringing.
> . . . .
> Blessed is your resurrection which has made the gloomy earth joyful.[171]

Jacob places families in parallel to churches: human units in which troubled relations between and among the constituent members afflict the health and well-being of all, from the youngest to the eldest. If one analyzes Jacob's (lengthy and here much condensed) prayer on behalf of the world, it is clear that a peaceful church resembles a peaceful family, which in turn mirrors a peaceful creation. When everything and everyone is in their right place, the image resounds with the song of rightly ordered liturgy: "The choirs in the assemblies stand firm in their splendor" (l. 228) among the whole.

Within that liturgy, women's choirs offered their song, voicing chants Jacob tells us elsewhere were sweet-sounding and "instructive": female teachers (*malphanyatha*) instructing the gathered church with the wisdom of sacred teaching-songs (*madrashe*).[172] I suggest that when Jacob summoned women to be teachers of divine instruction for their households in the likeness of the Shilumite Woman, as we saw above, he was once again recalling his favored image of the human-divine relationship as a marriage with its household. We might think of this as the "liturgification" of family life.

For Jacob tells us that liturgy was a school for the household of God. In it, women could be wise teachers of divine knowledge. To this simple point, liturgy offered (1) *models* from scripture, with the imagined voices of remembered women of the biblical past; (2) *exemplification* by and in the voices of women's choirs, whom Jacob called "female teachers" (*malphanyatha*); and (3) *affirmation* in sermons like Jacob's, wherein the pattern could be seen, time and again, to recur. Like the Shilumite Woman, the good wife was a teacher of divine instruction; like the Shilumite's husband, a good husband took heed of what she said. And like their household, a good congregation—including its female laity—sang their resounding response.

Afterword

Subsequently the record thins, yet it continues. After the seventh century, it becomes increasingly difficult to distinguish the office of daughter of the covenant from that of deaconess or nun.[1] Mention of their liturgical singing becomes rare. The twelfth-century pontifical of the West Syrian patriarch Michael the Great and a few more recent West Syriac manuscripts refer to, and in at least two cases contain, a consecration service for the office of deaconess, also identified as "singer."[2] Whether or not this service was still in use when any of these manuscripts were copied is unknown but seems unlikely. The assignment of the madrashe to the daughters of the covenant was twice cited in the thirteenth century by Gregory Bar Hebraeus, in his *Ethicon* and his *Nomocanon*.[3]

The term *bart qyama* gradually became synonymous with "nun," as we have noted. Further, since the tenth century and consistently since the early modern period, *bart qyama* has generally signified a priest's wife because it often fell to her to perform the liturgical assistance required for women.[4] These shifts in meaning need not have precluded the tradition of women's liturgical singing, but the terminological inconsistencies and lack of concrete liturgical descriptions over these later centuries make it difficult to find evidence for whether and how women's choirs continued. The service books now in use by the Syriac Orthodox Church include a rite for the blessing or consecration of a female singer (*mzamranitha*), among other services for deaconess, presbytress (*qashishtha*), and *bart qyama* (priest's wife).[5]

Beyond their homelands in the Middle East, out along the Silk Road of central Asia and as far away as China, Syriac communities flourished over long centuries. Medieval grave inscriptions identify Syriac Christian women sometimes with biblical names such as Sarah or those of saints such as Febronia, in communities for

FIGURE 14. Nativity scene. Manuscript illumination, British Library Add. 7170, fol. 21, Gospel lectionary, 13th cent. From the British Library Archive.

which we have virtually no other evidence, material or otherwise.[6] Liturgical manuscripts from western China include the celebration of the Sasanian convert queen Mart Shir, and her companions the priest Mar Barshabba and female attendant Zarvandokht, as missionaries who brought Christianity to Merv and established its lasting presence. Liturgical practices carried their memories, whatever else was lost from our view.[7] Liturgical poetry steadily continued as a locus for Syriac creativity. Often, in Syriac communities under the Ottomans, female patrons commissioned the copying and transmission of liturgical manuscripts.[8] Liturgically knowledgeable, did they also sing? We do not know.

Yet even a millennium's silence can be deceptive. In the late twentieth century and now in the twenty-first, an energetic revival and renewal of these choirs has taken place in local churches of the Middle East, Europe, Scandinavia, and North America for both Syriac Orthodox and Church of the East communities. In the wrenching contexts of war, displacement, and diaspora, these choirs have gained additionally charged echoes of meaning.[9] Their voices continue to be valued as significant within their communities, even as their roles change to accommodate the circumstances of multicultural, multireligious, and highly secularized social contexts.[10]

In recent decades, Syriac churches of both the East and West Syriac traditions are reviving the practice of women's choirs in their parishes. In many churches now, one finds their place, presentation, and role significantly enhanced in comparison to what it was even in the late twentieth century.[11] Syriac Orthodox women's choirs now often wear white robes, with white lace headscarves; sometimes they wear a single stole with the name of their parish. The women are generally young, including young girls. They stand in front of the congregation on the left-hand side, facing the altar, balancing the (male) deacons on the right. They lead the congregation in singing the major Syriac hymns of the liturgy; they sing with bold, strong, full-throated voices. In Sweden and Germany, annual competitions have been held between choirs (at least until the COVID-19 pandemic, beginning in 2020), recorded on DVD and online for distribution among the communities.[12] The choir directors, or sometimes lead singers, may be tonsured or specially consecrated in some way.[13] In Germany in May 2003, a choir of seventy girls was consecrated by their bishop in a thrilling service of praise.[14] These choirs are honored with immense pride among their people.

Much has changed, to be sure. The context for Syriac-speaking communities in Europe and Scandinavia, as well as North America, currently is one of intense focus on identity politics, as a recent, ongoing, and often well-educated immigrant population works to establish itself in new places. Renewal of the women's liturgical choirs is part of a larger effort to preserve language, tradition, culture, and religion in wholly changed circumstances, well documented in the scholarship of Sarah Bakker Kellogg.[15] Women's choirs or women singing in mixed parish choirs or skilled female chanters are traditions and practices valued in local communities. But there continue to be delicate gender politics to be negotiated, whether in the Middle East or in new homelands. As Tala Jarjour has emphasized, learned female singers may be recognized as worthy teachers, but may also find their work strictly circumscribed.[16] For East Syriac tradition, where again there are deep reservoirs of women's musical gifts, the work of Eve Sada demonstrates how greatly needed is the study of this music and its performative heritage, often barely acknowledged by scholars of Christian musicology.[17]

There is perhaps no greater measure of what has changed and what remains at stake for the Syriac women's choirs, over the long duration of their history, than

FIGURE 15. Harrowing of Hell/Resurrection with Adam and Eve.
Manuscript illumination, British Library Add. 7170, fol. 156v,
Gospel lectionary, 13th cent. From the British Library Archive.

the simple fact of the language that defines them. Today, these choirs sing the
ancient hymns in their original language—a language most often unknown and
unrecognized by those who sing, those who listen, or those who join them in song.
The teaching ministry of these choirs, in consequence, has taken a poignant, even
haunting turn. In new homelands, amid new and varied cultures, languages, and
religious communities, the Syriac women's choirs now perform a ministry to teach
an identity, a language, a history, in addition to the doctrinal and biblical content
of their hymns. They perform, with ever-changing ramifications.[18] Their continuing commitment to their inherited musical traditions offers hope for the future.

For some years now, I have given talks about the Syriac women's choirs in
Syriac church contexts and those of other Orthodox jurisdictions, both in North
America and abroad. It has been deeply moving to see how much people cherish
their heritage.

Invariably, after the official part of the event has ended, after the questions and discussions have moved over to an informal reception, one or two or several women will take me aside. They tell me their stories. They are daughters or sisters or wives of priests. They learned to sing the hymns of the liturgy out of love for this traditional music, or (initially) out of jealousy that a brother was learning and they were not; or they learned because help was needed in the services. Sometimes there was a mixed choir of men and women; sometimes they needed to take a more prominent role as a lead chanter. Sometimes, quite literally, there was no one else to do this important job. Liturgies do not happen without people; churches do not continue without congregations. Meaningful liturgical singing by chanters and choirs is key to religious community. Often this singing, when done by women, has had no official recognition.

One such encounter continues to haunt me, more than twenty years later. I spoke at a Syriac Orthodox church about Ephrem the Syrian and the ancient Syriac women's choirs. Afterward, the women's choir of the parish gathered round me, with some tumult and clearly much emotion. Some were in tears; I asked what I had done wrong. The woman who served as choir director said: "No one ever told us that what we do is important." When I left the event that night (a Friday, close to midnight), I could hear, loud and clear coming from the nave, the women's choir rehearsing for Sunday's liturgy.

In this way, I am sure, women have always sung in Syriac and other Orthodox liturgies. It is a local matter, dependent on the needs at a given time. It is normal to the point that people do not recognize it as something either unusual or often disallowed, hence even transgressive. Yet there continue to be parishes in all of these traditions (including in North America) where women are forbidden from taking a lead chanting role, or to sing at all.

When women's singing happens in such a way—as a local event, not marked as notable—it falls outside the institutional history of the church. It is not part of the ecclesiastical record. It is easily missed. It is not part of the history that scholars write; it is not part of the tradition that people remember. This kind of silence has occluded a great deal of women's history, whether in Christianity or more generally.

In the case of Syriac, however, whether by accident or design, women's liturgical singing made it into the official records of their churches. A handful of ecclesiastical canons institutionalized the practice during late antiquity; a handful of authors—as it happens, of particularly celebrated memory—highlighted their work. The women were there; and they continue to be there now. Their priests and parishes are glad for the help, and the life of the churches continues.[19] Yet the memory of these voices is fragile. It has been easy to write the story of Syriac Christians without them, despite the poetry of saints like Ephrem the Syrian or Jacob of Sarug.

And what happens when we do forget, or fail to take notice? A distorted history appears, in which women have had little to contribute to liturgical worship;

in which women are scarcely evident. The damage of patriarchal oppression is furthered through a continuing process of erasure that mischaracterizes everyone, inflating the importance of some and marginalizing or wholly excluding others.

In this book, I have taken the very slender threads of surviving evidence for Syriac women's liturgical choirs and asked what they can show us. I have argued that the evidence—however thin—indicates that these choirs received religious schooling in addition to musical instruction in order to perform their task of liturgical singing effectively. Their task as choirs was not to provide aesthetic adornment to the liturgy. This was not music for the purpose of beauty—although, as Jacob of Sarug wrote, beauty could be its outcome. Instead, their task was to educate. The church was the place where God's truth resided, available to any who sought it if they were rightly instructed. For the ancient Syriac churches, women's liturgical choirs were key transmitters of that truth and its holy wisdom.

Why does this matter?

First, there is the point of Syriac tradition in and of itself. The history of Christianity has long been dominated by the study of Greek and Latin, and the literary, doctrinal, and liturgical material from those language traditions: a Eurocentric view. Happily, for some time now scholars have come to appreciate Christianity as a global religion throughout its history, and hence to value the evidence that appears in other languages and literatures. Language traditions do not flourish in isolation. The richness of ancient Christian thought cannot be grasped if we confine ourselves to the study of Greek and Latin sources, or if we think of other language traditions as marginal. These were not peripheral histories. They were themselves centers of creative literary, liturgical, and theological activity. Syriac is a shining example. The material about women's voices real and imagined helps us to see this situation with particular clarity.

Second, consideration of Syriac women's choirs as transmitters of sacred knowledge provides us evidence for important religious leadership exercised by women. Their leadership was conducted in a prominent, publicly visible and audible role, authorized by the ecclesiastical institution, governed by ecclesiastical canons, at times supported by eminent saints like Ephrem the Syrian or Jacob of Sarug, in civic as distinct from monastic contexts. Their singing instructed every level of liturgical participant: ordained or not, high status or low, rich or poor, young or old, important or ordinary. These choirs were basic to the life of the ancient believing community. They were a daily part of that history. Women did this work, and if we do not make the effort to see it, these women and their work are erased from the historical record.

Scholarship on eastern Christian liturgies has been dominated by focus on the bishop or priest: their homilies, their sacramental actions. The spotlight shines on their pulpit or altar. To argue as I am doing that choirs played an important liturgical role is to see that liturgy is much more than sacramental acts or doctrinal instruction. It requires people, and meaningful—even useful—ways for them to participate. The scene shifts from pointed spotlight to panoramic view. Suddenly, instead of one or two key ritual actors (exclusively male), we see many ritual agents, female as well as male. For not only do the choirs themselves step into view, but also the congregation: those who sing the refrains and responses, and who complete the work of the choirs and other ritual agents. Liturgy becomes a composite of different contributing voices, each with its distinctive role—not competing or even equal, but complementary. Everyone has a role, and each is crucial, since none can be performed fully without the others. Above all, "everyone" includes *everyone*, including reckoning by gender, class, race, ethnicity, age, social and religious status. The significance of such consideration cannot be overstated, especially in a historical record that has largely ignored many of these people. If we do not include the presence and actively contributing voices of women, whether as choir or laity, we miss a huge part of what we need to see if we are going to understand ancient Christianity or its history.

Finally, the importance of liturgy as inclusive of women's history is also worth noting. For Syriac, we have no surviving evidence written by women until modernity (perhaps nothing of which we can be sure until the nineteenth century). If we take the liturgical role of women into account, then what we have here, in the witness of these ancient choirs, is a clear reminder that women were there, every day, publicly seen and heard, singing to and teaching their communities, dispensing the truths of their faith. We do not know anything about these women: who they were, what they thought or experienced. But because the choirs are mentioned in our sources, however rarely or briefly, we know these women were there.

I suggest a further result of this study. The evidence collected here indicates that women did more than sing. The striking heroines of Syriac sacred memory (whether the Bible or hagiography) could be imagined as such because those who told their stories had seen and known such women. They lived among them. Some of them sang in the choirs. This evidence shows us a very different history of women than what we have long been told was the case, whether by scholars or by ecclesiastical leaders. Women in their bold and loud singing, their wise teaching, and their persistent ministries are an indelible part of how and why Syriac Christianity (or any Christianity) survives and continues to flourish. We cannot underestimate the significance of this record.

For reasons such as these—Syriac as a language and tradition, liturgy as a mode of social history, and the remembrance of women's contributions in history—it is important to remember Syriac women's choirs as teachers and transmitters of traditions both sacred and human. They surely were in the ancient past, and they continue to be now as history moves forward.

NOTES

INTRODUCTION: A FORGOTTEN HISTORY

1. Jacob of Sarug, "On Mar Ephrem," v. 46b in Amar, trans., 37.

2. Jacob of Sarug, "On Mar Ephrem," vv. 108, 111, 113 in Amar, trans., 50–53.

3. Jacob of Sarug, "Homily 1 on the Nativity," l. 405 in Kollamparampil, trans., 56–57.

4. Jacob of Sarug, "On the Partaking," ll. 131, 214, 243–244 in Harrak, trans., 18–19, 28–29, 30–31.

5. See now Kellogg, *Sonic Icons*; Kellogg, "Ritual Sounds, Political Echoes"; Kellogg, "Perforating Kinship." Tala Jarjour incisively articulates the issues of liturgical singing, ethnicity, and religious identity for Syriac Orthodox Christians in Jarjour, *Sense and Sadness*, and specifically on challenges for women (53–55, 150–158); Jarjour, "Chant as the Articulation."

6. Brock and Harvey, *Holy Women*, offers a starting point.

7. See Brock, "Two Syriac Verse Homilies," 98–99.

8. British Library Add. 14652. See Wright, *Catalogue of Syriac Manuscripts*, 2:651–652 (no. 731).

9. The availability of ancient and medieval Syriac manuscripts has been dramatically improved in recent years with the digitization of many manuscript collections. There is much work to be done as this material becomes accessible. We do not know what may appear that might be relevant for women in the history of Syriac Christianity.

10. The complexity of this situation is evident, for example, in the case of the late nineteenth- and early twentieth-century poet Anne of Telkepe. Alessandro Mengozzi cites Anne of Telkepe as "the only Chaldean poetess we know of . . . described as a pious lady, illiterate, passably instructed in religious matters, but able to compose original verses" (Mengozzi, *Religious Poetry*, CSCO 628/Scr. Syr. 241, xxi–xxii). He includes her vivid *dorekta*, "On the Famine in the Year 1898," in his collection *Religious Poetry* (CSCO 627/Scr. Syr. 240, 67–82 for the Syriac; CSCO 628/Scr. Syr. 241, 79–93 for the English). Similarly, Heleen

Murre-van den Berg has stressed the importance of women as patrons and commissioners of liturgical books in East Syriac communities of the early modern period; see Murre-van den Berg, *Scribes and Scriptures*, 130–131. Such evidence flags what we are missing. I discuss further at the end of chapter 3, in the section "Sounding Voices: Sensing the Issues."

11. Late antique mosaics in the region of Edessa give ample indication of a lively familiarity with Greek and Roman stories, including their "extracanonical" forms, such as the post-Homeric stories of Achilles pictured in the Zeugma mosaics at Gaziantep, Turkey. See Possekel, "Orpheus"; Önal, *Mosaics*; Ross, *Roman Edessa*.

12. For the deep imprint of Greek and Roman sacred legends on late antique theater and civic culture in the eastern Mediterranean, see Webb, *Demons and Dancers*. For the impact of theater on liturgy, see now Lieber, *Staging the Sacred*. For the pervasive impact of oratorical training, Ludlow, *Art, Craft, and Theology*; Cribiore, *Gymnastics of the Mind*.

13. By the late third century CE, occasional Greek epigraphic evidence names especially beloved or prominent male chanters and liturgical singers. See Page, *The Christian West and Its Singers*, 87, no. 22 (Epitaph of Gaios); and 1–171 for the earliest evidence and development of Christian liturgical singing. I discuss this broader context in chapter 1.

14. Dixon, *Reading Roman Women*. Dixon here includes an astute survey of how feminist scholarship regarding ancient women has developed since the 1970s. The book is useful on multiple levels.

15. Kraemer, *Unreliable Witnesses*.

16. Clark, "The Lady Vanishes"; Clark, "Holy Women, Holy Words"; Clark, "Ideology, History, and the Construction of 'Woman.'"

17. Such perspective is concisely and helpfully mapped in Berger, *Gender Differences*.

18. For complaints on the sounds of lamenting women, see Jacob of Sarug, "On the Partaking," ll. 157–158 in Harrak, trans., 22–23; Jacob of Sarug, "On the Reposed," ll. 90–114 in Miller, trans., 45–46. For the distracting sound of women's weaving rods: Thomas of Marga, *Book of Governors*, 1.9 in Budge, ed. and trans., 1:29, 2:53. For examples of the sounds of ascetic women chanting their prayers: "Mary of Qidun," sec. 29, trans. in Brock and Harvey, *Holy Women*, 36; "Mary and Euphemia," trans. in Brock and Harvey, *Holy Women*, 126–128; "Shirin," secs. 74–75, trans. in Brock and Harvey, *Holy Women*, 180.

19. Berger, *Gender Differences*, 1–33 is an astute guide; I have already noted works by Kraemer, Clark, and Dixon. More will be cited. Useful studies may also be found in Holmes, *Gender*; and Penner and Vander Stichele, *Mapping Gender*, with its especially perceptive introduction by Burrus, "Mapping as Metamorphosis."

1. SINGING VOICES: WOMEN'S MINISTRY, WOMEN'S AUTHORITY

1. Ephrem, *Hymns on Resurrection* 2.2, 4, 6, 8, 9, where the singing women are termed *nakpatha*, "chaste women"; Brock and Kiraz, ed. and trans., *Select Poems*, 169–179.

2. On the relationship between Christian and Jewish practices of reading scripture at communal gatherings, see Rouwhorst, "The Reading of Scripture." On the biblicization of culture and society at this time, see Krueger, "Christian Piety and Practice."

3. Teresa Berger has argued that traditional scholarship of liturgical study has missed (or occluded) the experiences of many Christians, especially women, because of such focus. Her thesis is wholly substantiated in the case of the Syriac women's choirs. See her two important studies: *Gender Differences* and *Women's Ways of Worship*.

4. Helpful for a broad understanding of religion in the ancient Mediterranean relevant to late antiquity are, e.g., Rives, *Religion in the Roman Empire*; Beard, North, and Price, *Religions of Rome*.

5. Among the most helpful overviews, see Kraemer, *Women's Religions*. For the pre-Christian context of west Asia, see Chatonnet et al., *Femmes, cultures et sociétés*.

6. There has been excellent work on the Greek pre-Christian traditions for women's choirs and religious singing by Stehle, *Performance and Gender*; Goff, *Citizen Bacchae*; and Calame, *Choruses of Young Women*.

7. Kallimachos, *Hymn* 6.119–120 in Clayman, *Callimachus*, 368–371.

8. Power, "The Sound of the Sacred," esp. 26–27.

9. Ingalls, "Ritual Performance"; Calame, *Choruses of Young Women*, 221–244.

10. See, e.g., Dillon, *Girls and Women*, 212–215; *Homeric Hymns* 1.56.

11. Pausanias, *Description of Greece*, Elis 1.20.2–3; Plutarch, *Greek Questions* 36.299; Diodorus Siculus, *Library of History* 4.3.2–5. Multiple examples are included in the texts collected in Kraemer, *Women's Religions*, 12–65; and Lefkowitz and Fant, *Women's Life in Greece and Rome*, 353–390. Stehle, *Performance and Gender*; Goff, *Citizen Bacchae*; Calame, *Choruses of Young Women*; and Dillon, *Girls and Women* all contain copious examples.

12. Stehle, *Performance and Gender*, 26–118, is especially important on this point. Also noteworthy is Kowalzig, *Singing for the Gods*.

13. Stehle, *Performance and Gender*, 17–22 and 69–73; Goff, *Citizen Bacchae*, 85–98.

14. Beard, North, and Price, *Religions of Rome*, 70–71, 203, 296–299.

15. Beard, North, and Price, *Sourcebook*, 139–145, at 143.

16. Hanninen, "Juna Regina and the Roman Matrons."

17. Harland, *Associations, Synagogues, and Congregations*, esp. 44–52, 72–73, 107, 124, attempts to identify the presence of female participants, as far as the evidence enables. Van Nijf, *Professional Associations*, 165–170, and Price, *Rituals and Power*, e.g., 70 and 209, consider some of the same evidence (particularly Pergamum) without discussing gender, or else presuming male participants.

18. Pliny, *Letters* 10.96 in Radice, ed. and trans., 2:284–291.

19. In addition to the sources already cited, Robin Lane Fox provides lively descriptions of cultic events in his *Pagans and Christians*, e.g., 64–101.

20. Especially important here is Horbury, "Women in the Synagogue." Horbury is attuned to the significance of musical participation, and offers astute, insightful interpretation of the evidence.

21. On Miriam leading the women's singing: Horbury, "Women in the Synagogue," 379 and n58; on Philo's considerable attention to the incident: Kraemer, *Unreliable Witnesses*, 83–109. It is interesting that Miriam's prophetic voice—as distinct from her singing voice—seemed to carry problems for rabbinic authors; see Siquans, "She Dared to Reprove Her Father."

22. Reif, "The Early Liturgy of the Synagogue."

23. The literature is extensive. For Qumran, there is much helpful material in Chazon, *Liturgical Perspectives*; for the early synagogues, see Fine, *Sacred Realm*. For the relation between these locales and the Jerusalem temple, including the matters of singing and prayer, see Cohen, "The Temple and the Synagogue."

24. Philo, "On the Contemplative Life" sec. 8–11 in Colson, ed. and trans., 150–169.

25. See now Kraemer, *Unreliable Witnesses*, 57–116.

26. A point noted in the insightful discussion by Wilson, "Early Christian Music."

27. Horbury, "Women in the Synagogue," 375–388 and 398–399, rightly stresses the significance of this broader cultural context.

28. Above all, see Levine, *The Ancient Synagogue*. Yet, in chapter 14, "Women in the Synagogue" (499–519), Levine does not consider the evidence for hymnody or sung prayer at all. In this respect, the essays by Horbury, "Women in the Synagogue," and Reif, "The Early Liturgy of the Synagogue," cited above, remain perspicacious models for considering the liturgical evidence.

29. On the emergence of piyyut: Fleischer, "Piyyut"; Van Bekkum, "Hebrew Liturgical Poetry." On the significant comparative issues: Münz-Manor, "Liturgical Poetry."

30. On the structural elements that may suggest congregational or choral responses in the piyyutim, see the groundbreaking work by Laura Lieber: "Rhetoric of Participation"; "With One Voice"; "Call and Response." Ahuvia, *On My Right Michael*, 118–142, reads the tenuous evidence in its most positive terms.

31. The pioneering work of Brooten, *Women Leaders*, does not include a category for choirs or singers. Similarly, the plentiful scholarship on early Christian women's offices rarely takes liturgical singing into account. See, e.g., Eisen, *Women Officeholders*; Madigan and Osiek, *Ordained Women*. The categories used in these instances do not include singing as a classification or an indicator.

32. Reif, "The Early Liturgy of the Synagogue," esp. 339–347. Although dealing with a later period, Taitz, "Kol Ishah—The Voice of Woman," is relevant for highlighting the importance of Jewish women's singing in domestic and civic contexts, for childbirth, weddings, and funerals, and for considering lullabies, children's songs, work songs, and lamentation. All were forms of religious singing, and all contributed to the ritual life of the worshipping community as a whole, a point underscored in Shelemay, "The Power of Silent Voices," and Shelemay, *Let Jasmine Rain Down*. Yet again, the foundational work of Hauptman, *Rereading the Rabbis*, does not include women's singing in its discussions, even in chapter 10 ("Ritual," at 221–243), where one might have expected it.

33. See Rives, *Religion in the Roman Empire*, 4–7, 13–53, presenting in compelling terms why he chose to use the term "religion" (singular) for his book. For a cogent statement in terms of music, see Page, *The Christian West and Its Singers*, e.g., at 42: "The musical legacy of the synagogue, whatever it may have been, should be assessed with the mounting evidence that Jews and Christians in many Mediterranean cities maintained some forms of festive and cultic contact into at least the fourth century.... The history of Christian negotiations with any music used when Jews assembled as Jews in their gatherings or 'synagogues' is not necessarily a story of influence followed by independent Christian development; we should be looking instead for an evolving relationship in the matter of ritual singing between sibling commitments during some four hundred years."

34. Such was the profoundly influential view of Quasten, "Liturgical Singing"; Quasten, *Music and Worship*, 75–86. At the same time, Quasten's scholarship demonstrated the prevalence of women and girls singing in religious contexts across the ancient Mediterranean, as explored in the more recent scholarship cited above. One sees the impact of Quasten's characterization in scholarship such as MacMullen, *The Second Church*, 15; or Moss, "Severus of Antioch on Gender," 265–270.

35. See especially Webb, *Demons and Dancers*.

36. As Suzanne Dixon has pointed out for Roman sources, depictions of women in ancient sources must always be evaluated with a view to literary genre, rhetorical convention, and rhetorical strategy (Dixon, *Reading Roman Women*). Also important here is Knust, *Abandoned to Lust*, esp. 15–50; Drake, *Slandering the Jew*, esp. 78–98.

37. Tertullian, *Spectacles* 10.2, trans. Arbesmann et al., 73.

38. Tertullian, *To His Wife* 2.6, trans. Le Saint, 31.

39. Tertullian, *To His Wife*, 2.8, trans. Le Saint, 35.

40. E.g., John Chrysostom, "Against the Jews, Oration 1" in Mayer and Allen, trans., *John Chrysostom*, 148–167. This homily begins with John's praise for his own congregation when their devotional fervor turned the liturgy into a theater resounding with joyous acclamations.

41. E.g., John Chrysostom, "After the Remains of Martyrs" in Mayer and Allen, trans., *John Chrysostom*, 85–92; "On Martyrs" in Mayer and Allen, trans., *John Chrysostom*, 93–97, where John warns against Christian celebration getting out of hand. On boisterous Christian misbehavior, see Taft, *Through Their Own Eyes*, 29–131; Sheerin, *The Eucharist*, 319–348.

42. Basil of Caesarea, Homily 14.1 in Holman and DelCogliano, trans., 83–84.

43. For excellent discussion of gendered tropes for invective, see Knust, *Abandoned to Lust*, 15–50, including the association of music and sexual promiscuity at 38–39 and attendant endnotes.

44. Livy, *History of Rome* 39.8–18 (spread of Bacchic rites to Rome) in Yardley, ed. and trans., 11:228–261; and Livy, *History of Rome* 29.14 (arrival of the Great Mother to Rome) in Yardley, ed. and trans., 8:242–247.

45. See Beard, North, and Price, *Sourcebook*, 298; Wilson, "Early Christian Music."

46. For an illuminating musical analysis of Philo's depiction, see Jeffrey, "Philo's Impact on Christian Psalmody."

47. Eusebios, *History of the Church* 7.29–30 in Schott, trans., 372–380.

48. Eusebios, *History of the Church* 7.30.10 in Schott, trans., 377.

49. Methodios of Olympos, *Symposium* in Musurillo, trans. 150–157.

50. Horbury, "Women in the Synagogue," 380, 383, 387, 398–399, stresses this point very effectively. Both Ephrem and Jacob of Sarug identify the place and role of women's choirs in exactly these terms of ordered arrangement of the entire community of worship: Ephrem, *Hymns on Resurrection* 2.9; Jacob of Sarug, *Against the Jews* 7.528–542. The notion of *taxis* (order) is the fundamental reasoning by which Robert Taft accounts for the gendered elements of Byzantine liturgical practice: Taft, "Women at Church," esp. 79–86.

51. See now the magisterial discussion in Page, *The Christian West and Its Singers*, 9–87. Page expands on the still indispensable collection of McKinnon, *Music*. Both give only limited attention to Syriac sources. Also helpful is Cosgrove, "Clement of Alexandria and Early Christian Music."

52. Lattke, *Odes of Solomon*; Charlesworth, *The Earliest Christian Hymnbook*. Portions survive also in Greek, Coptic, and Latin. There is still no agreement on their original language, provenance, or date, although scholars generally agree on the second century. Sebastian Brock has commented on the significant differences in poetic form, as compared with the abundant wealth of poetry otherwise extant in Syriac, in Brock, "Poetry and Hymnography (3): Syriac." For the critical edition of the Syriac, see Charlesworth, *Odes of Solomon*.

53. E.g., Odes 6.1, 12.1, 16.1–2, 18.1–3, 21.1–4, 26.1–4, 35.5–6, 40.1–4.

54. Varghese, *Early History*, 22–33.

55. Münz-Manor, "Liturgical Poetry"; Page, *The Christian West and Its Singers*, 9–198.

56. In general, see Bradshaw, *Origins of Christian Worship*; Bradshaw and Johnson, *Feasts, Fasts, and Seasons*.

57. Leonhard, "Which Hymns Were Sung?" makes the point that the composition and chanting of literarily sophisticated hymns followed the creation of large-scale, public forms of Christian liturgy.

58. Page, *The Christian West and Its Singers*, 89–171. See also Ravolainen, *The Singer in the Ecclesiastical Hierarchy*.

59. See Vööbus, *Didascalia*; and Vööbus, *The [West Syrian] Synodicon*, which includes canons from the *Testament of Our Lord*, Hippolytus, the *Apostolic Constitutions*, and other early canon collections circulating in Greek and Latin, in addition to more localized Syriac canons.

60. Especially important are Madigan and Osiek, *Ordained Women in the Early Church*; Eisen, *Women Officeholders in Early Christianity*. Important historical context is provided in Chryssavgis et al., *Deaconesses*; see also Martimort, *Les diaconesses*.

61. For the Syriac developments, see Jajé, *Diaconesses*; Brock, "Deaconesses."

62. Especially helpful here is Penn, "'Bold and Having No Shame.'"

63. Vööbus, *Didascalia*, ch. XIV–XV, XVIII, vol. 1, CSCO 402/Scr. Syr. 176, 141–155, 162–167. Canons related to widows are also given in those from the *Testament of the Lord*, in Vööbus, *The [West Syrian] Synodicon*, vol. 1, CSCO 368/Scr. Syr. 162, at 34–35, 39, 42, 43–45, 50, 56, 57, 61. The criteria for appointment and the prayer of consecration are given at 43–45.

64. The discussion on the female diaconate is now critically enhanced by Pylvänäinen, *Agents in Liturgy*. Pylvänäinen's discussion, at 58–72, of literary genre and the nature of these churches' orders (or compilations) as "living literature" is especially helpful. For the Syriac, see further Jajé, *Diaconesses*; Brock, "Deaconesses"; Harvey, "Women's Service."

65. Vööbus, *Didascalia*, ch. IX, vol. 1, CSCO 402/Scr. Syr. 176, 100. See the discussion of terminology in Brock, "Deaconesses," 204–205.

66. Pylvänäinen, *Agents in Liturgy*, 196–205, offers insightful discussion of this analogy.

67. See Harvey, "Feminine Imagery for the Divine"; Brock, "The Holy Spirit as Feminine."

68. E.g., Vööbus, *Didascalia*, ch. XVI, vol. 1, CSCO 402/Scr. Syr. 176, 155–158. Detailed discussion is found in Brock, "Deaconesses"; Jajé, *Diaconesses*. The Syriac terminology for ordination can be confusing, as different terms were used with different senses ("laying on of hands," "ordination," "consecration"). For the service in the current Syrian Orthodox *Penqitho* (2009), see Varghese, *Ordination*, 16–39, 94–95. As for other Orthodox churches, there is considerable debate and discussion at present about whether and how to revitalize the order of deaconesses: Jajé, *Diaconesses*, 105–108; Pylvänäinen, *Agents in Liturgy*, 15–17; Chryssavgis et al., *Deaconesses*, passim.

69. Various sources in the canonical collections for both the West and East Syriac churches contain canons for the deaconesses. For the West Syriac canons, see Vööbus, *The [West Syrian] Synodicon*; for the East, Chabot, *Synodicon Orientale*. See also Hélou, "Les diaconesses moniales." For the Byzantine tradition, see Chryssavgis et al., *Deaconesses*; Karras, "Female Deacons."

70. I discuss the current practice for women's offices in the Syriac Orthodox Church in the afterword.

71. Tavolieri, "Una vita tra silenzio e canto."

72. The term "office," often used to interpret the sons and daughters of the covenant as a designation, suggests a clearer institutional identity than the early evidence supports. Scholars should resist anachronistic notions of ecclesiastical roles and titles especially in handling fourth-century evidence, but thereafter as well.

73. The literature on the covenanters is extensive; further references follow below. For close attention to the early evidence, see Griffith, "Monks, 'Singles', and the 'Sons of the Covenant'"; Murray, "Circumcision of the Heart"; Nedungatt, "Covenanters," 191–215, 419–444.

74. Aphrahat, *Demonstration* 6, "On the Covenanters" in Lehto, trans., 169–198.

75. E.g., John of Dalyatha, *Letter* 4.2, 18.28 in Hansbury, trans., 20, 92; Becker, *Fear of God*, 86.

76. For Aphrahat in context, and particularly his notion of the vow or "yoke" of holiness: Bumazhnov, "Qyama Before Aphrahat"; Koltun-Fromm, *Hermeneutics of Holiness*, esp. 129–174; Koltun-Fromm, "Yokes of the Holy-Ones."

77. Aphrahat, *Demonstration* 6.2 in Lehto, trans., 177.

78. Aphrahat, *Demonstration* 6.6 in Lehto, trans., 182.

79. Aphrahat, *Demonstration* 6.6 in Lehto, trans., 183.

80. Aphrahat, *Demonstration* 6.6 in Lehto, trans., 181.

81. Aphrahat, *Demonstration* 6.7 in Lehto, trans., 183–184.

82. The earliest examples would be references to the persecution of sons and daughters of the covenant in the martyrdoms of Shmona and Guria, sec. 1, sec. 70 in Burkitt, trans., 90, 109; and daughters of the covenant named and unnamed in the early acts of the Persian martyrs, set during the reign of Shapur II in the mid-fourth century: some are collected in Brock and Harvey, *Holy Women*, 63–82. Similar incidents are cited for later military atrocities as well: a sixth-century account of an attack of Huns on Edessa recalled in the anonymous *Life of Ephrem*, ch. 36 (on this episode, see Amar, CSCO 630/Scr. Syr. 243, 92n1); the sixth-century Najran martyrs on the Arabian peninsula, also collected in Brock and Harvey, *Holy Women*, 100–121; an incident listed for 773–774 CE in the *Chronicle of Zuqnin* in Harrak, trans., 302.

83. The account of the Forty Martyrs of Beth Kashkraye under Shapur II lists (with their names) two bishops, sixteen priests, nine deacons, six sons of the covenant, and seven daughters of the covenant: Harvey et al., *Three Persian Martyr Acts*, 84–85.

84. E.g., (Ps.-)Joshua the Stylite, *Chronicle*, ch. 36 and ch. 100 in Trombley and Watt, trans., 35 and 117, respectively. Such a list could, of course, be employed as a literary convention; undoubtedly, this could be the case in some of the texts in notes 82–83 above. However, I would argue that the point holds for the earliest of the texts, the Edessan martyrs and the earliest of the Persian acts. And whether a historical fact or a trope of memory that served to imbue collective suffering with liturgical meaning, these lists nonetheless signaled a public visibility for covenanters, with civic connotations.

85. Russell, "Betrothed of Christ," argues for nuanced awareness of the issues in the Zoroastrian context.

86. "Martyrdom of Martha," trans. in Brock and Harvey, *Holy Women*, 67–73 (Syriac edited in Bedjan, *AMS*, 2:233–241).

87. "Martyrdom of Martha," trans. in Brock and Harvey, *Holy Women*, 68 (Syriac edited in Bedjan, *AMS*, 2:234).

88. Ephrem, *Memre on Nicomedia* 8.553–570 and 667–678 in Renoux, ed. and trans., Éphrem de Nisibe, 146–147 and 152–155, respectively.

89. Ephrem, *Hymns in Armenian* 46 in Mariès and Mercier, trans., 214–217; English translation in Murray, "A Marriage for All Eternity," 65–69. For the influence of the Syriac covenanters on the development of Armenian Christianity, see Zakarian, *Women, Too, Were Blessed.*

90. Murray, "A Marriage for All Eternity," 68 (commentary on ll. 53–56), notes the similarity between this hymn and Aphrahat's *Demonstration* 6.1 in their allusions to the parable of the wise and foolish virgins in Mt 25:1–13, "applying it precisely to consecrated virgins and understanding the wedding feast as the general resurrection."

91. E.g., Ephrem, *Hymns on the Nativity* 4.62b-63, 22, N23; *Hymns on Resurrection* 2.2, 4, 6, 8, 9.

92. Ephrem, *Hymns on Virginity* 25.17 in McVey, trans., 374. See also, e.g., Ephrem, *Hymns on Virginity* 1–3 and *Hymns on the Nativity* 12.

93. *Hymns on Resurrection* 2.2, 4, 7 in Brock and Kiraz, eds. and trans., *Select Poems*, 171, 173, 175, respectively.

94. *Hymns on Resurrection* 2.2, 7, 8, 9.

95. Ephrem, *Hymns on the Nativity* 22.1, G9 in McVey, trans., 179, 181.

96. Ephrem, *Hymns on the Nativity* 4.62b in McVey, trans., 94.

97. The most influential presentation of this view was Vööbus, *Celibacy.*

98. Recalibration of Vööbus's argument began in earnest with Murray, "Exhortation to Candidates." See further the studies noted above, notes 73 and 76, and below, note 116.

99. From this perspective, there appears a certain parallel with the Jewish *Ma'amadot* during the Second Temple period: a group of men who stood (*ma'amad*, "in standing position") in representation of the local community at the Jerusalem temple; and who stood to read Torah, representing the Jerusalem liturgy, in the local synagogue. See Tabory, "Ma'amadot."

100. See now the commentary, edition, and translation by Phenix and Horn, "Commandments and Admonitions for the Priests and the Children of the Covenant," xcvii–cxiii, ccii–ccxiv, ccxxi–ccxxix, 102–117, in their volume *Rabbula Corpus* (hereafter cited as "Canons for Priests and Covenanters"). See also Vööbus, *Syriac and Arabic Documents*, 34–50 ("The Rules of Rabbula for the Clergy and the Qeiama"). Closely related, but separate, are Rabbula canons for monks in Phenix and Horn, *Rabbula Corpus*, 94–101, and Vööbus, *Syriac and Arabic Documents*, 24–33. These do not mention the covenanters, although the canons for clergy and covenanters include rules regarding monastics and monasteries.

101. "Canons for Priests and Covenanters," in Phenix and Horn, eds. and trans., *Rabbula Corpus*: canons 3 and 4 at 103; canon 20 at 107; canon 27 at 109. As noted by Phenix and Horn (at 197n18) the canon is ambiguous in its wording as to whether or not the daughters of the covenant were to also sing the Psalms. However, subsequently "Maruta Canons" 41.2 makes this clear; Vööbus, trans., CSCO 440/Scr. Syr. 192, 72.

102. "The Life of Rabbula," bilingual edition in Phenix and Horn, eds. and trans., *Rabbula Corpus*, xxvii–lviii, 2–83. The Phenix and Horn volume is the first scholarly effort to bring together the Rabbula materials as a corpus; their extensive introductory section is helpful. The translation "Heroic Deeds of Mar Rabbula" in Doran, trans., *Stewards of the Poor*, 41–105, also includes insightful commentary.

103. "Life of Rabbula," sections 22–23, 50, 54 in Phenix and Horn, eds. and trans., *Rabbula Corpus*, 36–39, 74–75, 78–79, respectively; "Heroic Deeds of Mar Rabbula," trans. in Doran, *Stewards of the Poor*, 79, 80, 101, 104.

104. *Teaching of Addai* in Howard, trans., 101. I have modified Howard's translation by noting the Syriac terms (Howard's book includes the Syriac edition by George Phillips). Howard's translation does not include a term for *qyama*, nor does he qualify the word "service," whereas *teshmeshta* would normally denote liturgy. This is a very interesting passage in Syriac. The adjectives and nouns are the basic technical vocabulary for the ascetic life, strongly in place by the early fifth century.

105. Burkitt, "Early Syriac Lectionary System," 301–339. On this important source, see now Rouwhorst, "Epiphany."

106. Burkitt, "Early Syriac Lectionary System," 312, 320.

107. Jacob of Sarug, "On the Death of a Bart Qyama," in Bedjan and Brock, eds., *Homilies of Mar Jacob*, 5:821–836. On this homily, see Kitchen, "Pearl of Virginity."

108. Jacob, "On the Death of a Bart Qyama," sec. 5 in Bedjan and Brock, eds., *Homilies of Mar Jacob*, 5:826–827.

109. Robert Kitchen, "Pearl of Virginity," notes that Jacob's homily shares a number of prominent themes and images with a burial service for nuns copied in eastern Turkey in 1980, edited and translated in Brock, *Burial Service for Nuns*.

110. (Ps.-)Ephrem, *Necrosima* 33. The *Necrosima* are a collection of eighty-five burial hymns wrongly ascribed to Ephrem. The generic, even stereotypical content of these hymns in no way masks the poignancy of the occasions for their use. Indeed, their lack of high artistry speaks to their utility and accessibility, at the ready in any instance. Found in Assemani, "Necrosima, seu Funebres Canones"; a partial translation of the collection is offered in Burgess, *Select Metrical Hymns and Homilies*. *Necrosima* 33 was not included in Burgess's volume. I am grateful to Maria Doerfler for bringing this material to my attention and discussing her own research with me at length. See Doerfler, "Translating Eve."

111. See the discerning discussion in Doerfler, "Translating Eve," esp. 178–179 on *Necrosima* 33.

112. Wolff, "Drei Begräbnisgesänge Narsais," at 20–21.

113. Brock, *Burial Service for Nuns*, 17 (madrasha 11.4).

114. Covenanter status sometimes appeared in legal texts. The official records of the Second Council of Ephesos in 449 include a report by the governor, Chaereas of Osrhoene, on recent riots in the city of Edessa, during which public acclamations were performed by the city in its ranks, including daughters of the covenant. A number of those interviewed for the report were identified as covenanters. For discussion and translation, see Doran, *Stewards of the Poor*, 109–188, esp. 148, 159, 166, 167, 168. The Syriac version of the Acts is edited in Flemming, *Akten der Ephesinischen Synode*.

115. One has to wonder about enslaved women identified as daughters of the covenant. The Persian martyr Tarbo, a daughter of the covenant, had an unnamed servant "also a daughter of the covenant, and who had been instructed by Tarbo in the excellent teaching of Christ" (Brock and Harvey, *Holy Women*, 73). Did this enslaved woman choose this vocation? Was her purpose to accompany Tarbo in her public ministries, including liturgical singing, for reasons of social decorum or protection?

116. See especially Stewart, "Ascetic Taxonomy"; Elm, *Virgins of God*, 25–59, 137–83.

117. "Canons for Priests and Covenanters," canons 28, 29 in Phenix and Horn, eds. and trans., *Rabbula Corpus*, 108–111. Compare John Chrysostom, "Treatises on the Subintroductae," also in the late fourth century; and see Leyerle, *Theatrical Shows and Ascetic Lives*.

118. On the philoponoi, see, above all, Wipszycka, "Les confrèries." There is close association with the *spoudaioi*. See Pétridès, "Spoudæi et Philopones." Again, the tradition of the Maʿamadot comes to mind, as an analogous form of devotion and service, liturgically expressed: Tabory, "Maʿamadot."

119. Wipszycka, "Les confrèries," also finds the evidence for the philoponoi falling largely between the fourth and ninth centuries, analogous to that for the covenanters. At 514, she discusses the importance of their liturgical participation.

120. Various of the Persian Martyr Acts from the fifth or sixth century seem to use the terminology of sons and daughters of the covenant to indicate monastic communities; the distinction is not always clear. In the case of Mar Pinhas, the terms are used together (in sec. 14) for the same woman—she is termed *dayrayatha* and *bart qyama*—and also for her companions (in McCollum, ed. and trans., *Mar Pinhas*, 16–17). Geoffrey Herman chooses to translate *bar qyama* as "monk" in his collection *Persian Martyr Acts*: e.g., at 2–3 for the martyr Narseh, and at 42–43 in the account of the martyrs of Beth Garmai; Mar Tataq enters a *dayra* (monastery), at 28–29.

121. John of Ephesos, *Lives*, ch. 16 (Brooks, ed. and trans., *PO* 17, 246–247). Stressing the liturgical over and against the monastic, see Pierre, "Les 'membres de l'ordre'"; Harvey, "Revisiting the Daughters of the Covenant"; Tabé, "Les bnay wa bnoth Qyomo"; Macina, "Les bnay et bnat Qyama"; Jargy, "Les 'fils et filles du pacte'"; Fiey, "Cénobitisme féminine ancien."

122. "Canons for Priests and Covenanters," canons 20, 27 in Phenix and Horn, eds. and trans., *Rabbula Corpus*, 106–109.

123. On the translation of *madrasha* as "teaching song," see Palmer, "Merchant of Nisibis."

124. Jacob of Sarug, "On Mar Ephrem," vv. 151–154 in Amar, ed. and trans., 62–65; and *Life of Ephrem*, ch. 31 in Amar, ed. and trans., *Syriac "Vita" Tradition*, CSCO 629/Scr. Syr. 242, 70–74 (Syriac), CSCO 630/Scr. Syr. 243, 76–80 (English).

125. *Life of Ephrem*, ch. 31 in Amar, ed. and trans., *Syriac Vita Tradition*, 77–78 (Syr. in CSCO 629/Scr. Syr. 242, 73).

126. Jacob of Sarug, "On Mar Ephrem," v. 152 in Amar, ed. and trans., 64–65. Varghese, *Early History of the Syriac Liturgy*, 55–60, reads these passages in Jacob of Sarug's homily "On Mar Ephrem" as referring to the singing of laywomen in the liturgy, not choirs. In contrast, I see this memra as consonant with other textual evidence for Syriac women's choirs, particularly given its close correspondence to the passage on Ephrem's recruitment of the daughters of the covenant in the *Life of Ephrem*, ch. 31. I fully concur that the singing participation of laywomen was important in ancient Syriac worship, and address it below, especially in chapters 5 and 6.

127. Jacob of Sarug, "On the Partaking," l. 131 in Harrak, ed. and trans., 18.

128. Jacob of Sarug, "On Mar Ephrem," vv. 99–101 in Amar, trans., 48–49. Compare the *Life of Ephrem*, ch. 31.

129. Vööbus, trans., "Maruta Canons," 26.1–4, in CSCO 439/Scr. Syr. 191, 76 (Syriac), CSCO 440/Scr. Syr. 192, 65 (English).

130. Vööbus, trans., "Maruta Canons," 26.1–4, in CSCO 439/Scr. Syr. 191, 76 (Syriac), CSCO 440/Scr. Syr. 192, 65 (English).

131. Vööbus, trans., "Maruta Canons," 41.1–3, in CSCO 439/Scr. Syr. 191, 85 (Syriac), CSCO 440/Scr. Syr. 192, 72 (English).

132. E.g., "Maruta Canons," 41.3, in CSCO 440/Scr. Syr. 192, 72. Compare the *Synod of Mar George I* in 676 CE, canon 9: Chabot, ed. and trans., *Synodicon Orientale*, 221–222 (Syriac), 486 (French).

133. Vööbus, trans., "Canons of Johannon bar Qursos," canon 27, in CSCO 368/Scr. Syr. 162, 151.

134. Chabot, ed. and trans., *Synodicon Orientale*, 221–222 (Syriac) and 486 (French).

135. See the account of the education of Bar ʿIdta, under the supervision of his sister Hanah-Isho, herself a nun, in Budge, ed. and trans., "The Life of Bar-ʿIdtâ," ll. 59–135.

136. Becker, *Fear of God*, esp. 88–93 on the important place of liturgical music in this training. Also important are Possekel, "'Go and Set Up for Yourselves Beautiful Laws'"; Possekel, "Selbstverständnis und Bildungsauftrag."

137. Becker, *Fear of God*, 163–166. Becker argues persuasively for a typology of East Syriac schools in three categories: independent schools, monastic schools, and village schools (155–168). But there was also disagreement in Syriac monastic circles as to music's value: Tavolieri, "Body and Soul."

138. Tavolieri, "Una vita tra silenzio e canto."

139. John of Ephesos, *Lives*, ch. 16 in Brooks, ed. and trans., *PO* 17, 229–247, esp. 246–247.

140. On women's literacy in ancient Christianity, see now Haines-Eitzen, *The Gendered Palimpsest*; Brown, "Psalmody and Socrates." Specifically on the literacy and training necessary for Byzantine choir nuns, see Garland, "'Til Death Do Us Part?'"

141. John of Ephesos, *Lives*, ch. 12, trans. in Brock and Harvey, *Holy Women*, 122–133, esp. 126, 128, 129.

142. John of Ephesos, *Lives*, ch. 54 in Brooks, ed. and trans., *PO* 19, 185–191. Some of Caesaria's correspondence is included in Severus, *The Sixth Book of Select Letters*. One of Severos's letters to Caesaria is preserved in the *The [West Syrian] Synodicon*, ed. and trans. Vööbus, CSCO 367/Scr. Syr. 161, 143–145 (Syriac), CSCO 368/Scr. Syr. 162, 141–142 (English) (Document 17).

143. Sahdona (Martyrios), "Shirin," *Book of Perfection*, 69–79, trans. in Brock and Harvey, *Holy Women*, 177–181.

144. An especially prominent theme in the *Life of Febronia*, trans. in Brock and Harvey, *Holy Women*, 150–176. For this aspect of Syriac women's monasticism, see Jullien, "Le monaschisme feminine"; Hélou, "La vie monastique féminine."

145. Burris and Van Rompay, "Thecla in Syriac Christianity"; Burris, "The Syriac 'Book of Women'"; Van Rompay, "*No Evil Word About Her.*"

146. Wright, *Catalogue of Syriac Manuscripts*, 2:651a–652a (no. 731). The manuscript also included the *Life of Rabbula*, as well as two of his canon collections and the sermon he preached in Constantinople. These sources, too, would be suitable for female monastic readers, since Rabbula's *Life* and his canons gave important attention to the daughters of the covenant (as discussed above).

147. *The Life of Bar-ʿIdtâ*, ll. 59–120 in Budge, ed. and trans., 9–10.

148. Compare the accounts in the *Life of John Bar-Aphtonia* in Nau, ed. and trans.; "Life of John of Tella by the Monk Elijah," in Brooks, ed. and trans., CSCO 7–8/Scr. Syr. 7–8; CSCO 7/ Scr. Syr. 7, 29–95, at 39–45 (Syriac), and CSCO 8/Scr. Syr. 8, 21–60, at 27–31 (Latin); Thomas of Marga, *The Book of Governors*, in Budge, ed. and trans, 1:116–117 (Syriac),

2:251–252 (English). For comparative rabbinic evidence, see Marks, "Bayit versus Beit Midrash."

149. Vööbus, trans. "Maruta Canons," canon 58, in CSCO 440/Scr. Syr. 192, 85.

150. "Life of Rabbula," sec. 22, 23, 25 in Phenix and Horn, eds. and trans., *Rabbula Corpus*, 36–41.

151. Vööbus, *Syriac and Arabic Documents*, 35.

152. Vööbus, *The [West Syrian] Synodicon*, CSCO 368/Scr. Syr. 162, 11–12.

153. "Further Canons of Jaʿqob of Edessa [Jacob of Edessa]," canon 22, in Vööbus, ed. and trans., *The [West Syrian] Synodicon*. CSCO 367/Scr. Syr. 161, 272 (Syriac); and CSCO 368/Scr. Syr. 162, 247 (English).

154. Pseudo-George of Arbela, as cited by Mateos, *Lelya-Sapra*, 408; on the women's choirs, citing East Syriac sources, see Mateos, *Leyla-Sapra*, 408–410.

155. Again, especially helpful on the religious presence of female voices in ancient civic life are Stehle, *Performance and Gender*; Goff, *Citizen Bacchae*; and Calame, *Choruses of Young Women*.

156. Quasten, "Liturgical Singing"; Quasten, *Music and Worship*, 75–86. Berger, *Women's Ways of Worship*, 59–60, reads Quasten with nuance and suggests that the historical record shows women's liturgical singing to have been a contested issue in late antiquity, even while continuing in different forms.

157. Eusebios, *History of the Church* 7.29–30 in Schott, trans., 372–380.

158. Cyril of Jerusalem, *Procatechesis*, sec. 14 in McKinnon, *Music*, 75–76 (no. 154).

159. Isidore of Pelusium, *Ep.* 1.90 in McKinnon, *Music*, 61 (no. 121); Jerome, *Dial. c. pel.* 1.25 in McKinnon, *Music*, 145 (no. 334). Elsewhere, Jerome speaks with warm enthusiasm for women's monastic singing and psalmody in their private chambers: e.g., *Ep.* 54 in McKinnon, *Music*, 141 (no. 320) and *Ep.* 107.12 in McKinnon, *Music*, 142–143 (no. 326).

160. *Cave of Treasures*, XI.8^1; XII.1, 16, 17; XV.1, 3^2; XVIII.15^2; XXVI.14^1. Serge Ruzer suggested to me that there could be an interesting pun here, on the terms *bnat Qaina* (daughters of Cain) and *bnat qyama* (daughters of the covenant).

161. (Ps.-)Athanasios, "On Virginity," sec. 45 in Brakke, trans., CSCO 592/Scr. Syr. 232, 18; CSCO 593/Scr. Syr. 233, 17.

162. Ephrem, *On Fasting* 3.4 in Brock and Kiraz, eds. and trans., *Select Poems*, 100–101; Narsai, *Homily on Creation* 1, ll. 246–249 in Gignoux, ed. and trans., *Homélies de Narsai*, 123 [541].

163. Libanios, *Autobiography*, sec. 22 in Norman, ed. and trans., *Libanius*, 78–79.

164. Jerome, *Ep.* 54, as cited in Quasten, *Music*, 127.

165. Severos of Antioch, *Homily* 83 (xv.419), as cited in Cuming, "Liturgy of Antioch," 96. See now Moss, "Severus of Antioch on Gender."

166. E.g., Ambrose, *Explan. Ps.* 1.9 in McKinnon, *Music*, 126–127 (no. 276); Ambrose, *De vir. ad Marcelliam* 1.10.60, 3.4.19 in McKinnon, *Music*, 133 (nos. 300–301).

167. Paulinus of Nola, *Poem* 21, ll. 60–83 and 272–277 in Walsh, trans., 175–176, 121–122, respectively.

168. Asterios of Amaseia, *Homily* 4.8.6 in Anderson and Goodspeed, trans., 126. I am grateful to Daniel Caner for drawing my attention to this passage and several others in the present discussion.

169. Victricius of Rouen, *In Praise of Saints*, sec. 5 in Clark, trans., 382.

170. Leontios of Constantinople, *Homily* 2, "On Palm Sunday," 10 [112] in Allen and Datema, trans., 43.

171. Cyril of Skythopolis, "Life of Cyriacus," ch. 18 in Price, trans., 257; Greek in Schwartz, *Kyrillos von Skythopolis*, 233, at ll. 29–33. Price translates the Greek term *psaltria* as "cantor." This tale was one of many variations on the story of Saint Mary of Egypt. For discussion, see Ward, *Harlots of the Desert*, 26–35.

172. Basil, *Ep.* 2.12, 207.3 in McKinnon, *Music*, 68–69 (nos. 138–139); Gregory of Nyssa, *Life of Macrina*, 3, 33 in McKinnon, *Music*, 73–74 (nos. 151–152). See also the anonymous *De virg.*, 20 in McKinnon, *Music*, 74 (no. 153). There is much more in the *Life of Macrina* than McKinnon includes: see Callahan's translation, *Ascetical Works*, 171, 178, 182–183, 186–187. For women's liturgical singing in later Byzantine hagiographic and monastic texts, see Talbot, "The Devotional Life of Laywomen"; Talbot, "Bluestocking Nuns."

173. Gregory of Nyssa, *Life of Macrina*, 182–183, 186–187. Gregory's description of psalmody has elicited a number of insightful scholarly studies: Krueger, "Hagiography as Liturgy"; Rousseau, "The Pious Household"; Burrus, "Gender, Eros, and Pedagogy."

174. Athanasios, "Canons," cited by Brakke, *Athanasius and the Politics of Asceticism*, 27.

175. Jerome, *Ep.* 107.4, 8, 9, 12 in McKinnon, *Music*, 142 (nos. 322–326).

176. Compare (Ps.-)Athanasios, "On Virginity," secs. 8, 11 in Brakke, trans., 305–306.

177. (Ps.-)Athanasios, "On Syncletica" in Castelli, trans., 277, 283. See also, e.g., Gerontios, *Melania the Younger*, 42, 46, 47 in Clark, trans., 56, 59–60; Jerome, *Ep.* 108.20 in McKinnon, *Music*, 143 (no. 327).

178. Psalmody is important in several places in the magisterial hagiography of Matrona of Perge, including for the conversion of pagan girls to Christian monasticism. See especially "Life of Matrona," secs. 2, 36, 38 in Featherstone, trans., *Holy Women of Byzantium*, ed. Talbot, 20, 52–53.

179. Scholarship on the practice of psalmody in Jewish and Christian traditions is vast. Two recent excellent examples would be Daley and Kolbet, *Harp of Prophecy*; and Attridge and Fassler, *Psalms in Community*. For the ascetic practice of psalmody, see the insightful studies by Kolbet, "Athanasius, the Psalms"; Frank, "The Memory Palace of Marcellinus."

180. The terms *psalmoi, hymnoi,* and *odai* in Ephesians 5:19 and Colossians 3:16 were apparently used interchangeably. See Wilson, "Early Christian Music"; Smith, "First-Century Christian Singing"; Smith, "The Ancient Synagogue"; Bastiaensen, "*Psalmi, Hymni,* and *Cantica.*"

181. E.g., John Chrysostom, "After the Remains of Martyrs" in Mayer and Allen, trans., *John Chrysostom*, 90–91; John Chrysostom, "On St. Phocas" 2 in Meyer and Neil, trans., *Saint John Chrysostom*, 78.

182. Theodoret of Cyrrhos, *Ecclesiastical History* 3.19.1–4.

183. Gregory of Nyssa, *Letter* 6.10 in Silva, trans., 142.

184. "Life of Rabbula," sec. 55 in Horn and Phenix, eds. and trans., *Rabbula Corpus*, 80–81.

185. Egeria, *Diary of a Pilgrimage*, 24 in Gingras, trans., 89–93. Key passages are included in McKinnon, *Music*, 112–117 (nos. 242–254), with helpful commentary.

186. I am grateful to Alexander Lingas for his insight on this point. See further Taft, *Through Their Own Eyes*, 29–67, esp. 56–67.

187. Karras, "Female Deacons," esp. 283–285; Karras, "Liturgical Functions"; Karras, "Liturgical Participation," 153–162; and Taft, *Through Their Own Eyes*, 60–67, follow the evidence through to the late Byzantine period. See also Ciggaar, *Western Travelers to Constantinople*, 51.

188. E.g., Mateos, *Typikon de la Grande Église*, 1:4–5, 154–155; 2:52, 287; Arranz, "L'office de l'Asmatikos Hesperinos," 408.

189. Justinian, *Novels*, 3 (preface) and 3.1 in Miller and Sarris, trans., *Novels of Justinian*, 1:76–78. Criteria for the ordination of these women is specified in *Novels* 6.6 in Miller and Sarris, trans., *Novels of Justinian*, 1:105–106. For the Greek: Kroll and Schoell, eds., *Novellae*, vol. 3. See also Lingas, "From Earth to Heaven," 312, 321.

190. Justinian, *Novels* 59.2–4 in Miller and Sarris, trans., *Novels of Justinian*, 1:454–456.

191. In "On the Resurrection (6)," strophe 15, Romanos calls the myrrh-bearing women at the tomb a *choros*. Romanos, Kontakion 29, in Maas and Trypanis, eds., 223–33 (Greek); Lash, trans., *On the Life of Christ*, 167–179. Himself from Syria, Romanos brought strong influence from the Syriac liturgical poets to his own compositions; he was no doubt familiar with the Syriac women's choirs.

192. A number of Greek scholars are now working on this evidence, most importantly Evangelia Spyrakou: *Οι Χοροί Ψαλτών κατά την βυζαντινή*, 182–197; "The Byzantine Choral System Until 1204," 144–156; "Did Women Chant Professionally?" See also Chaldaeakes, "The 'Woman Figure.'" I am grateful to Sevi Mazera-Mamali for introducing me to this scholarship.

193. (Ps.-)Zachariah Rhetor, *Chronicle* 4.11.b in Greatrex et al., trans., 152; Taft, *Through Their Own Eyes*, 61; Lingas, "From Earth to Heaven," 312–313.

194. Sources for the Myrrophores are distressingly rare. See Ernst, *Martha from the Margins*, esp. 152–158.

195. Anna Komnena, *Alexiad* 15.7, trans. Sewter and Frankopan, 452–455.

196. *Timarion*, sec. 10 in Baldwin, trans., 48–49. See also Lingas, "Sunday Matins," 188–190. Important for the larger context of women's presence and roles in Byzantine liturgy is Taft, "Women at Church."

197. Consider Radle, "The Veiling of Women," 1074–1075, which cites a frequent prayer from medieval Byzantine manuscripts that refers to women who, "covering the head, adorn themselves in good works and bring hymns and prayers to [the Lord's] glory with modesty and sobriety."

198. Page, *The Christian West and Its Singers*, 89–115.

199. Page, *The Christian West and Its Singers*, 131–154.

200. Ravolainen, *The Singer in the Ecclesiastical Hierarchy*, 107–158.

201. "Rules of Hippolytus/Simon the Canaanite" in Vööbus, ed. and trans., *The [West Syrian] Synodicon*, CSCO 368/Scr. Syr. 162, 85 (English); CSCO 367/Scr. Syr. 161, 73–74 (Syriac).

202. On the early canonical prescriptions for singers circulating in Greek and Latin, see Page, *The Christian West and Its Singers*, 89–174; Ravolainen, *The Singer in the Ecclesiastical Hierarchy*, 91–210. Also helpful is the account of these rulings as they became part of subsequent Byzantine canon law and liturgical commentaries in Moran, *Singers*, 14–50.

203. As noted, I will discuss madrashe more specifically in chapter 3. For the basic literary forms, see Brock, "Poetry and Hymnography (3): Syriac"; Griffith, "'Denominationalism'"; Rouwhorst, "Hymns and Prayers."

2. SINGING WOMEN: PORTRAITS AND MEANINGS

1. As noted in chapter 1, historians have often focused on the negative statements or portraits, without attending to the positive ones. The continuing reliance on Quasten's seminal article, "Liturgical Singing," is the strongest indication of this. See, e.g., MacMullen, *The Second Church*, 15; Page, *The Christian West and Its Singers*, 5; Moss, "Severus of Antioch on Gender," 265–270. In this same study, Quasten cited the Syriac evidence as indicative of the practice of women's choirs in some areas, but considered it unilateral, unrepresentative, and insignificant.

2. The methodological issues straddle late antique rhetorical habits and also literary conventions for the representation of women. See, e.g., Cameron, *History as Text*; Dixon, *Reading Roman Women*; Kraemer, *Unreliable Witnesses*.

3. Ephrem, *Hymns on Resurrection* 2.8, here citing the translation by Sidney H. Griffith, in McKinnon, *Music*, 93. See also the translation in Brock and Kiraz, *Select Poems*, 174–177.

4. Ephrem, *Hymns on Resurrection* 2.8–9, trans. Griffith, in McKinnon, ed., *Music*, 93–94.

5. Ephrem, *Hymns on Virginity* 5.10 in McVey, trans., 284 (adjusted for clarity).

6. Ephrem, *Hymns on the Nativity* 22, N23 in McVey, trans., 183; the refrain is on 180.

7. Ephrem, *Hymns on Heresies* 2.6 in Beck, ed. and trans., *Hymnen contra Haereses*, CSCO 169/Scr. Syr. 73, 7 (Syriac), CSCO 170/Scr. Syr. 74, 8 (German).

8. Ephrem, *Hymns on the Nativity* 4.62–63 in McVey, trans., 93.

9. Ephrem himself seems to have made a collection of Nativity hymns he titled "lullabies," depicting Mary's songs to her newborn son. Starting in the sixth century, editors added other Marian hymns by Ephrem, eventually bringing the collection to twenty-eight in total; hymns 5–20 in the present collection are those compiled by Ephrem. McVey argues for authenticity of the entire cycle, with the final hymn as a composite of Ephrem's verses. See the discussion in McVey, *Ephrem the Syrian*, 29; Beck, *Des Heiligen Ephraem des Syrers Hymnen de Nativitate*, CSCO 187/Scr. Syr. 83, v–vi.

10. Passages in first-person speech for Mary: Ephrem, *Hymns on Nativity* 2.7, 5.19–24, 6.1–6, 9.4–16, 15 (entire), 16.1–14, 17 (entire), 19 (entire). We have no direct evidence for performance, other than Ephrem's own mention in *Hymns on Resurrection* 2.8 that women sing the madrashe. We should imagine various styles: perhaps Ephrem sang the verses and the women led the congregation in the refrains; or perhaps the women sang the verses directly.

11. Ephrem, *Hymns on Nativity* 19.8–9 in McVey, trans., 168.

12. Ephrem, *Hymns on the Nativity* 5.22 in McVey, trans., 109.

13. Ephrem, *Hymns on the Nativity* 5.24 in McVey, trans., 109.

14. Ephrem, *Hymns on the Nativity* 2.7 in McVey, trans., 77; see also Ephrem, *Hymns on the Nativity* 17.6.

15. See especially Ephrem, *Hymns on the Nativity* 16, 17, and 19.

16. Ephrem, *Hymns on the Nativity* 15.1, 4–5 in McVey, trans., 145–146.

17. Ephrem's emphasis on "a new song" perhaps follows the prevalent biblical theme found especially in the Psalms: e.g., Ps 40:3, Ps 96:1, Ps 98:1–9, Ps 144:9.

18. Ephrem, *Hymns on the Nativity* 16.8–9 in McVey, trans., 150.

19. E.g., Ephrem, *Hymns on the Nativity* 6.4; 10; 12; 13.13; 14.11–13; 15.2–3, 7; 25.12.

20. Ephrem, *Hymns on the Nativity* 15.7 in McVey, trans., 146–147.

21. Especially Ephrem, *Hymns on the Nativity* 12, in which the entire hymn is devoted to defending the reputations of the slandered virgins. See also Ephrem, *Hymns on the Nativity* 17.4–11, in defense of virginity.

22. Ephrem, *Hymns on the Nativity* 6.4 in McVey, trans., 111.

23. I am grateful to Niki Kasumi Clements for her insight on these nested images of virginity.

24. Ephrem, *Hymns on the Nativity* 17.11 in McVey, trans., 155–156.

25. Contestation over Mary's virginity was present from earliest Christianity, and continued unabated during late antiquity. Matthew 1:1–25 expresses this through the choice of women the Gospel writer includes in his genealogy (all guilty of pregnancy by unconventional means) and the story of Joseph's doubts, without offering Mary's voice in self-defense. There are numerous references in the ancient sources. See, e.g., Rubin, *Mother of God*, 12–16; Schaberg, *The Illegitimacy of Jesus*. On Ephrem's anti-Jewish polemic, see Shepardson, *Anti-Judaism and Christian Orthodoxy*.

26. Ephrem, *Hymns on the Nativity* 12.9, 11 in McVey, trans., 135.

27. Crucial now is the work of Julia Kelto Lillis, *Virgin Territory*; the rhetorical significance was stressed in Cameron, *Christianity and the Rhetoric of Empire*, 171–180; Cameron, "Virginity as Metaphor."

28. For an example of the debates as Ephrem might have heard them, see Aphrahat, *Demonstration* 18.

29. Ephrem's concern about sexual slander indicates the use of the standard gendered tropes of invective to impugn the entire Christian community. See Knust, *Abandoned to Lust*, 115–150 and passim; Dixon, *Reading Roman Women*, 29–65.

30. Historians sometimes forget how controversial vows of celibacy continued to be during late antiquity. A concise presentation of the situation is Brown, "The Notion of Virginity." For the broader picture, see Brown, *The Body and Society*.

31. Ephrem embeds the biblical image into the incarnational one: Ephrem, *Hymns on the Nativity* 15.5; compare Ps 40:3, Ps 96:1, Ps 98:1–9, and Ps 144:3.

32. There are several examples in Brock, *Bride of Light*, at 42, 47: e.g., Prayer Song 9.1 (= *Hymns on Mary* 4.1), Prayer Song 11.1 (= Hymns on Mary 6.1). The anonymous Syriac dialogue hymns (*sughyatha*) that include female characters are further examples: e.g., the hymns on Mary in Brock, *Mary and Joseph*.

33. Jacob of Sarug, *On the Mother of God*, Homily 3 in Hansbury, trans., 83. Jacob, like Ephrem, also exalted the church as most glorious when the whole, in its ordered, gathered ranks, brought their gifts of voice in offering to God that the liturgy might be fulfilled. That offering included "the voice of handmaids grouped in choirs to make a joyful noise," and "the voice of women who exalt Him with their madrashe" (Jacob of Sarug, *Against the Jews* 7.529–542, here my translation); in Albert, ed. and trans., *Jacques de Saroug*, 216–217. This passage will be discussed further in other chapters below.

34. Andrew Palmer points to other types of female personifications that Ephrem placed in the voices of his women's choir: personified cities such as Nisibis or Bethlehem, the personified Church, all imaged in the feminine. Palmer, "A Single Human Being Divided," 129–130.

35. Jacob of Sarug, "On Mar Ephrem." On this homily, see the important essay by McVey, "Ephrem the Kitharode."

36. See now Amar, *The Syriac "Vita" Tradition*. For convenience, I will cite this text as the anonymous *Life of Ephrem*.

37. In his edition of Jacob's homily, Amar dates it to the late fifth century, arguing that it shows no knowledge of the multiple calamities that afflicted Edessa between 494 and 506; see the discussion in Amar, ed. and trans., "On Mar Ephrem," 16. For a graphic account of these disasters, see (Ps.-)Joshua the Stylite, *Chronicle*. However, as Kathleen McVey has pointed out, Jacob did not die until 521, and nothing precludes a composition date for this homily closer to that time; see McVey, "Ephrem the Kitharode," 248n5. Like many of Jacob's homilies, this one is simply impossible to date.

38. While Amar in his introduction to Jacob of Sarug, "On Mar Ephrem," 15, posits that the homily was written for Ephrem's feast day, McVey, "Ephrem the Kitharode," 245, is not convinced that the evidence indicates a feast day rather than other prompting circumstances—for example, a need to defend the women's choirs from critique or attack.

39. The genres of memre, madrashe, and related forms (or subgroups), especially the sughyatha, will be discussed more thoroughly in chapter 3.

40. See Brock, "Ephrem in the Eyes of Later Syriac," 13–15, for later West Syriac liturgical notices in the Fenqitho (collection of hymns for Sundays and feast days) that specifically mention Ephrem and the women's choirs. The East Syriac Hudra (collection of liturgical variables) preserves the portrait of Ephrem as a fighter of heresy without mentioning the women's choirs (Brock, "Ephrem in the Eyes of Later Syriac," 12–13). This perhaps makes sense, given the often bitter contestation between West and East Syriac churches over much of their history. At the same time, Jacob's homilies in some instances were transmitted in both East and West Syriac manuscripts. For the most part, Jacob's homilies scrupulously avoided Christological polemics related to the miaphysite–dyophysite debates that split the Syriac-speaking churches in the fifth century and thereafter. Many of his homilies would have presented no problems whatsoever, even when the rivalry was at its most vitriolic. It is in fact a tribute to Jacob's poetic brilliance that his memre could be valued for their form and content when church polemics could be sidestepped. See now Forness, *Preaching Christology*, 9–18. Verses about the women's choirs from Jacob's homily are often cited in current scholarship on Ephrem. E.g., Griffith, *"Faith Adoring the Mystery,"* 13; Brock, *The Luminous Eye*, 168–169; Outtier, "Saint Éphrem d'après ses biographies," 25.

41. Outtier, "Saint Éphrem d'après ses biographies," 25.

42. Outtier, "Saint Éphrem d'après ses biographies," 28; Brock, *The Luminous Eye*, 168–172. Ephrem's positive portrayal of women is uncommon among patristic authors of late antiquity.

43. Kellog, *Sonic Icons*, ch. 4; Jarjour, *Sense and Sadness*, 54.

44. Late antique sources include Epiphanios, Jerome, Palladios, the *Sayings of the Desert Fathers*, Sozomen, Theodoret, Sokrates, Gennadios, Pseudo-Amphilochios; Arabic,

Armenian, and Georgian versions of the anonymous Syriac *vita*; and a number of spurious "autobiographical" Syriac compositions. The sources are admirably discussed in Amar, *The Syriac "Vita" Tradition*, CSCO 630/Scr. Syr. 243, v–xxix. See also Outtier, "Saint Éphrem d'après ses biographies"; Brock, "Ephrem in the Eyes of Later Syriac."

45. McVey, "Ephrem the Kitharode."

46. Jacob of Sarug, "On Mar Ephrem," vv. 24, 40–50, 58–59, 77–84, 96–116, 152.

47. McVey, "Ephrem the Kitharode," esp. 245–248, where McVey posits a variety of contributing circumstances that might possibly have brought women's ecclesial leadership into question in the early sixth century.

48. Jacob of Sarug, "On Mar Ephrem," vv. 3, 6, 7 in Amar, trans., 25, 27. I will use Amar's translation throughout, although occasionally I have added clarifications in square brackets.

49. Jacob of Sarug, "On Mar Ephrem," vv. 153–154 in Amar, trans., 64–65.

50. Jacob of Sarug, "On Mar Ephrem," vv. 24–25 in Amar, trans., 30–31. For the image of "new wine," see Acts 2:13.

51. Jacob of Sarug, "On Mar Ephrem," vv. 40–43 in Amar, trans., 34–35.

52. Sokoloff, *A Syriac Lexicon*, 647–648; Payne Smith, *A Compendious Syriac Dictionary*, 225. Compare the Greek *kerygma*; Lampe, *A Patristic Greek Lexicon*, 751–752.

53. As noted in Payne Smith, *A Compendious Syriac Dictionary*, 279, often used for the great theologians of the church such as Ephrem and Jacob of Sarug. The term is still used in neo-Aramaic for respected teachers; Jarjour, *Sense and Sadness*, 50–51.

54. Jacob of Sarug, "On Mar Ephrem," v. 44 in Amar, trans., 34–35.

55. On Ephrem's anti-Judaism, see Shepardson, *Anti-Judaism and Christian Orthodoxy*; Murray, *Symbols of Church and Kingdom*, 41–68; Young, "The 'Church from the Nations,'" 111–121.

56. Jacob of Sarug, "On Mar Ephrem," vv. 47–48 in Amar, trans., 36–37.

57. Jacob of Sarug, "On Mar Ephrem," vv. 81–84 in Amar, trans., 44–45.

58. Jacob of Sarug, "On Mar Ephrem," vv. 45–84 in Amar, trans., 34–45.

59. Jacob of Sarug, "On Mar Ephrem," vv. 108–113 in Amar, trans., 50–53.

60. Varghese, *Early History*, 55–60, reads both Jacob and the anonymous *Life of Ephrem* as advocating for increased congregational singing, not separate choirs. He sees the entire liturgical tradition as relying on a less formalized mode of singing by deacons and others in minor orders, rather than trained choirs.

61. Jacob of Sarug, "On Mar Ephrem," vv. 96–97 in Amar, trans., 48–49.

62. Jacob of Sarug, "On Mar Ephrem," vv. 98–101 in Amar, trans., 48–49.

63. Jacob of Sarug, "On Mar Ephrem," vv. 102–114 in Amar, trans., 48–53. Verse 114 is, literally, "to give voices/melodies (*qale*) of instruction (*malputha*) to their songs (*l-zmiratheyn*)."

64. Jacob of Sarug, "On Mar Ephrem," v. 176 in Amar, trans., 68–69.

65. Moss, "Severus of Antioch on Gender," 266–268, suggests an analogous perspective between this passage of Jacob's and Severus of Antioch's Cathedral Homily 83. He then argues for significant differences between the two texts. The similarities are indeed intriguing, but I would still argue for Jacob's singularity.

66. Amar, "Byzantine Ascetic Monasticism"; Griffith, "Images of Ephraem."

67. In recent scholarship, Ephrem is commonly referred to as a deacon, or sometimes as a son of the covenant. As Sidney Griffith has pointed out (*"Faith Adoring the Mystery,"* 7–9), Ephrem's terminology for his own role is ambiguous. What is clear is that he worked

in ministerial service to three successive bishops in the cities of Nisibis and Edessa. See now the nuanced analysis of Rouwhorst, "Deacons."

68. Excellent summaries of the historical information on Ephrem are included in the introduction to Amar's edition of the *Life of Ephrem*; Brock, "Ephrem in the Eyes of Later Syriac"; Outtier, "Saint Éphrem d'après ses biographies"; and Griffith, *"Faith Adoring the Mystery,"* 1–29. On the use of Ephrem's hymns for instructional purposes in nonliturgical settings, see now Rouwhorst, "Original Setting"; Wickes, *Bible and Poetry*; Wickes, "Between Liturgy and School."

69. Such is the suggestion of Salvesen, "Themes in Ephrem's Exodus Commentary," 39–40. The depiction in Jacob of Sarug and the *Life of Ephrem* of Ephrem instructing the daughters of the covenant accords with such a possibility. See Brock, *Luminous Eye*, 168–172.

70. In addition to Amar's critical edition of the *Life of Ephrem*, see the important discussions in Brock, "Ephrem in the Eyes of Later Syriac"; and Outtier, "Saint Éphrem d'après ses biographies." The transformation of Ephrem from civic teacher to desert ascetic was accompanied by the emergence in Greek of a substantial corpus of metrical homilies on biblical and ascetic themes attributed to Ephrem. Sozomen, *Ecclesiastical History* 3.16 claims that Ephrem was translated into Greek during his own lifetime. However, the only correlation between the authentic corpus of Ephrem and the extensive corpus of Ephrem Graecus appears to be a portion of one memra on Noah. See now Pino, "Ephrem Graecus." These homilies proved highly influential in subsequent Byzantine and Russian monastic traditions.

71. *Life of Ephrem*, ch. 31; in Amar, CSCO 629/Scr. Syr. 242, 70–74 (Syriac) and CSCO 630/Scr. Syr. 243, 76–80 (English).

72. For Bardaisan and his influence, see Possekel, "Bardaisan's Influence"; on hymns and poetry specifically, 94–96.

73. *Life of Ephrem*, ch. 31 in Amar, trans., CSCO 630/Scr. Syr. 243, 76–77. For this chapter, Amar's text and translation alternate paragraphs of the three primary recensions: Paris Syr. 235, fols. 125r–142v (P); Damascus Syriac Orthodox Patriarchate 12/17, fols. 220v–226r (D); and Vatican Syr. 117, fols. 187v–194r (V). The three versions proceed independently but with close repetition of phraseology. In quotation, I attempt to cite from all three at different points; sometimes elision between them is necessary for the sake of clarity. The account of heretical hymns is partly based on Ephrem's own presentation in *Hymns Against Heresies* 53.5–6. But the tradition that Ephrem mimicked Greek poetic forms is based on the contrived report in Sozomen, *Ecclesiastical History* 3.16. For critical analysis of this misrepresentation, see Brock, "Syriac and Greek Hymnography."

74. *Life of Ephrem*, ch. 31 (V) in Amar, trans., CSCO 630/Scr. Syr. 243, 79.

75. *Life of Ephrem*, ch. 31 (D) in Amar, trans., CSCO 630/Scr. Syr. 243, pp. 77–78.

76. *Life of Ephrem*, ch. 31 (V) in Amar, trans., CSCO 630/Scr. Syr. 243, 80; for the Syriac, CSCO 629/Scr. Syr. 242, 73.

77. *Life of Ephrem*, ch. 31 (V) in Amar, trans., CSCO 630/Scr. Syr. 243, 80.

78. Syriac *Didascalia Apostolorum*, ch. 15 in Vööbus, trans., CSCO 408/Scr. Syr. 180, 144–145.

79. *Life of Ephrem*, ch. 31 (P), (D), and (V) in Amar, trans., CSCO 630/Scr. Syr. 243, 78 and 80.

80. *Life of Ephrem*, ch. 31 (D) in Amar, trans., CSCO 630/Scr. Syr. 243, 78. Following citations are from the same ch. 31.

81. *Life of Ephrem*, ch. 31 (P), (D), (V) in Amar, trans., CSCO 630/Scr. Syr. 243, 78 and 80. While chapter 31 is the only place to mention the daughters of the covenant, chapter 32 is a tribute to Ephrem's hymnographic victory over Bardaisan.

82. See the discussion in chapter 1 at "Syriac Women's Service and Syriac Women's Song."

83. Terminology for Syriac poetic forms, including hymnography, is confusing in this early period. The same terms can have varied meanings, and may or may not refer to particular hymn types in different texts. See the comments in Brock, "Poetry and Hymnography (3): Syriac." The range of meanings for each term as listed in Sokoloff, *A Syriac Lexicon*, is helpful. See also the descriptions in Barsoum, *Scattered Pearls*, 93–96. Although dealing with a later period and some differences in hymn types, there is pertinent and perceptive discussion in Murre-van den Berg, *Scribes and Scriptures*, 156–181.

84. Sozomen, *Ecclesiastical History* 3.16, Hartranft, trans., 295–297; Theodoret, *Ecclesiastical History* 4.29.1–3 in McKinnon, *Music*, 105 (no. 226).

85. *Life of Rabbula*, esp. secs. 40, 41, 43, 45. The anonymous author also combines this imagery of poetry and music with that of archery, as we have seen used in Jacob of Sarug's "On Mar Ephrem," and the anonymous *Life of Ephrem*. The close similarities are striking; see further discussion below.

86. Barhadbeshabba, *Ecclesiastical History* 31 in Becker, trans., *School of Nisibis*, 69.

87. E.g., Ephrem, *Hymns Against Heresies* 53.5–6.

88. Jacob of Sarug, "On the Spectacles, 3" in Moss, ed. and trans., 105. These homilies match well with other late antique homiletic objections to the theater, and with Jacob's own in "On the Partaking," ll. 155–164 in Harrak, ed. and trans., 22–23. On the dangers of the songs of the theater: e.g., John Chrysostom, "Against the Games and the Theatres," in Mayer and Allen, trans., *John Chrysostom*, 121–122; Severos of Antioch, *Homily* 18.28 in Allen and Hayward, trans., 124.

89. Basil of Caesarea, *Homilia in psalmum i*, in McKinnon, *Music*, 65 (no. 130).

90. John Chrysostom, *In psalmum xli* 1, in McKinnon, *Music*, 79–80 (no. 164). On this theme in Chrysostom, with many resonances to the Syriac material, see Wylie, "Musical Aesthetics."

91. *Life of Rabbula*, secs. 43, 45; in Horn and Phenix, eds. and trans., *Rabbula Corpus*, 62–69. Consider a passage on monks as spiritual warriors, attributed to Isaac of Antioch, "On the Perfection of Monks," stanza 320 (as cited in Caner, *Wandering, Begging Monks*, 116): "Their prayers are arrows, which they aim at the target of mercy; their lips are bows, with which they fire to astonishing heights. The words of the Holy Spirit are their armaments, since their struggle is directed against a spiritual fortress."

92. John Chrysostom, "Juventius and Maximinus," sec. 7 in Mayer and Neil, trans., *Saint John Chrysostom*, 97; Pseudo-Martyrius, *Funerary Speech for John Chrysostom*, sec. 26 in Barnes and Bevan, trans., 54. Compare Gregory of Nyssa, *Life of Moses*, 2.260.8 in Malherbe and Ferguson, trans., 121.

93. For the range of meanings for *belos*, see *The Online Liddell-Scott-Jones Greek-English Lexicon*, s.v. "βέλος," http://stephanus.tlg.uci.edu/lsj.

94. Jacob of Sarug, "On Mar Ephrem," vv. 116, 152 in Amar, trans., 53, 65.

95. The phrase was famously used by Palladios about Melania the Elder, in Palladios, *Lausiac History*, ch. 9. See Krawiec, "The Memory of Melania"; and e.g., Cloke, *This Female Man of God*.

96. There is useful discussion in Neyrey, "Jesus, Gender, and the Gospel of Matthew."

97. The discussion in Krawiec, "The Memory of Melania," provides an instructive paradigm on this point.

98. Lillis, *Virgin Territory*, discusses this as a shift during late antiquity; see especially 97–164, and 110–113 (on Ephrem).

99. See now Butts, "Manuscript Transmission."

100. Van Rompay, "Society and Community," offers a trenchant overview.

101. Van Rompay, "Mallpânâ dilan Suryâyâ."

102. Considerable scholarly attention has been given to the problem of Ephrem's hymns in later liturgical manuscripts. Butts, "Manuscript Transmission," does a masterful job in assessing both the scholarship and the evidence, and drawing out the polemical contexts dominating the early scribal decisions.

103. See now Hartung, "Collection and Transmission."

104. Brock, "The Transmission of Ephrem's Madrashe"; de Halleux, "La transmission des hymnes d'Éphrem"; Gribomont, "La tradition liturgique des hymnes pascales de S. Éphrem."

105. Philo, "On the Contemplative Life," secs. 64–90 in Colson, trans., 150–169. On the significance of the entire passage for the history of music, see Jeffrey, "Philo's Impact"; Wilson, "Early Christian Music."

106. See now Kraemer, *Unreliable Witnesses*, 57–116.

107. Philo, "On the Contemplative Life," secs. 85–87.

108. Jeffrey, "Philo's Impact."

109. Eusebios, *History of the Church* 2.17.

110. E.g., Barnes, *Constantine and Eusebius.*

111. In addition to the commentary Eusebios provides on Philo and the Therapeutae in *History of the Church* 2.17, consider, for example, his presentation of Origen of Alexandria in *History of the Church* 6, and of the martyrs in *History of the Church* 8.3–13 or throughout his *Martyrs of Palestine.*

112. On Eusebios's interaction with the writings of Philo in a climate of philosophical competition, see Urbano, *The Philosophical Life*, 107–111.

113. The Syriac of Eusebios's *History of the Church* is edited in Wright and McLean, *The Ecclesiastical History of Eusebius*. There seems to be no evidence that Philo was translated directly into Syriac. However, late antique Syriac scholars in both West and East Syriac contexts knew of Philo's works; their knowledge of Greek authors was extensive. See Runia, *Philo in Early Christian Literature*, 28, 265–266.

114. Philo, "On the Contemplative Life," secs. 40–63 in Colson, trans., 136–151. See the discussion in Jeffrey, "Philo's Impact," 162–164.

115. Philo, "On the Contemplative Life," secs. 30–32.

116. Philo, "On the Contemplative Life," secs. 80–81 in Colson, trans., 162–163.

117. Philo, "On the Contemplative Life," sec. 83 in Colson, trans., 164–165.

118. Philo, "On the Contemplative Life," sec. 88 in Colson, trans., 166–167.

119. Peter Jeffrey provides incisive analysis of Philo's terminology, its classical background, as well as its misinterpretation by fourth- and fifth-century Christian writers based on their reading of Eusebios's version of Philo's work; see Jeffrey, "Philo's Impact."

120. Kraemer, *Unreliable Witnesses*, 83–114, provides detailed analysis, including the variations between the Hebrew of the biblical text and the Greek of the Septuagint, on which Philo's discussions were based.

121. Jacob of Sarug, "On Mar Ephrem," v. 33 in Amar, trans., 32–33.

122. Jacob of Sarug, "On Mar Ephrem," vv. 153–157 in Amar, trans., 64–65.

123. Edited by Musurillo in *Méthode d'Olympe: Le banquet*. I follow the translation by Musurillo, *St. Methodius, The Symposium*, with additional references to the section numbers of the Greek. I have occasionally adapted for sense, marked in square brackets.

124. Methodios, *Symposium*, Logos 8, prologue in Musurillo, trans., 104–105.

125. Methodios, *Symposium*, Logos 11 in Musurillo, trans., 149–151.

126. See now Norman, *Aesthetics of Hope*, for a complete reassessment of Methodios. Her discussion of the *Symposium*, at 163–200, and of Thekla's hymn, at 201–240, attend to the literary boldness, including issues of gender and speech, in the context of the vibrant changes in Greek poetry of the third century. Her treatment of Thekla's hymn raises intriguing notions of liturgical and eschatological time. König, "Sympotic Dialogue," places Methodios within the literary tradition of sympotic literature, demonstrating Methodios's active originality in employing this genre for his own theological and philosophical purposes.

127. Burrus, "From Diotima to Thecla"; Hylen, *A Modest Apostle*, 105–107; Haines-Eitzen, *Gendered Palimpsest*, 96–112. Relevant also is Muehlberger, "Perpetual Adjustment."

128. Burrus, "From Diotima to Thecla"; Muehlberger, "Perpetual Adjustment."

129. Halperin, "Why Is Diotima a Woman?"

130. The discussion in Burrus, "From Diotima to Thecla," is especially important. Consider also the paradigms in Jarratt and Ong, "Aspasia"; and Swearingen, "A Lover's Discourse."

131. Methodios, *Symposium*, Logos 1.5 (sec. 26) in Musurillo, trans., 48.

132. Methodios, *Symposium*, Logos 3.6 (sec. 64), in Musurillo, trans., 62–63. The notion that creation ideally established a perfect and ceaseless liturgy composed of angelic, human, and natural voices was common in early Christian literature, and much loved in Syriac tradition. See now Harvey, "Creation, Order, Beauty." I will return to this theme in chapter 4.

133. As Musurillo remarks, "Methodius pictures the ideal worship of God as a liturgical hymn of praise sung by angels and men dividing the verses antiphonally, or perhaps singing alternately strophe and refrain as do Thecla and the virgins in *Symp*. 11" (*St. Methodius*, 199n22).

134. Methodios, *Symposium*, Logos 4.1 (sec. 94) in Musurillo, trans., 75.

135. Methodios, *Symposium*, Logos 8, prologue in Musurillo, trans., 105.

136. Methodios, *Symposium*, Logos 8.1 (sec. 172) in Musurillo, trans., 105–106.

137. Methodios, *Symposium*, Logos 11 (sec. 284) in Musurillo, trans., 151.

138. Methodios, *Symposium*, Logos 11, refrain in Musurillo, trans., 151–157.

139. Musurillo, *St. Methodius*, 236–237n1.

140. Compare the discussions in Lillis, *Virgin Territory*, esp. 97–164; Shaw, *Burden of the Flesh*, esp. 161–253; Burrus, "The Heretical Woman as Symbol"; and Sissa, *Greek Virginity*.

141. See now Anagnostou-Laoutides, "Drinking New Wine."

142. Consider the discussion in Norman, "Methodius and Methodologies."

143. Letter 22 is dated to approximately 384, prior to Jerome's final move with Paula and Eustochium to Bethlehem. I follow the translation in Petersen, *Handmaids of the Lord*, 171–217; Latin in Gorce, *Lettres spirituelles de Saint Jérome*.

144. Letter 22 is notorious in this regard. Particularly insightful are Miller, "The Blazing Body"; Burrus, *The Sex Lives of Saints*, 19–20; and Clark, *Reading Renunciation*, 87–88.

145. Jerome, Letter 22 in Petersen, trans., 207–208 (modified for clarity).

146. E.g., Gregory of Nyssa, "On Virginity" (19) in Callahan, trans., 60–62. John Chrysostom cites Miriam and Exodus 15 to praise the empress Eudoxia leading the people of Constantinople in procession to the martyrs' shrine at Drypia ("After the Remains of Martyrs" in Mayer and Allen, trans., *John Chrysostom*, 90–91).

147. While Ephrem also used the phrase "a new song," the book of Revelation was not part of the Syriac Bible versions during late antiquity. The phrase "All generations shall call me blessed" (Lk 1:48) is cited in a number of the anonymous hymns set in Mary's voice in Brock, *Bride of Light*: e.g., Prayer Song 13.2 (= Hymns on Mary 8.2) and Prayer Song 17.5 (= Hymns on Mary 12.5), Prayer Song 23.10 (= Sughitha 2.10), and the "Dialogue Between Mary and the Angel," v. 48 (at 51, 66, 84, and 131, respectively).

148. Methodios, *Symposium*, Logos 8.2. Musurillo discusses the ambiguity of the Greek here, where it is not clear if the angelic chorus proceeds "in solemn silence" or "with much rejoicing": *meta polles euphemias*. See his discussion in Musurillo, trans., 220–221n14; for the Greek text, see Musurillo, *Le banquet*, 206 (and note 1, on the same page).

149. As discussed in chapter 1; see Egeria, *Diary of a Pilgrimage*, 24 in Gingras, trans., 89–93.

150. E.g., Page, *The Christian West and Its Singers*, 134–135.

151. It is intriguing to consider the later rabbinic injunction of R. Joseph, "If men sing and women respond (i.e. by singing after them, or joining in the chorus) it is a breach of law, but if women sing and men respond it is as if a fire was raging in a field of flax." B.T. Sotah 48a, cited by Taitz, "Kol Ishah," 47.

152. Portions of Ephrem's madrashe continued to be included in liturgical books (and to the present day still are), but often only in units of one or two verses together, and often without his authorship identified. See Butts, "Manuscript Transmission"; Brock, "The Transmission of Ephrem's Madrashe"; de Halleux, "La transmission des hymnes d'Éphrem"; Gribomont, "La tradition liturgique des hymnes pascales de S. Ephrem."

153. Jacob describes this liturgical sequence in his homily "On the Partaking," ll. 129–188 in Harrak, trans., 18–25. How precisely one should interpret this liturgical description remains an unresolvable question.

154. Jacob of Sarug's homily "On Mar Ephrem" is extant in at least twelve manuscripts, a high number for a Syriac text. See the discussion in Amar, "A Metrical Homily on Holy Mar Ephrem," 11–13. On the collection and circulation of Jacob's homilies, see Forness, *Preaching Christology*, 22–55; for their continuing use in vesper and vigil services, and in monastic communities, see Barsoum, *Scattered Pearls*, 59, 77, 92.

155. There are charming portraits of what such monastic, meditative study would have involved. Jacob of Sarug describes the monk with a book fighting off the demons of sleepiness, distraction, and boredom; Jacob, "On the Solitaries 2," ll. 373–384 in Scott and Reed, eds. and trans., 92–93. The anonymous "Forty Martyrs" begins with a gentle pastoral encouragement on how to read and contemplate such a text: in Harvey et al., trans., 84–127, at 88–96.

156. On religious rivalry expressed through competing song, see Harvey, "Patristic Worlds"; Shaw, *Sacred Violence*, 441–489.

157. Jacob of Sarug, "Homily 4 on Elisha," ll. 21–30 in Kaufman, trans., 177.

158. For the contrasting record for male singers and choirs, see Page, *The Christian West and Its Singers*, passim. The earliest citation of a named male singer is an epitaph from

Dineksarai in south-central Turkey, dating to the third or fourth century, for a singer or composer named Gaios: Page, *The Christian West and Its Singers*, 87. Compare, further, the occasional but detailed evidence for Byzantine (male) choirs, which sometimes includes information on titles for ranks or roles within the choir, vestments (including special armbands and hats), salaries, and the like. See Avdokhin, "Singers Silently Speaking"; Moran, *Singers*, 14–50.

3. SINGING VOICES, VOICES SUNG:
PERFORMANCE, GENRE, BIBLICAL MODELS

1. As will be apparent throughout this book, my treatment of liturgy is influenced in particular by Bell, *Ritual Theory, Ritual Practice*; McCall, *Do This*; Searle, "Ritual"; Berger, *Women's Ways of Worship*; Berger, *Gender Differences*.

2. Chatonnet, "Les églises dans les textes," esp. 11–20.

3. Chatonnet, "Les églises dans les textes," 20–28; Cassingena-Trévedy and Jurasz, *Les liturgies syriaques*. For building designs, Kayaalp, *Church Architecture*. For a basic introduction to the different Syriac rites within the larger family of eastern liturgies, see now Alexopoulos and Johnson, *Eastern Christian Liturgies*, and the bibliographies there at 413–419.

4. In general, but helpful also for Syriac: Bradshaw, *Daily Prayer in the Early Church*, 72–110; Taft, *Liturgy of the Hours in East and West*, esp. 225–248; Mateos, *Lelya-Sapra*.

5. These kinds of allusions are scattered throughout Ephrem's madrashe, but consider his *Hymns on the Nativity*: these are replete with references to singing, participation, and the evening context. Ephrem is also one of our earliest sources on the Christian liturgical use of incense, for which see Harvey, *Scenting Salvation*, 75–83.

6. Ephrem, *Hymns on the Nativity* 1.63–83 in McVey, trans., 71–73. McVey accepts the authenticity of this hymn, following Beck's lead: McVey, *Ephrem the Syrian*, 29n121.

7. Brock, "Seeds of Liturgical Drama in Syriac?"; Brock, "Dispute Between the Cherub and the Thief"; and below.

8. For example, Ephrem, *Hymns on Nativity* 5.6, 7, 9; 21.2.

9. On the development of Syriac liturgies within a broader context of eastern Christianity, see, in general, Varghese, *Early History*; Mateos, *La célébration de la parole*; Sheerin, "Eucharistic Liturgy"; Talley, *Origins of the Liturgical Year*; Bradshaw and Johnson, *Origins of Feasts, Fasts, and Seasons*.

10. For a trenchant example, see Rouwhorst, "Celebration of Holy Week in Early Syriac-Speaking Churches," and for a wisely cautionary note, Rouwhorst, "Original Setting."

11. Jacob of Sarug, "On the Partaking."

12. Burkitt, "The Early Syriac Lectionary System"; Rouwhorst, "Epiphany"; Brock, "Use of the Syriac Versions"; Jenner, "The Development of Syriac Lectionary Systems."

13. Merras, "The Date of the Earliest Syriac Lectionary."

14. Rouwhorst, "Liturgical Reading of the Bible in the Syriac Church," is an especially perceptive study.

15. Jacob of Sarug, "On the Partaking," ll. 129–188 in Harrak, trans., 18–25.

16. In addition to the above references, see Yousif, *L'Eucharistie chez saint Éphrem*; and for Jacob's own explication, Jacob of Sarug, "On the Partaking," ll. 201–354 in Harrak, trans., 26–43. Varghese, *West Syrian Liturgical Theology*, 35–47, has a helpful discussion of the

liturgical vocabulary (such as *qurbono*, at 44–45), although he draws heavily on sources after late antiquity.

17. Jacob of Sarug, "On the Partaking," ll. 189–200 in Harrak, trans., 24–27.

18. See the discussion in chapter 5 for examples.

19. Crucial now is Kayaalp, *Church Architecture.*

20. Palmer and Rodley, "The Inauguration Anthem"; McVey, "The Domed Church as Microcosm."

21. Translated in Palmer, "The Inauguration Anthem," 131–133.

22. John of Ephesos, *Lives*, ch. 12 (Mary and Euphemia) describes a small chapel with "likenesses and pictures and chests [for relics and sacred vessels] . . . the oblation and Scriptures . . . mats and curtains and rugs" (in Brooks, ed. and trans., *PO* 17: 177); ch. 55 (John and Sosiana) mentions converting rich clothing into liturgical items: "cloths and veils and napkins . . . men came who were occupied with gilding and decorating them in a marvellous manner . . . linen cloths and Persian cambrics . . . all overlaid [with gold]. . . . and fine figures made of various silks and raw silks and pure silk" and a copious donation of silver from which "chalices and patens were made, and many dishes and spoons" (in Brooks, ed. and trans., *PO* 19: 194–195).

23. See the discussion and references in Harvey, "Interior Decorating." An example of canons dealing with cleaning and restoration of liturgical utensils is the sixth-century document "Answers of Johannan [John of Tella] to Sargis," in Vööbus, ed. and trans., *The [West Syrian] Synodicon* 1, CSCO 367/Scr. Syr. 161, 211–221 (Syriac), CSCO 368/Scr. Syr. 162, 197–205 (English).

24. Especially well known is Mango, *Silver from Early Byzantium.*

25. Cassingena-Trévedy, "Constructions, Destructions, Inhabitation Divine."

26. Narsai, "On the Sanctification" in Harrak, ed. and trans.

27. Narsai, "On the Sanctification," in Harrak, ed. and trans., passim. Interestingly, this memra has a refrain at the beginning ("O Church of the Nations pay homage to Christ, for he planted you on earth and registered you in heaven") and at the end ("Blessed are you, Christ the Bridegroom by your Church redeemed by your blood") (in Harrak, ed. and trans., 10–11 and 54–55, respectively), indicating a pattern of performative recitation and response.

28. Beautifully captured in Debié, "Le bruissement des ailes des anges."

29. For detailed description based on several different madrashe, see Palmer, "A Single Human Being Divided," esp. 128–133.

30. Ephrem, *Memre on Nicomedia* 8.553–570, 667–678, in Renoux, ed. and trans., *Éphrem de Nisibe*, 146–147, 152–155.

31. Loosely, *Architecture and Liturgy of the Bema*, 27–30, 33, 103–133. On the continuity with Jewish use of the bema, see Rouwhorst, "Jewish Liturgical Traditions," esp. 74–78.

32. See further the important discussions in Sodini, "Archéologie des églises"; Cassis, "The Bema in the East Syriac Church," and the citations below.

33. Synod of Laodicea, canon 15 in Vööbus, ed. and trans., *The [West Syrian] Synodicon*, CSCO 367/Scr. Syr. 161, 118 (Syriac), CSCO 368/Scr. Syr. 162, 121 (English).

34. See the helpful discussion in Donceel-Voûte, *Les pavements des églises byzantines*, 503–540; and Taft, "Some Notes on the Bema." Taft's article was reprinted in Taft, *Liturgy in Byzantium and Beyond*, 326–359, with updated evidence on the bema; see 3–5 of the addendum for a still valid and trenchant summary of the issues.

35. The bema of Syrian churches has received enormous scholarly attention over the past century. The studies I have found most helpful are Sodini, "Archéologie des églises"; Janeras, "Le bêma syrien"; Loosely, *Architecture and Liturgy of the Bema*, 27–30, 33, 103–133; Rouwhorst, "Jewish Liturgical Traditions"; Cassis, "The Bema in the East Syriac Church"; Donceel-Voûte, *Les pavements des églises byzantines*, 503–540; and Taft, "Some Notes on the Bema." All contain extensive bibliographies.

36. On the gendered spatial arrangements of Syrian naves, see Sodini, "Archéologie des églises." Taft, "Women at Church in Byzantium," 27–87, focuses most heavily on Constantinople, but includes some Syriac sources. His discussion raises analogous issues for Syriac churches, especially at 79–87, where he considers the reasoning behind a gendered organization of the liturgical space. Extremely important is his observation that while women had a designated space (in an upper gallery or on one side of the nave), there is little evidence to indicate that women would not have been present during liturgy in other areas of the church where the laity were permitted; or in the case of liturgical assistance, where deacons or other designated ritual agents performed their duties. Liturgical order was an organizational principle, not a rigid system. Even the sanctuary, the most ritually exclusive space of the church building, could be entered by women (usually deaconesses) for purposes of cleaning or for liturgical assistance, a principle still followed in Orthodox canon law. For examples from late antique Syriac, see "Answers of Johannan [John of Tella] to Sargis," canons 33–40 and "Answers of Ja'qob [Jacob of Edessa] to Addai," canon 41 in Vööbus, ed. and trans., *The [West Syrian] Synodicon*, CSCO 367/Scr. Syr. 161, 218–219, 266 (Syriac) and CSCO 368/Scr. Syr. 162, 203–204, 242 (English).

37. Ephrem, *Hymns against Heresies* 2.6. This passage rings of the classic trope in which "heretics" are identified as disordered, evidenced by their granting leadership to women. See Burrus, "The Heretical Woman as Symbol."

38. On the significance of architectural design, gendered ordering of space, and participant location, see Branham, "Women as Objects of Sacrifice?"

39. See the discussion in chapter 1, "Syriac Christian Ministry: Daughters of the Covenant."

40. "Canons of Johannan bar Qursos [John of Tella]," canon 27 in Vööbus, ed. and trans., *The [West Syrian] Synodicon*, CSCO 367/Scr. Syr. 161, 156 (Syriac) and CSCO 368/Scr. Syr. 162, 151 (English).

41. "Canons of Johannan bar Qursos [John of Tella]," canon 27 in Vööbus, ed. and trans., *The [West Syrian] Synodicon*, CSCO 367/Scr. Syr. 161, 55 (Syriac) and CSCO 368/Scr. Syr. 162, 151 (English).

42. "The Synod of Laodicea," canon 23, "Canons of Johannan bar Qursos [John of Tella]," canon 27 in Vööbus, ed. and trans., *The [West Syrian] Synodicon*, CSCO 367/Scr. Syr. 161, 119 (Syriac) and CSCO 368/Scr. Syr. 162, 122 (English). On the Laodicean canons, see Page, *The Christian West and Its Singers*, 90–95; Ravolainen, *The Singer in the Ecclesiastical Hierarchy*, 107–112.

43. For excellent examples of the array of social significations cued by dress in late antiquity, see Upson-Saia, Daniel-Hughes, and Batten, *Dressing Judeans and Christians*. Also helpful is the material insightfully discussed in Ball, "Decoding the Habit of the Byzantine Nun."

44. Compare the issues raised in Mayer, "John Chrysostom: Extraordinary Preacher, Ordinary Audience," esp. 126–133.

45. A number of instances are cited in (Ps.-)Joshua the Stylite, *Chronicle*, secs. 31, 35, 36, 43, 100 in Trombley and Watt, trans., 30, 34–36, 45, 117–118. These and others are discussed at length in chapter 5.

46. See, for example, McKinnon, *Music*, 72 (no. 148, Gregory of Nazianzos on the congregation at Caesarea); 101–102 (no. 218, Sokrates on Nicenes and Arians in Constantinople); 102–103 (no. 219, Sozomen on factions in Antioch); 105–106 (no. 227, Theodoret on Melitians in Alexandria). The public ethos of polemic may have contributed to the development of Jewish liturgical poetry, particularly piyyutim. See van Bekkum, "Anti-Christian Polemics."

47. See now Falcasantos, *Constantinople*; Shepardson, *Controlling Contested Places*; Shaw, *Sacred Violence*, 441–489, specifically on singing as a form of hostile religious rivalry. Baldovin, *The Urban Character of Christian Worship* remains foundational. See, further, e.g., Mathews, *The Clash of Gods*; Andrade, "Processions of John Chrysostom."

48. Jacob of Sarug, "Homily 4 on Elisha," ll. 21–30 in Kaufman, trans., 176–177.

49. Here, as throughout my discussion of ritual, I am much influenced by Bell, *Ritual Theory, Ritual Practice*. On the ritual body specifically, see Bell, 94–117.

50. McVey, "Were the Earliest *Madrase* Songs or Recitations?" For the development of Syriac hymnography overall, see Cassingena-Trévedy, "L'hymnographie syriaque."

51. Lattke, "Sind Ephraems *Madrashe* Hymnen?"; McVey, "Were the Earliest *Madrase* Songs or Recitations?"; Brock, "Poetry and Hymnography (3): Syriac"; Palmer, "A Single Human Being Divided."

52. On metrical recitation in late antique schools, see Wickes, "Between Liturgy and School"; Becker, *Fear of God*, 89–90, 92–93, 189, 204–209.

53. Roueché, "Acclamations"; Lieber, *Staging the Sacred*; Lieber, "Theater of the Holy"; Torres, "'*Polla eti eis polla.*'" The custom of public acclamations will be discussed further in chapter 5.

54. On the possible locations for Ephrem's madrashe, see Rouwhorst, "Original Setting"; Wickes, *Bible and Poetry*.

55. See Rouwhorst, "Hymns and Prayers in the Apocryphal Acts," esp. 210–212.

56. Sometimes the titles of the original melodies provided the organizational principles for Ephrem's hymns as they were transmitted in cycles (largely organized by later editors, although in a few cases by Ephrem himself) within the manuscripts. See de Halleux, "Une clé pour les hymnes d'Ephrem"; de Halleux, "La transmission des hymnes d'Ephrem." For an example, see McVey, *Ephrem the Syrian*, 39–40, on the collection loosely titled "Hymns on Virginity and on the Symbols of Our Lord."

57. For the medieval developments, with possible remnants of earlier melodic patterns, see Cody, "Early History of the Octoechos in Syria"; Velimirović, "Christian Chant"; Husmann, "Syrian Church Music."

58. Suggestive and thoughtful efforts have been made by Ibrahim and Kiraz, "Ephrem's *Madroshe* and the Syrian Orthodox *Beth Gazo*." See also Brock and Kiraz, *Select Poems*, xiii–xvi.

59. Chatonnet, "Les églises dans les textes," 28–32.

60. I am helped by issues raised in McCall, *Do This*, as well as the suggestive parallels in Goff, *Citizen Bacchae*, and Stehle, *Performance and Gender*.

61. In portions of what follows, I draw on Harvey, "On Mary's Voice."

62. Ephrem, *Hymns on the Nativity* 6.1–2 in McVey, trans., 111.

63. For Ephrem's primary themes and images, see Brock, *The Luminous Eye*; Murray, *Symbols of Church and Kingdom.*

64. E.g., Shoemaker, *Mary in Early Christian Devotion and Faith*; Limberis, *Divine Heiress*, 121–143. For the larger ramifications of the theme in cultural terms, see Cameron, *Christianity and the Rhetoric of Empire*, 155–188, on the rhetoric of paradox. For the broader context of early Marian devotion, see Rubin, *Mother of God*, 3–49.

65. The tradition was most prevalent for the Holy Spirit, since in Syriac the term *ruha*, "spirit," is a feminine noun. But the imagery of Christ's breasts, or God's womb, was also found elsewhere in Syriac texts. See, e.g., Harvey, "Feminine Imagery for the Divine"; Drijvers, "The 19th Ode of Solomon"; McVey, *Ephrem the Syrian*, 10n28; McVey, "Images of Joy in Ephrem's Hymns." The image of Christ as a nursing mother, in particular, enjoyed wider exploration in early Christian literature: e.g., Clement of Alexandria, *Paedagogos* 2.6 in Wood, trans., 24–49.

66. Ephrem, *Hymns on the Nativity* 4.143–214; cf. *Hymns on the Nativity* 11.6–8.

67. Ephrem, *Hymns on the Nativity* 8.20–21 in McVey, trans., 123.

68. Ephrem, *Hymns on the Nativity* 8, refrain in McVey, trans., 119.

69. Ephrem, *Hymns on the Nativity* 15.2–3 in McVey, trans., 146.

70. Ephrem, *Hymns on the Nativity* 6.3–6; 8.9; 12.4–11; 13.13; 14, passim; 15.7–8; 16.12–13; 17.7.

71. Rubin, *Mother of God*, charts the Byzantine and medieval glory with great insight.

72. On narrative as an inherently moralizing form of discourse, see White, "The Value of Narrativity."

73. Ephrem, *Hymns on the Nativity* 17.11 with refrain, in McVey, trans., 154–155.

74. I am much influenced by Bell, *Ritual Theory, Ritual Practice*, 109–124.

75. Ephrem, *Hymns on the Nativity* 25.14 in McVey, trans., 203.

76. Ephrem, *Hymns on the Nativity* 25, refrain in McVey, trans., 200.

77. See now Mengozzi, *L'invenzione del dialogo*; Brock, "The Dispute Poem"; Brock, "Dramatic Dialogue Poems"; Brock, "Syriac Dispute Poems"; Murray, "Aramaic and Syriac Dispute Poems." Reinink and Vanstiphout, *Dispute Poems and Dialogues*, is helpful for the larger literary context.

78. There is a useful inventory of extant sughyatha, with available editions and translations, in Brock, *Mary and Joseph*, 97–104.

79. On the liturgical setting for these dialogue hymns and its impact on their exegetical process, see Mengozzi, *L'invenzione del dialogo*, 55–83; Upson-Saia, "Caught in a Compromising Position"; Brock, "Syriac Dialogue Poems," 37. For the intersection of dramatic dialogue and liturgy in Greek tradition of the same period, see especially Dobrov, "Dialogue with Death." Also important for the broader traditions of literary and rhetorical disputes, see Reinink and Vanstiphout, *Dispute Poems and Dialogues*, and especially Cameron, "Disputations, Polemical Literature."

80. I use the examples collected and translated in Brock, *Bride of Light*, 125–150 (nos. 41–44). These same sughyatha on Mary are also presented in a bilingual Syriac-English edition in Brock, *Mary and Joseph*.

81. On the Virgin Mary rather than Mary Magdalene for this gospel episode, see Murray, *Symbols of Church and Kingdom*, 146–148; Shoemaker, *Mary in Early Christian Faith and Devotion*, 30–63; Shoemaker, "Rethinking the 'Gnostic Mary.'"

82. Eg., Prayer Song 24, "On Simeon the Old Man" (Sughitha 3) in Brock, *Bride of Light*, 87–94. Brock's collection *Bride of Light* offers numerous examples of these various encounters retold in hymns.

83. "Mary and the Angel," v.1 2 (41.12) in Brock, *Bride of Light*, 127.

84. "Mary and the Angel," v. 17 (41.17) in Brock, *Bride of Light*, 127.

85. "Mary and the Angel," v. 23 (41.23) in Brock, *Bride of Light*, 128.

86. "Mary and the Angel," v. 24 (41.24) in Brock, *Bride of Light*, 128.

87. "Mary and the Angel," v. 25 (41.25) in Brock, *Bride of Light*, 128.

88. "Mary and the Angel," vv. 51–54 (41.51–54) in Brock, *Bride of Light*, 131–132.

89. "Mary and Joseph," vv. 9–13 (42.9–13) in Brock, *Bride of Light*, 134–135.

90. "Mary and the Angel," vv. 21, 25 (41.21, 25); "Mary and Joseph," vv. 9, 11 (42.9, 11) both in Brock, *Bride of Light*, 128, 134, respectively.

91. "Mary and Joseph," v. 1, Response (42.1, Response) in Brock, *Bride of Light*, 133.

92. "Mary and the Magi," v. 12 (43.12) in Brock, *Bride of Light*, 140.

93. "Mary and the Gardener" (a) v. 13 (44(a).13) in Brock, *Bride of Light*, 147.

94. In comparing the narrative aspects of Ephrem's hymns, the sughyatha, and the verse homilies of Jacob of Sarug (below), I have been much helped by the essays in Mitchell, *On Narrative*, especially White, "The Value of Narrativity," 1–24; Kermode, "Secrets and Narrative Sequence," 79–98; Ricoeur, "Narrative Time," 165–186; and Scholes, "Language, Narrative, and Anti-Narrative," 200–208. See also Dubrov, "Dialogue with Death."

95. On the memra as poetic form, see Griffith, "Poetics of Scriptural Reasoning"; Brock, "Poetry and Hymnography (3): Syriac".

96. Forness, "The Construction of Metrical Poetry"; Papoutsakis, "Formulaic Language."

97. On the sung performance of memre, see Harvey, "Holy Sound."

98. Narsai (d. ca. 502) would be the other obvious Syriac writer to consider. However, Narsai makes little use of dialogue in his verse homilies, in contrast to Jacob. The difference in presentation is strikingly clear in Narsai's "Homily on Our Lord's Birth from the Holy Virgin," which covers the episodes from Luke, from the Annunciation all the way through to the presentation to Simeon (Lk 1–2). In this long homily (of 508 lines), Narsai has Mary speak only three lines: an immediate acceptance of Gabriel's announcement of her conception! The text is edited with translation by McLeod, *Narsai's Metrical Homilies*, 36–69.

99. Jacob's homilies on Mary are edited in Bedjan and Brock, *Homilies of Mar Jacob of Sarug*, 6:2–220. I cite the homilies as numbered and translated by Mary Hansbury in her collection, *Jacob of Serug, On the Mother of God*. Since Hansbury does not give line numbers, I indicate the page in her translation. Relevant here are two recent studies: Kollamparampil, *Salvation in Christ*; and Puthuparampil, *Mariological Thought of Mar Jacob*.

100. Jacob of Sarug, "On the Partaking," ll. 129–188 in Harrak, trans., 18–25.

101. Compare especially "Mary and the Angel" and "Mary and Joseph" in Brock, *Bride of Light*, 125–138, with Jacob of Sarug, "On the Nativity," ll. 155–325, 571–734 in Kollamparampil, trans., 28–49, 74–93, respectively. Some of the dialogue hymns may have been composed in the fifth century, earlier than Jacob's homilies. It is also possible, of course, that over time the dialogue portions of Jacob's Marian homilies might have given rise to sughyatha of similar content.

102. It is difficult to know the precise occasions for these different performed pieces in late antique services. The sughyatha were probably sung in vigil services, as were Ephrem's hymns. But Jacob's description in his homily "On the Partaking," ll. 129–188, gives the

impression that the choirs sang madrashe in the eucharistic liturgy as well (perhaps portions of them: select verses). Jacob's Marian memre would likely have accompanied the liturgical commemoration associated with the gospel story he was telling.

103. Jacob of Sarug, *On the Mother of God*, "Homily 1," in Hansbury, trans., 29.

104. For the larger theme in Syriac tradition, see Murray, "Mary, the Second Eve."

105. Jacob of Sarug, *On the Mother of God*, "Homily 1" in Hansbury, trans., 33.

106. Jacob of Sarug, *On the Mother of God*, "Homily 1" in Hansbury, trans., 33.

107. Jacob of Sarug, *On the Mother of God*, "Homily 1" in Hansbury, trans., 33.

108. Jacob of Sarug, *On the Mother of God*, "Homily 2" in Hansbury, trans., 53–54.

109. Jacob of Sarug, *On the Mother of God*, "Homily 2" in Hansbury, trans., 55.

110. Jacob of Sarug, *On the Mother of God*, "Homily 2" in Hansbury, trans., 57.

111. Jacob of Sarug, *On the Mother of God*, "Homily 3" in Hansbury, trans., 78.

112. Jacob of Sarug, *On the Mother of God*, "Homily 3" in Hansbury, trans., 82–83.

113. Jacob of Sarug, "On Mar Ephrem," esp. vv. 40–45 in Amar, ed. and trans., 34–35.

114. Jacob of Sarug, "On Mar Ephrem," v. 43 in Amar, ed. and trans., 34–35.

115. Helpful comparative material is considered in McClure, *Spoken Like a Woman*; Lardinois and McClure, *Making Silence Speak*.

116. Thomas, "Stories Without Texts and Without Authors."

117. Brock, "Syriac Dialogue Poems," raises especially important issues relevant to this point; for a specific example, see 45–46; also Brock, "The Sinful Woman and Satan."

118. Particularly for major feasts, phrases and words recur across different compositions. A "new" hymn could be composed from portions of already familiar verses or lines. While not exactly analogous, other liturgical texts show a similar tendency. Sebastian Brock has described the composition of anaphoras in similar terms: utilizing something like "formulaic building blocks, rather on the analogy of the formulaic features that have been isolated in the composition of oral epic poetry" (Brock, "Invocations to/for the Holy Spirit," 398; see, further, Brock, "Towards a Typology of the Epiclesis").

119. Consider the observations of Murre-van den Berg, *Scribes and Scriptures*, 156–183.

120. For incisive articulations of the positions for and against female authorship of ancient Christian texts, see Kraemer, "Women's Authorship"; Clark, *Women in Late Antiquity*, 119–138. The same question holds, for example, for apocryphal literature, martyrs' passions, or hagiography. See Harvey, "Women and Words."

121. There are important comparanda from the huge corpus of Byzantine hymnography, where, unlike in Syriac, we know about several women composers. Best known is the nun Kassia (d. 865); her renowned hymn on the Sinful Woman continues in use to the present day in churches of the Byzantine rite, sung annually in the Bridegroom Orthros for Holy Wednesday. One of her hymns, a canon for Holy Saturday, was wrongly attributed to Cosmas of Maiouma, because the propriety of singing a hymn by a woman on such a holy day was questioned. See McGuckin, "Poetry and Hymnography (2): The Greek World"; Topping, *Sacred Songs*.

4. VOICES SUNG: WOMEN'S VOICES IN CONTEXTUAL NARRATIVES

1. Portions of the following pages draw on Harvey, *Song and Memory*.

2. The groundwork on biblical figures was laid among ancient Jewish writers especially between the second century BCE and the first century CE. See, e.g., Kraemer, *When*

Aseneth Met Joseph; Wills, *The Jewish Novel in the Ancient World*; Kugel, *The Bible as It Was.* The study of biblical figures outside the Bible has produced a vast scholarship in recent decades, with attention to literature, hymnography, and art. For the pagan parallels, consider the use of female characters in literary and rhetorical exercises, as seen widely from Ovid's *Heroides* to Libanios's *Progymnasmata.*

3. Tkacz, "Singing Women's Words."

4. Rouwhorst, "Les lectionaires syriaques."

5. There is much important scholarship: den Beisen, *Simple and Bold*; Kollamparampil, *Salvation in Christ*, 49–104; Murray, *Symbols of Church and Kingdom*; Murray, "The Theory of Symbolism"; Bou Mansour, *La pensée symbolique de saint Ephrem*; Brock, *The Luminous Eye*; Griffith, *"Faith Adoring the Mystery"*; McCarron, "An Epiphany of Mystical Symbols."

6. Overview in Harvey, "Spoken Words, Voiced Silence." Greek liturgical poets of the fifth and sixth centuries, both homilists and hymnographers, shared the interest in imagined dialogue. See Barkhuizen, "Proclus of Constantinople"; and Allen, "The Sixth-Century Greek Homily." The culmination on the Greek side was the kontakion as crafted by Romanos the Melodist in the sixth century. See now Gador-Whyte, *Theology and Poetry in Early Byzantium*; and Arentzen, *The Virgin in Song.*

7. Expansion of biblical stories, with imagined speech, was a common feature of both Christian and Jewish writings of this era. Consider Pseudo-Philo, *Liber Antiquitatum*, which often provided names for the unnamed women of the Bible. Among the copious scholarship, see now Lieber, *Staging the Sacred*; Siquans, *Biblical Women in Patristic Reception.* The common factor, as Lieber signals, may have been the schools, and the way in which declamations and progymnasmata dominated education in the Roman and late antique periods. These exercises often involved imagined speeches for female characters of Greek or Roman myth. See Webb, "Poetry and Rhetoric"; Kaster, *Emotion, Restraint, and Community.* There is further discussion in chapter 6.

8. E.g., Lieber, *Staging the Sacred*; Butts and Gross, *Jews and Syriac Christians*; Grypeou and Spurling, *The Exegetical Encounter*; Frishman and Van Rompay, *Book of Genesis*; Rouwhorst, "Biblical Stories About the Prophet Elijah"; Kamesar, "Evaluation of the Narrative Aggada"; Brock, "Jewish Traditions in Syriac Sources."

9. For example, Brock, "Creating Women's Voices"; Brock, "Genesis 22 in Syriac Tradition"; Heal, "Reworking the Biblical Text"; Rodrigues Pereira, "Two Syriac Verse Homilies on Joseph." The point is highlighted in Van Rompay, "Christian Syriac Tradition of Interpretation," 641.

10. Ephrem, *Commentary on Genesis* in Amar and Mathews, trans.; Wickes, "Ephrem's Interpretation of Genesis," focuses specifically on Ephrem's crafting of speeches in this commentary, using the examples of Ephrem's treatment of Lot's daughters (Gen 19:30–38) and of Tamar (Gen 38); Brock, "Saint Ephrem on Women." For Ephrem's method in this commentary, see also Van Rompay, "Antiochene Biblical Interpretation"; and Hidal, *Interpretatio Syriaca.* Ephrem's "Commentary on Exodus" in Amar and Mathews, trans., *Selected Prose Works*, 217–265, offers similar material. See Salvesen, "Some Themes"; and Salvesen, "The Exodus Commentary of St. Ephrem."

11. Of those extant, Ephrem's commentaries on Genesis, Exodus, and the Diatessaron are the most important, both in their impact on subsequent Syriac theologians and in their richness of interaction with the biblical texts.

12. Portions of the following draw on Harvey, "Holy Impudence."

13. Talley, *Origins of the Liturgical Year*, 17–27.

14. We cannot be sure of the lectionary guiding Ephrem's hymns; on the contrary, I am arguing here that we should use his hymns to help reconstruct what the readings may have been for the services in which he participated.

15. Ephrem discoursed against all these opponent groups at length in all his literary genres: madrashe, memre, and prose discourses. But for a specific reflection on the competing biblical canons of these groups, see Ephrem, *Hymns on Virginity* 27–30 in McVey, trans., 382–397, where he sings on the theme of the three harps of revelation: the Old Testament, the New Testament, and the natural world.

16. Ephrem speaks of these women especially in *Hymns on Nativity* 1, 9, 15, and 16.

17. See, above all, Kronholm, "Holy Adultery"; Botha, "Ephrem the Syrian's Treatment of Tamar"; Menn, *Judah and Tamar*; Petit, "Exploitations non bibliques des themes de Tamar."

18. The madrashe collected as Ephrem's *Hymns on the Nativity* raise the issue of performative variation particularly well. Some of them are presented in the voice of the poet, suggesting that the verses were sung by Ephrem while the choir responded, leading the congregation in the refrain. Consider, e.g., Ephrem, *Hymns on the Nativity* 1–4. Those presented in Mary's first-person voice would suggest that the choir sang the verses, with the congregation responding: see, e.g., Ephrem, *Hymns on the Nativity* 6, 9, 15, 16, 17. Ephrem does not supply the evidence to resolve the question, but it appears that all combinations of voiced exchange were possible.

19. Ephrem, *Hymns on the Nativity* 1.12–13, 33 in McVey, trans., 65, 68.

20. And elsewhere in Ephrem, as cited in Brock, "Jacob of Serugh's Verse Homily on Tamar," 309, in the commentary to line 98. Tamar's deceit is a major theme in Ephrem's *Hymns on Virginity* 22 (coupled with that of the Samaritan Woman).

21. Ephrem, *Hymns on the Nativity* 9.7 in McVey, trans., 126.

22. Ephrem, *Hymns on the Nativity* 9.8–11 in McVey, trans., 126.

23. On the significance of this rhetoric of paradox and its strong Syriac representation, see Cameron, *Christianity and the Rhetoric of Empire*, 155–188.

24. Ephrem, *Hymns on the Nativity* 9.12–14 in McVey, trans., 126–127.

25. Ephrem, *Hymns on the Nativity* 9.16 in McVey, trans., 127.

26. Ephrem, *Hymns on the Nativity* 8.14–16 in McVey, trans., 122. For the biblical accounts: Gen 16:1–6, 17:15–17, 18:9–15 (Sarah); Gen 25:21 (Rebecca); Gen 30:1 (Rachel); 1 Sam 1:9–20 (Hannah); Lk 1:5–25 (Elizabeth).

27. Ephrem, *Hymns on the Nativity* 8.16 in McVey, trans., 122.

28. The scriptural summons to "sing to the Lord a new song" recurs in the Hebrew Bible and the New Testament: e.g., Ps 33:3, 40:3, 96:1, 98:1, 144:9, 149:1; Isa 42:10; Rev 5:9, 14:3. Ephrem would not have known Revelation, but he captures the prophetic and eschatological quality of the theme, as well as its liturgical aptness, when he applies it to Mary's song.

29. Ephrem, *Hymns on the Nativity* 15.8 in McVey, trans., 147.

30. Ephrem, *Hymns on the Nativity* 4.62–63 in McVey, trans., 94.

31. For the polemical intent of Ephrem's establishment of the women's choirs, see chapter 2.

32. Ephrem's *Prose Refutations* are well known. His focus on Arians (of various kinds) is especially strong in his *Hymns on Heresies, Hymns on Faith*, and *Homilies on Faith*. See Griffith, "'Denominationalism'"; Griffith, "Setting Right the Church of Syria"; Griffith, "Faith Adoring the Mystery."

33. E.g., Ephrem, *Hymns on the Nativity* 11, 13, 19.

34. On the emergence of Syriac monasticism, see Griffith, "Asceticism in the Church of Syria."

35. Jacob of Sarug, "On Tamar."

36. Rouwhorst, "Les lectionaires syriaques"; Burkitt, "Early Syriac Lectionary System."

37. Jacob of Sarug, "On Tamar," ll. 51–52 in Brock, ed. and trans., 294.

38. The earliest extant Syriac lectionary list, in British Library Add. 14528, does not include Mt 1:1–16 anywhere, but Lk 3:21–38 is listed in at least one early manuscript for Epiphany. See Burkitt, "Early Syriac Lectionary System"; Rouwhorst, "Epiphany.

39. Jacob of Sarug, "On Tamar," ll. 73–90 in Brock, ed. and trans., 295.

40. Jacob of Sarug, "On Tamar," ll. 93–104 in Brock, ed. and trans., 295.

41. Jacob of Sarug, "On Tamar," ll. 111–117 in Brock, ed. and trans., 295–296.

42. Jacob of Sarug, "On Tamar," ll. 137–157 in Brock, ed. and trans., 296. The key to Jacob's exegetical retelling probably lay in the pertinent passage from Ephrem's "Commentary on Genesis": "Tamar thought, 'How can I make the Hebrews realize that it is not marriage for which I am hungering, but rather that I am yearning for the blessing that is hidden in them? . . . I ought then to have relations with Judah so that by the treasure I receive, I might enrich my poverty, and in the widowhood I preserve, I might make it clear that I did not desire marriage." Ephrem, "Commentary on Genesis" 34.2 in Amar and Mathews, trans., 183.

43. Jacob of Sarug, "On Tamar," ll. 186, 205–206 in Brock, ed. and trans., 297–298.

44. This passage is an interesting reversal of a common late antique literary topos in which the penitent harlot (whether of scripture or hagiography) removes her finery and dons sackcloth and ashes instead. In Syriac, clothing is an important theological metaphor. See Brock, "Clothing Metaphors." On the literary function of garments in the Genesis narratives, see Furman, "His Story Versus Her Story."

45. Jacob of Sarug, "On Tamar," ll. 233–253 in Brock, ed. and trans., 298–299. The scene is highly reminiscent of another hagiographic motif of concealed sanctity, presented by the perfect ascetic in the guise of a reckless dissolute.

46. Jacob of Sarug, "On Tamar," ll. 311–314 in Brock, ed. and trans., 300.

47. Jacob of Sarug, "On Tamar," ll. 341–348 in Brock, ed. and trans., 301.

48. Jacob of Sarug, "On Tamar," ll. 362–420 in Brock, trans., 301–302.

49. For the religious context of Jacob's times, see Van Rompay, "Society and Community." For Jacob's Christology, see now Forness, *Preaching Christology*.

50. So argues McVey, "Ephrem the Kitharode." E.g., John of Ephesos, *Lives of the Eastern Saints*, chs. 12 and 27. See Harvey, "Women's Service," and for the texts, Brock and Harvey, *Holy Women*, 124–133, 133–141, respectively.

51. Jacob of Sarug, "On Mar Ephrem."

52. E.g., the interesting study of Cunningham, "Women and Preaching in the Patristic Age."

53. Coon, *Sacred Fictions*; Constantinou, *Female Corporeal Performances*.

54. E.g., Constantinou, *Female Corporeal Performances*, 19–58.

55. Compare Forness, *Preaching Christology*.

56. Portions of the following follow Harvey, "Bearing Witness."

57. Ephrem, *Hymns on Virginity* in McVey, trans., 261–468. This collection is a compilation of single hymns and other, smaller collections; see McVey, *Ephrem the Syrian*, 39–41. If the *Hymns on Virginity* discussed in this chapter were intended by Ephrem for teaching his

students rather than for liturgical performance, then we may well be glimpsing the training of women for the choir.

58. Ephrem, *Hymns on Virginity* 26.3 in McVey, trans., 377. The verb here, *ethra'am*, meaning "sounded forth/ proclaimed," could also be translated "was indignant"; the sense then elides Martha's indignation in the biblical account with her sounding voice in the hymn.

59. Ephrem, *Hymns on Virginity* 26.5 in McVey, trans., 378.

60. Ephrem, *Hymns on Virginity* 26.9 in McVey, trans., 377–381.

61. Ephrem, *Hymns on Virginity* 34 in McVey, trans., 411–415.

62. Ephrem, *Hymns on Virginity* 26.3 in McVey, trans., 377–378. Sarah's service to the angels: Gen 18:6.

63. Ephrem, *Hymns on Virginity* 22.2 in McVey, trans., 355.

64. Ephrem, *Hymns on Virginity* 22.5 in McVey, trans., 356.

65. Ephrem, *Hymns on Virginity* 22.6 in McVey, trans., 356.

66. Ephrem, *Hymns on Virginity* 22.21 in McVey, trans., 360.

67. Ephrem, *Hymns on Virginity* 22.17, 20, 21 in McVey, trans., 359–360.

68. Ephrem, *Hymns on Virginity* 23.4 in McVey, trans., 362.

69. Ephrem, *Hymns on Virginity* 22.5 in McVey, trans., 362.

70. Ephrem, *Hymns on Virginity* 23.1 in McVey, trans., 361.

71. Ephrem, *Hymns on Virginity* 16.7 in McVey, trans., 331.

72. Ephrem, *Hymns on Virginity* 19.2 in McVey, trans., 342.

73. Ephrem, *Hymns on Resurrection* 2.2 in Brock and Kiraz, eds. and trans., *Select Poems*, 171. The entire hymn makes this point.

74. The following draws on Harvey et al., *Women Whom Jesus Met*.

75. Jacob of Sarug, "On the Samaritan Woman" in Harvey et al., trans., 51–124.

76. Jacob of Sarug, "On the Samaritan Woman," l. 192 in Harvey et al., trans., 76–77.

77. Jacob of Sarug, "On the Samaritan Woman," ll. 278–288 in Harvey et al., trans., 86–87.

78. Jacob of Sarug, "On the Samaritan Woman," ll. 299–302 in Harvey et al., trans., 88.

79. Jacob of Sarug, "On the Samaritan Woman," ll. 344–350 in Harvey et al., trans., 92.

80. Jacob of Sarug, "On the Samaritan Woman," ll. 611–634 in Harvey et al., trans., 118–122.

81. Jacob of Sarug, "On Mar Ephrem," esp. vv. 41–42, 105, 107, 108 in Amar, trans., 34–35, 50–51.

82. Jacob of Sarug, "On the Canaanite Woman," in Harvey et al., trans., 1–49.

83. Jacob of Sarug, "On the Canaanite Woman," ll. 84, 101–102 in Harvey et al., trans., 66, 68.

84. Jacob of Sarug, "On the Canaanite Woman," ll. 119, 157, 183, 379 in Harvey et al., trans., 18–19, 22–23, 26–27, 44–45.

85. Jacob of Sarug, "On the Canaanite Woman," l. 36 and variant in Harvey et al., trans., 10–11.

86. Jacob of Sarug, "On the Canaanite Woman," ll. 47–48 in Harvey et al., trans., 12–13.

87. Jacob of Sarug, "On the Canaanite Woman," ll. 111–113 in Harvey et al., trans., 18–19.

88. Jacob of Sarug, "On the Canaanite Woman," l. 127 in Harvey et al., trans., 20–21.

89. Jacob of Sarug, "On the Canaanite Woman," l. 157 in Harvey et al., trans., 22–23.

90. Jacob of Sarug, "On the Canaanite Woman," l. 256 in Harvey et al., trans., 32–33.

91. Jacob of Sarug, "On the Canaanite Woman," l. 387 in Harvey et al., trans., 46–47.

92. Jacob of Sarug, "On the Canaanite Woman," ll. 386–368 in Harvey et al., trans., 46.

93. Harvey, "Why the Perfume Mattered."

94. Heal, "The Syriac History of Joseph"; Heal, "Reworking the Biblical Text." Here, too, there is a crucial passage in Ephrem, "Commentary on Genesis" 35.1–2, and 79 in Amar and Mathews, trans., 185 and 197–198, respectively.

95. Harvey, "Encountering Eve." For a complementary perspective from Greek and Latin sources, see Ellison, "Reimagining and Reimaging Eve."

96. Jacob of Sarug, "On the Nativity 3," ll. 358–359 in Kollamparampil, trans., 226–227.

97. Good examples would be the depiction of Delilah as "the second Eve" in Jacob of Sarug, "On Samson," ll. 333–412 in Miller, trans., 46–55; and the presentation of Jezebel as a model for Zion (= the Synagogue)—a vitriolic anti-Jewish diatribe—in Jacob of Sarug, "On the Transfiguration," ll. 445–466, in Kollamparampil, trans., 54–59.

98. Tertullian, "On the Apparel of Women" 1.1–2 in Quain, trans., *Tertullian*, 117–118.

99. Aphrahat, *Demonstration* 6, "On Covenanters" in Lehto, trans., 160–198.

100. Aphrahat, *Demonstration* 6.3 in Lehto, trans., 177–179.

101. For the scant historical information, see Lehto, *Demonstrations of Aphrahat*, 1–24.

102. Compare, for example, Cyrus of Edessa, *Explanation of the Resurrection* 6.5 in Macomber, ed. and trans., 103 (CSCO 355–356/Scr. Syr. 155–156).

103. Murray, "Rhetorical Patterns."

104. Aphrahat, *Demonstrations* 4.8 and 3.10 in Lehto, trans., 134 and 118, respectively.

105. Aphrahat, *Demonstration* 16.6 in Lehto, trans., 381–382.

106. Aphrahat, *Demonstration* 14, "An Argument in Response to Dissension," in Lehto, trans., 305–360.

107. Murray, "Some Rhetorical Patterns."

108. See the summary by Van Rompay, "Narsai."

109. Van Rompay, "Society and Community."

110. Barhadbeshabba, *Ecclesiastical History*, ch. 31 in Becker, trans., *Sources*, 69.

111. While not as extensive a corpus as those of Ephrem or Jacob of Sarug, more than eighty memre by Narsai are extant. See now Butts et al., *Narsai*; and Brock, "Published Verse Homilies: Index."

112. Narsai, "Homily on Our Lord's Birth" in McLeod, ed. and trans., 36–69.

113. Such as those collected in Brock, *Bride of Light*. Consider also the standard invocations to Mary included in the hymns and liturgical prayers attributed to Rabbula: for texts and translations, see Phenix and Horn, eds., *Rabbula Corpus*, 286–409. See further Smelova, "Melkite Syriac Hymns." For Jacob's most important homilies on Mary, see Kollamparampil, ed. and trans., *Jacob of Sarug's Homilies on the Nativity*; and Hansbury, trans., *Jacob of Serug on the Mother of God*.

114. The danger from Narsai's perspective was not only from miaphysite circles, but also from dyophysites, whose affirmation of the title Theotokos, "Mother of God," at the Council of Ephesos in 431 appeared heretical to the followers of Nestorios and Theodore of Mopsuestia.

115. Narsai, "Homily on Our Lord's Birth," ll. 191–196 in McLeod, ed. and trans., 49.

116. Narsai, "Homily on Our Lord's Birth," ll. 389–508 in McLeod, ed. and trans., 60–69.

117. Narsai, "Homily on Our Lord's Birth," l. 455 in McLeod, ed. and trans., 66–67.

118. Narsai, "Homily on Our Lord's Birth," ll. 425–434 in McLeod, ed. and trans., 64–65.

119. Narsai, "Homily on Our Lord's Birth," ll. 461–490 in McLeod, ed. and trans., 66–69.

120. Narsai, "On the Canaanite Woman" in Walsh, trans., 69–87; the manuscript witness is discussed at 70.

121. Walsh, "Holy Boldness"; Walsh, "From Sketches to Portraits"; Walsh, "How the Weak Rib Prevailed!" Interesting technical similarities are examined in Forness, "The Construction of Metrical Poetry."

122. Ephrem, *Commentary of the Diatessaron* 12.13 in McCarthy, trans., 196–197. For a sense of other patristic exegetical themes, see Oden and Hall, *Ancient Christian Commentary on Scripture*, 100–102. Ephrem's influence was profound on both East and West Syriac traditions. See, e.g., Jansma, "Narsai and Ephrem."

123. Narsai, "On the Canaanite Woman," ll. 102, 103, 149 in Walsh, trans., 75–77.

124. Narsai, "On the Canaanite Woman," ll. 216, 223, 226 in Walsh, trans., 79.

125. Narsai, "On the Canaanite Woman," l. 239 in Walsh, trans., 80.

126. Narsai, "On the Canaanite Woman," l. 242 in Walsh, trans., 80.

127. Narsai, "On the Canaanite Woman," ll. 243–272 in Walsh, trans., 80–81.

128. Narsai, "On the Canaanite Woman," ll. 214, 217 in Walsh, trans., 79.

129. Narsai, "On the Canaanite Woman," ll. 299–311 in Walsh, trans., 82.

130. Narsai, "On the Canaanite Woman," ll. 315–318 in Walsh, trans., 83.

131. Narsai, "On the Canaanite Woman," ll. 323–326 in Walsh, trans., 83.

132. Narsai, "On the Canaanite Woman," ll. 353–360 in Walsh, trans., 84.

133. Narsai, "On the Canaanite Woman," ll. 375–420 in Walsh, trans., 85–86.

134. Narsai, "On the Canaanite Woman," ll. 421–431 in Walsh, trans., 87.

135. Narsai, "On the Reproof of Eve's Daughters" in Molenberg, trans., "Narsai's Memra," 65–87.

136. Barhadbeshabba, *Ecclesiastical History*, ch. 31 in Becker, trans., *Sources*, 66–68.

137. Molenberg, "Narsai's Memra," 66–75.

138. Molenberg, "Narsai's Memra," 66–75. Becker, *Sources*, 86n147, suggests Molenberg overreads the evidence.

139. The homily was firmly part of Narsai's transmission history. It was preserved in six manuscripts containing his memre. See Molenberg, "Narsai's Memra," 65; Macomber, "Manuscripts of the Metrical Homilies of Narsai," 305, no. 80.

140. Narsai, "On the Reproof of Eve's Daughters," v. 151 in Molenberg, trans., "Narsai's Memra," 84.

141. Narsai, "On the Reproof of Eve's Daughters," vv. 179–181 in Molenberg, trans., 85.

142. Narsai, "On the Reproof of Eve's Daughters," v. 51 in Molenberg, trans., 78.

143. Narsai, "On the Reproof of Eve's Daughters," vv. 205–208 in Molenberg, trans., 86. I have added square brackets for clarification; the parenthetical inserts are the translator's.

144. Narsai, "On the Reproof of Eve's Daughters," vv. 213–219 in Molenberg, trans., 87.

145. Bou Mansour, *Le ministère sacerdotal*, 568–574, has an interesting discussion on women and priesthood in ancient Syriac sources, with a strongly positive assessment of Narsai's ability to grant full equality to women and men without any lingering consequences from the sin of Eve.

146. Fiey, "Diptyques nestoriens."

147. Edited with detailed commentary in Fiey, "Une hymne nestorienne."

148. See Connolly, "The Book of Life"; Palmer, "The Book of Life in the Syriac Liturgy."

149. Harvey, "Encountering Eve." Bou Mansour, *Le ministère sacerdotal*, 568–574, sees Narsai as more promising than Jacob of Sarug in this respect.

150. There are multiple examples in Brock, *Bride of Light*: e.g., Prayer Song 6.12–14 ("Hymns on Mary" 1.12–14), Prayer Song 7.7–9 ("Hymns on Mary" 2.7–9), Prayer Song 23.19–24 ("Sughitha" 2.19–24), at 38, 40, 85–86.

151. E.g., "Liturgia Sancti Jacobi Syrorum," in Hammond, ed., *Antient Liturgies*, 61; "The Liturgy of the Syrian Jacobites," in Brightman, *Eastern Liturgies*, 73–74.

152. See the examples in Harvey, "Encountering Eve."

153. Christensen, "Holy Women as Humble Teachers." Christensen examines the *vitae* of Macrina, Melania the Younger, Syncletica, Febronia, and Radegund, along with some discussion of Jerome's letters about Paula and Marcella.

154. Maxwell, *Simplicity and Humility*, concisely lays out the issues. She does not directly address women or gender except in a short discussion on Macrina at 140–144. This paradox for women was articulated especially well in Elizabeth Clark's groundbreaking article, "Ascetic Renunciation and Feminine Advancement." See also Gillian Clark, *Women in Late Antiquity*, 119–141.

155. Fundamental for the lifting of this situation into common scholarly discussion were pioneering works such as Daly, *The Church and the Second Sex*; Ruether, *Religion and Sexism*; Clark, *Women in the Early Church*.

156. I am mindful here, as elsewhere, of the issues raised so helpfully by Berger, *Gender Differences* and Berger, *Women's Ways of Worship*.

5. SINGING VOICES: WOMEN AMONG THE ASSEMBLY

1. Jacob of Sarug disparaged those heads of households who sent a female slave or other servant to the church to take the memorial offering for the departed, rather than bringing it themselves: Jacob of Sarug,"On the Reposed," ll. 265–272 in Miller, trans., 52–53; Syriac in Bedjan and Brock, *Homilies of Mar Jacob*, 1:535–550.

2. The inconsistency of ecclesiastical terminology in the early Syriac—and, indeed, all early Christian—texts must be kept in mind. Designated terminology for church offices varied in usage for centuries. Two relevant discussions here are Pylvänäinen, *Agents in Liturgy*, and Rouwhorst, "Deacons."

3. Points stressed with deep discernment by Teresa Berger in her two books, *Gender Differences* and *Women's Ways of Worship*.

4. Torjesen, "Clergy and Laity."

5. Ephrem, *Hymns on Easter* 2.8–9, trans. Griffith, in McKinnon, ed., *Music*, 93–94.

6. Jacob of Sarug, "On the Love of God Towards Humanity," ll. 453–464 in Sirgy, ed. and trans., 54–55.

7. *Book of Steps*, Memre 12.4 in Kitchen and Parmentier, trans., 122.

8. Hagiographies often mention liturgical attendance by laity visiting local or distant monastic communities. Such occasions were not necessarily eucharistic liturgies; they might be daily or evening offices, or homiletic exhortations by holy men or women offered to visitors. For example, in the *Life of Febronia*, sec. 38, the women of the convent "and many other people" gathered annually for the saint's memorial, especially for "the prayers of the night office," when the saint sometimes appeared (trans. in Brock and Harvey, *Holy Women*,

173–174). John of Ephesos, *Lives of the Eastern Saints*, ch. 4, "Abraham and Maro," describes how the stylite Maro would preach often "not to us [monks] only, but to laymen also as well, and even to women and children and fathers and all classes" (in Brooks, ed. and trans., *PO* 17, 77). Various church canons address questions regarding the sacramental authority of stylites in such circumstances: "Answers from the Orient Fathers," canon 14; "Again, Ja'qob to Johannan 'Estunara," canons 4 and 5; "Further Canons of Jacob of Edessa," canon 7 in Vööbus, ed. and trans., *The [West Syrian] Synodicon*, CSCO 368/Scr. Syr. 162, 160, 227–228, 245 (English); CSCO 367/Scr. Syr. 161, 166–167, 247–249, 270 (Syriac).

9. For a concise presentation of the scholarly debates, see Bradshaw, *Origins of Christian Worship*, 73–97. Still useful as summaries of the key documents are several chapters in O'Connell, trans., *Roles in the Liturgical Assembly*: Arranz, "Functions of the Christian Assembly," 29–59; Botte, "Christian People and Hierarchy," 61–72; Braniste, "The Liturgical Assembly," 73–100.

10. For nuanced consideration of how to use these texts, see now Pylvänäinen, *Agents in Liturgy*; and for a truly creative rereading, Doerfler, *Constituting the Past*.

11. Vööbus, ed. and trans., *Didascalia Apostolorum in Syriac, I: Chapters I–X*, CSCO 401–402/Scr. Syr. 175–176; and Vööbus, ed. and trans., *Didascalia Apostolorum in Syriac, II: Chapters XI–XXVI*, CSCO 407–408/Scr. Syr. 179–180.

12. *Didascalia*, ch. 9 in Vööbus, ed. and trans., CSCO 402/Scr. Syr. 176, 99–110, at 100 (English), CSCO 401/Scr. Syr. 175, 103–116, at 104 (Syriac). I have added text in square brackets for clarification; additions in parentheses are the translator's.

13. *Didascalia*, ch. 9 in Vööbus, ed. and trans., CSCO 402/Scr. Syr. 176, 101 (English), CSCO 401/Scr. Syr. 175, 105 (Syriac).

14. *Didascalia*, ch. 9 in Vööbus, ed. and trans., CSCO 402/Scr. Syr. 176, 107 (English), CSCO 401/Scr. Syr. 175, 112 (Syriac).

15. *Didascalia*, ch. 9 in Vööbus, ed. and trans., CSCO 402/Scr. Syr. 176, 109 (English), CSCO 401/Scr. Syr. 175, 114 (Syriac).

16. *Didascalia*, ch. 13 in Vööbus, ed. and trans., CSCO 408/Scr. Syr. 180, 135–141 (English), CSCO 407/Scr. Syr. 179, 148–154 (Syriac).

17. "Testament of the Lord" in Vööbus, ed. and trans., *The [West Syrian] Synodicon*, CSCO 368/Scr. Syr. 162, 37 (English), CSCO 367/Scr. Syr. 161, 14 (Syriac).

18. "Testament of the Lord" in Vööbus, ed. and trans., *The [West Syrian] Synodicon*, CSCO 368/Scr. Syr. 162, 40–45 (English), CSCO 367/Scr. Syr. 161, 18—25 (Syriac).

19. "Testament of the Lord" in Vööbus, ed. and trans., *The [West Syrian] Synodicon*, CSCO 368/Scr. Syr. 162, 46 (English), CSCO 367/Scr. Syr. 161, 25–26 (Syriac).

20. "Testament of the Lord, Book II of Clement" in Vööbus, ed. and trans., *The [West Syrian] Synodicon*, CSCO 368/Scr. Syr. 162, 47–57 (English), CSCO 367/Scr. Syr. 161, 27–39 (Syriac).

21. "Testament of the Lord, Book II of Clement" in Vööbus, ed. and trans., *The [West Syrian] Synodicon*, CSCO 368/Scr. Syr. 162, 50 (English), CSCO 367/Scr. Syr. 161, 31 (Syriac).

22. "Canons of the Testament of the Lord," canons 4–5 in Vööbus, ed. and trans., *The [West Syrian] Synodicon*, CSCO 368/Scr. Syr. 162, 57–58 (English), CSCO 367/Scr. Syr. 161, 40–41 (Syriac).

23. "Canons of the Testament of the Lord," canon 36 in Vööbus, ed. and trans., *The [West Syrian] Synodicon*, CSCO 368/Scr. Syr. 162, 61 (English), CSCO 367/Scr. Syr. 161, 44 (Syriac).

24. "Canons of Johannan bar Qursos," canon 16 in Vööbus, ed. and trans., *The [West Syrian] Synodicon*, CSCO 368/Scr. Syr. 162, 149 (English), CSCO 367/Scr. Syr. 161, 153 (Syriac).

25. For prominent examples, see MacMullen, *The Second Church*, 1–32, 117–124 (interestingly thin on Syriac evidence); Maxwell, *Christianization and Communication*; Tannous, *The Making of the Medieval Middle East*, 1–198.

26. Maxwell, *Christianization and Communication*, and Leyerle, *The Narrative Shape of Emotion*, both on John Chrysostom in Antioch, make interesting comparison with the material considered here.

27. The groundbreaking work on such perspective is Krueger, *Liturgical Subjects*.

28. Portions of this section follow Harvey, "Liturgy and Ethics in Ancient Christianity."

29. Ephrem, *Hymns on Virginity* 14.2 in McVey, trans., *Ephrem the Syrian*, 321.

30. See especially Brock, *The Luminous Eye*, 99–114; Murray, *Symbols of Church and Kingdom*, 89–91, 199–203.

31. Ephrem, *Hymns on the Nativity* 3.1 in McVey, trans., 82–83.

32. Ephrem adds further: "Blessed is the Physician who descended and cut painlessly / and healed the sores with a mild medicine" (*Hymns on the Nativity* 3.19, 3.20 in McVey, trans., 87.) Compare *Hymns on the Nativity* 4.24–26 in McVey, trans., 91: the Nativity feast was itself "a treasure of medicine" for a humanity "severely wounded," healing "our blindness," feeding "our hunger."

33. Ephrem, *Hymns on Virginity* 37.9 in McVey, trans., 426.

34. Ephrem, *Hymns on the Nativity* 15.2–3 in McVey, trans., 146. This theme is stressed throughout Ephrem's Nativity hymns; see especially Ephrem, *Hymns on the Nativity* 11.7–8, 13, 15, 18, and 19.

35. Ephrem, *Hymns on the Nativity* 18.20 in McVey, trans., 122.

36. Ephrem, *Hymns on Virginity* 37.3 in McVey, trans., 425.

37. McVey, following Beck, accepts the authenticity of this hymn (although my point here does not actually require Ephrem's authorship): McVey, *Ephrem the Syrian*, 29 and at n121.

38. Ephrem, *Hymns on the Nativity*, 1.63–72 in McVey, trans., 71–72.

39. Ephrem, *Hymns on the Nativity*, 1.73–74 in McVey, trans., 72.

40. Ephrem, *Hymns on the Nativity*, 1.74–92, in McVey, trans., 72–74.

41. Ephrem, *Hymns on the Nativity*, 1.93–99 in McVey, trans., 74.

42. E.g., Ephrem, *Hymns on Virginity* 2.14–15, 37.2 in McVey, trans., 270 and 425, respectively.

43. Ephrem, *Hymns on the Nativity* 4.50 in McVey, trans., 93.

44. Portions of what follows draw on Harvey, "Creation, Order, Beauty."

45. Jacob of Sarug, "On the Fashioning of Creation," ll. 190–194, 201–202 in Mathews, ed. and trans., 68–69. Also Jacob of Sarug, "On the Love of God Towards Humanity."

46. Jacob of Sarug, "On the Fashioning of Creation," ll. 180–233, 465–482 in Mathews, ed. and trans., 66–73 and 94–97, respectively.

47. Jacob of Sarug, "On the Lord's Prayer," ll. 433–449 in Reed, ed. and trans., 58–61.

48. Jacob of Sarug, "On the Giving of Praise," ll. 69–78 in Holy Transfiguration Monastery [Dana Miller], trans., 62.

49. For example, Jacob of Sarug, "On the Fashioning of Creation," ll. 1805–1920 in Mathews, ed. and trans., 250–263.

50. Jacob of Sarug, "On Palm Sunday," ll. 237–240, in Kollamparampil, ed. and trans., 28–29.

51. Jacob of Sarug, "On Palm Sunday," ll. 275–304, in Kollamparampil, ed. and trans., 32–36.

52. Compare, e.g., Jacob of Sarug, "Homily 3 on the Nativity," ll. 27–34, 342–370, in Kollamparampil, *Jacob of Sarug's Homilies on the Nativity*, trans., 188–189, 224–227.

53. Such processional lists were traditional in ancient Mediterranean societies. For an example comparable here, see Proclus of Constantinople, *Homily* 1.1 and *Homily* 4.2 in Constas, ed. and trans., *Proclus of Constantinople*, 136–137, 228–231; and the discussion, including the pre-Christian traditions, in Limberis, *Divine Heiress*, 7–29.

54. Narsai, "On the Sanctification of the Church," v. 157 in Harrak, ed. and trans., 46–47.

55. Jacob of Sarug, "On the Love of God Towards Humanity," ll. 465–470 in Sirgy, ed. and trans., 56–57.

56. Ephrem, *Hymns on the Nativity* 6.21–23 in McVey, trans., 114.

57. Crucial to this theme is Brock, "The Priesthood of the Baptised."

58. (Ps.-)Joshua the Stylite, *Chronicle*, sec. 31 in Trombley and Watt, trans., 30.

59. (Ps.-)Joshua the Stylite, *Chronicle*, sec. 35 in Trombley and Watt, trans., 34.

60. (Ps.-)Joshua the Stylite, *Chronicle*, sec. 36 in Trombley and Watt, trans., 35–36.

61. (Ps.-)Joshua the Stylite, *Chronicle*, sec. 43 in Trombley and Watt, trans., 45.

62. (Ps.-)Joshua the Stylite, *Chronicle*, sec. 100 in Trombley and Watt, trans., 117–118.

63. *Life of Rabbula*, sec. 55 in Phenix and Horn, eds. and trans., 81.

64. Khouri-Sarkis, "Réception d'un évêque syrien au VIᵉ siècle"; Taft, *Through Their Own Eyes*, 40–41. See now Brock, "An Episcopal *adventus*," for the full text.

65. It is worth considering these events through the lens of "resonance," the notion of the embodied, sonic interaction within and among the congregation, and between the congregation and other liturgical performers, whether singers or listeners: e.g., Porter, "Back and Forth"; Porter, *Ecologies of Resonance*.

66. Compare the even more extensive processions with responses conducted by the Byzantine imperial court: Torres, "'*Polla eti eis polla*.'"

67. Cyrillona, "On the Scourges," ll. 67–82 in Griffin, ed. and trans., 136–143. On this text, see the important discussion in Griffin, *Cyrillona: A Critical Study*, 179–230. Curiously, the manuscript identifies this as a hymn (in fact, "madrashe" in the plural), but Griffin points out it is clearly a sermon, directly focused on the preacher and his afflicted congregation (179–180).

68. Cyrillona, "On the Scourges," ll. 634–637 in Griffin, ed. and trans., 186–187.

69. Ephrem, *Hymns on the Resurrection* 2.9 in Brock and Kiraz, eds. and trans., *Select Poems*, 177.

70. Ephrem, *Hymns on the Resurrection* 2.2 in Brock and Kiraz, eds. and trans., *Select Poems*, 171.

71. Ephrem, *Hymns on the Resurrection* 2.3 in Brock and Kiraz, eds. and trans., *Select Poems*, 173.

72. Ephrem, *Hymns on the Resurrection* 2.7 in Brock and Kiraz, eds. and trans., *Select Poems*, 175.

73. Ephrem, *Hymns on the Resurrection* 2.6 and 2.8 in Brock and Kiraz, eds. and trans., *Select Poems*, 175.

74. Prayer Song 20. Response and verse 4 (= Hymns on Mary 15, response and verse 4), trans. in Brock, *Bride of Light*, 70.

75. John of Ephesos, *Lives*, ch. 31 in Brooks, ed. and trans., *PO* 18, 576–585, at 581–583.

76. Ephrem, *Hymns on the Resurrection* 2.2 in Brock and Kiraz, eds. and trans., *Select Poems*, 171.

77. Jacob's attention to listening as a formative moral and ethical category was consonant with the broader Mediterranean culture of education. See especially Harrison, *The Art of Listening*.

78. On the legacy of Plato and Aristotle for late antique Christian culture, see Harrison, *The Art of Listening*, 23–60. Chidester, *Word and Light*, remains foundational.

79. Jacob of Sarug, "The Conversion of the Apostle Paul," l. 192, in Hansbury and Parakkott, trans., *Jacob of Sarug's Homilies on Paul*, 24–25.

80. The capacity of hearing to encounter sound across distance was noted by the late fourth-century Syrian bishop Nemesios of Emesa: *On the Nature of Man*, secs. 62, 80 in Sharples and van der Eijk, trans., 108 and 139, respectively. As Chidester noted about Plato and Aristotle, "Basically, hearing was associated with a relatively discontinuous relationship between the object of perception and the perceiving subject" (Chidester, *Word and Light*, 7).

81. Again, the work of Mark Porter and others is relevant. Porter, "Back and Forth"; Porter, *Ecologies of Resonance*; Hackett, "Sound, Music, and the Study of Religion"; Laack, "Sound, Music and Religion."

82. Jacob of Sarug, "On the Tower of Babel," ll. 69–74 in Butts, trans., 14.

83. Note especially Plutarch, "On Listening to Lectures," sec. 14: "For [the hearer] is a participant in the discourse and a fellow-worker with the speaker" (in Babbitt, ed. and trans., *Plutarch's Moralia*, 1:244–245). See, further, Harrison, "Playing Ball"; Harrison, *The Art of Listening*. From the Syriac side, groundbreaking work may now be seen in Wickes, *Bible and Poetry*; and Forness, *Preaching Christology*.

84. Jacob of Sarug, "On Elisha: About Namaan the Edomite and His Disciple, Gahzi," l. 4 in Kaufman, trans., *Jacob of Sarug's Homilies on Elisha*, 174.

85. Jacob of Sarug, "On the Ascension of Elijah," ll. 25–28 in Kaufman, trans., *Jacob of Sarug's Homilies on Elijah*, 358.

86. Brock, "Poetry and Hymnography (3): Syriac," 663; Harvey, "The Poet's Prayer" (on which portions of this discussion draw).

87. Jacob of Sarug, "On Pentecost," ll. 1–6 in Kollamparampil, trans., 4–5.

88. Jacob of Sarug, "On the Fashioning of Creation," ll. 18–20 in Mathews, ed. and trans., 46–47.

89. Jacob of Sarug, "On the Fashioning of Creation," ll. 53–54; Mathews, ed. and trans., 50–51.

90. On ritual agents, see, for example, Bell, *Ritual Theory, Ritual Practice*, 118–142.

91. Jacob of Sarug, "On Elisha the Prophet," ll. 19–20 in Kaufman, trans., *Jacob of Sarug's Homilies on Elisha*, 10–11.

92. Jacob of Sarug, "On Elisha the Prophet," ll. 33–40 in Kaufman, trans., *Jacob of Sarug's Homilies on Elisha*, 10–11.

93. Jacob of Sarug, "On Elisha the Prophet," ll. 34–35 in Kaufman, trans., *Jacob of Sarug's Homilies on Elisha*, 10–11.

94. Jacob of Sarug, "On Elijah When He Fled from Jezebel," ll. 61–65 in Kaufman, trans., *Jacob of Sarug's Homilies on Elijah*, 124–125.

95. Jacob of Sarug, "On the Partaking," l. 123 in Harrak, trans., 18–19.

96. Jacob of Sarug, "On the Famine That Was in Samaria," ll. 29–30 in Kaufman, trans., *Jacob of Sarug's Homilies on Elisha*, 250.

97. Harvey, "To Whom Did Jacob Preach?"

98. Jacob of Sarug, "Homily 61, On Paul," ll. 183–186 in Hansbury and Parakkott, trans., *Jacob of Sarug's Homilies on Paul*, 24–25.

99. Jacob of Sarug, "On Mar Ephrem," vv. 128–146 in Amar, ed. and trans., 57–63. The entire passage, continuing through verse 169 on p. 67, is a frank expression of pastoral frustration.

100. Jacob of Sarug, "On the Lord's Prayer," l. 126 in Reed, ed. and trans., 128–129.

101. Jacob of Sarug, "Homily 61, On Paul," ll. 57–60 in Hansbury and Parakkott, trans., *Jacob of Sarug's Homilies on Paul*, 12–13.

102. Compare the broader Syriac theological view: Brock, "On the Priesthood of the Baptised."

103. Jacob of Sarug, "Concerning the Red Heifer," ll. 55–56 in Alibertius, ed. and trans., 20–21.

104. Jacob of Sarug, "On the Partaking," ll. 129–142 in Harrak, trans., 18–21.

105. Jacob of Sarug, "On the Partaking," ll. 155–156 in Harrak, trans., 22–23.

106. Jacob of Sarug, "On the Partaking," ll. 163–166 in Harrak, trans., 22–23.

107. Jacob of Sarug, "On the Partaking," ll. 171–176 in Harrak, trans., 22–23.

108. Jacob, "On Mar Ephrem," vv. 114, 152 in Amar, ed. and trans., 53, 65.

109. Jacob of Sarug, "On the Partaking," ll. 317–320 and l. 214 in Harrak, trans., 38–39 and 28–29, respectively.

110. Jacob of Sarug, "On the Prodigal Son," ll. 15–64, trans. Holy Transfiguration Monastery [Dana Miller], 12–14.

111. Jacob of Sarug, "Homily 1 on the Nativity," ll. 1037–1038 in Kollamparampil, trans., 126–127.

112. Jacob of Sarug, *Against the Jews* 7.529–542 in Albert, ed., 216 (my translation).

113. Foundational for the Syriac context is Brock, "On the Priesthood of the Baptised." Bou Mansour, *Le ministère sacerdotal*, is the starting point on priesthood in Syriac tradition. In an interesting appendix, "Annexe: Le sacerdoce common et le role de la femme dans le sacerdoce," 559–574, Bou Mansour responds to Brock's article and considers ramifications of the ancient theological witness for present-day questions of laity and women in the Syriac churches.

114. Syriac tradition is very rich on the Sinful Woman. See Harvey, "Why the Perfume Mattered"; and for a nuanced reading of the Syriac influence on the larger Orthodox heritage, Kalish, *She Who Loved Much*.

115. Ephrem, *Hymns on Virginity* 35.5 in McVey, trans., 417.

116. Ephrem, *Hymns on Virginity* 35.7 in McVey, trans., 418.

117. Ephrem, *Hymns on Virginity* 35.8 in McVey, trans., 418. Ephrem here conflates the unnamed woman of Lk 7:36–50 with Mary of Bethany in Jn 12:3.

118. Ephrem, *Hymns on Virginity* 26.4 in McVey, trans., 378.

119. Ephrem, "Homily on Our Lord" 44.1 in Amar and Mathews, trans., 219.

120. Ephrem, "Homily on Our Lord" 46.1 in Amar and Mathews, trans., 322.

121. Coon, *Sacred Fictions*, has argued that hagiographic texts about female saints particularly emphasize the healing aspect of Christ's ministry, while those of male saints stress the combative aspect of spiritual war against Satan.

122. Jacob of Sarug, "On the Sinful Woman," ll. 205–206 in Johnson, ed., 46–47 (my translation).

123. Jacob of Sarug, "On the Sinful Woman," ll. 175–178 in Johnson, ed., 44–45 (my translation).

124. Jacob of Sarug, "On the Sinful woman," l. 277 in Johnson, ed. and trans., 54–55.

125. Jacob of Sarug, "On the Sinful Woman," ll. 281–284 in Johnson, ed. 54–57 (my translation).

126. Jacob of Sarug, "Homily 1 on the Nativity," ll. 387–418 in Kollamparampil, trans., 54–59. For discussion of this extraordinary passage, see Harvey, "Interior Decorating."

127. Jacob of Sarug, "On the Lord's Prayer," ll. 391–420 in Reed, ed. and trans., 54–57.

128. For example, Harvey, "Bearing Witness."

129. "Life of Eugenia," sec. 8 in Papaioannou, ed. and trans., *Christian Novels*, 184–261, at 190–191. In the text the monks are singing Ps 96:5 (LXX 95:5): "All the gods of the nations are demons; but the Lord made the heavens."

130. John the Stylite, "Eugenia," in Smith Lewis, ed. and trans., Studia Sinaitica 9, fols. 21a–52b, at fol. 23b (Syriac), Studia Sinaitica 10, 1–35, at 4 (English).

131. John the Stylite, "Eugenia," in Smith Lewis, ed. and trans., Studia Sinaitica 9, at fol. 25a (Syriac), Studia Sinaitica 10, 5 (English). Perhaps alluding to Isa 26:7.

132. John the Stylite, "Eugenia," in Smith Lewis, ed. and trans., Studia Sinaitica 9, at fol. 25a–b (Syriac), Studia Sinaitica 10, 6 (English).

6. MODELS FOR LAITY, MODELS FOR FAITH

1. "Life of Pelagia," trans. in Brock and Harvey, *Holy Women*, 40–62.

2. "Life of Pelagia," sec. 17, trans. in Brock and Harvey, *Holy Women*, 47.

3. "Life of Pelagia," sec. 18, trans. in Brock and Harvey, *Holy Women*, 47–48; the passage alludes to Lk 7:36–50.

4. "Life of Pelagia," secs. 20–21, trans. in Brock and Harvey, *Holy Women*, 48–49. The scriptural citations are Jn 4:1–26 (the Samaritan Woman); Mt 15:22–28 (the Canaanite Woman); Mk 5:25–34 (the Hemorrhaging Woman); Lk 10:38–42 and Jn 11 (Mary and Martha of Bethany, and the raising of Lazarus).

5. The Syriac version of this hagiography differs, for example, from the Latin, both in the detail it accords to the description of this liturgy, and to the cluster of biblical exempla cited by Pelagia in her letter to Nonnos. For the versions in the ancient Christian languages, see Petitmangin and the Séminaire d'Histoire des textes, *Pélagie la Pénitente*. For an English translation of the Latin, see Ward, *Harlots of the Desert*, 57–75.

6. "Life of Pelagia," sec. 29, trans. in Brock and Harvey, *Holy Women*, 52: "'I believe that God is merciful and will not look upon the multitude of my sins—just as he did not look upon the sin of that sinful woman in the Gospels, or that of the Canaanite woman or the one from Samaria: he did not shut his door in their faces but had pity and compassion upon them; he held them to be worthy of healing in their bodies and of forgiveness of their sins.'"

7. On the way that lectionary readings could guide biblical interpretation, see Harvey, "Bride of Blood, Bride of Light."

8. Ward, *Harlots of the Desert*, remains a concise yet insightful explication of the theme, relevant across the whole of ancient Christian literature.

9. Jacob of Sarug, "On the Sinful Woman" in Johnson, ed. and trans.

10. Jacob of Sarug, "On the Sinful Woman," ll. 421–430 in Johnson, ed. and trans., 70–71; "Life of Pelagia," sec. 24, trans. in Brock and Harvey, *Holy Women*, 49–50.

11. Jacob of Sarug, "On the Sinful Woman," ll. 55–56, 87–90, and 302, in Johnson, ed. and trans., 32–33, 36–37, 58–59.

12. "The Sinful Woman and Satan," trans. in Brock, *Treasure-House of Mysteries*, 201–210. This text is also edited and translated as "Soghitha 1" in Brock, "The Sinful Woman and Satan," 23–54. There is a rich treasure of Syriac liturgical poetry about the Sinful Woman. See Harvey, "Why the Perfume Mattered"; and for the broader impact of the Syriac themes, Kalish, *She Who Loved Much*.

13. "The Sinful Woman and Satan," vv. 46–47, trans. in Brock, *Treasure-House of Mysteries*, 208.

14. Jacob of Sarug, "On the Canaanite Woman," ll. 369–370, 387 in Harvey et al., trans., 46–49.

15. Jacob of Sarug, "On the Canaanite Woman," ll. 337–410 in Harvey et al., trans., 46–49.

16. Contrast Derek Krueger's fine work on the "guilty conscience" cultivated by Byzantine monastic liturgies through different scripts of liturgical practice: Krueger, *Liturgical Subjects*.

17. "Ahay ba-ktobe," v. 29 in Brock, ed. and trans., *Stanzaic Poems of Jacob of Serugh*, 150–151; the attribution to Jacob is unlikely (135).

18. "Hymns Attributed to Rabbula" VI.2.4 in Phenix and Horn, eds. and trans., *Rabbula Corpus*, 380–381. The hymn is referencing the biblical characters in Lk 18:9–14 (the Publican and the Pharisee), Lk 23:39–43 (the Penitent Thief on the cross), Lk 7:36–50 (the Sinful Woman and Simon the Pharisee), and Jn 4 (the Samaritan Woman). These hymns were widely transmitted, continuing into modern service books. See the discussion in Phenix and Horn, eds. and trans., *Rabbula Corpus*, ccl–cclviii.

19. For another Syriac example, consider the case of Potiphar's Wife from Gen 39, for which see now Heal, *Genesis 37 and 39 in the Syriac Tradition*, 179–190 ("Making a Syriac Woman Sinful [Gen. 39]"). Compare Libanios of Antioch's prose exercise "What Words Would a Prostitute Say upon Gaining Self-Control?" in Gibson, trans., *Libanius' Progymnasmata*, 402–405.

20. Jacob of Sarug, "Homily 1 on the Nativity," in Kollamparampil, trans., 10–139. The passage in question is ll. 1033–1056, at 124–129. I have also treated this material in Harvey, "The Despised Woman."

21. Jacob of Sarug, "Homily 1 on the Nativity," ll. 1033–1056 in Kollamparampil, trans., 124–129.

22. On the Church as Bride in Syriac tradition, and this particular clustering of images, see Murray, *Symbols of Church and Kingdom*, 131–142. There is an important Jewish development of this imagery, identifying the barren and redeemed woman with Sarah, as an allegory for Israel as the Bride of God. See Münz-Manor, "All About Sarah," esp. 346–351.

23. For these supersessionist typologies in early Syriac, see Murray, *Symbols of Church and Kingdom*, 41–68, 131–142.

24. The Syriac habit of titles for Christ is well charted in Murray, *Symbols of Church and Kingdom*, 354–363 (Table III: Titles of Christ); see, further, Brock, "Divine Titles and Epithets."

25. Jacob of Sarug, "On Epiphany," ll. 3 and 5 in Kollamparampil, trans., 6–7.

26. Jacob of Sarug, "On the Ascension," ll. 95–96 in Kollamparampil, trans., 16–17.

27. Jacob of Sarug, "On the Ascension," ll. 173, 174–178 in Kollamparampil, trans., 24–27.

28. Jacob of Sarug, "On the Partaking," ll. 89–110 in Harrak, trans., 14–17; see also the homilies attributed to Jacob of Sarug, "On the Spectacles."

29. Forness, "The Construction of Metrical Poetry"; Papoutsakis, "Formulaic Language."

30. Harvey, "Bride of Blood, Bride of Light."

31. E.g., Brock and Hopkins, "Verse Homily on Abraham and Sarah." For Mary as Daughter of the Poor, see, e.g., Ephrem, *Hymns on the Nativity* 4.2, 15.2; Jacob of Sarug, "Homily 1 on the Nativity" 1. 42. See also Jacob of Sarug, Homilies 1 and 3 in Hansbury, trans., *Jacob of Serug on the Mother of God*, 19, 29 and 70, respectively. For the Church as Daughter of the Poor, see Jacob of Sarug, "On Epiphany," l. 20 (and passim) in Kollamparampil, trans., 8–9.

32. Jacob of Sarug, *On the Mother of God*, Homily 3 in Hansbury, trans., 82; Prayer Song 7.7 (= Hymns on Mary 2.7), trans. in Brock, *Bride of Light*, 36; Prayer Song 23.19 (= Soghitha 2.19), trans. in Brock, *Bride of Light*, 85.

33. For Elizabeth: e.g., Ephrem, *Hymns on Virginity* 15.1, 22.14 in McVey, trans., 325, 358; *Hymns on the Nativity* 2.20, 6.16, 21.16–18 in McVey, trans., 80, 113, 177. Compare Jacob of Sarug, *On the Mother of God*, Homily 2 in Hansbury, trans., 48, 52 (Elizabeth as the Sterile One).

34. E.g., Jacob of Sarug, "On Tamar," l. 205 in Brock, trans., 297. There are further references in Harvey, "Holy Impudence."

35. Susannah's story (Dan 13 LXX) is transmitted in Syriac not only as part of the Peshitta Syriac text, but also in the Syriac "Book of Women." See Burris, "The Syriac 'Book of Women.'" The text may be found in *The Antioch Bible: The Book of Women*, 24–41.

36. Ephrem, *Hymns on Virginity* 22.16–17 in McVey, trans., 359, which presents Sarah in this episode from Genesis 12 as "deceitful." Her designation as "humiliated" is presented in the anonymous memra, in Brock and Hopkins, ed. and trans., "A Verse Homily on Abraham and Sarah in Egypt."

37. Ephrem, *Hymns on Virginity* 35.5–7 in McVey, trans., 417–418; Brock, "The Sinful Woman and Satan"; Jacob of Sarug, "On the Sinful Woman," esp. ll. 185, 188, 313, 316, 320, 431, and 409–432 in Johnson, trans., 44–47, 58–61, 68–71; in this same homily, Jacob titles the Sinful Woman "the Wise Woman" (*ta'manatha*) at ll. 171, 272, Johnson, trans., 44–45, 54–55.

38. Ephrem, *Hymns on Virginity* 22.9 in McVey, trans., 357.

39. The theme is present throughout Jacob of Sarug, "On the Canaanite Woman."

40. Jacob of Sarug, "On the Afflicted Woman": she is the "Wretched Woman" (ll. 117, 131, 197, 217, 228 in Brock, trans., 188–191, 196–201), "sick and tormented" (ll. 257, 314, 336, 338, 413, 512 in Brock trans., 202–203, 208–211, 218–19, 228–229), "afflicted" (l. 343 in Brock, trans., 212–213), "unclean" (l. 355 in Brock, trans., 212–213); she titles herself all of these in lines 465–470 in Brock, trans., 224–225.

41. Tkacz, "Women as Types of Christ."

42. E.g., Ephrem, *Hymns on Virginity* 22, 26, 34 in McVey, trans., 355–360, 377–381, 411–415. See, further, Harvey, "Why the Perfume Mattered."

43. Though not specifically focusing on Syria, see the important discussions in Spier, *Picturing the Bible*, and Jensen, *Understanding Early Christian Art*.

44. On biblical memory, see Harvey, *Song and Memory*.

45. For some recent examples: Walsh, "From Sketches to Portraits"; Walsh, "Giving Voice to Pain"; Walsh, "The Gendered Body in Verse"; Walsh, "'How the Weak Rib Prevailed!'"; Doerfler, *Jephthah's Daughter, Sarah's Son*; and many references in this chapter.

46. Much important work is happening here. Especially helpful are Ludlow, *Art, Craft, and Theology*; Doerfler, "Listen to Her"; Brock, "Creating Women's Voices"; Lardnois and McClure, *Making Silence Speak*.

47. Brock, "Creating Women's Voices," discusses this conundrum.

48. Crucial to any consideration of whether or how women's actual voices might be present in ancient Christian texts remains the groundbreaking work of Clark, "The Lady Vanishes."

49. Brock, "The Dispute Poem: From Sumer to Syriac"; Brock, "Syriac Dispute Poems: The Various Types."

50. There is a useful list in Brock, *Mary and Joseph*, 97–104 ("Appendix: Dialogue *Sughyotho*").

51. Brock, "Joseph and Potiphar's Wife." In other Syriac literature, the character of Potiphar's Wife is presented as repenting and exonerated, worthy of mercy. The source appears to be Ephrem, *Commentary on Genesis* 35.1–2, 7–9. For the development, see Heal, *Genesis 37 and 39 in the Syriac Tradition*.

52. Brock, ed. and trans., "St. Marina and Satan." For Marina's impressive liturgical tradition in Syriac, see Hélou, *Sainte Marina*.

53. "St. Marina and Satan," vv. 20–23 in Brock, 42 (Syriac) and 47 (translation).

54. It is interesting to compare the sughyatha with the larger category of late antique Christian literary dialogues, for which see Rigolio, *Christians in Conversation*. Rigolio does not include hymnography in his extensive study; hence neither the kontakia of Romanos the Melodist nor the sughyatha are treated. But the comparative features are intriguing.

55. Ephrem, *Hymns on the Nativity*, esp. 6.1–6; 9.4–16; 15; 16.1–14; 17; 19 in McVey, trans., 111–112, 125–127, 145–147, 149–151, 153–157, 166–170.

56. Brock and Harvey, trans., "Lament of Mary," in *Holy Women*, 37–39; the Syriac is edited with translation in Brock, "The Lament of Mary."

57. Compare the insightful discussion by Purpura, "Beyond the Binary."

58. Concisely and effectively laid out in Ludlow, *Art, Craft, and Theology*, 119–143, 161–181. For training in imaginative dialogue as well as monologues, see Rigolio, *Christians in Conversation*, 16–21. For ancient Christian literary habits for the presentation of women, see Wicker, "Mulierum Virtutes." Underscoring the depth of social orientation on the proper roles and locations for women, see Beauchamp, "Discours et norms"; Beauchamp, "Le vocabulaire de la faiblesse feminine."

59. Most often cited in this regard by ancient Christian authors is 1 Cor 14:26–40, supplemented by the so-called household codes of Eph 5:22–6:9 and Col 3:18–4:1. There is extensive scholarship: e.g., Osiek, "Family Matters." For a sense of the older Greek literary

traditions, wherein women's voices were restricted to the household or else to particular types of utterances—curses and ritual laments—see Giordano, "Women's Voice and Religious Utterances."

60. The empress Eudokia addressed the people of Antioch when she passed through on pilgrimage to the Holy Land in 438, but only a brief statement from her speech was recorded: Evagrios Scholasticos, *Ecclesiastical History* 1.20 in Whitby, trans., 47–48. Again, Prokopios of Caesarea included a short speech by the empress Theodora before Justinian's court on the occasion of the Nika Riots in 532: Prokopios, *History of the Wars* 1.24, in Dewing, ed. and trans., 230–232.

61. Ludlow, *Art, Craft, and Theology*, 119–143, 161–181; Doerfler, "Listen to Her." Clark, *Women in Late Antiquity*, 94–181, is immensely useful.

62. Prominent examples would be Macrina, the sister of Gregory of Nyssa, as portrayed in Greogry's treatises the *Life of Macrina* and *On the Soul and Resurrection*; Gorgonia, the sister of Gregory of Nazianzos, as portrayed in his oration "On His Sister Gorgonia"; and the teachings attributed to Synkletica of Alexandria in the "Life of Synkletica" (Pseudo-Athanasios). See Harvey, "Women and Words."

63. An excellent example in Syriac is the noblewoman Ruhm, martyred with her three daughters, among the women martyrs of Najran. The account from the letter by Simeon of Beth Arsham stresses the shocking abnormality of her public speech on the occasion. See the translation and discussion in Brock and Harvey, *Holy Women*, 100–121, esp. 111–115.

64. E.g., Wicker, "Mulierum Virtutes."

65. For these, see Brock and Hopkins, "Verse Homily on Abraham and Sarah"; Brock, "Verse Homilies on the Binding of Isaac"; Heal, "The Syriac History of Joseph"; Brock, "Verse Homily on Elijah and the Widow of Sarepta"; Brock, "The Queen of Sheba's Questions to Solomon."

66. E.g., Ephrem, *Commentary on Genesis* 16.5–13 (imagined speeches for Lot's daughters, exonerating them), 34 (Tamar the daughter-in-law of Judah, with her internal speech of righteous motivation), 35.1–2, 7–9 (Potiphar's Wife, with her speech of exoneration and faith) in Amar and Mathews, trans., *Selected Prose Works*, 161–164, 182–185, 187–188. See, further, Brock, *Singer of the Word of God*, 141–151 (chapter 13, "St. Ephrem on Women in the Old Testament").

67. The issue of preaching and exemplarity requires careful treatment. Consider the perceptive study by Heal, "Narsai and the Scriptural Self." Extremely helpful are Roller, "Exemplarity in Roman Culture"; Wicker, "Mulierum Virtutes." The contrast between a preacher like Jacob of Sarug, who employs both expansive narrative and the condensed or abbreviated stories signaled by short descriptive titles, and one like John Chrysostom, who embeds biblical stories in his pastoral exhortations, is illuminating. For astute analysis of Chrysostom's methods, see Leyerle, *The Narrative Shape of Emotion*.

68. The homilies on the theater attributed to Jacob give evidence for how easily sacred and secular storytelling intersected: see Moss, "Homilies on the Spectacles of the Theater." Late antique mosaics in the region of Edessa, adorned with Syriac inscriptions, give ample indication of lively familiarity with Greek and Roman sacred stories, including their "extracanonical" forms, such as the post-Homeric stories of Achilles. E.g., Possekel, "Orpheus Among the Animals"; Önal, *Mosaics of Zeugma*; Ross, *Roman Edessa*. For the deep imprint of Greek and Roman sacred stories on late antique theater, see Webb, *Demons and Dancers*.

For the impact of theater on liturgy, see now Lieber, *Staging the Sacred*; Lieber, "Theater of the Holy"; Leyerle, *Theatrical Shows and Ascetic Lives*.

69. The intersection between hagiography and liturgical poetry is receiving exciting scholarly attention. See, for example, Taylor, "Hagiographie et liturgie syriaque"; Brock, "L'hagiographie versifiée." Compare Efthymiadis, "Greek Byzantine Hagiography in Verse"; Giannouli, "Byzantine Hagiography and Hymnography."

70. Jacob of Sarug, "On Elisha the Prophet" in Kaufman, trans., *Jacob of Sarug's Homilies on Elisha*, 1–73.

71. Jacob of Sarug, "On Elisha the Prophet," ll. 496–503 in Kaufman, trans., *Jacob of Sarug's Homilies on Elisha*, 54–57.

72. Jacob of Sarug, "On Elisha the Prophet," ll. 511–516 in Kaufman, trans., *Jacob of Sarug's Homilies on Elisha*, 56–57.

73. Jacob of Sarug, "On Elisha the Prophet," ll. 517–520 in Kaufman, trans., *Jacob of Sarug's Homilies on Elisha*, 58–59.

74. Jacob here uses different forms of the root *shin- ʿe-beth-dalath*, both for the Widow's "forcing" of Elisha's action and for the threatened enslavement of her sons: ll. 512, 514, 518, 521, 522.

75. Jacob of Sarug, "On Elisha the Prophet," ll. 569–570 in Kaufman, trans., *Jacob of Sarug's Homilies on Elisha*, 62–63.

76. Jacob of Sarug, "On Elisha the Prophet," ll. 613–638 in Kaufman, trans., *Jacob of Sarug's Homilies on Elisha*, 68–70.

77. It is often difficult to adduce Jacob's audience for a given homily. In certain cases, however, he clearly addresses a monastic congregation: e.g., Scott and Reed, trans., Jacob of Sarug, *Homilies on the Solitaries*; Jacob of Serug, "On Simeon the Stylite."

78. In the case of widows, these same stereotypes could impact ecclesiastical practice. See Penn, "'Bold and Having No Shame.'"

79. Jacob of Sarug, "On Elisha the Prophet," ll. 501–506 in Kaufman, trans., *Jacob of Sarug's Homilies on Elisha*, 56–57.

80. Jacob of Sarug, "Homily 3, on Elisha and the Shilumite Woman" in Kaufman, trans., *Jacob of Sarug's Homilies on Elisha*, 113–167.

81. Jacob of Sarug, "Homily 3, on Elisha and the Shilumite Woman," l. 36 in Kaufman, trans., *Jacob of Sarug's Homilies on Elisha*, 124–125.

82. Jacob of Sarug, "Homily 3, on Elisha and the Shilumite Woman," ll. 35, 52–54 in Kaufman, trans., *Jacob of Sarug's Homilies on Elisha*, 124–125.

83. Jacob of Sarug, "Homily 3, on Elisha and the Shilumite Woman," ll. 55–74 in Kaufman, trans., *Jacob of Sarug's Homilies on Elisha*, 124–126.

84. Jacob of Sarug, "Homily 3, on Elisha and the Shilumite Woman," ll. 61–62 in Kaufman, trans., *Jacob of Sarug's Homilies on Elisha*, 125–126. The verse is reminiscent of Jacob's comment "Yonder in the kingdom [of heaven] men and women are equal" in his homily "On Mar Ephrem," v. 43b in Amar, ed. and trans., 34–35.

85. Plutarch, "Advice to Bride and Groom" in Babbitt, ed. and trans., 295–343.

86. Prov 31:26 (NRSV).

87. Sir 26:1–27 (NRSV).

88. Jacob of Sarug, "Homily 3, on Elisha and the Shilumite Woman," ll. 75–84 in Kaufman, trans., *Jacob of Sarug's Homilies on Elisha*, 126–128.

89. Jacob of Sarug, "Homily 3, on Elisha, and the Shilumite Woman," ll. 185–209 in Kaufman, trans., *Jacob of Sarug's Homilies on Elisha*, 136–138.

90. Jacob of Sarug, "Homily 3, on Elisha and the Shilumite Woman," l. 361 in Kaufman, trans., *Jacob of Sarug's Homilies on Elisha*, 154.

91. Jacob of Sarug, "On the Afflicted Woman," in Brock, trans., in Harvey et al., 171–233.

92. Jacob of Sarug, "On the Afflicted Woman," ll. 77–82 in Brock, trans., in Harvey et al., 184–187.

93. Jacob of Sarug, "On the Afflicted Woman," ll. 455–460 in Brock, trans., in Harvey et al., 222–225.

94. Jacob of Sarug, "On the Afflicted Woman," ll. 465–447 in Brock, trans., in Harvey et al., 224–225.

95. Jacob of Sarug, "On the Afflicted Woman," ll. 489–490 in Brock., trans., in Harvey et al., 226–227.

96. Brock and Harvey, trans., *Holy Women*, 122–141, 177–181.

97. John of Ephesos, "Euphemia and Maria," trans. in Brock and Harvey, *Holy Women*, 130–131.

98. Sahdona, "Shirin," secs. 71, 77–79, trans. in Brock and Harvey, *Holy Women*, 179–181.

99. Jacob of Sarug, "On Jairus' Daughter," ll. 167–170 in Brock, trans., in Harvey et al., 256–257.

100. Hope, "Vocal Expression"; Habinek, *The World of Roman Song*, 233–243.

101. There is important recent scholarship, particularly the brilliant work by Doerfler, *Jephthah's Daughter, Sarah's Son*. In broader terms, see Rebillard, *Care of the Dead in Late Antiquity*, esp. 89–139; Samellas, *Death in the Eastern Mediterranean*.

102. See, further, Bear, "Funeral Music in Early Christianity," comparing the cases represented by Gregory of Nyssa on the death of his sister Macrina, John Chrysostom on lay family practices, and Pachomios on monastic grief. In each of these cases, Bear emphasizes that church leaders were at odds with the desires—and behaviors—of their congregations.

103. Harvey, "Guiding Grief."

104. Rush, *Death and Burial in Christian Antiquity*, remains foundational.

105. See "Ber(y) Habibo" in Brock, ed. and trans., *Stanzaic Poems of Jacob of Serugh*, 279–285.

106. "Ber(y) Habibo," vv. 1.1, 3.1, 4.2, 7.1, 8.1 in Brock, ed. and trans., *The Stanzaic Poems of Jacob of Serugh*, 280–285.

107. "Ber(y) Habibo," vv. 1.5, 3.5, 4.2, 7.5 in Brock, ed. and trans., *Stanzaic Poems of Jacob of Serugh*, 280–285.

108. "Ber(y) Habibo," v 8.5 in Brock, ed. and trans., *The Stanzaic Poems of Jacob of Serugh*, 285.

109. Jacob of Sarug, "On Women" in Akhrass and Syryani, eds., *160 Unpublished Homilies*, 2:533–535. See the insightful analysis and translation in Walsh, "Mourning Eve." As Walsh points out, there are a number of problems with the attribution to Jacob.

110. Jacob of Sarug, "On Women," l. 25 Akhrass and Syryani, eds., *160 Unpublished Homilies*, 2:534; trans. Walsh, "Mourning Eve," 57.

111. Jacob of Sarug, "On Women," ll. 32–36, Akhrass and Syryani, eds., *160 Unpublished Homilies*, 2:534; trans. Walsh, "Mourning Eve," 57–58.

112. For an especially perceptive treatment of such texts, see Doerfler, "Translating Eve."

113. Jacob of Sarug, "On the Reposed" in Holy Transfiguration Monastery [Miller], trans., 42, 52–53.

114. Jacob of Sarug, "On the Reposed," ll. 265–282 in Holy Transfiguration Monastery [Miller], trans., 52–53.

115. Jacob specified, "I shall now speak particularly to the women's side," indicating the gender segregation of the congregation; "On the Reposed," ll. 89–114 in Holy Transfiguration Monastery [Miller], trans., 45–46.

116. Jacob of Sarug, "On the Reposed," ll. 91–120 in Holy Transfiguration Monastery [Miller], trans., 45–46 (altered for sense).

117. Jacob of Sarug, "On the Partaking," ll. 157–158 in Harrak, trans., 22.

118. Doerfler, "Emotional Communities."

119. Doerfler, "Gone But Not Forgotten"; Rebillard, *Care of the Dead in Late Antiquity*, 111–122.

120. See the hauntingly tender portrait of the deaths of wilderness solitaries, in the anonymous memra "On Hermits and Desert Dwellers" in Beck, ed., *Des Heiligen Ephraem des Syrers*, 16–28; Amar, trans., "On Hermits and Desert Dwellers," 66–80.

121. As in the anonymous Syriac *vita* of the Man of God, for which see Doran, *Stewards of the Poor*; Amiaud, *La légende syriaque de Saint Alexis*.

122. Powerfully presented in Doerfler, *Jephthah's Daughter, Sarah's Son*.

123. A classic example would be Jer 9:17–21, with its description of wailing and lamenting women teaching their daughters how to mourn. The biblical book of Lamentations, purporting to be those of Jeremiah at the fall of Jerusalem, consists of five laments in the prophet's voice. In 2 Sam 1:11–27, David laments the deaths of Saul and Jonathan; vv. 19–27 present the words of his lament, which call also for women to take their part in the grieving process. See Olyan, *Biblical Mourning*.

124. E.g., Jacob of Sarug, "On Cain and Abel: Homily 3"; Brock, "Two Syriac Verse Homilies on the Binding of Isaac"; Brock, "Dinah in a Syriac Poem on Joseph"; Jacob of Sarug, "On Jephthah's Daughter."

125. Brock and Hopkins, "A Verse Homily on Abraham and Sarah in Egypt"; Jacob of Sarug, "On the Sinful Woman"; and Harvey, "Why the Perfume Mattered."

126. Brock and Harvey, eds. and trans., "Lament of Mary, the Niece of Abraham of Qidun," in *Holy Women*, 37–39; the text is edited in Brock, "The Lament of Mary, Niece of Abraham Qidunaya."

127. "Lament of Mary, the Niece of Abraham of Qidun," refrain (following v. Alaph), v. 'E, v. Shin, trans. in Brock and Harvey, *Holy Women*, 37–39.

128. Brock, "Dinah in a Syriac Poem on Joseph"; Heal, *Tradition and Transformation*, 235–257.

129. Brock, "Dinah in a Syriac Poem on Joseph," 231.

130. Mk 15:33; Mt 27:45; Lk 23:44.

131. "Abel and Cain," trans. in Brock, *Treasure-House of Mysteries*, 51–59.

132. For example, Jacob of Sarug, "On Simeon the Stylite" in Bedjan and Brock, eds., *Homilies of Mar Jacob*, 4:664–665; trans. Harvey, 26–27. The trope is there in the early martyr accounts, e.g., Eusebios of Caesarea, *Martyrs of Palestine* 4.15 and 9.12, where sea and earth alike are unable to endure these deaths (in Lawlor and Oulton, trans., 351–352, 375).

133. Jacob of Sarug, "On Cain and Abel: Homily 3" in Bedjan and Brock, eds., *Homilies of Mar Jacob*, 5:32–47. Translations from this are my own.

134. Jacob of Sarug, "On Cain and Abel: Homily 3," in Bedjan and Brock, eds., *Homilies of Mar Jacob*, 5:44, l. 21.

135. Jacob of Sarug, "On Cain and Abel: Homily 3," in Bedjan and Brock, eds., *Homilies of Mar Jacob*, 5:44, ll. 6–7.

136. Jacob of Sarug, "On Cain and Abel: Homily 3," in Bedjan and Brock, eds., *Homilies of Mar Jacob*, 5:44, l. 17.

137. Jacob of Sarug, "On Cain and Abel: Homily 3," in Bedjan and Brock, eds., *Homilies of Mar Jacob*, 5:45, ll. 7–13. In the Syriac *Life of Abel* by Symmachos, the author crafts poignant lamentations for Eve, Adam, and even a repentant Cain. For the portrayal of Eve mourning her sons as a distinctive literary feature of Syriac authors, see Glenthøj, *Cain and Abel*, 210–216.

138. Jacob of Sarug, "The Fourth Homily on Cain and Abel," ll. 69–105 trans. Forness, in Walters, *Eastern Christianity*, 60–61.

139. Jacob of Sarug, "On Jephthah's Daughter" in Harvey and Münz-Manor, eds. and trans.

140. Jacob of Sarug, "On Jephthah's Daughter," ll. 227–283, 346–375 in Harvey and Münz-Manor, trans., 34–41, 46–49.

141. Jacob of Sarug, "On Jephthah's Daughter," ll. 378–387 in Harvey and Münz-Manor, trans., 48–51.

142. Jacob of Sarug, "On Jephthah's Daughter," ll. 422–423 in Harvey and Münz-Manor, trans., 52–53.

143. Jacob of Sarug, "On Jephthah's Daughter," ll. 460–509 in Harvey and Münz-Manor, trans., 56–61.

144. Jacob of Sarug, "On the Judgment of Solomon," ll. 292–297 in Kaufman, trans., 30–31.

145. Kraus, "Rehearsing the Other Sex"; Lieber, "Theater of the Holy"; Russell, *Greek Declamation*, 87–105.

146. Consider the instructive parallel from late antique Jewish hymnography: Lieber, "Stages of Grief"; and for the particular case of maternal grief: Lieber, "On the Road with the Mater Dolorosa."

147. Romanos, "On the Lament of the Mother of God," in Maas and Trypanis, eds., *Sancti Romani Melodi Cantica*, 142–149; trans. in Lash, *St. Romanos the Melodist*, 141–150.

148. Above all, Alexiou, *The Ritual Lament in Greek Tradition*; Alexiou, "The Lament of the Virgin"; Constas, "Poetry and Painting in the Middle Byzantine Period"; Dobrov, "A Dialogue with Death."

149. There are at least two extant. One poem, "Sleq la-slibo," is attributed to Jacob of Sarug: in Brock, ed. and trans., *Stanzaic Poems of Jacob of Serugh*, 251–263. See also the anonymous "Prayer Song 40"/"Lament of Mary at the Cross," trans. in Brock, *Bride of Light*, 122–123.

150. A sizable number of Greek hymns to the Virgin Mary were translated into Syriac between the ninth and eleventh century. See Smelova, "Melkite Syriac Hymns to the Mother of God."

151. Harvey, "Encountering Eve."

152. Prayer Song 7.7, 9 (= *Hymns on Mary* 2.7, 9), trans. in Brock, *Bride of Light*, 39–40.

153. Prayer Song 6.14 (= *Hymns on Mary* 1.14), trans. in Brock, *Bride of Light*, 38.

154. Dodd, *Medieval Painting in Lebanon*, 158–163. For the Byzantine iconography of Abel with Eve and Adam, with which the Syriac tradition shows interaction, see Kartsonis, *Anastasis*, esp. 209–213.

155. Murray, *Symbols of Church and Kingdom*, 146–150; and for two anonymous dialogue hymns of Mary's exchange with the gardener, who is the risen Christ, see Brock, *Mary and Joseph*, 69–85.

156. Jacob of Sarug, "On the Partaking," ll. 339–340 in Harrak, trans., 40–41 (altered).

157. Jacob of Sarug, "The Fourth Homily on Cain and Abel," ll. 207–208, 235–236, trans. Forness, in Walters, *Eastern Christianity*, 65–66.

158. Jacob of Sarug, "On the Reposed," ll. 283–296, in Holy Transfiguration Monastery [Miller], trans., 53.

159. Jacob of Sarug, "On Epiphany," in Kollamparampil, trans.

160. Jacob of Sarug, "On the Death of a Bart Qyama," in Bedjan and Brock, ed., 5:821–836.

161. Jacob of Sarug, *Homilies on Praise at Table*, in Childers, trans. For further background on meals as an occasion for early Christian singing, see Rouwhorst, "Table Community in Early Christianity."

162. Jacob of Sarug, "Praise at Table 2," ll. 41–50 in Childers, trans., 44.

163. Childers, "Jacob of Sarug's Memra 9 On Praise at Table." This memra is newly edited in Akhrass and Syryany, *160 Unpublished Homilies*, 1:451–453.

164. Childers, "'This is why brides in their bridal chambers evoke great desire,'" p. 182.

165. Jacob of Sarug, "Praise at Table 1," ll. 41–64 in Childers, trans., 32–35.

166. Jacob of Sarug, "Praise at Table 6," ll. 56–58 in Childers, trans., 94–95.

167. Jacob of Sarug, "Homily 3 on the Nativity," ll. 23–32 in Kollamparampil, ed. and trans., *Jacob of Sarug's Homilies on the Nativity*, 188–190.

168. Jacob of Sarug, "On the Judgment of Solomon," ll. 39–44 in Kaufman, trans., 6–9.

169. Jacob of Sarug, "On the Fashioning of Creation," ll. 2295–2299 in Mathews, trans., 312–313.

170. Jacob of Sarug, "On the Fashioning of Creation," ll. 2303–2312 in Mathews, trans., 314–315.

171. Jacob of Sarug, "Homily 2 on the Resurrection of Our Lord," ll. 201–238 in Kollamparampil, ed. and trans., *Jacob of Sarug's Homilies on the Resurrection*, 60–64.

172. Jacob of Sarug, "On Mar Ephrem," v. 115b (here referring to the madrashe as *malphanutha l-zmiratha*) in Amar, trans. 52–53.

AFTERWORD

1. Consider the confusion between the titles "daughter of the covenant" and "deaconess" acknowledged in canonical sources in Martimort, *Les diaconesses*. Already in the Persian martyr texts there can be elision or confusion of the terms *bnay* and *bnat qyama* and those for monastics, *dayraya/dayraytha*: e.g., the texts collected in Herman, *Persian Martyr Acts*.

2. The service for ordination of a deaconess from Mingana Syriac MS 166 is translated in Brock, "Deaconesses in the Syriac Tradition," 213–217.

3. Gregory Bar Hebraeus, *Ethicon, Memra I*, 5.3 in Teule, ed. and trans., CSCO 534/Scr. Syr. 218, 72 (Syriac), CSCO 535/Scr. Syr. 219, 61 (English). Teule here (CSCO 535/Scr. Syr. 219,

61n24) cites the *Nomocanon*, noting that Bar Hebraeus in this instance substitutes "nuns" (*dayrayatha*) for "daughters of the Covenant" (*bnat qyama*). However, the entire passage reprises the Rabbula canons, and both terms, *dayrayatha* and *bnat qyama*, are used. See Bedjan, *Nomocanon Gregorii Barhebraei*, 111.

4. The evolution of the term *bart qyama* is discussed in Jajé, *Diaconesses*, 51–76, where he includes a translation (76–104) of a rite of ordination for a daughter of the covenant, here designated by the term *qashishtha*. In modern times, *bart qyama* and *qashishtha* have often been used interchangeably.

5. These services are usefully collected and translated in Varghese, *Ordination of Women*, along with helpful discussion of the historical record and canonical traditions behind them. The consecration service for nuns may be found in Aydin, *The Syriac Order of Monastic Profession*, 222–241. The current Syriac Orthodox Pontifical was compiled and edited by Metropolitan Yuhanon Dolabani of Mardin in 1947. It is now used in the version published in 2009 by the Syrian Orthodox Patriarchate, *Fenqito d-Khirtounias* (Book of Priestly Ordinations), and available at their website: dss-syriacpatriarchate.org. I am grateful to Ephrem Ishac for his patient assistance on these matters.

6. For example, Tang, "Christian Communities in Medieval Central Asia." The Salzburg International Conference series on Syriac Christianity in China and Central Asia has been held triennially since 2003, publishing their findings in the useful orientalia–patristica–oecumenica series of LIT Verlag.

7. Hunter, "Commemorating the Saints at Turfan." Hunter points out that the liturgical commemoration of Mart Shir highlighted this female saint in a manner not shared in other historical sources that reference her. For the texts, see Hunter and Coakley, *A Syriac Service-Book from Turfan*.

8. Murre-van den Berg, *Scribes and Scriptures*, 113–142, 143–183; Murre-van den Berg, "Generous Devotion."

9. Kellogg, *Sonic Icons*. For the context of an apparent revival of attention to hymn singing by young girls for the Syriac Orthodox in the first half of the twentieth century, see Murre-van den Berg, "Classical Syriac," 139.

10. Kellogg, "Ritual Sounds, Political Echoes"; Kellogg, "Perforating Kinship." For the renewal of Syriac women's choirs in the context of the vibrant contemporary Syriac musical culture, see Brock and Witakowski, *The Hidden Pearl*, 125–126.

11. Moran Mor Ignatius Zakka-I Iwas, "The Role of Women in the Syrian Orthodox Church of Antioch," (1998/2005), http://www.malankaraworld.com/library/History/WomeninSOC-by-Patriarch.pdf.

12. E.g., "Gesangswettbewerb der Kirchenchöre der syrisch-orthodoxen Kirche von Antiochien in NRW," (as recorded on 9 December 2006, Apostel St. Johannes Kireche, Rheda-Wiedenbrück).

13. The services collected in Varghese, *Ordination of Women*, are examples and templates for these occasions.

14. "Weihe der Subdiakonen, Lektoren (*Qoruye*) and Messdienerinen am Weissen-Sontag den, 5. Mai 2003," St. Johannes Apostel Kirche, Rheda-Wiedenbrück (videotape).

15. Kellogg, "A Racial-Religious Imagination"; Kellogg, "Perforating Kinship"; Mack, *The Construction of Equality*; Atto, *Hostages in the Homeland*; Cetrez, *Meaning-Making Variations*; Romeny, "From Religious Association to Ethnic Community."

16. Jarjour, *Sense and Sadness*, 31–32, 52–55, 90–91, 150–159; Kellogg, *Sonic Icons*, esp. chapter 4, "Daughters of the Covenant."

17. Sada, "Assyrian Syriac Chants."

18. Kellogg, *Sonic Icons*; Kellogg, "Ritual Sounds, Political Echoes." Tala Jarjour, while not discussing the women's choirs, incisively articulates the issues of liturgical singing, ethnicity, and religious identity for Syriac Orthodox Christians in Jarjour, "Chant as the Articulation."

19. Significantly, Syriac women's choirs provide important models for the liturgical participation of women in other Oriental Orthodox Churches. See now Rizk-Asdourian, "Women and Their Position Within the Liturgical Life."

BIBLIOGRAPHY

ABBREVIATIONS

AB	*Analecta Bollandiana*
ACW	Ancient Christian Writers
AMS	*Acta Martyrum et Sanctorum*
BMGS	*Byzantine and Modern Greek Studies*
CCSL	Corpus Christianorum, Series Latina
CH	*Church History*
CHR	*Catholic Historical Review*
CSCO	Corpus Scriptorum Christianorum Orientalium
	Scr. Syr. Scriptores Syrii
	Sub. Subsidia
CSEL	Corpus Scriptorum Ecclesiasticorum Latinorum
DOML	Dumbarton Oaks Medieval Library
DOP	*Dumbarton Oaks Papers*
ESTE	Estonian Theological School in Exile
FC	Fathers of the Church
GCS	Griechischen christlichen Schriftsteller der ersten Jahrhunderte
GNO	*Gregorii Nysenii Opera*
GRBS	*Greek, Roman, and Byzantine Studies*
HTR	*Harvard Theological Review*
JAAR	*Journal of the American Academy of Religion*
JAJ	*Journal of Ancient Judaism*
JCSSS	*Journal of the Canadian Society of Syriac Studies*
JECH	*Journal of Early Christian History*
JECS	*Journal of Early Christian Studies*
JOR	*Journal of Religion*

JSS   *Journal of Semitic Studies*
JTS   *Journal of Theological Studies*
LCL   Loeb Classical Library
LXX   The Septuagint
NPNF   Nicene and Post-Nicene Fathers
NRSV   New Revised Standard Version (*HarperCollins Study Bible*)
OCA   Orientalia Christiana Analecta
OCP   *Orientalia Christiana Periodica*
OLA   Orientalia Liturgica Analecta
PETSE   Papers of the Estonian Theological School in Exile
PG   *Patrologia Graeca*
PO   *Patrologia Orientalis*
SC   *Sources Chrétiennes*
SVTQ   *St. Vladimir's Theological Quarterly*
TTH   Translated Texts for Historians
TU   Texte und Untersuchungen
VC   *Vigiliae Christianae*
WUNT   Wissenschaftliche Untersuchungen zum Neuen Testament 2. Reihe
ZAC   *Zeitschrift für Antikes Christentum/Journal of Ancient Christianity*

ANCIENT SOURCES

Acta Martyrum et Sanctorum. Edited by Paul Bedjan. *Acta Martyrum et Sanctorum Syriace*. 7 vols. Paris: Otto Harrassowitz, 1890–1897. Reprint, Hildesheim: Georg Olms, 1968.

Acts of the Council of Ephesos. Edited and translated by Johannes Flemming. *Akten der ephesinischen Syonode vom Jahre 449: Syrisch mit Georg Hoffman's deutscher Übersetzung und seinen Anmerkungen*. Berlin: Weidmann, 1917.

Anna Komnena. *Alexiad*. Edited and translated by Bernard Leib with Paul Gautier. *Anne Comnène, Alexiade (Règne de l'empereur Alexis Comnène, 1081–1118)*. 4 vols. Paris: Société d'Édition "Les Belle Lettres," 1937–1976. Translated by E. R. A. Sewter. Rev. ed. by Peter Frankopan. London: Penguin, 2009.

"Answers from the Orient Fathers." Edited and translated by Arthur Vööbus. *The Synodicon in the West Syrian Tradition*. CSCO 367/Scr. Syr. 161, 163–176 (Syriac), CSCO 368/Scr. Syr. 162, 157–168 (English). Louvain: Secrétariat du CorpusSCO, 1975–1976.

"Answers of Ja'qob [Jacob of Edessa] to Addai." Edited and translated by Arthur Vööbus. *The Synodicon in the West Syrian Tradition*. CSCO 367/Scr. Syr. 161, 258–269 (Syriac), CSCO 368/Scr. Syr. 162, 235–244 (English). Louvain: Secrétariat du CorpusSCO, 1975–1976.

"Answers of Johannan [John of Tella] to Sargis." Edited and translated by Arthur Vööbus. *The Synodicon in the West Syrian Tradition*. CSCO 367 Scr. Syr. 161, 211–221 (Syriac), CSCO 368/Scr. Syr. 162, 197–205 (English). Louvain: Secrétariat du CorpusSCO, 1975–1976.

The Antioch Bible: The Book of Women: Ruth, Susanna, Esther, and Judith. Translated by Donald M. Walter, Gillian Greenberg, and Eric Tully. Edited by George Kiraz and Joseph Bali. Piscataway, NJ: Gorgias Press, 2020.

Aphrahat. *Demonstrations*. Edited by D. I. Parisot. *Aphraatis Sapientis Persae, Demonstrationes, I–XXII*, 241–311. *Patrologia Syriaca* 1.1. Paris: Firmin-Didot, 1894. Translated by Adam Lehto. *The Demonstrations of Aphrahat, the Persian Sage*. Piscataway, NJ: Gorgias Press, 2010.

Asterios of Amaseia. *Homilies*. Edited in J.–P Migne, *PG* 40:155–480. Translated by Galusha Anderson and Edgar Johnson Goodspeed. *Ancient Sermons for Modern Times*. New York: Pilgrim Press, 1904.

(Ps.-)Athanasios. "On Synkletica." Edited in J.–P. Migne, *PG* 28:1487–1558. Translated by Elizabeth Castelli. "Pseudo-Athanasius, The Life and Activity of the Holy and Blessed Teacher Syncletica," in *Ascetic Behavior in Greco-Roman Antiquity: A Sourcebook*, edited by Vincent L. Wimbush, 265–311. Minneapolis: Fortress Press, 1990.

(Ps.-)Athanasios. "On Virginity." Edited by J. Lebon. "Athanasiana Syriaca I: Un *logos peri parthenias* attribué à saint Athanase d'Alexandrie." *Le Muséon* 40 (1927): 205–248, at 209–28. Translated by David Brakke. *Athanasius and the Politics of Asceticism*, 303–309. Oxford: Clarendon Press, 1995.

Barhadbeshabba. *Ecclesiastical History*. Edited by François Nau. *Barhadbeshabba ʿArbaye, La première partie de l'historie*. PO 23.2. Paris: Firmin-Didot, 1932. Chapters 31 and 32 translated in Becker, *Sources for the Study of the School of Nisibis*, 47–85.

Barhadbeshabba ʿArbaye. *The Cause of the Foundation of the Schools*. Edited by Addai Scher. *Mar Barhadbeshabba ʿArabaya, Cause de la fondation des écoles*. PO 4.4. Paris: Firmin-Didot, 1908. Translated in Becker, *Sources for the Study of the School of Nisibis*, 86–160.

Basil of Caesarea. Homily 14. Edited in J.–P. Migne, *PG* 31:444–64. Translated by Susan R. Holman and Mark DelCogliano. "Homily Against Drunkards," in *Saint Basil the Great, On Fasting and Feasts*, 83–95. Yonkers: St. Vladimir's Seminary Press, 2013.

Basil of Caesarea. *Letters*. Edited and translated by R. J. Deferrari. *Saint Basil: The Letters*. 4 vols. LCL 190, 215, 243, 270. Cambridge, MA: Harvard University Press, 1970.

Book of Steps. Edited by M. Kmosko. *Liber Graduum*. *Patrologia Syriaca* 3. Paris: Firmin-Didot, 1926. Translated by Robert Kitchen and Martin Parmentier. *The Book of Steps: The Syriac Liber Graduum*. Kalamazoo, MI: Cistercian Publications, 2004.

Burial Service for Nuns. Edited and translated by Sebastian P. Brock. *Burial Service for Nuns: Syriac Text with Translation*. Moran Etho 4. Kottayam: St. Ephrem Ecumenical Research Institute, 1992.

"Canons of Johannon bar Qursos [John of Tella]." Edited and translated by Arthur Vööbus. *The Synodicon in the West Syrian Tradition*. CSCO 367/Scr. Syr. 161, 145–156 (Syriac), CSCO 368/Scr. Syr. 162, 142–151 (English). Louvain: Secrétariat du CorpusSCO, 1975–1976.

"Canons of the Synod of Laodicea." Edited and translated by Arthur Vööbus. *The Synodicon in the West Syrian Tradition*. CSCO 367/Scr. Syr. 161, 115–125 (Syriac), CSCO 368/Scr. Syr. 162, 119–126 (English). Louvain: Secrétariat du CorpusSCO, 1975–1976.

"Canons of the Testament of Our Lord." Edited and translated by Arthur Vööbus. *The Synodicon in the West Syrian Tradition*. CSCO 367/Scr. Syr. 161, 40–49 (Syriac), CSCO 368/Scr. Syr. 162, 57–64 (English). Louvain: Secrétariat du CorpusSCO, 1975–1976.

Cave of Treasures. Edited and translated by Su-Min Ri. *La caverne des trésors: Les deux recensions syriaques*. CSCO 486–487/Scr. Syr. 207–208. Leuven: Peeters, 1987.

Chronicle of Zuqnin. Edited by J. B. Chabot. *Incerti auctoris Chronicon anonymum pseudo-Dionysianum, II*. CSCO 104/Scr. Syr. 53. Paris: E Typographeo Reipublicae, 1933.

Translated by Amir Harrak. *The Chronicle of Zuqnin, Parts III and IV, A.D. 488–775.* Toronto: Pontifical Institute of Mediaeval Studies, 1999.

Clement of Alexandria. *Paedagogus.* Edited and translated by H.-I. Marrou, M. Harl, C. Mondésert, and C. Matray. *Clément d'Alexandrie, Le pédagogue.* 3 vols. SC 70, 108, 158. Paris: Éditions du Cerf, 1960–1970. Translated by Simon P. Wood. *Clement of Alexandria, Christ the Educator.* FC 23. Washington, DC: The Catholic University of America Press, 1954.

Cyril of Jerusalem. "Procatechesis." Edited and translated by Maxwell E. Johnson. *Lectures on the Christian Sacraments: The Procatechesis and the Five Mystagogical Catecheses Ascribed to St. Cyril of* Jerusalem, 64–83. Yonkers: St. Vladimir's Seminary Press, 2017.

Cyril of Skythopolis. "Life of Cyriacus." Edited by Eduard Schwartz. *Kyrillos von Skythopolis,* 222–235. TU 49.2. Leipzig: J.C. Hinrichs Verlag, 1939. Translated by Richard Price. *Lives of the Monks of Palestine,* 245–261. Kalamazoo, MI: Cistercian Publications, 1991.

Cyrillona. "On the Scourges." Edited and translated by Carl Griffin. *The Works of Cyrillona,* 136–194. Piscataway, NJ: Gorgias Press, 2016.

Cyrus of Edessa. *Explanation of the Resurrection.* Edited and translated by William F. Macomber. *Six Explanations of the Liturgical Feasts: An East Syrian Theologian of the Mid-Sixth Century.* CSCO 355–356/Scr. Syr. 155–156. Louvain: Secrétariat du CorpusSCO, 1974.

Didascalia Apostolorum. Edited and translated by Arthur Vööbus. *The Didascalia Apostolorum in Syriac.* CSCO 401–402, 407–408/Scr. Syr. 175–176, 179–180. Louvain: Secrétariat du CorpusSCO, 1979.

Diodorus Siculus. *Library of History.* Edited and translated by C. H. Oldfather, C. L. Sherman, R. M. Greer, and F. R. Walton. 12 vols. LCL. Cambridge, MA: Harvard University Press, 1935–1967.

Egeria. *Diary of a Pilgrimage.* Edited by Pierre Maraval. *Égerie, Journal de voyage: Itinéraire.* Paris: Éditions du Cerf, 1982. Translated by George E. Gingras. *Diary of a Pilgrimage.* ACW 38. New York: Paulist Press, 1970.

Ephrem. *Commentary on Genesis.* Edited by R. M. Tonneau. *Sancti Ephraem Syri in Genesim et in Exodum commentarii.* CSCO 152–153/Scr. Syr. 71–72. Louvain: L. Durbecq, 1955. Translated by Joseph P. Amar and Edward G. Mathews. *Ephrem the Syrian: Selected Prose Works,* 59–213. FC 91. Washington, DC: The Catholic University of America Press, 1994.

Ephrem. *Commentary on the Diatessaron.* Translated by Carmel McCarthy. *Saint Ephrem's Commentary on Tatian's Diatessaron.* JSS Supplement 2. Oxford: Oxford University Press/University of Manchester, 1993.

Ephrem. "Homily on Our Lord." Edited by Edmund Beck. *Des Heiligen Ephraem des Syrers Sermo de Domino Nostro.* CSCO 270–271/Scr. Syr. 116–117. Louvain: Secretariat du CorpusSCO, 1966. Translated by Joseph P. Amar and Edward G. Mathews. *Ephrem the Syrian: Selected Prose Works,* 269–332. FC 91. Washington, DC: The Catholic University of America Press, 1994.

Ephrem. *Hymns Against Heresies.* Edited and translated by Edmund Beck. *Des Heiligen Ephraem des Syrers Hymnen contra Haereses.* CSCO 169–170/Scr. Syr. 76–77. Louvain: Durbecq, 1955.

Ephrem. *Hymns in Armenian*. Edited and translated by Louis Mariès and Charles Mercier. *Hymnes de Saint Éphrem conservées en version arménienne*. PO 30. Paris: Firmin-Didot, 1963.

Ephrem. *Hymns on Faith*. Edited and translated by Edmund Beck. *Des Heiligen Ephraem des Syrers Hymnen de Fide*. CSCO 154-155/Scr. Syr. 73-74. Louvain: Secrétariat du CorpusSCO, 1955. Translated by Jeffrey Wickes. *St. Ephrem the Syrian: The Hymns on Faith*. FC 130. Washington, DC: The Catholic University of America Press, 2015.

Ephrem. *Hymns on Julian Saba*. Edited and translated by Edmund Beck. *Des heiligen Ephraem des Syrers Hymnen auf Abraham Kidunaya und Julianos Saba*. CSCO 322-323/ Scr. Syr. 140-141. Louvain: Peeters, 1972.

Ephrem. *Hymns on the Nativity*. Edited and translated by Edmund Beck. *Des Heiligen Ephraem des Syrers Hymnen de Nativitate (Epiphania)*. CSCO 186-187/Scr. Syr. 82-83. Louvain: Secrétariat du CorpusSCO, 1959. Translated by Kathleen McVey. *Ephrem the Syrian: Hymns*, 61-217. Mahwah, NJ: Paulist Press, 1989.

Ephrem. *Hymns on the Resurrection*. Edited and translated by Edmund Beck. *Des Heiligen Ephraem des Syrers Paschahymnen (De azymis, De Crucifixione, De Resurrectione)*. CSCO 248/Scr. Syr. 84. Louvain: Secrétariat du CorpusSCO, 1964.

Ephrem. *Hymns on Virginity*. Edited and translated by Edmund Beck. *Des Heiligen Ephraem des Syrers Hymnen de Virginitate*. CSCO 223-224/Scr. Syr. 94-95. Louvain: Secrétariat du CorpusSCO, 1962. Translated by Kathleen McVey. *Ephrem the Syrian: Hymns*, 259-468. Mahwah, NJ: Paulist Press, 1989.

Ephrem. *Memre on Nicomedia*. Edited and translated by Charles Renoux. *Éphrem de Nisibe, Memre sur Nicomédie*. PO 37.2-3. Turnhout: Brepols, 1975.

(Ps.-)Ephrem. *Necrosima*. Edited by J.S. Assemani. "Necrosima, seu Funebres Canones," in *Sancti patris nostri Ephraem Syri Opera omnia quae exstant Graece, Syriace, Latine*, 6:225-359. Rome: 1743. Select translation by Henry Burgess. *Select Metrical Hymns and Homilies of Ephrem Syrus*. London: Robert S. Blackader, 1853.

Ephrem. *Prose Refutations*. Edited and translated by C.W. Mitchell. *S. Ephraim's Prose Refutations of Mani, Marcion, and Bardaisan*. 2 vols. London: Williams and Norgate, 1912. Repr. Farnborough: Gregg, 1969.

Euphemia and the Goth. Edited and translated by F.C. Burkitt. *Euphemia and the Goth with the Acts of the Martyrdom of the Confessors of Edessa*. London: Williams and Norgate, 1913.

Eusebios. *History of the Church*. Edited by Eduard Schwartz, Theodor Mommsen, and Friedhelm Winkelmann. *Eusebius Werke, 2: Die Kirchengeschichte*. GCS n.f. 6. Berlin: Akademie Verlag, 1999. Translated by Jeremy M. Schott. *Eusebius of Caesarea, History of the Church*. Oakland: University of California Press, 2019. Syriac edited by William Wright and Norman McLean. *The Ecclesiastical History of Eusebius, in Syriac*. Cambridge: Cambridge University Press, 1898.

Eusebios. *Martyrs of Palestine*. Translated by Hugh Jackson Lawlor and J.E.L. Oulton. *Eusebius of Caesarea, The Ecclesiastical History and the Martyrs of Palestine*. London: SPCK, 1954.

Evagrios Scholasticos. *Ecclesiastical History*. Edited by J. Bidez and L. Parmentier. *Evagrius Scholasticus, Historia Ecclesiastica*. London: Methuen, 1898. Translated by Michael

Whitby. *The Ecclesiastical History of Evagrius Scholasticus.* TTH 33. Liverpool: Liverpool University Press, 2000.

"Forty Martyrs." Edited in Bedjan. *AMS*, 2:325–347. Translated by Susan Ashbrook Harvey, Reyhan Durmaz, Michael L. Payne, Daniel Picus, and Noah Tetenbaum. "The Forty Martyrs of Beth Kashkraye," in Harvey et al., *Three Persian Martyr Acts*, 81–127.

"Further Canons of Jaʿqob of Edessa [Jacob of Edessa]." Edited and translated by Arthur Vööbus. *The Synodicon in the West Syrian Tradition.* CSCO 367/Scr. Syr. 161, 269–272 (Syriac), CSCO 368/Scr. Syr. 162, 245–247 (English). Louvain: Secrétariat du CorpusSCO, 1975–1976.

Gerontius. *Melania the Younger.* Edited and translated by Denys Gorce. *Vie de Sainte Melanie.* SC 90. Paris: Éditions du Cerf, 1962. Translated by Elizabeth A. Clark. *The Life of Melania, the Younger: Introduction, Translation, and Commentary.* New York: E. Mellen Press, 1984.

Gregory Bar Hebraeus. *Ethicon, Memra I.* Edited and translated by Herman G. B. Teule. CSCO 534–535/Scr. Syr. 218–219. Louvain: Peeters, 1993.

Gregory Bar Hebraeus. *Nomocanon.* Edited by Paul Bedjan. *Nomocanon Gregorii Barhebraei.* Leipzig: Harrassowitz, 1898.

Gregory of Nazianzos. "On His Sister Gorgonia." Edited in J.-P. Migne, *PG* 35, 789–816 (Or. 8). Translated by Leo P. McCauley. *Funeral Orations: Ambrose of Milan and Gregory of Nazianzus,* translated by Leo P. McCauley, John J. Sullivan, Martin R. P. McGuire, and Roy J. Deferrari, 101–118. FC 22. New York: The Catholic University of America Press, 1953.

Gregory of Nyssa. *Letters.* Edited by Georgius Pasquali. *Gregorii Nysenni Epistolae.* Editio altera. In Werner Jaeger, ed., *GNO*, 87.2. Leiden: E.J. Brill, 1959. Translated by Anna Silva. *Gregory of Nyssa: The Letters.* Supplements to *VC* 83. Leiden: Brill, 2007.

Gregory of Nyssa. *Life of Macrina.* Edited by Pierre Maraval. *Grégoire de Nysse: Vie de Sainte Macrine.* SC 178. Paris: Éditions de Cerf, 1971. Translated by Virginia Callahan. *Saint Gregory of Nyssa: Ascetical Works,* 163–191. FC 58. Washington, DC: The Catholic University of America Press, 1967.

Gregory of Nyssa. *Life of Moses.* Edited by Jean Daniélou. *Gregoire de Nysse, Vie de Moïse.* SC 1. Paris: Éditions de Cerf, 1955. Translated by Abraham J. Malherbe and Everett Ferguson. *Gregory of Nyssa: Life of Moses.* New York: Paulist Press, 1978.

Gregory of Nyssa, *On the Soul and Resurrection.* Edited in J.-P. Migne, *PG* 46, 11–160. Translated by Catharine Roth. *St. Gregory of Nyssa, On the Soul and the Resurrection.* Crestwood: NY: St. Vladimir's Seminary Press, 1993.

Gregory of Nyssa. "On Virginity." Edited by John P. Carvanos. In Werner Jaeger, ed., *GNO*, 8.1. Leiden: E.J. Brill, 1952. Translated by Virginia Callahan. *Saint Gregory of Nyssa: Ascetical Works,* 1–76. FC 58. Washington, DC: The Catholic University of America Press, 1967.

The HarperCollins Study Bible: New Revised Standard Version with the Apocryphal/Deuterocanonical Books. Edited by Wayne A. Meeks and Jouette M. Bassler with the Society of Biblical Literature. New York: HarperCollins, 1993.

Homeric Hymns. Edited and translated by Hugh Gerard Evelyn-White. *Hesiod, the Homeric Hymns, and Homerica.* LCL 57. Cambridge, MA: Harvard University Press, 1914.

Isaac of Antioch. "On the Vigil Which Took Place in Antioch." Edited by Paul Bedjan. *Homiliae S. Isaaci Syri Antiocheni,* Memra 68, 815–821. Leipzig: Harrassowitz, 1903. Translated by Robert Kitchen. In Glenn Peers, "Isaac of Antioch's Organ and the Media of Musical Subjects." *JECS* 26.1 (2018): 75–109, at 103–109.

Jacob of Sarug. *Against the Jews*. Edited and translated by Micheline Albert. *Jacques de Saroug: Homélies contre les juifs: Édition critique, introduction, traduction et notes*. PO 38.1. Paris: Firmin-Didot, 1976.

Jacob of Sarug. "Concerning the Red Heifer." Edited and translated by Demetrios Alibertius. *Jacob of Sarug's Homily Concerning the Red Heifer and the Crucifixion of Our Lord*. Piscataway, NJ: Gorgias Press, 2022.

Jacob of Sarug. "The Fourth Homily on Cain and Abel." Edited in Bedjan and Brock, *Homilies of Mar Jacob*, 5:47–61. Translated by Philip Michael Forness. *Eastern Christianity: A Reader*, edited by J. Edward Walters, 55–68. Grand Rapids, MI: Eerdmans, 2021.

Jacob of Sarug. *Homilies of Mar Jacob*. Edited by Paul Bedjan and Sebastian P. Brock. *Homilies of Mar Jacob of Sarug/Homiliae Selectae Mar-Jacobi Sarugensis*. 6 vols. Piscataway, NJ: Gorgias Press, 2006.

Jacob of Sarug. *Homilies on Elijah*. Edited and translated by Stephen A. Kaufman. *Jacob of Sarug's Homilies on Elijah*. Piscataway, NJ: Gorgias Press, 2009.

Jacob of Sarug. *Homilies on Elisha*. Edited and translated by Stephen A. Kaufman. *Jacob of Sarug's Homilies on Elisha*. Piscataway, NJ: Gorgias Press, 2010.

Jacob of Sarug. *Homilies on Women Whom Jesus Met*. Edited and translated by Susan Ashbrook Harvey, Sebastian P. Brock, Reyhan Durmaz, Rebecca Stephens Falcasantos, Michael L. Payne, and Daniel Picus. *Jacob of Sarug's Homilies on Women Whom Jesus Met*. Piscataway, NJ: Gorgias Press, 2016.

Jacob of Sarug. "Homily 1 on Paul." Edited by Mary Hansbury and translated by Raju Parakkott. *Jacob of Sarug's Homilies on Paul*, 6–67. Piscataway, NJ: Gorgias Press, 2021.

Jacob of Sarug. "Homily 2 on Elisha." Edited and translated in Kaufman, *Jacob of Sarug's Homilies on Elisha*, 75–111.

Jacob of Sarug. "Homily 3, on Elisha and the Shilumite Woman." Edited and translated in Kaufman, *Jacob of Sarug's Homilies on Elisha*, 113–167.

Jacob of Sarug. "Homily 4 on Elisha." Edited and translated in Kaufman, *Jacob of Sarug's Homilies on Elisha*, 169–205.

Jacob of Sarug. "Homily 1 on the Nativity." Edited and translated by Thomas Kollamparampil. *Jacob of Sarug's Homilies on the Nativity*, 3–139. Piscataway, NJ: Gorgias Press, 2010.

Jacob of Sarug. "Homily 3 on the Nativity." Edited and translated by Thomas Kollamparampil. *Jacob of Sarug's Homilies on the Nativity*, 181–227. Piscataway, NJ: Gorgias Press, 2010.

Jacob of Sarug, "Homily 2 on the Resurrection of Our Lord." Edited and translated by Thomas Kollamparampil. *Jacob of Sarug's Homilies on the Resurrection*, 37–65. Piscataway, NJ: Gorgias Press, 2008.

Jacob of Sarug. "On Cain and Abel: Homily 3." Edited in Bedjan and Brock, *Homilies of Mar Jacob of Sarug*, 5:32–47.

Jacob of Sarug. "On Elisha the Prophet." Edited and translated in Kaufman, *Jacob of Sarug's Homilies on Elisha*, 1–73.

Jacob of Sarug. "On Epiphany." Edited and translated by Thomas Kollamparampil. *Jacob of Sarug's Homily on Epiphany*. Piscataway, NJ: Gorgias Press, 2008.

Jacob of Sarug. "On Jairus' Daughter." Edited and translated by Sebastian P. Brock. In Harvey et al., *Jacob of Sarug's Homilies on Women Whom Jesus Met*, 235–271.

Jacob of Sarug. "On Jephthah's Daughter." Edited and translated by Susan Ashbrook Harvey and Ophir Münz-Manor. *Jacob of Sarug's Homily on Jephthah's Daughter*. Piscataway, NJ: Gorgias Press: 2010.

Jacob of Sarug. "On Mar Ephrem." Edited and translated by Joseph P. Amar. *A Metrical Homily on Holy Mar Ephrem by Mar Jacob of Sarug*. PO 47.1. Turnhout: Brepols, 1995.

Jacob of Sarug. "On Palm Sunday." Edited and translated by Thomas Kollamparampil. *Jacob of Sarug's Homily on Palm Sunday*. Piscataway, NJ: Gorgias Press, 2008.

Jacob of Sarug. "On Pentecost." Edited and translated by Thomas Kollamparampil. *Jacob of Sarug's Homily on the Holy Sunday of Pentecost*. Piscataway, NJ: Gorgias Press, 2010.

Jacob of Sarug, "On Samson." Edited and translated by Dana Miller and Mary Hansbury. *Jacob of Sarug's Homily on Samson*. Piscataway, NJ: Gorgias Press, 2021.

Jacob of Sarug. "On Simeon the Stylite." Edited in Bedjan and Brock, *Homilies of Mar Jacob of Sarug*, 4:650–665. Translated by Susan Ashbrook Harvey. "Jacob of Serug, Homily on Simeon the Stylite," in *Ascetic Behavior in Greco-Roman Antiquity: A Sourcebook*, edited by Vincent L. Wimbush, 15–28. Minneapolis: Fortress Press, 1990.

Jacob of Sarug. "On Simon Peter." Edited and translated by Adam Carter McCollum. *Jacob of Sarug's Homily on Simon Peter, When Our Lord Said "Get Behind Me, Satan."* Piscataway, NJ: Gorgias Press, 2009.

Jacob of Sarug. "On Tamar." Edited and translated by Sebastian P. Brock. "Jacob of Serugh's Verse Homily on Tamar (Gen. 38)." *Le Muséon* 115 (2002): 279–315.

Jacob of Sarug. "On Women." Edited in Akhrass and Syryani, *160 Unpublished Homilies of Jacob of Serugh*, 2:533–535. Translated by Erin Galgay Walsh. "Mourning Eve: The Homily on Women as Attributed to Jacob of Serugh." *Studia Patristica Nordica* 33 (2018): 31–59.

Jacob of Sarug, "On the Afflicted Woman." Edited and translated by Sebastian P. Brock. In Harvey et al., *Jacob of Sarug's Homilies on Women Whom Jesus Met*, 171–233.

Jacob of Sarug. "On the Ascension." Edited and translated by Thomas Kollamparampil. *Jacob of Sarug's Homily on the Ascension of Our Lord*. Piscataway, NJ: Gorgias Press, 2009.

Jacob of Sarug. "On the Canaanite Woman." Edited and translated by Susan Ashbrook Harvey, Reyhan Durmaz, Rebecca Stephens Falcasantos, Michael Payne, and Daniel Picus. In Harvey et al., *Jacob of Sarug's Homilies on Women Whom Jesus Met*, 46–49.

Jacob of Sarug. "On the Death of a Bart Qyama." Edited in Bedjan and Brock. *Homilies of Mar Jacob*, 5:821–836.

Jacob of Sarug. "On the Famine That Was in Samaria." Edited and translated in Kaufman, *Jacob of Sarug's Homilies on Elisha*, 243–285.

Jacob of Sarug. "On the Fashioning of Creation." Edited and translated by Edward G. Mathews. *Jacob of Sarug's Homily on the Fashioning of Creation*. Piscataway, NJ: Gorgias Press, 2021.

Jacob of Sarug. "On the Giving of Praise for the Morning and Evening." Edited in Bedjan and Brock, *Homilies of Mar Jacob*, 3:907–912. Translated by Holy Transfiguration Monastery [Dana Miller]. *The True Vine* 26 (1998): 59–64.

Jacob of Sarug. "On the Judgment of Solomon." Edited and translated by Stephen A. Kaufman. *Jacob of Sarug's Homily on the Judgment of Solomon*. Piscataway, NJ: Gorgias Press, 2008.

Jacob of Sarug. "On the Lord's Prayer." Edited and translated by Morgan Reed. *Jacob of Sarug's Homily on the Lord's Prayer*. Piscataway, NJ: Gorgias Press, 2016.

Jacob of Sarug. "On the Love of God Towards Humanity." Edited and translated by Dominique Sirgy. *Jacob of Sarug's Homily on the Love of God Towards Humanity and of the Just Towards God*. Piscataway, NJ: Gorgias Press, 2022.

Jacob of Sarug. *On the Mother of God.* Edited in Bedjan and Brock, *Homilies of Mar Jacob*, 6:1–107. Translated by Mary Hansbury. *Jacob of Serug, On the Mother of God.* Crestwood, NY: St. Vladimir's Seminary Press, 1998.

Jacob of Sarug. "On the Partaking of the Holy Mysteries." Edited and translated by Amir Harrak. *Jacob of Sarug's Homily on the Partaking of the Holy Mysteries.* Piscataway, NJ: Gorgias Press, 2009.

Jacob of Sarug. "On the Prodigal Son." Edited in Bedjan and Brock, *Homilies of Mar Jacob*, 1:267–299. Translated by Holy Transfiguration Monastery [Dana Miller]. "A Homily on the Son Who Squandered His Riches by Mar Jacob, Bishop of Serugh." *The True Vine* 20 (1994): 11–37.

Jacob of Sarug. "On the Reposed." Edited in Bedjan and Brock, *Homilies of Mar Jacob*, 1:535–550. Translated by Holy Transfiguration Monastery [Dana Miller]. "A Homily on the Commemoration of the Reposed, by Mar Jacob, Bishop of Serugh." *The True Vine* 5 (1990): 41–53.

Jacob of Sarug. "On the Samaritan Woman." Edited and translated by Susan Ashbrook Harvey, Reyhan Durmaz, Rebecca Stephens Falcasantos, Michael Payne, and Daniel Picus. In Harvey et al., *Jacob of Sarug's Homilies on Women Whom Jesus Met*, 51–124.

Jacob of Sarug. "On the Sinful Woman." Edited and translated by Scott Fitzgerald Johnson. *Jacob of Sarug's Homily on the Sinful Woman.* Piscataway, NJ: Gorgias Press, 2013.

Jacob of Sarug. "On the Solitaries." Edited and translated by Colby A. Scott and Morgan Reed. *Jacob of Sarug's Homilies on the Solitaries.* Piscataway, NJ: Gorgias Press, 2016.

Jacob of Sarug. "On the Spectacles." Edited and translated by Cyril Moss. "Jacob of Serugh's Homilies on the Spectacles of the Theatre." *Le Muséon* 48 (1935): 87–112.

Jacob of Sarug. "On the Tower of Babel." Edited and translated by Aaron Michael Butts. *Jacob of Sarug's Homily on the Tower of Babel.* Piscataway, NJ: Gorgias Press, 2009.

Jacob of Sarug. *160 Unpublished Homilies of Jacob of Serugh.* Edited by R. Akhrass and I. Syryany. *160 Unpublished Homilies of Jacob of Serugh.* 2 vols. Damascus: Department of Syriac Studies-Syriac Orthodox Patriarchate, 2017.

Jacob of Sarug. "Praise at Table." Edited and translated by Jeff W. Childers. *Jacob of Sarug's Homilies on Praise at Table.* Piscataway, NJ: Gorgias Press, 2016.

Jacob of Sarug. *Stanzaic Poems.* Edited and translated by Sebastian P. Brock. *The Stanzaic Poems of Jacob of Serugh: A Collection of His Madroshe and Sughyotho.* Piscataway, NJ: Gorgias Press, 2022.

Jerome. Letter 22, "To Eustochium." Edited by Denys Gorce. *Lettres spirituelles de Saint Jérome*, 1:17–68. Paris: Librairie Lecoffre, 1932. Translated by Joan Petersen. *Handmaids of the Lord: Contemporary Descriptions of Feminine Asceticism in the First Six Christian Centuries*, 171–217. Kalamazoo, MI: Cistercian Publications, 1996.

John Chrysostom. "After the Remains of Martyrs." Edited in J.-P. Migne, *PG* 63, 467–472. Translated in Allen and Mayer, *John Chrysostom*, 85–92.

John Chrysostom. "Against the Games and the Theatres." Edited in J.-P. Migne, *PG* 56, 263–270. Translated in Mayer and Allen, *John Chrysostom*, 118–125.

John Chrysostom. "Against the Jews." Edited in J.-P. Migne, *PG* 48, 843–856. Translated in Mayer and Allen, *John Chrysostom*, 148–167.

John Chrysostom. *The Cult of Saints.* Translated by Wendy Mayer and Bronwen Neil. *St. John Chrysostom: The Cult of Saints.* Crestwood, NY: St. Vladimir's Seminary Press, 2006.

John Chrysostom. "On Martyrs." Edited in J.-P. Migne, *PG* 50, 661–666. Translated in Mayer and Allen, *John Chrysostom*, 93–97.

John Chrysostom. "On Saints Juventius and Maximinus." Edited in J.-P. Migne, *PG* 50, 571–578. Translated in Mayer and Neil, *Saint John Chrysostom: The Cult of Saints*, 91–99.

John Chrysostom. "On St. Phocas." Edited in J.-P. Migne, *PG* 50, 699–706. Translated in Mayer and Neil, *St. John Chrysostom: The Cult of Saints*, 75–87.

John Chrysostom. "Treatises on the Subintroductae." Edited by Jean Dumortier. *Saint Jean Chrysostom: Les cohabitations suspectes; Comment observer la virginité*. Paris: Société d'Éditions "Les Belles Lettres," 1955. Translated by Elizabeth Clark. *Jerome, Chrysostom, and Friends*, 158–248. Lewiston, NY: Edwin Mellen Press, 1979.

John of Dalyatha. *Letters*. Edited and translated by Mary Hansbury. *The Letters of John of Dalyatha*. Piscataway, NJ: Gorgias Press, 2006.

John of Ephesos. *Lives of the Eastern Saints*. Edited and translated by E. W. Brooks. *John of Ephesus, Lives of the Eastern Saints. PO* 17–19. Paris: Firmin-Didot, 1923–1925.

John the Stylite. *Select Narratives*. Edited and translated by Agnes Smith Lewis. *Select Narratives of Holy Women by John the Stylite of Beth-Mari-Qanun*. Studia Sinaitica 9–10. London: C.J. Clay and Sons, 1900.

(Ps.-)Joshua the Stylite. *Chronicle*. Edited by William Wright. *The Chronicle of Joshua the Stylite, Composed in Syriac A.D. 507, with a Translation into English and Notes*. Cambridge: Cambridge University Press, 1882. Translated by Frank Trombley and John W. Watt. *The Chronicle of Pseudo-Joshua the Stylite*. TTH 32. Liverpool: Liverpool University Press, 2000.

Justinian. *Novels*. Edited by W. Kroll and R. Schoell. *Corpus Iuris Civilis: Novellae*. Hildesheim: Weidmann, 1993. Translated by David J. D. Miller and Peter Sarris. *The Novels of Justinian: A Complete Annotated English Translation*. Cambridge: Cambridge University Press, 2018.

Kallimachos. *Hymn* 6. Edited and translated by Dee L. Clayman. *Callimachus, Hecale, Hymns, Epigrams*, 356–377. LCL 129. Cambridge, MA: Harvard University Press, 2022.

Leontios of Constantinople. *Homilies*. Edited and translated by Pauline Allen and Cornelis Datema. *Leontius, Presbyter of Constantinople: Fourteen Homilies*. Byzantina Australiensia 9. Brisbane: Australian Association for Byzantine Studies, 1991.

Libanios. *Autobiography*. Edited and translated by A. F. Norman. *Libanius: Autobiography and Selected Letters*, vol. 1. LCL 478. Cambridge, MA: Harvard University Press, 1992.

Libanios. *Progymnasmata*. Edited and translated by Craig A. Gibson. *Libanius' Progymnasmata: Model Exercises in Greek Prose Composition and Rhetoric*. Atlanta: Society of Biblical Literature, 2008.

Libanios. "What Words Would a Prostitute Say upon Gaining Self-Control?" Edited and translated by Craig A. Gibson. *Libanius' Progymnasmata: Model Exercises in Greek Prose Composition and Rhetoric*, 402–405. Atlanta: Society of Biblical Literature, 2008.

"Life of Bar-'Idtâ." Edited and translated by E. A. Wallis Budge. *The Histories of Rabban Hormizd the Persian and Rabban Bar-'Idtâ*. Luzac's Semitic Text and Translation Series 9 (Syriac) and 10 (English). London: Luzac, 1902.

"Life of Ephrem." Edited and translated by Joseph P. Amar. *The Syriac "Vita" Tradition of Ephrem the Syrian*. CSCO 629–630/Scr. Syr. 242–243. Leuven: Peeters, 2011.

"Life of Eugenia." Greek text edited and translated in Papaioannou, *Christian Novels*, 184–261. Syriac text in John the Stylite, *Select Narratives*, edited and translated by Agnes

Smith Lewis, Studia Sinaitica 9, fols. 21a–52b (Syriac); Studia Sinaitica 10, 1–35 (English). London: C.J. Clay and Sons, 1900.

"Life of Febronia." Edited in Bedjan, *AMS* 5:573–615. Translated in Brock and Harvey, *Holy Women of the Syrian Orient*, 150–176.

"Life of John Bar-Aphtonia." Edited and translated by F. Nau. "Histoire de Jean bar Aphtonia." *Revue de l'Orient Chrétien* 7 (1902): 97–135.

"Life of John of Tella" (by Elias). Edited and translated by E. W. Brooks. "Vita Iohannis Episcopi Tellae," in *Vitae virorum apud Monophysitas celeberrimorum.* CSCO 7/Scr. Syr. 7, 29–95 (Syriac), CSCO 8/Scr. Syr. 8, 21–60 (Latin). Paris: E typographeo reipublicae, 1907.

"Life of Mary, the Niece of Abraham of Qidun." Edited in Bedjan, *AMS* 6, 465–499. Translated in Brock and Harvey, *Holy Women of the Syrian Orient*, 29–39.

"Life of Matrona." Edited in *Acta Sanctorum Novembris*, 3:790–813. Brussels: Société des Bollandistes, 1910. Translated by Jeffrey Featherstone. "Life of St. Matrona of Perge," in *Holy Women of Byzantium: Ten Saints' Lives in English Translation*, edited by Alice-Mary Talbot, 18–64. Washington, DC: Dumbarton Oaks Research Library and Collection, 1996.

"Life of Pelagia." Edited in Bedjan, *AMS* 6:616–649. Translated in Brock and Harvey, *Holy Women of the Syrian Orient*, 40–62.

"Life of Rabbula." Edited and translated in Phenix and Horn, *The Rabbula Corpus*, 2–83.

"Liturgy of S. James (Syriac)." Translated by C. E. Hammond. *Antient Liturgies*, 56–81. Piscataway, NJ: Gorgias Press, 2004.

"Liturgy of the Syrian Jacobites." Translated by F. E. Brightman. *Eastern Liturgies: Being the Texts Original or Translated of the Principal Liturgies of the Church*, 69–110. Piscataway, NJ: Gorgias Press, 2004.

Livy. *History of Rome.* vol. 1, Books 1–2. Edited and translated by B. O. Foster. LCL 114. Cambridge, MA: Harvard University Press, 1976.

Livy. *History of Rome.* vol. 8, Books 28–30. Edited and translated by John C. Yardley. LCL 381. Cambridge, MA: Harvard University Press, 2021.

Livy. *History of Rome.* vol. 11, Books 38–40. Edited and translated by John C. Yardley. LCL 313. Cambridge, MA: Harvard University Press, 2018.

"Mar Pinhas." Edited and translated by Adam Carter McCollum. *The Story of Mar Pinhas.* Piscataway, NJ: Gorgias Press, 2013.

"Martyrdom of Martha." Edited in Bedjan, *AMS* 2:233–241. Translated in Brock and Harvey, *Holy Women of the Syrian Orient*, 67–73.

"Maruta Canons." Edited and translated by Arthur Vööbus. *The Canons Ascribed to Maruta of Maipherqat and Related Sources.* CSCO 439–440/Scr. Syr. 191–192. Louvain: Secrétariat du CorpusSCO, 1982.

Methodios of Olympos. *Symposium.* Edited by Herbert Musurillo. *Méthode d'Olympe: Le banquet.* SC 95. Paris: Les Éditions du Cerf, 1963. Translated by Herbert Musurillo. *St. Methodius, The Symposium; A Treatise on Chastity.* ACW 27. Westminster, MD: Newman Press, 1958.

Narsai. *Homilies on Creation.* Edited and translated by Philippe Gignoux. *Homélies de Narsai sur la Création.* PO 34.3–4. Turnhout: Brepols, 1968.

Narsai. "On Our Lord's Birth." Edited and translated by F. G. McLeod. *Narsai's Metrical Homilies on the Nativity, Epiphany, Passion, Resurrection and Ascension*, 36–69. PO 40.1. Turnhout: Brepols, 1979.

Narsai. "On the Caananite Woman." Edited and translated by Erin Galgay Walsh. *Eastern Christianity: A Reader*, edited by J. Edward Walters, 69–87. Grand Rapids, MI: Eerdmans, 2021.

Narsai. "On the Reproof of Eve's Daughters." Edited by Alphonse Mingana. *Selected Works of Narsai/Narsai Doctoris Syri Homiliae et Carmina*, 2:353–365. Piscataway, NJ: Gorgias Press, 2008. Translated by Corrie Molenberg. "Narsai's Memra on the Reproof of Eve's Daughters and the 'Tricks and Devices' They Perform." *Le Muséon* 106.1–2 (1993): 65–87.

Narsai. "On the Sanctification of the Church." Edited and translated by Amir Harrak. *Mar Narsai: Homily 33 on the Sanctification of the Church*. Piscataway, NJ: Gorgias Press, 2018.

Nemesios of Emesa. *On the Nature of Man*. Edited by Moreno Morani. *Nemesii Emeseni. De natura hominis*. Leipzig: B.G. Teubner, 1987. Translated by R.W. Sharples and P.J. van der Eijk. *Nemesius, On the Nature of Man*. TTH 49. Liverpool: Liverpool University Press, 2008.

Odes of Solomon. Edited and translated by James H. Charlesworth. *The Odes of Solomon: The Syriac Texts*. Missoula, MT: Scholars Press, 1978.

"On Hermits and Desert Dwellers." Edited and translated by Edmund Beck. *Des Heiligen Ephraem des Syrers, Sermones*, 4:16–28. CSCO 334–335/Scr. Syr. 148–149. Louvain: Sécretariat du CorpusSCO, 1973. Translated by Joseph P. Amar. "On Hermits and Desert Dwellers," in *Ascetic Behavior in Greco-Roman Antiquity: A Sourcebook*, edited by Vincent L. Wimbush, 66–80. Minneapolis: Fortress Press, 1990.

Ovid. *Heroides*. Edited and translated by Grant Showerman and G.P. Goold. *Ovid, Heroides and Amores*. LCL 41. Cambridge, MA: Harvard University Press, 1996.

Palladios. *Lausiac History*. Edited and translated by Cuthbert Butler. *The Lausiac History of Palladius*. 2 vols. Hildesheim: Georg Olms, 1967 [1898–1904]. Translated by R.T. Meyer. *Palladius, The Lausiac History*. ACW 34. New York: Paulist Press, 1964.

Paulinus of Nola. *Poems*. Edited by Franz Dolveck. *Paulini Nolani Carmina*. CCSL 21. Turnhout: Brepols, 2015. Translated by P.G. Walsh. *The Poems of St. Paulinus of Nola*. ACW 40. New York: Newman Press, 1975.

Philo. "On the Contemplative Life." Edited and translated by Francis Henry Colson. *Philo*, vol. 9, 112–169. LCL 363. Cambridge, MA: Harvard University Press, 1941.

Pliny. *Letters*. Edited and translated by Betty Radice. *Pliny the Younger, Letters*, vol. 2, Books 8–10. LCL 59. Cambridge, MA: Harvard University Press, 1975.

Plutarch. "Advice to Bride and Groom." Edited and translated by F.C. Babbitt. *Plutarch, Moralia*, vol. 2, 295–343. LCL 222. Cambridge, MA: Harvard University Press, 1928.

Plutarch. "On Listening to Lectures." Edited and translated by F.C. Babbitt. *Plutarch's Moralia*, vol. 1, 199–260. LCL 197. Cambridge, MA: Harvard University Press, 1927.

Plutarch. "The Greek Questions." Edited and translated by F.C. Babbit. *Plutarch, Moralia*, vol. 4, 176–249. LCL 305. Cambridge, MA: Harvard University Press, 1936.

Proclus of Constantinople. *Homilies*. Edited and translated by Nicholas Constas. *Proclus of Constantinople and the Cult of the Virgin in Late Antiquity*, 125–272. Leiden: Brill, 2003.

Prokopios of Caesarea. *History of the Wars*. Edited and translated by H.B. Dewing. *Procopius of Caesarea, History of the Wars*, vol. 1, Books 1–2 (Persian War). LCL 48. Cambridge. MA: Harvard University Press, 1914.

Pseudo-Dionysios of Tel-Mahre. *Chronicle*. Edited by J.B. Chabot. *Incerti auctoris chronicon anonymum pseudo-Dionysianum, II*. CSCO 104/Scr. Syr. 53. Paris: E Typographeo Reipublicae, 1933. Translated by Witold Witakowski. *Pseudo-Dionysius of Tel-Mahre, Chronicle, Part III (Known Also as the Chronicle of Zuqnin)*. TTH 22. Liverpool: Liverpool University Press, 1996.

Pseudo-Martyrius. *Funerary Speech for John Chrysostom*. Edited by M. Wallraff. *Oratio funebris in laudem Sancti Johannis Chrysostomi: Epitaffio attribuito a Martirio di Antiochia (BHG 871, CPG 6517)*. Spoleto: Centro italiano di studi sull'alto medioevo, 2007. Translated by Timothy D. Barnes and George Bevan. *Funerary Speech for John Chrysostom*. TTH 60. Liverpool: Liverpool University Press, 2013.

Rabbula. "Commandments and Admonitions for the Priests and the Children of the Covenant." Edited and translated in Phenix and Horn, *The Rabbula Corpus*, 102–117.

Rabbula. "Hymns." Edited and translated in Phenix and Horn, *The Rabbula Corpus*, 286–409.

Romanos. *Kontakia*. Edited by Paul Maas and Constantine Athanasius Trypanis. *Sancti Romani Melodi Cantica: Cantica Genuina*. Oxford: Oxford University Press, 1963. Partial translation by Ephrem Lash. *St. Romanos the Melodist: Kontakia on the Life of Christ*. San Francisco: HarperCollins, 1995.

Sahdona. "Shirin." Edited by A. de Halleux. Martyrius (Sahdona), *Oeuvres spirituelle* I: *Livre de la perfection*, I.iii.64, 69–79. CSCO 200–201/Scr. Syr. 86–87, Louvain, Secrétariat du CorpusSCO, 1960. Translated in Brock and Harvey, *Holy Women of the Syrian Orient*, 178–182.

The Septuagint with Apocrypha: Greek and English. Edited and translated by Lancelot C. L. Brenton. London: 1851. Reprint, Carol Stream, IL: Hendrickson Publishers, 2009.

Severos of Antioch. *Homily 18*. Edited by Maurice Brière and François Graffin. *Les "Homiliae cathedrales" de Sévère d'Antioche: Homélies XVIII à XXV*. PO 37.1, 6–23. Turnhout: Brepols, 1975. Translated by Pauline Allen and C. T. R. Hayward. *Severus of Antioch*, 118–126. New York: Routledge, 2004.

Severos of Antioch. *Letters*. Edited and translated by E. W. Brooks. *The Sixth Book of Select Letters of Severus, Patriarch of Antioch by Athanasius of Nisibis*. 4 vols. Oxford: Williams and Norgate, 1902.

Sozomen. *Ecclesiastical History*. Edited by J. Bidez and G. C. Hanson. *Sozomenus, Kirchengeschichte*. Berlin: Akademie Verlag, 1995. Translated by Chester Hartranft. NPNF, 2nd ser., vol. 2. Buffalo: Christian Literature, 1890.

Statutes of the School of Nisibis. Edited and translated by Arthur Vööbus. *The Statutes of the School of Nisibis*. PETSE 12. Stockholm: Estonian School of Theology in Exile, 1961.

Symmachus. *Life of Abel*. Edited and translated by Sebastian P. Brock. "A Syriac Life of Abel." *Le Muséon* 87.3–4 (1974): 467–492.

Synodicon Orientale. Edited by Jean-Baptiste Chabot. *Synodicon Orientale, ou, Recueil de synodes nestoriens*. Paris: Imprimerie Nationale, 1902.

Synod of Mar George I. Edited and translated in Chabot, *Synodicon Orientale*, 215–225 (Syriac), 480–490 (French).

Syriac and Arabic Documents. Edited and translated by Arthur Vööbus. *Syriac and Arabic Documents Regarding Legislation Relative to Syrian Asceticism*. PETSE 11. Stockholm: Estonian School of Theology in Exile, 1960.

Teaching of Addai. Edited and translated by George Howard. *The Teaching of Addai*. Chico, CA: Society of Biblical Literature, 1981.

"Testament of the Lord." Edited and translated by Arthur Vööbus. *The Synodicon in the West Syrian Tradition*. CSCO 367/Scr. Syr. 161, 1–26 (Syriac), CSCO 368/Scr. Syr. 162, 27–47 (English). Louvain: Secrétariat du CorpusSCO, 1975–1976.

"Testament of the Lord, Book II of Clement." Edited and translated by Arthur Vööbus. *The Synodicon in the West Syrian Tradition*. CSCO 367/Scr. Syr. 161, 27– 39 (Syriac), CSCO 368/Scr. Syr. 162, 47–57 (English). Louvain: Secrétariat du CorpusSCO, 1975–1976.

Tertullian. "On the Apparel of Women." Edited by Emil Kroymann. *Quinti Septimi Florentis Tertulliani Opera.* CSEL 70, 59–95. Vienna: Hoelder-Pichler-Tempsky, 1942. Translated by Edwin A. Quain. *Tertullian: Disciplinary, Moral, and Ascetical Works,* 117–152. FC 40. Washington, DC: The Catholic University of America Press, 1959.

Tertullian. "Spectacles." Edited by August Reifferscheid et Georg Wissowa. *Quinti Septimi Florentis Tertulliani Opera.* CSEL 20, 1–29. Vienna: Hoelder-Pichler-Tempsky, 1890. Translated by Rudolphus Arbesmann, Emily Joseph Daly, and Edwin A. Quain. *Tertullian: Disciplinary, Moral, and Ascetical Works,* 31–108. FC 40. Washington, DC: The Catholic University of America Press, 1959.

Tertullian. "To His Wife." Edited by Emil Kroymann. *Quinti Septimi Florentis Tertulliani Opera.* CSEL 70, 96–124. Vienna: Hoelder-Pichler-Tempsky, 1942. Translated by William P. Le Saint. *Tertullian: Treatises on Marriage and Remarriage,* 10–36. ACW 13. Westminster, MD: Newman Press, 1951.

Theodoret of Cyrrhos. *Ecclesiastical History.* Edited and translated by L. Parmentier, G. C. Hansen, J. Bouffartigue, and Pierre Canivet. *Theodoret de Cyr, Histoire Ecclésiastique,* vol. 2: Livres III–V. SC 530. Paris: Cerf, 2009. Translated by Blomfield Jackson. *The Ecclesiastical History of Theodoret.* NPNF, 2nd ser., vol. 3, 33–159. Grand Rapids, MI: Eerdmans, 1989.

Theodoret of Cyrrhos. *History of the Monks of Syria.* Edited and translated by P. Canivet and A. Leroy-Molighen. *Théodoret de Cyr, Histoire des moines de syrie.* SC 243, 257. Paris: Éditions du Cerf, 1977–1979. Translated by R. M. Price, Theodoret of Cyrrhus, *History of the Monks of Syria.* Kalamazoo, MI: Cistercian Publications, 1985.

Thomas of Marga. *The Book of Governors.* Edited and translated by E. A. Wallis Budge. *The Book of Governors: The Historia Monastica of Thomas, Bishop of Margâ A.D. 840, Edited from Syriac Manuscripts in the British Museum and Other Libraries.* 2 vols. London: Kegan, Paul, Trench, Trübner, 1893.

Timarion. Edited and translated by Barry Baldwin. *Timarion: Translated with Introduction and Commentary.* Detroit: Wayne State University Press, 1984.

Typikon de la Grande Église. Edited and translated by Juan Mateos. *Le Typikon de la Grande Église, Ms. Sainte-Croix No 40, Xe Siècle.* 2 vols. OCA 165–166. Rome: Pontificum Institutum Orientalium Studiorum, 1962–1963.

Victricius of Rouen. *In Praise of Saints.* Edited by I. Mulders and R. Demeulenaere. In R. Demeulenaere, *Foebadius, Victricius, Leporius, Vincentius Lerinensis, Evagrius, Ruricius.* CCSL 64, 53–93. Turnhout: Brepols, 1985. Translated by Gillian Clark. "Victricius of Rouen: Praising the Saints." *JECS* 7.3 (1999): 365–399.

(Ps.-)Zachariah Rhetor. *Chronicle.* Edited by E. W. Brooks. *Historia ecclesiastica Zachariae Rhetori vulgo adscripta.* 4 vols. CSCO 83–84/Scr. Syr. 38–39, CSCO 87–88/Scr. Syr. 41–42. Louvain: L. Durbecq, 1953. Translated by Geoffrey Greatrex, Robert R. Phenix, and Cornelia Horn. *Chronicle of Pseudo-Zachariah Rhetor: Church and War in Late Antiquity.* TTH 55. Liverpool: Liverpool University Press, 2011.

MODERN SOURCES

Ahuvia, Mika. *On My Right Michael, On My Left Gabriel: Angels in Ancient Jewish Culture.* Oakland: University of California Press, 2021.

Alexiou, Margaret. "The Lament of the Virgin in Byzantine Literature and Modern Greek Folk-Song." *BMGS* 1 (1975): 111–140.

Alexiou, Margaret. *The Ritual Lament in Greek Tradition.* 2nd ed., rev. by Dimitrios Yatromanolakis and P. Roilos. Lanham, MD: Rowman and Littlefield, 2002.

Alexopoulos, Stefanos, and Maxwell E. Johnson. *Introduction to Eastern Christian Liturgies.* Collegeville, MN: Liturgical Press, 2022.

Allen, Pauline. "The Sixth-Century Greek Homily: A Re-Assessment." In Cunningham and Allen, *Preacher and Audience*, 201–226.

Amar, Joseph P. "Byzantine Ascetic Monasticism and Greek Bias in the Vita Tradition of Ephrem the Syrian." *OCP* 58 (1992): 123–156.

Amiaud, Arthur. *La légende syriaque de Saint Alexis, l'homme de Dieu.* Paris: Vieweg, 1889.

Anagnostou-Laoutides, Eva. "Drinking New Wine (Acts 2:13): Drinking Wine from Plato to the Eucharist Tradition of Early Christian Thinkers." In *Eastern Christianity and Late Antique Philosophy*, edited by Eva Anagnostou-Laoutides and Ken Parry, 81–109. Leiden: Brill, 2020.

Andrade, Nathanael. "The Processions of John Chrysostom and the Contested Spaces of Constantinople." *JECS* 18.2 (2010): 161–189.

Arranz, Miguel. "L'office de l'Asmatikos Hesperinos ('vêpres chantées') de l'ancien Euchologe byzantine." *OCP* 44 (1978): 107–130, 391–419.

Arranz, Miguel. "The Functions of the Christian Assembly in the *Testament of the Lord*." In Semaine d'études liturgiques, *Roles in the Liturgical Assembly*, 29–60.

Arentzen, Thomas. *The Virgin in Song: Mary and the Poetry of Romanos the Melodist.* Philadelphia: University of Pennsylvania Press, 2017.

Atto, Naures. *Hostages in the Homeland, Orphans in the Diaspora.* Leiden: Leiden University Press, 2011.

Attridge, Harold W., and Margot Elsbeth Fassler. *Psalms in Community: Jewish and Christian Textual, Liturgical, and Artistic Traditions.* Leiden: Brill, 2004.

Avdokhin, Arkadiy. "Singers Silently Speaking: Psalmists in Inscriptions from Late Antique Middle Egypt (Bawit)." *JECS* 29.4 (2021): 607–636.

Aydin, Polycarpus Augin. *The Syriac Order of Monastic Profession and the Order of Baptism: Common Structure, Imagery, and Theological Themes.* Piscataway, NJ: Gorgias Press, 2017.

Baldovin, John F. *The Urban Character of Christian Worship: The Origins, Development, and Meaning of Stational Liturgy.* OCA 228. Rome: Pontificium Institutum Orientalium Studiorum, 1987.

Ball, Jennifer. "Decoding the Habit of the Byzantine Nun." *Journal of Modern Hellenism* 27 (2009/10): 25–52.

Barkhuizen, John. "Proclus of Constantinople: A Popular Preacher in Fifth-Century Constantinople." In Cunningham and Allen, *Preacher and Audience*, 179–200.

Barnes, Timothy David. *Constantine and Eusebius.* Cambridge, MA: Harvard University Press, 1981.

Barsoum, Ignatius Aphram I. *The Scattered Pearls: A History of Syriac Literature and Sciences.* Translated by Matti Moosa. Piscataway, NJ: Gorgias Press, 2003.

Bastiaensen, A. A. "*Psalmi, Hymni*, and *Cantica* in Early Jewish-Christian Tradition." *Studia Patristica* 21 (1989): 15–26.

Bear, Carl. "Funeral Music in Early Christianity." *Cross Accent* 22.3 (2014): 4–14.

Beard, Mary, John North, and Simon Price. *Religions of Rome*. vol. 1, *A History*. Cambridge: Cambridge University Press, 1998.

Beard, Mary, John North, and Simon Price. *Religions of Rome*. vol. 2, *A Sourcebook*. Cambridge: Cambridge University Press, 1998.

Beauchamp, Joëlle. "Discours et norms: La faiblesse feminine dans les texts protobyzantins." *Cahiers du Centre Gustave Glotz* 5 (1994): 199–220.

Beauchamp, Joëlle. "Le vocabulaire de la faiblesse féminine dans les texts juridique romains du IIIe au Ve siècle." *Revue historique du droit français et étranger*, ser. 4, vol. 54.4 (1976): 485–508.

Becker, Adam H. *Fear of God and the Beginning of Wisdom: The School of Nisibis and the Development of Scholastic Culture in Late Antique Mesopotamia*. Philadelphia: University of Pennsylvania Press, 2006.

Becker, Adam H. *Sources for the Study of the School of Nisibis*. TTH 50. Liverpool: Liverpool University Press, 2008.

Bell, Catherine. *Ritual Theory, Ritual Practice*. New York: Oxford University Press, 1992.

Berger, Teresa. *Gender Differences and the Making of Liturgical History: Lifting a Veil on Liturgy's Past*. Farnham, UK: Ashgate, 2011.

Berger, Teresa. *Women's Ways of Worship: Gender Analysis and Liturgical History*. Collegeville, MN: Liturgical Press, 1999.

Binggeli, André, ed. *L'hagiographie syriaque*. Études Syriaque 9. Paris: Geuthner, 2012.

Botha, Phil J. "Ephrem the Syrian's Treatment of Tamar in Comparison to That in Jewish Sources." *Acta Patristica et Byzantina* 6 (1995): 15–26.

Botte, Bernard. "Christian People and Hierarchy in the *Apostolic Traditions* of St. Hippolytus." In Semaine d'études liturgiques, *Roles in the Liturgical Assembly*, 61–72.

Bou Mansour, Tantios. *Le ministère sacerdotal dans la tradition syriaque primitive: Aphraate, Éphrem, Jacques de Saroug et Narsaï*. Supplements to *VC* 156. Leiden: Brill, 2019.

Bou Mansour, Tantios. *La pensée symbolique de saint Ephrem le syrien*. Bibliothèque de l'Université Saint-Ésprit 16. Kaslik: Université Saint Esprit, 1988.

Bradshaw, Paul F. *Daily Prayer in the Early Church*. Oxford: Oxford University Press, 1982.

Bradshaw, Paul F. *The Search for the Origins of Christian Worship: Sources and Methods for the Study of Early Liturgy*. 2nd ed. New York: Oxford University Press, 2002.

Bradshaw, Paul F., and Maxwell E. Johnson. *The Origins of Feasts, Fasts, and Seasons in Early Christianity*. Collegeville, MN: Liturgical Press, 2011.

Brakke, David. *Athanasius and the Politics of Asceticism*. Oxford: Clarendon Press, 1995.

Branham, Joan R. "Women as Objects of Sacrifice? An Early Christian 'Chancel of the Virgins.'" In *La cuisine et l'autel: Les sacrifices en questions dans les sociétés de la Méditerranée ancienne*, edited by Stella Georgoudi, Renée Koch Piettre, and Francis Schmidt, 372–385. Turnhout: Brepols, 2005.

Braniste, Ene. "The Liturgical Assembly and Its Functions in the *Apostolic Constitutions*." In Semaine d'études liturgiques, *Roles in the Liturgical Assembly*, 73–100.

Brock, Sebastian P. *Bride of Light: Hymns on Mary from the Syriac Churches*. Moran 'Etho 6. Piscataway, NJ: Gorgias Press, 2010.

Brock, Sebastian P. "Clothing Metaphors as a Means of Theological Expression in Syriac Tradition." In *Typus, Symbol, Allegorie bei den östlichen Vätern und ihren Parallelen im Mittelalter*, edited by Margot Schmidt, 11–40. Eichstätt: Pustet, 1982.

Brock, Sebastian P. "Creating Women's Voices: Sarah and Tamar in Some Syriac Narrative Poems." In Grypeou and Spurling, *The Exegetical Encounter*, 125–141.

Brock, Sebastian P. "Deaconesses in the Syriac Tradition." In *Woman in Prism and Focus: Her Profile in Major World Religions and in Christian Traditions*, edited by Prasanna Vazheeparampil, 205–218. Rome: Mar Thoma Yogam, 1996.

Brock, Sebastian P. "Dinah in a Syriac Poem on Joseph." In *Semitic Studies in Honour of Edward Ullendorff*, edited by Geoffrey Khan, 222–235. Studies in Semitic Languages and Linguistics 47. Leiden: Brill, 2005.

Brock, Sebastian P. "The Dispute Between the Cherub and the Thief." *Hugoye: Journal of Syriac Studies* 5.2 (2002): 169–193.

Brock, Sebastian P. "The Dispute Poem: From Sumer to Syriac." *JCSSS* 1 (2001): 3–20.

Brock, Sebastian P. "Divine Titles and Epithets in Syriac Writings: Some Approaches." *Parole de l'Orient* 38 (2013): 35–48.

Brock, Sebastian P. "Dramatic Dialogue Poems." In *Symposium Syriacum IV*, edited by H. J. W. Drijvers, R. Lavenant, C. Molenberg, and G. J. Reinink, 135–147. OCA 229. Rome: Pontificio Instituto Orientale, 1987.

Brock, Sebastian P. "Ephremiana in Manuscript Sinai Syr. 10." *Le Muséon* 129.3–4 (2016): 285–322.

Brock, Sebastian P. "An Episcopal *adventus* in Syriac." In *A Journey Along the Christian Way: Festschrift for the Right Rev. Kallistos Ware on His 85th Anniversary*, edited by E. Ene D-Vasilescu, 52–61. Beau Bassin, Mauritius: Scholars Press, 2018.

Brock, Sebastian P. "Genesis 22 in Syriac Tradition." In *Mélanges Dominique Barthélemy: Études bibliques offertes a l'occasion de son 60e anniversaire*, edited by Pierre Casetti, Othman Keel, and Adrian Schenker, 1–30. Göttingen: Vandenhoeck & Ruprecht, 1981.

Brock, Sebastian P. "The Holy Spirit as Feminine in Early Syriac Literature." In *After Eve: Women, Theology and the Christian Tradition*, edited by Janet Soskice, 73–88. London: Collins, 1990.

Brock, Sebastian P. "Invocations To/For the Holy Spirit in Syriac Liturgical Texts: Some Comparative Approaches." In *Comparative Liturgy: Fifty Years After Anton Baumstark*, edited by Robert F. Taft and Gabriele Winkler, 377–406. OCA 265. Rome: Pontificium Institutum Orientalium Studiorum, 2001.

Brock, Sebastian P. "Jewish Traditions in Syriac Sources." *Journal of Jewish Studies* 30.2 (1979): 212–232.

Brock, Sebastian P., "Joseph and Potiphar's Wife: Two Anonymous Dispute Poems." In *Syriac Polemics: Studies in Honour of Gerrit Jan Reinink*, edited by W. J. van Bekkum, J. W. Drijvers, and Alexander C. Klugkist, 41–57. OLA 170. Leuven: Peeters, 2007.

Brock, Sebastian P. "The Lament of Mary, Niece of Abraham Qidunaya." *Syriac Annals of the Romanian Academy* 1 (2020–2021): 9–30.

Brock, Sebastian P. "L'hagiographie versifiée." In Binggeli, *L'hagiographie syriaque*, 113–126.

Brock, Sebastian P. *The Luminous Eye: The Spiritual World Vision of Saint Ephrem*. Kalamazoo, MI: Cistercian Publications, 1992.

Brock, Sebastian P. *Mary and Joseph, and Other Dialogue Poems on Mary*. Piscataway, NJ: Gorgias Press, 2011.

Brock, Sebastian P. "Poetry and Hymnography (3): Syriac." In Harvey and Hunter, *The Oxford Handbook of Early Christian Studies*, 657–671.

Brock, Sebastian P. "The Priesthood of the Baptised: Some Syriac Perspectives." *Sobornost/ Eastern Churches Review* 9.2 (1987): 14–22.

Brock, Sebastian P. "The Published Verse Homilies of Isaac of Antioch, Jacob of Serugh, and Narsai: Index of Incipits." *JSS* 32.2 (1987): 279–313.

Brock, Sebastian P. "The Queen of Sheba's Questions to Solomon: A Syriac Version." *Le Muséon* 92.3–4 (1979): 331–345.

Brock, Sebastian P. "Saint Ephrem on Women in the Old Testament." In *Saint Éphrem, un poète pour notre temps*, 35–44. Patrimoine Syriaque, Actes du Colloque XI. Antélias, Lebanon: Centre d'Études et de Recherches Orientales, 2007.

Brock, Sebastian P. "The Seeds of Liturgical Drama in Syriac?" In *Études bibliques et Proche-Orient ancien: Mélanges offerts au Père Paul Feghali*, edited by Ayoub Chehwan and Antoine Kassis, 323–341. Beirut: Fédération Biblique, 2001.

Brock, Sebastian P. "The Sinful Woman and Satan: Two Syriac Dialogue Poems." *Oriens Christianus* 72 (1988): 21–62.

Brock, Sebastian P. *Singer of the Word of God: Saint Ephrem and His Significance in Late Antiquity*. Piscataway, NJ: Gorgias Press, 2020.

Brock, Sebastian P. "St. Ephrem in the Eyes of Later Syriac Liturgical Tradition." *Hugoye: Journal of Syriac Studies* 2.1 (1999 [2010]): 5–25.

Brock, Sebastian P. "St. Marina and Satan: A Syriac Dialogue Poem." *Collectanea Christiana Orientalia* 5 (2008): 35–57.

Brock, Sebastian P. "Syriac and Greek Hymnography: Problems of Origins." *Studia Patristica* 16 (1985): 77–81. Reprinted in Sebastian P. Brock, *Studies in Syriac Christianity*, 77–81. Aldershot: Variorum, 1992.

Brock, Sebastian P. "Syriac Dialogue Poems: Marginalia to a Recent Edition." *Le Muséon* 97.1–2 (1984): 29–58.

Brock, Sebastian P. "Syriac Dispute Poems: The Various Types." In Reinink and Vanstiphout, *Dispute Poems and Dialogues*, 109–112.

Brock, Sebastian P. "A Syriac Verse Homily on Elijah and the Widow of Sarepta." *Le Muséon* 102.1–2 (1989): 93–113.

Brock, Sebastian P. "The Transmission of Ephrem's Madrashe in the Syriac Liturgical Tradition." *Studia Patristica* 33 (1997): 490–505.

Brock, Sebastian P. "Towards a Typology of the Epiclesis in the West Syrian Anaphoras." In *Crossroad of Cultures: Studies in Liturgy and Patristics in Honor of Gabriele Winkler*, edited by Hans-Jürgen Feulner, Elena Velkovska, and Robert F. Taft, 173–192. OCA 260. Rome: Pontificium Institutum Orientalium Studiorum, 2000.

Brock, Sebastian P. *Treasure-House of Mysteries: Explorations of the Sacred Text Through Poetry in the Syriac Tradition*. Yonkers: St. Vladimir's Seminary Press, 2012.

Brock, Sebastian P. "Two Syriac Verse Homilies on the Binding of Isaac." *Le Muséon* 99.1–2 (1986): 61–129.

Brock, Sebastian P. "The Use of the Syriac Versions in the Liturgy." In Haar Romeny, *The Peshitta*, 3–25.

Brock, Sebastian P., and Susan Ashbrook Harvey. *Holy Women of the Syrian Orient*. Berkeley: University of California Press, 1998.

Brock, Sebastian P., and Simon Hopkins. "A Verse Homily on Abraham and Sarah in Egypt: Syriac Original with Early Arabic Translation." *Le Muséon* 105 (1992): 87–146.

Brock, Sebastian P., and George Kiraz. *Ephrem the Syrian: Select Poems*. Provo, UT: Brigham Young University Press, 2006.

Brock, Sebastian P., and Witold Witakowski. *The Hidden Pearl: The Syrian Orthodox Church and Its Ancient Aramaic Heritage*. vol. 3, *At the Turn of the Third Millennium: The Syrian Orthodox Witness*. Edited by David G. K. Taylor and Sebastian P. Brock. Rome: Trans World Film Italia via Massimo Meliconi, 2001.

Brooten, Bernadette J. *Women Leaders in the Ancient Synagogue: Inscriptional Evidence and Background Issues*. Chico, CA: Scholars Press, 1982.

Brown, Amelia. "Psalmody and Socrates: Female Literacy in the Byzantine Empire." In Neil and Garland, *Questions of Gender*, 57–76.

Brown, Peter. *The Body and Society: Men, Women, and Sexual Renunciation in Early Christianity*. New York: Columbia University Press, 1988.

Brown, Peter. "The Notion of Virginity in the Early Church." In *Christian Spirituality: Origins to the Twelfth Century*, edited by Bernard McGinn, John Meyendorff, and Jean Leclercq, 427–443. World Spirituality 16. New York: Crossroad, 1985.

Bumazhnov, Dmitrij. "Qyama Before Aphrahat: The Development of the Idea of Covenant in Some Early Syriac Documents." In *Syrien im 1.–7. Jahrhundert nach Christus: Akten der 1. Tübinger Tagung zum Christlichen Orient (15.–16. Juni 2007)*, edited by Dmitrij Bumazhnov and Hans Reinhard Seeliger, 65–81. Tübingen: Mohr Siebeck, 2011.

Burgess, Henry. *Select Metrical Hymns and Homilies of Ephraem Syrus*. London: Blackadder and Low, 1853.

Burkitt, Francis C. "The Early Syriac Lectionary System." *Proceedings of the British Academy* 10 (1923): 301–339.

Burris, Catherine. "The Syriac 'Book of Women': Text and Metatext." In *The Early Christian Book*, edited by William E. Klingshirn and Linda Safran, 86–98. Washington, DC: The Catholic University of America Press, 2007.

Burris, Catherine, and Lucas Van Rompay. "Thecla in Syriac Christianity: Preliminary Observations." *Hugoye: Journal of Syriac Studies* 5.2 (2002): 225–236.

Burrus, Virginia. "From Diotima to Thecla and Beyond: Virginal Voice in the Lives of Helia and Constantina." In *Thecla and Medieval Sainthood: The Acts of Paul and Thecla in Eastern and Western Hagiography*, edited by Ghazzal Dabiri and Flavia Ruani, 233–255. Cambridge: Cambridge University Press, 2022.

Burrus, Virginia. "Gender, Eros, and Pedagogy: Macrina's Pious Household." In Leyerle and Young, *Ascetic Culture*, 167–181.

Burrus, Virginia. "The Heretical Woman as Symbol in Alexander, Athanasius, Epiphanius, and Jerome," *HTR* 84 (1991): 229–248.

Burrus, Virginia. "Mapping as Metamorphosis: Initial Reflections on Gender and Ancient Religious Discourses." In Penner and Vander Stichele, *Mapping Gender*, 1–10.

Burrus, Virginia. *The Sex Lives of Saints: An Erotics of Ancient Hagiography*. Philadelphia: University of Pennsylvania Press, 2004.

Butts, Aaron Michael. "Manuscript Transmission as Reception History: The Case of Ephrem the Syrian (d. 373)." *JECS* 25.2 (2017): 281–306.

Butts, Aaron Michael, and Simcha Gross, eds. *Jews and Syriac Christians: Intersections Across the First Millenium.* Tübingen: Mohr Siebeck, 2020.

Butts, Aaron Michael, Kristian S. Heal, and Robert A. Kitchen, eds. *Narsai: Rethinking His Work and His World.* Tübingen: Mohr Siebeck, 2020.

Calame, Claude. *Choruses of Young Women in Ancient Greece: Their Morphology, Religious Role, and Social Functions.* Translated by Derek Collins and Janice Orion. Lanham, MD: Rowman and Littlefield, 2001.

Cameron, Averil. *Christianity and the Rhetoric of Empire: The Development of Christian Discourse.* Berkeley: University of California Press, 1991.

Cameron, Averil. "Disputations, Polemical Literature, and the Formation of Opinion." In Reinink and Vanstiphout, *Dispute Poems and Dialogues,* 91–108.

Cameron, Averil, ed. *History as Text: The Writing of Ancient History.* Chapel Hill: University of North Carolina Press, 1990.

Cameron, Averil. "Virginity as Metaphor: Women and the Rhetoric of Early Christianity." In Cameron, *History as Text,* 181–205.

Caner, Daniel. *Wandering, Begging Monks: Spiritual Authority and the Promotion of Monasticism in Late Antiquity.* Berkeley: University of California Press, 2002.

Cassingena-Trévedy, François. "Constructions, Destructions, Inhabitation Divine: Mystère et vie des églises à travers les écrits des premiers auteurs syriaque (IVᵉ–VIᵉ siècles)." In Chatonnet, *Les églises en monde syriaque,* 521–539.

Cassingena-Trévedy, François. "L'hymnographie syriaque." In Cassingena-Trévedy and Jurasz, *Les liturgies syriaques,* 185–218.

Cassingena-Trévedy, François, and Izabela Jurasz, eds. *Les liturgies syriaques.* Études Syriaques 3. Paris: Geuthner, 2006.

Cassis, Marica. "The Bema in the East Syriac Church in Light of New Archaeological Evidence." *Hugoye: Journal of Syriac Studies* 5.2 (2002): 195–211.

Cetrez, Önver. *Meaning-Making Variations in Acculturation and Ritualization: A Multi-Generational Study of Suroyo Migrants in Sweden.* Psychologica et Sociologica Religionum 17. Uppsala: Acta Universitatis Upsaliensis, 2005.

Chaldaeakes, Achilleus G. "The 'Woman Figure' in Byzantine Melopoeia." In *Psaltike: Neue Studien zur Byzantinischen Musik; Festschrift für Gerda Wolfram,* edited by Nina-Maria Wanek, 67–101. Vienna: Praesens Verlag, 2011.

Charlesworth, James H. *The Earliest Christian Hymnbook: The Odes of Solomon.* Eugene, OR: Cascade Books, 2009.

Chatonnet, Françoise Briquel. "Les églises dans les textes." In Chatonnet, *Les églises en monde syriaque,* 11–40.

Chatonnet, Françoise Briquel, ed. *Les églises en monde syriaque.* Études Syriaques 10. Paris: Geuthner, 2013.

Chatonnet, Françoise Briquel, Saba Farès, Brigitte Lion, et Cécile Michel, eds. *Femmes, cultures et sociétés dans les civilisations méditerranéennes et proches-orientales de l'Antiquité.* Topoi: Orient-Occident Supplément 10. Lyon: 2009.

Chazon, Esther G., ed. *Liturgical Perspectives: Prayer and Poetry in Light of the Dead Sea Scrolls.* Leiden: Brill, 2003.

Chidester, David. *Word and Light: Seeing, Hearing, and Religious Discourse.* Urbana: University of Illinois Press, 1992.

Childers, Jeff W. "Jacob of Sarug's Memra 9 On Praise at Table: A Newly Published Syriac Text." *Studia Patristica* 125, edited by Markus Vinzent, 149–156. Leuven: Peeters, 2021.

Childers, Jeff W. "'This Is Why Brides in Their Bridal Chambers Evoke Great Desire'—Some Performative Aspects of a Memrā Attributed to Jacob of Serugh (Praise at Table 9)." In Elkhoury and Kitchen, *The Year of Jacob of Serugh*, 179–196.

Christensen, Maria Munkholt. "Holy Women as Humble Teachers. An Investigation of Hagiographical Texts from Late Antiquity." In *Teachers in Late Antique Christianity*, edited by Peter Gemeinhardt, Olga Lorgeoux, and Maria Munkholt Christensen, 165–183. Tübingen: Mohr Siebeck, 2018.

Chryssavgis, John, Niki Papageorgiou, Marilyn Rouvelas, and Petros Vassiliadis, eds. *Deaconesses: A Tradition for Today and Tomorrow*. Brookline, MA: Holy Cross Orthodox Press, 2023.

Ciggaar, Krijnie N. *Western Travelers to Constantinople: The West and Byzantium, 962–1204; Cultural and Political Relations*. Leiden: Brill, 1996.

Clark, Elizabeth A. "Ascetic Renunciation and Feminine Advancement: A Paradox of Late Ancient Christianity." *Anglican Theological Review* 63 (1981): 240–257. Reprinted in Elizabeth A. Clark, *Ascetic Piety and Women's Faith: Essays on Late Ancient Christianity*, 175–208. Lewiston/Queenston: Edwin Mellen Press, 1986.

Clark, Elizabeth A. "Holy Women, Holy Words: Early Christian Women, Social History, and the Linguistic Turn." *JECS* 6.3 (1998): 413–430.

Clark, Elizabeth A. "Ideology, History, and the Construction of 'Woman' in Late Ancient Christianity." *Journal of Early Christianity* 2.1 (1994): 155–184.

Clark, Elizabeth A. "The Lady Vanishes: Dilemmas of a Feminist Historian After the 'Linguistic Turn.'" *CH* 67.1 (1998): 1–31.

Clark, Elizabeth A. *Reading Renunciation: Asceticism and Scripture in Early Christianity*. Princeton, NJ: Princeton University Press, 1999.

Clark, Elizabeth A. *Women in the Early Church*. Wilmington, DE: Michael Glazier, 1983.

Clark, Gillian. *Women in Late Antiquity: Pagan and Christian Lifestyles*. Oxford: Clarendon Press, 1993.

Cloke, Gillian. *This Female Man of God: Women and Spiritual Power in the Patristic Age, AD 350–450*. New York: Routledge, 1995.

Cody, Aelred. "The Early History of the Octoechos in Syria." In *East of Byzantium: Syria and Armenia in the Formative Period*, edited by Nina G. Garsoïan, Thomas F. Mathews, and Robert W. Thomson, 89–113. Washington, DC: Dumbarton Oaks, 1982.

Cohen, Shaye J. D. "The Temple and the Synagogue." In Davies, Sturdy, and Horbury, *The Cambridge History of Judaism*, 3:298–325.

Cohen, Shaye J. D. "Were Pharisees and Rabbis the Leaders of Communal Prayer and Torah Study in Antiquity? The Evidence of the New Testament, Josephus, and the Early Church Fathers." In Kee and Cohick, *Evolution of the Synagogue*, 89–105.

Connolly, Richard H. "The Book of Life." *JTS* 13.51 (1912): 580–594.

Constantinou, Stavroula. *Female Corporeal Performances: Reading the Body in Byzantine Passions and Lives of Holy Women*. Uppsala: Acta Universitatis Upsaliensis, 2005.

Constas, Fr. Maximos. "Poetry and Painting in the Middle Byzantine Period: A Bilateral Icon from Kastoria and the *Stavrotheotokia* of Joseph the Hymnographer." In *Viewing*

Greece: Cultural and Political Agency in the Medieval and Early Modern Mediterranean, edited by Sharon Gerstel, 12–32. Turnhout: Brepols, 2016.

Coon, Lynda L. *Sacred Fictions: Holy Women and Hagiography in Late Antiquity*. Philadelphia: University of Pennsylvania Press, 1997.

Cosgrove, Charles. "Clement of Alexandria and Early Christian Music." *JECS* 14.3 (2006): 255–282.

Cribiore, Raffaella. *Gymnastics of the Mind: Greek Education in Hellenistic and Roman Egypt*. Princeton, NJ: Princeton University Press, 2005.

Cuming, G. J. "The Liturgy of Antioch in the Time of Severus (513–518)." In *Time and Community*, edited by J. Neil Alexander, 83–103. Washington, DC: The Pastoral Press, 1990.

Cunningham, Agnes. "Women and Preaching in the Patristic Age." In *Preaching in the Patristic Age: Studies in Honor of Walter J. Burghardt, S.J.*, edited by David G. Hunter, 53–72. New York: Paulist Press, 1989.

Cunningham, Mary B., and Pauline Allen, eds. *Preacher and Audience: Studies in Early Christian and Byzantine Homiletics*. Leiden: Brill, 1998.

Daley, Brian E., and Paul R. Kolbet. *The Harp of Prophecy: Early Christian Interpretation of the Psalms*. Notre Dame, IN: University of Notre Dame Press, 2014.

Daly, Mary. *The Church and the Second Sex*. New York: Harper and Row, 1968.

Davies, William David, John Sturdy, and William Horbury, eds. *The Cambridge History of Judaism*. vol. 3, *The Early Roman Period*. Cambridge: Cambridge University Press, 1984.

Debié, Muriel. "Le bruissement des ailes des anges: La vue et l'ouïe convoqués à l'autel dans la tradition syriaques." In *Rituels religieux et sensorialité (Antiquité et Moyen Âge): Parcours de recherche*, edited by Béatrice Caseau Chevallier and Elisabetta Neri, 203–220. Milan: SilvanaEditoriale, 2021.

de Halleux, André. "La transmission des hymnes d'Éphrem d'après les ms. Sinaï syr. 10, f. 165v–178r." In *Symposium Syriacum*, edited by Ignacio Ortiz de Urbina, 21–62. OCA 197. Rome: Pontificio Instituto Orientale, 1974.

de Halleux, André. "Une clé pour les hymnes d'Ephrem dans le ms Sinai syr. 10." *Le Muséon* 85 (1972): 171–199.

den Beisen, Kees. *Simple and Bold: Ephrem's Art of Symbolic Thought*. Piscataway, NJ: Gorgias Press, 2006.

den Boeft, Jan, and Antonius Hilhorst, eds., *Early Christian Poetry: A Collection of Essays*. Leiden: Brill, 1993.

Dillon, Matthew. *Girls and Women in Classical Greek Religion*. New York: Routledge, 2003.

Dixon, Suzanne. *Reading Roman Women: Sources, Genres, and Real Life*. London: Duckworth, 2001.

Dobrov, Gregory W. "A Dialogue with Death: Ritual Lament and the *Threnos Theotokou* of Romanos Melodos." *GRBS* 35.4 (1994): 387–405.

Dodd, Erica Cruikshank. *Medieval Painting in Lebanon*. Wiesbaden: Reichert Verlag, 2004.

Doerfler, Maria. *Constituting the Past: Law and the Creation of Sacred Histories*. Oakland: University of California Press (forthcoming).

Doerfler, Maria. "Emotional Communities and the Loss of an Individual." In *Managing Emotions in Byzantium: Passions, Affects and Imaginings*, edited by Margaret Mullett and Susan Ashbrook Harvey, 292–313. London: Routledge, 2023.

Doerfler, Maria. "Gone But Not Forgotten: Retrieving the Migrant in Late Antiquity." *JAAR* 87.4 (2019): 1153–1177.

Doerfler, Maria. *Jephthah's Daughter, Sarah's Son: The Death of Children in Late Antiquity.* Oakland: University of California Press, 2019.

Doerfler, Maria. "Listen to Her: Women as Avatars of Wisdom in Late Ancient Homiletic Discourse." *JECH* 8.3 (2018): 28–56.

Doerfler, Maria. "Translating Eve: Death and Female Identity in a Funerary Hymn Ascribed to Ephrem." *JTS* 73.1 (2022): 167–194.

Doerfler, Maria, Emanuel Fiano, and Kyle Smith, eds. *Syriac Encounters: Papers from the Sixth North American Syriac Symposium, Duke University, 26–29 June 2011.* Leuven: Peeters, 2015.

Donceel-Voûte, Pauline. *Les pavements des églises byzantines de Syrie et du Liban: Décor, archeology et liturgie.* Louvain-la-Neuve: Département d'archéologie et d'histoire de l'art, Collège Érasme, 1988.

Doran, Robert. *Stewards of the Poor: The Man of God, Rabbula, and Hiba in Fifth-Century Edessa.* Kalamazoo, MI: Cistercian Publications, 2006.

Drake, Susanna. *Slandering the Jew: Sexuality and Difference in Early Christian Texts.* Philadelphia: University of Pennsylvania Press, 2013.

Drijvers, H. J. W. "The 19ᵗʰ Ode of Solomon: Its Interpretation and Place in Syrian Christianity." *JTS* 31.2 (1980): 337–355.

Efthymiades, Stephanos, ed. *The Ashgate Research Companion to Byzantine Hagiography.* vol. 2, *Genres and Contexts.* Burlington, VT: Ashgate, 2014.

Efthymiadis, Stephanos. "Greek Byzantine Hagiography in Verse." In *The Ashgate Research Companion to Byzantine Hagiography*, vol. 2, *Genres and Contexts*, edited by Stephanos Efthymiadis, 161–179. Burlington, VT: Ashgate, 2014.

Eisen, Ute E. *Women Officeholders in Early Christianity: Epigraphical and Literary Studies.* Collegeville, MN: Liturgical Press, 2000.

Elkhoury, Armando, and Robert Kitchen, eds. *The Year of Jacob of Serugh: Essays in Commemoration of the 1500th Anniversary of His Death.* Washington, DC: The Hidden Pearl Press, 2023.

Ellison, Mark. "Reimagining and Reimaging Eve in Early Christianity." In *Material Culture and Women's Religious Experience in Antiquity: An Interdisciplinary Symposium*, edited by Mark D. Ellison, Catherine Gines Taylor, and Carolyn Osiek, 213–256. Lanham, MD: Lexington Books/Fortress Academic, 2021.

Elm, Susanna. *Virgins of God: The Making of Asceticism in Late Antiquity.* Oxford: Clarendon Press, 1994.

Ernst, Allie M. *Martha from the Margins: The Authority of Martha in Early Christian Tradition.* Supplements to *VC* 98. Leiden: Brill, 2009.

Falcasantos, Rebecca Stephens. *Constantinople: Ritual, Violence, and Memory in the Making of a Christian Imperial Capital.* Oakland: University of California Press, 2020.

Fiey, J.-M. "Cénobitisme féminine ancien dans les églises syriennes orientale et occidentale." *L'Orient Syrien* 10 (1965): 281–306.

Fiey, J.-M. "Diptyques nestoriens du XIVe siècle." *AB* 81 (1963): 371–413.

Fiey, J.-M. "Une hymne nestorienne sur les saintes femmes." *AB* 84 (1966): 77–110.

Fine, Steven, ed. *Sacred Realm: The Emergence of the Synagogue in the Ancient World.* New York: Oxford University Press; Yeshiva University Museum, 1996.

Fleischer, Ezra. "Piyyut." In *The Literature of the Sages*, edited by Shmuel Safrai, Peter J. Tomson, Zeev Safrai, and Joshua Schwartz, 363–374. Minneapolis: Fortress Press, 2006.

Forness, Philip M. "The Construction of Metrical Poetry in the Homilies of Narsai of Nisibis and Jacob of Serugh." In Butts, Heal, and Kitchen, *Narsai*, 93–115.

Forness, Philip M. *Preaching Christology in the Roman Near East: A Study of Jacob of Serugh.* Oxford: Oxford University Press, 2018.

Fox, Robin Lane. *Pagans and Christians.* London: Viking, 1986.

Frank, Georgia. "The Memory Palace of Marcellinus: Athanasius and the Mirror of the Psalms." In Leyerle and Young, *Ascetic Culture*, 97–124.

Frishman, Judith, and Lucas Van Rompay, eds. *The Book of Genesis in Jewish and Oriental Interpretation.* Leuven: Peeters, 1997.

Furman, Nelly. "His Story Versus Her Story: Male Genealogy and Female Strategy in the Jacob Cycle." In *Feminist Perspectives on Biblical Scholarship*, edited by Adela Yarbo Collins, 107–116. Chico, CA: Scholar's Press, 1985.

Gador-Whyte, Sarah. *Theology and Poetry in Early Byzantium: The* Kontakia *of Romanos the Melodist.* Cambridge: Cambridge University Press, 2017.

Garland, Lynda. "'Til Death Do Us Part?': Family Life in Byzantine Monasteries." In Neil and Garland, *Questions of Gender*, 29–55.

Gavrili, Paraskevi. "A New Approach to the Mosaic from Mariamin, Syria, with Female Musicians: Theatrical Performance or Private Banqueting Concert?" *Studien zur Musikarchäologie* VII, edited by R. Eichmann, E. Hickmann, and L. C. Koch (2010): 9–16.

Giannouli, Antonia. "Byzantine Hagiography and Hymnography: An Interrelationship." In Efthymiadis, *The Ashgate Research Companion to Byzantine Hagiography*, 2:285–312.

Giordano, Manuela. "Women's Voice and Religious Utterances in Ancient Greece." *Religions* 2.4 (2011): 729–743.

Glenthøj, Johannes B. *Cain and Abel in Syriac and Greek Writers (4th–6th Centuries).* CSCO 567/Sub. 95. Leuven: Peeters, 1997.

Goff, Barbara. *Citizen Bacchae: Women's Ritual Practice in Ancient Greece.* Oakland: University of California Press, 2004.

Gordley, Matthew E. *Teaching Through Song in Antiquity: Didactic Hymnody Among Greeks, Romans, Jews, and Christians.* WUNT 302. Tübingen: Mohr Siebeck, 2011.

Gribomont, Jean. "La tradition liturgique des hymnes pascales de S. Ephrem." *Parole de l'Orient* 4.1–2 (1973): 191–246.

Griffin, Carl. *Cyrillona: A Critical Study and Commentary.* Piscataway, NJ: Gorgias Press, 2016.

Griffith, Sidney H. "Asceticism in the Church of Syria: The Hermeneutics of Early Syrian Monasticism." In *Asceticism*, edited by Vincent Wimbush and Richard Valantasis, 220–245. New York: Oxford University Press, 1995.

Griffith, Sidney H. "'Denominationalism' in Fourth-Century Syria: Readings in Saint Ephrem's *Hymns Against Heresies*, Madrashe 22–24." In *The Garb of Being: Embodiment and the Pursuit of Holiness in Late Ancient Christianity*, edited by Georgia Frank, Susan R. Holman, and Andrew S. Jacobs, 79–100. New York: Fordham University Press, 2020.

Griffith, Sidney H. *"Faith Adoring the Mystery": Reading the Bible with St. Ephraem the Syrian.* Milwaukee: Marquette University Press, 1997.

Griffith, Sidney H. "'Faith Seeking Understanding' in the Thought of St. Ephraem the Syrian." In *Faith Seeking Understanding: Learning and the Catholic Tradition*, edited by George C. Berthold, 35–55. Manchester, NH: Saint Anselm College Press, 1991.

Griffith, Sidney H. "Images of Ephraem: The Syrian Holy Man and His Church." *Traditio* 45 (1989): 7–33.

Griffith, Sidney H. "Julian Saba, 'Father of the Monks' of Syria." *JECS* 2.2 (1994): 185–216.

Griffith, Sidney H. "The Marks of the 'True Church' According to Ephraem's *Hymns Against Heresies*." In Reinink and Klugkist, *After Bardaisan*, 125–140.

Griffith, Sidney H. "Monks, 'Singles,' and the 'Sons of the Covenant': Reflections on Syriac Ascetic Terminology." In *Eulogema: Studies in Honor of Robert Taft*, edited by Ephrem Carr, 141–160. Studia Anselmiana 110; Analecta Liturgica 17. Rome: Pontificio Ateneo San Anselmo, 1993.

Griffith, Sidney H. "The Poetics of Scriptural Reasoning: Syriac *Mêmrê* at Work." In Wickes and Heal, *Literature, Rhetoric, and Exegesis in Syriac Verse*, 5–24.

Griffith, Sidney H. "Setting Right the Church of Syria: Saint Ephraem's *Hymns Against Heresies*." In *The Limits of Ancient Christianity: Essays on Late Antique Thought and Culture in Honor of R. A. Markus*, edited by William Klingshirn and Mark Vessey, 97–114. Ann Arbor: University of Michigan Press, 1999.

Groen, Bert, Steven Hawkes-Teeples, and Stephanos Alexopoulos, eds. *Inquiries into Eastern Christian Worship*. Eastern Christian Studies 12. Leuven: Peeters, 2012.

Grypeou, Emmanouela, and Helen Spurling, eds. *The Exegetical Encounter Between Jews and Christians in Late Antiquity*. Leiden: Brill, 2009.

Haar Romeny, Bas Ter. "From Religious Association to Ethnic Community: A Research Project on Identity Formation Among the Syrian Orthodox under Muslim Rule." *Islam and Christian-Muslim Relations* 16 (2005): 377–399.

Haar Romeny, Bas Ter, ed. *The Peshitta: Its Use in Literature and Liturgy; Papers Read at the Third Peshitta Symposium*. Leiden: Brill, 2006.

Habinek, Thomas. *The World of Roman Song: From Ritualized Speech to Social Order*. Baltimore: Johns Hopkins University Press, 2005.

Hackett, Rosalind. "Sound, Music, and the Study of Religion." *Temenos* 48.1 (2012): 11–17.

Haines-Eitzen, Kim. *The Gendered Palimpsest: Women, Writing, and Representation in Early Christianity*. Oxford: Oxford University Press, 2012.

Halperin, David M. "Why Is Diotima a Woman? Platonic Erōs and the Figuration of Gender." In *Before Sexuality: The Construction of Erotic Experience in the Ancient Greek World*, edited by David M. Halperin, John J. Winkler, and Froma I. Zeitlin, 257–308. Princeton, NJ: Princeton University Press, 1990.

Hanninen, Marja-Leena. "Juna Regina and the Roman Matrons." In *Female Networks and the Public Sphere in Roman Society*, edited by Päivi Setälä and Liisa Savunen, 39–52. Acta Instituti Romani Finlandiae 22. Rome: Institutum Romanum Finlandiae, 1999.

Harland, Philip A. *Associations, Synagogues, and Congregations: Claiming a Place in Ancient Mediterranean Society*. Minneapolis: Fortress Press, 2003.

Harrison, Carol. *The Art of Listening in the Early Church*. Oxford: Oxford University Press, 2013.

Harrison, Carol. "Playing Ball: Plutarch and Augustine on Capturing Wisdom." In *Being Christian in Late Antiquity: A Festschrift for Gillian Clark*, edited by Carol Harrison, Caroline Humfress, and Isabella Sandwell, 90–108. Oxford: Oxford University Press, 2014.

Hartung, Blake. "The Collection and Transmission of Late Antique Liturgical Poetry: A Comparative Approach." *JECS* 29.3 (2021): 415–444.

Harvey, Susan Ashbrook. "Bearing Witness: New Testament Women in Early Byzantine Hymnography." In *The New Testament in Byzantium*, edited by Derek Krueger and Robert Nelson, 205–221. Washington, DC: Dumbarton Oaks Publications, 2016.

Harvey, Susan Ashbrook. "Bride of Blood, Bride of Light: Biblical Women as Images of Church in Jacob of Serug." In *Malphono w-Rabo d-Malphone: Festschrift for Sebastian P. Brock*, edited by George A. Kiraz, 189–218. Piscataway, NJ: Gorgias Press, 2008.

Harvey, Susan Ashbrook. "Creation, Order, Beauty: Jacob of Serugh on Liturgical Aesthetics." In Elkhoury and Kitchen, *The Year of Jacob of Serugh*, 155–178.

Harvey, Susan Ashbrook. "The Despised Woman: Jacob of Serug at the Nativity Feast." In *Byzantine Religious Culture: Studies in Honor of Alice-Mary Talbot*, edited by Elizabeth Fisher, Denis Sullivan, and Eustratios Papaioannou, 3–18. Leiden: Brill, 2011.

Harvey, Susan Ashbrook. "Encountering Eve in Syriac Tradition." In *Syriac Encounters: Papers from the Sixth North American Syriac Symposium*, edited by Maria Doerfler, Emanuel Fiano, and Kyle Smith, 11–49. Leuven: Peeters, 2015.

Harvey, Susan Ashbrook. "Feminine Imagery for the Divine: The Holy Spirit, the Odes of Solomon, and Early Syriac Tradition." *SVTQ* 37 (1993): 111–139.

Harvey, Susan Ashbrook. "Guiding Grief: Liturgical Poetry and Ritual Lamentation in Early Byzantium." In *Greek Laughter and Tears: Antiquity and After; Proceedings of the 8th A. G. Leventis Conference in Greek, University of Edinburgh, November 2013*, edited by Douglas Cairns and Margaret Alexiou, 199–216. Edinburgh: University of Edinburgh Press, 2017.

Harvey, Susan Ashbrook. "Holy Impudence, Sacred Desire: The Women of Matthew 1:1–16 in Syriac Tradition." In *Studies on Patristic Texts and Archaeology: If These Stones Could Speak; Texts and Contexts*, edited by George Kalantzis and Thomas Martin, 27–48. Lewiston, NY: Edwin Mellen Press, 2009.

Harvey, Susan Ashbrook. "Holy Sound: Preaching as Divine Song in Late Antique Syriac Tradition." In *Jewish Roots of Eastern Christian Mysticism*, edited by Andrei A. Orlov, 226–239. Leiden: Brill, 2020.

Harvey, Susan Ashbrook. "Interior Decorating: Jacob of Serug on Mary's Preparation for the Incarnation." *Studia Patristica* 41, edited by Frances M. Young, Mark Edwards, and Peter Parvis, 23–28. Leuven: Peeters, 2006.

Harvey, Susan Ashbrook. "Liturgy and Ethics in Ancient Syriac Christianity: Two Paradigms." *Studies in Christian Ethics* 26.3 (2013): 300–316.

Harvey, Susan Ashbrook. "On Mary's Voice: Gendered Words in Syriac Marian Tradition." In *The Cultural Turn in Late Ancient Studies: Gender, Asceticism, and Hagiography*, edited by Dale B. Martin and Patricia Cox Miller, 63–86. Durham, NC and London: Duke University Press, 2005.

Harvey, Susan Ashbrook. "Patristic Worlds." In *Patristic Studies in the Twenty-First Century: Proceedings of an International Conference to Mark the 50th Anniversary of the International Association of Patristic Studies*, edited by Brouria Bitton-Ashkelony, Theodore de Bruyn, and Carol Harrison, 25–53. Turnhout: Brepols, 2015.

Harvey, Susan Ashbrook. "The Poet's Prayer: Invocational Prayers in the Memre of Jacob of Sarug." In Wickes and Heal, *Literature, Rhetoric, and Exegesis in Syriac Verse*, 51–60.

Harvey, Susan Ashbrook. "Revisiting the Daughters of the Covenant: Women's Choirs and Sacred Song in Ancient Syriac Christianity." *Hugoye: Journal of Syriac Studies* 8.2 (2005 [2010]): 125–149.

Harvey, Susan Ashbrook. *Scenting Salvation: Ancient Christianity and the Olfactory Imagination*. Berkeley: University of California Press, 2006.

Harvey, Susan Ashbrook. *Song and Memory: Biblical Women in Syriac Tradition*. Milwaukee: Marquette University Press, 2010.

Harvey, Susan Ashbrook. "Spoken Words, Voiced Silence: Biblical Women in Syriac Tradition." *JECS* 9 (2001): 105–131.

Harvey, Susan Ashbrook. "To Whom Did Jacob Preach?" In *Jacob of Serugh and His Times: Studies in Sixth-Century Syriac Christianity*, edited by George Anton Kiraz, 115–131. Piscataway, NJ: Gorgias Press, 2010.

Harvey, Susan Ashbrook. "Why the Perfume Mattered: The Sinful Woman in Syriac Exegetical Tradition." In *In Dominico Eloquio/In Lordly Eloquence: Essays on Patristic Exegesis in Honor of Robert Wilken*, edited by Paul Blowers, Angela Christman, David Hunter, and Robert Darling Young, 69–89. Grand Rapids, MI: Eerdmans, 2001.

Harvey, Susan Ashbrook. "Women and Words: Texts by and about Women." In *The Cambridge History of Early Christian Literature*, edited by Frances M. Young, Lewis Ayers, and Andrew Louth, 382–390. Cambridge: Cambridge University Press, 2004.

Harvey, Susan Ashbrook. "Women's Service in Ancient Syriac Christianity." In *Mother, Nun, Deaconess: Images of Women According to Eastern Canon Law*, edited by Eva Synek, 226–241. Kanon 16. Egling an der Paar: Kovar, 2001.

Harvey, Susan Ashbrook, Sebastian P. Brock, Reyhan Durmaz, Michael L. Payne, Daniel Picus, and Noah Tetenbaum, ed. and trans. *Three Persian Martyr Acts*. Piscataway, NJ: Gorgias Press, 2023.

Harvey, Susan Ashbrook, and David G. Hunter, eds. *The Oxford Handbook of Early Christian Studies*. Oxford: Oxford University Press, 2010.

Hauptman, Judith. *Rereading The Rabbis: A Woman's Voice*. Boulder, CO: Westview Press, 2008.

Heal, Kristian. *Genesis 37 and 39 in the Syriac Tradition*. Leiden: Brill, 2023.

Heal, Kristian S. "Narsai and the Scriptural Self." In Butts, Heal, and Kitchen, *Narsai*, 133–143.

Heal, Kristian. "Reworking the Biblical Text in the Dramatic Dialogue Poems on the Old Testament Patriarch Joseph." In Haar Romeny, *The Peshitta*, 87–98.

Heal, Kristian S. "The Syriac History of Joseph: A New Translation and Introduction." In *Old Testament Pseudepigrapha: More Noncanonical Scriptures*, vol. 1, edited by Richard Bauckham, James Davila, and Alexander Panayotov, 85–120. Grand Rapids, MI: Eerdmans, 2013.

Hélou, Clémence. "La vie monastique féminine dans la tradition syriaque." In *Le monachisme syriaque du VIIe siècle à nos jours*, 1:85–118. Patrimonie Syriaque Actes du Colloque VI. Antélias, Lebanon: Centre d'Études et de Recherches Orientales, 1999.

Hélou, Clémence. "Les diaconesses moniales dans la tradition Syriaque." In *Le monachisme syriaque: Aux premiers siècles de l'église, IIe-début VIIe siècle*, 1:167–190. Patrimonie Syriaque Actes du Colloque V. Antélias, Lebanon: Centre d'Études et de Recherches Orientales, 1998.

Hélou, Clémence. *Sainte Marina: Moniale déguisée en habit de moine dans la tradition maronite*. Patrimoine Syriaque 6. Kaslik: Parole de l'Orient, 2013.

Herman, Geoffrey. *Persian Martyr Acts Under King Yazdgird I*. Piscataway, NJ: Gorgias Press, 2016.

Hidal, Sten. *Interpretatio Syriaca: Die Kommentare des Heiligen Ephräm des Syrers zu Genesis und Exodus mit besondere[r] Berücksichtung ihrer auslegungsgeschichtlichen Stellung.* Lund: C.W.K. Gleerup, 1974.

Holmes, Brooke. *Gender: Antiquity and Its Legacy.* Oxford: Oxford University Press, 2012.

Horbury, William. "Women in the Synagogue." In Davies, Sturdy, and Horbury, *The Cambridge History of Judaism,* 3:358–401.

Hunter, Erica. "Commemorating the Saints at Turfan." In *Winds of Jingjiao: Studies on Syriac Christianity in China and Central Asia,* edited by Li Tang and Dietmar W. Winkler, 89–104. Zurich: LIT Verlag, 2016.

Hunter, Erica. "Turfan: Connecting with Seleucia-Ctesiphon." *Entangled Religions* 11.6 (2020). http://doi.10.46586/er.11.2020.8779.

Hunter, Erica, and J. F. Coakley. *A Syriac Service-Book from Turfan: Museum für Asiatische Kunst, Berlin MIK III 45.* Turnhout: Brepols, 2017.

Husmann, Heinrich. "Syrian Church Music." In *The New Grove Dictionary of Music and Musicians,* edited by Stanley Sadie, 18:472–480. London: Macmillan, 1980.

Hylen, Susan. *A Modest Apostle: Thecla and the History of Women in the Early Church.* Oxford: Oxford University Press, 2015.

Ibrahim, Gregorios Y., and George Kiraz. "Ephrem's *Madroshe* and the Syrian Orthodox *Beth Gazo*: A Loose, but Fascinating, Affinity." *Hugoye: Journal of Syriac Studies* 2.1 (1999 [2010]): 47–56.

Ingalls, Wayne B. "Ritual Performance as Training for Daughters in Archaic Greece." *Phoenix: Journal of the Classical Association of Canada* 54.1–2 (2000): 1–20.

Iwas, Moran Mor Ignatius Zakka-I. "The Role of Women in the Syrian Orthodox Church of Antioch." (1998/2005). http://www.malankaraworld.com/library/History/WomeninSOC -by-Patriarch.pdf.

Jajé, Ameer. *Diaconesses: Les femmes dans l'Église syriaque.* Toulouse: Domuni Press, 2016.

Janeras, Sebastia. "Le bêma syrien, icon de réalités supérieures." In *Les enjeux spirituels et théologiques de l'espace liturgique,* edited by C. Braga and A. Pistoia, 117–138. Rome: Edizioni liturgiche, 2005.

Jansma, Taeke. "Narsai and Ephrem: Some Observations on Narsai's Homilies on Creation and Ephrem's Hymns on Faith." *Parole de l'Orient* 1 (1970): 49–68.

Jargy, Simon. "Les 'Fils et Filles du Pacte' dans la littérature monastique syriaque." *OCP* 17.3–4 (1951): 304–320.

Jarjour, Tala. "Chant as the Articulation of Christian Aramaean Spirithood." In *The Oxford Handbook of World Christianities,* edited by Suzel Ana Reily and Jonathan M. Dueck, 187–207. New York: Oxford University Press, 2016.

Jarjour, Tala. *Sense and Sadness: Syriac Chant in Aleppo.* Oxford: Oxford University Press, 2018.

Jarratt, Susan, and Rory Ong. "Aspasia: Rhetoric, Gender, and Colonial Ideology." In Lunsford, *Reclaiming Rhetorica,* 9–24.

Jeffrey, Peter. "Philo's Impact on Christian Psalmody." In Attridge and Fassler, *Psalms in Community,* 147–187.

Jenner, Konrad. "The Development of Syriac Lectionary Systems." *The Harp* 10 (1997): 9–24.

Jensen, Robin M. *Understanding Early Christian Art.* New York: Routledge, 2002.

Jullien, Florence. "Le monachisme feminin en milieu Syriaque." In Jullien, *Le monachisme syriaque,* 65–87.

Jullien, Florence, ed. *Le monachisme syriaque*. Études Syriaques 7. Paris: Geuthner, 2010.

Kalish, Kevin. *She Who Loved Much: The Sinful Woman in Saint Ephrem the Syrian and the Orthodox Tradition*. Jordanville, NY: Holy Trinity Seminary Press, 2022.

Kamesar, Adam. "The Evaluation of the Narrative Aggada in Greek and Latin Patristic Literature." *JTS* 45.1 (1994): 37–71.

Karras, Valerie A. "Female Deacons in the Byzantine Church." *CH* 73.2 (2004): 272–316.

Karras, Valerie A. "The Liturgical Functions of Consecrated Women in the Byzantine Church." *Theological Studies* 66.1 (2005): 96–116.

Karras, Valerie A. "The Liturgical Participation of Women in the Byzantine Church." PhD diss., The Catholic University of America, 2002.

Kartsonis, Anna. *Anastasis: The Making of an Image*. Princeton, NJ: Princeton University Press, 1986.

Kaster, Robert. *Emotion, Restraint, and Community in Ancient Rome*. Oxford: Oxford University Press, 2005.

Kayaalp, Elif Keser. *Church Architecture of Late Antique Northern Mesopotamia*. Oxford: Oxford University Press, 2021.

Kee, Howard Clark, and Lynn H. Cohick. *Evolution of the Synagogue: Problems and Progress*. Harrisburg, PA: Trinity Press International, 1999.

Kellogg, Sarah Bakker. "Perforating Kinship: Syriac Christianity, Ethnicity, and Secular Legibility." *Current Anthropology* 60.4 (2019): 475–498.

Kellogg, Sarah Bakker. "A Racial-Religious Imagination: Syriac Christians, Iconic Bodies, and the Sensory Politics of Ethical Difference in the Netherlands." *Cultural Anthropology* 36.4 (2021): 618–648.

Kellogg, Sarah Bakker. "Ritual Sounds, Political Echoes: Vocal Agency and the Sensory Cultures of Secularism in the Dutch Syriac Diaspora." *American Ethnologist* 42.3 (2015): 431–445.

Kellogg, Sarah Bakker. *Sonic Icons: Relation, Recognition, and Revival in a Syriac World*. Notre Dame, IN: University of Notre Dame Press, 2024.

Kermode, Frank. "Secrets and Narrative Sequence." In *On Narrative*, edited by William J. T. Mitchell, 79–98. Chicago: University of Chicago Press, 1981.

Khouri-Sarkis, G. "Réception d'un évêque syrien au VIᵉ siècle." *L'Orient syrien* 2 (1957): 137–148.

Kitchen, Robert A. "The Pearl of Virginity: Death as the Reward of Asceticism in Memra 191 of Jacob of Serug." *Hugoye: Journal of Syriac Studies* 7.2 (2007 [2010]): 147–156.

Knust, Jennifer Wright. *Abandoned to Lust: Sexual Slander and Ancient Christianity*. New York: Columbia University Press, 2006.

Kolbet, Paul R. "Athanasius, the Psalms, and the Reformation of the Self." *HTR* 99.1 (2006): 85–101. Reprinted in *The Harp of Prophecy: Early Christian Interpretation of the Psalms*, edited by Brian E. Daley and Paul R. Kolbet, 75–96. Notre Dame, IN: University of Notre Dame Press, 2014.

Kollamparampil, Thomas. *Salvation in Christ According to Jacob of Serugh: An Exegetico-theological Study on the Homilies of Jacob of Serugh on the Feasts of Our Lord*. Piscataway, NJ: Gorgias Press, 2010.

Koltun-Fromm, Naomi. *Hermeneutics of Holiness: Ancient Jewish and Christian Notions of Sexuality and Religious Community*. Oxford: Oxford University Press, 2010.

Koltun-Fromm, Naomi. "Yokes of the Holy-Ones: The Embodiment of a Christian Vocation." *HTR* 94.2 (2001): 205–218.

König, Jason. "Sympotic Dialogue in the First to Fifth Centuries CE." In *The End of Dialogue in Antiquity*, edited by Simon Goldhill, 85–113. Cambridge: Cambridge University Press, 2008.

Kowalzig, Barbara. *Singing for the Gods: Performances of Myth and Ritual in Archaic and Classical Greece*. Oxford: Oxford University Press, 2007.

Kraemer, Ross Shepard. *Unreliable Witnesses: Religion, Gender, and History in the Greco-Roman Mediterranean*. Oxford: Oxford University Press, 2010.

Kraemer, Ross Shepard. *When Aseneth Met Joseph: A Late Antique Tale of the Biblical Patriarch and His Egyptian Wife, Revisited*. New York: Oxford University Press, 1998.

Kraemer, Ross Shepard. "Women's Authorship of Jewish and Christian Literature in the Greco-Roman Period." In *"Women Like This": New Perspectives on Jewish Women in the Greco-Roman World*, edited by Amy-Jill Levine, 221–242. Atlanta: Scholars Press, 1991.

Kraemer, Ross Shepard. *Women's Religions in the Greco-Roman World: A Sourcebook*. Oxford: Oxford University Press, 2004.

Kraus, Manfred. "Rehearsing the Other Sex: Impersonation of Women in Ancient Classroom Ethopoeia." In *Escuela y literatura en Gracia Antigua: Acta del Simposio Internacional, Universidad de Salamanca 17–19 Novembre de 2004*, edited by José A. F. Delgado, F. Pordomino, and A. Stramiglia, 455–468. Cassino: Edizioni dell'Università degli Studi di Cassino, 2007.

Krawiec, Rebecca. "The Memory of Melania." In *Melania: Early Christianity Through the Life of One Family*, edited by Catherine M. Chin and Caroline T. Schroeder, 130–147. Oakland: University of California Press, 2016.

Kronholm, Tryggve. "Holy Adultery: The Interpretation of the Story of Judah and Tamar (Gen. 38) in the Genuine Hymns of Ephrem Syrus." *Orientalia Suecana* 40 (1991): 149–163.

Krueger, Derek. "Christian Piety and Practice in the Sixth Century." In *The Cambridge Companion to the Age of Justinian*, edited by Michael Maas, 291–315. Cambridge: Cambridge University Press, 2005.

Krueger, Derek. "Hagiography as Liturgy: Writing and Memory in Gregory of Nyssa's *Life of Macrina*." In *Writing and Holiness: The Practice of Authorship in the Early Christian East*, 110–132. Philadelphia: University of Pennsylvania Press, 2004.

Krueger, Derek. *Liturgical Subjects: Christian Ritual, Biblical Narrative, and the Formation of the Self in Byzantium*. Philadelphia: University of Pennsylvania Press, 2014.

Kugel, James. *The Bible as It Was*. Cambridge, MA: Belknap Press, 1997.

Laack, Isabel. "Sound, Music and Religion: A Preliminary Cartography of a Transdisciplinary Research Field." *Method and Theory in the Study of Religion* 27.3 (2015): 220–246.

Lampe, G. W. H. *A Patristic Greek Lexicon*. Oxford: Clarendon Press, 1961.

Lange, Christian. *The Portrayal of Christ in the Syriac Commentary on the Diatessaron*. CSCO 616/Sub. 118. Leuven: Peeters, 2005.

Lardinois, André, and Laura McClure, eds. *Making Silence Speak: Women's Voices in Greek Literature and Society*. Princeton, NJ: Princeton University Press, 2001.

Lash, Ephrem. *St. Romanos the Melodist: Kontakia on the Life of Christ*. San Francisco: HarperCollins, 1995.

Lassus, Jean. *Sanctuaires chrétiens de Syrie: Essai sur la genèse, la forme et l'usage liturgique des édifices du culte chrétien, en Syrie, du IIIe siècle à la conquête musulmane*. Paris: Geuthner, 1947.

Lattke, Michael. *Odes of Solomon: A Commentary*. Edited by Harold W. Attridge. Translated by Marianne Ehrhardt. Minneapolis: Fortress Press, 2009.

Lattke, M. "Sind Ephraems *Madrashe* Hymnen?" *Oriens Christianus* 73 (1989): 38–43.

Lavenant, René, ed. *Symposium Syriacum VII*. OCA 256. Rome: Pontificum Institutum Orientalium Studiorum, 1998.

Lefkowitz, Mary R., and Maureen B. Fant, eds. *Women's Life in Greece and Rome: A Sourcebook in Translation*. 4th ed. Baltimore: Johns Hopkins University Press, 2016.

Leonhard, Clemens. "Which Hymns Were Sung in Ancient Christian Liturgies?" In Leonhard and Löhr, *Literature or Liturgy?* 175–194.

Leonhard, Clemens, and Hermut Löhr, eds. *Literature or Liturgy? Early Christian Hymns and Prayers in Their Literary and Liturgical Context in Antiquity*. Tübingen: Mohr Siebeck, 2014.

Levine, Lee I. *The Ancient Synagogue: The First Thousand Years*. New Haven, CT: Yale University Press, 2005.

Leyerle, Blake. *The Narrative Shape of Emotion in the Preaching of John Chrysostom*. Oakland: University of California Press, 2020.

Leyerle, Blake. *Theatrical Shows and Ascetic Lives: John Chrysostom's Attack on Spiritual Marriage*. Berkeley: University of California Press, 2001.

Leyerle, Blake, and Robin Darling Young, eds. *Ascetic Culture: Essays in Honor of Philip Rousseau*. Notre Dame, IN: University of Notre Dame Press, 2013.

Lieber, Laura S. "Call and Response: Antiphonal Elements in Jewish Palestinian Aramaic Poetry." *Aramaic Studies* 17.2 (2019): 127–144.

Lieber, Laura S. "On the Road with the Mater Dolorosa: An Exploration of Mother-Son Discourse Performance." *JECS* 24.2 (2016): 265–291.

Lieber, Laura S. "The Rhetoric of Participation: Experiential Elements of Early Hebrew Liturgical Poetry." *JQR* 90.2 (2010): 119–147.

Lieber, Laura S. "Stages of Grief: Enacting Lamentation in Late Ancient Hymnography." *Association of Jewish Studies Review* 40 (2016): 101–124.

Lieber, Laura S. *Staging the Sacred: Theatricality and Performance in Late Ancient Liturgical Poetry*. New York: Oxford University Press, 2023.

Lieber, Laura S. "Theater of the Holy: Performative Elements of Late Antique Hymnography." *HTR* 108.3 (2015): 327–355.

Lieber, Laura S. "With One Voice: Elements of Acclamations in Early Jewish Liturgical Poetry." *HTR* 111.3 (2018): 401–424.

Lillis, Julia Kelto. *Virgin Territory: Configuring Female Virginity in Early Christianity*. Oakland: University of California Press, 2022.

Limberis, Vasiliki. *Divine Heiress: The Virgin Mary and the Creation of Christian Constantinople*. London: Routledge, 1994.

Lingas, Alexander. "From Earth to Heaven: The Changing Musical Soundscape of Byzantine Liturgy." In *Experiencing Byzantium: Papers from the 44th Spring Symposium of Byzantine Studies, Newcastle and Durham, April 2011*, edited by Claire Nesbitt and Mark Jackson, 311–358. Farnham, UK: Ashgate, 2013.

Lingas, Alexander. "Sunday Matins in the Byzantine Cathedral Rite: Music and Liturgy." PhD diss., University of British Columbia, 1996.

Löhr, Helmut. "What Can We Know About the Beginnings of Christian Hymnody?" In Leonhard and Löhr, *Literature or Liturgy?* 157–174.

Loosely, Emma. *The Architecture and Liturgy of the Bema in Fourth to Sixth Century Syrian Churches*. Patrimoine Syriaque 2. Kaslik: Parole de l'Orient, 2003.

Ludlow, Morwenna. *Art, Craft, and Theology in Fourth-Century Christian Authors*. New York: Oxford University Press, 2020.

Lunsford, Andrea A., ed. *Reclaiming Rhetorica: Women in the Rhetorical Tradition*. Pittsburgh: University of Pittsburgh Press, 1995.

Macina, Menahem Robert. "Les bnay et bnat Qyama de l'Église syriaque: Une piste philologique périeuse." In *Le monachisme syriaque du VIIe siècle à nos jours*, 1:13–49. Patrimonie Syriaque Actes du Colloque VI. Antélias, Lebanon: Centre d'Études et de Recherches Orientales, 1999.

Mack, Jennifer. *The Construction of Equality: Syriac Immigration and the Swedish City*. Minneapolis: University of Minnesota Press, 2017.

MacMullen, Ramsay. *The Second Church: Popular Christianity A.D. 200–400*. Atlanta: Society of Biblical Literature, 2009.

Macomber, William F. "The Manuscripts of the Metrical Homilies of Narsai." *OCP* 38 (1973): 275–306.

Madigan, Kevin, and Carolyn Osiek, eds. *Ordained Women in the Early Church: A Documentary History*. Baltimore: Johns Hopkins University Press, 2005.

Mango, Marlia Mundell. *Silver from Early Byzantium: The Kaper Koraon and Related Treasures*. Baltimore: Trustees of the Walters Art Gallery, 1986.

Marks, Susan. "Bayit versus Beit Midrash: Jewish Mother as Teacher." In *A Most Reliable Witness: Essays in Honor of Ross Shepard Kraemer*, edited by Susan Ashbrook Harvey, Nathaniel P. DesRosiers, Shira Lander, Jacquline Z. Pastis, and Daniel Ulluci, 195–204. Providence, RI: Brown Judaic Studies, 2015.

Martimort, Aimé-Georges. *Les diaconesses: Essai historique*. Bibliotheca "Ephemerides Liturgicae" Subsidia. Rome: Pontificium Institutum Orientalium Studiorum, 1959.

Mateos, Juan. *La célébration de la parole dans la liturgie Byzantine*. OCA 191. Rome: Pontificium Institutum Orientalium Studiorum, 1971.

Mateos, Juan. *Lelya-Sapra: Essai d'interpretation des matines chaldéennes*. OCA 156. Rome: Pontificium Institutum Orientalium Studiorum, 1959.

Mathews, Thomas F. *The Clash of Gods: A Reinterpretation of Early Christian Art*. 2nd ed. Princeton, NJ: Princeton University Press, 1999.

Maxwell, Jaclyn. *Christianization and Communication in Late Antiquity: John Chrysostom and His Congregation in Antioch*. Cambridge: Cambridge University Press, 2006.

Maxwell, Jaclyn. *Simplicity and Humility in Late Antique Christian Thought: Elites and the Challenges of Apostolic Life*. Cambridge: Cambridge University Press, 2021.

Mayer, Wendy. "John Chrysostom: Extraordinary Preacher, Ordinary Audience." In *Preacher and Audience: Studies in Early Christian and Byzantine Homiletics*, edited by Mary B. Cunningham and Pauline Allen, 105–137. Leiden: Brill, 1998.

Mayer, Wendy, and Pauline Allen. *John Chrysostom*. London: Routledge, 2000.

McCall, Richard D. *Do This: Liturgy as Performance*. Notre Dame, IN: University of Notre Dame Press, 2007.

McCarron, Richard E. "An Epiphany of Mystical Symbols: Jacob of Sarug's *Mêmrâ* 109 on Abraham and His Types." *Hugoye: Journal of Syriac Studies* 1.1 (1998 [2010]): 57–78.

McClure, Laura R. *Spoken Like a Woman: Speech and Gender in Athenian Drama*. Princeton, NJ: Princeton University Press, 1999.

McGuckin, John A. "Poetry and Hymnography (2): The Greek World." In Harvey and Hunter, *The Oxford Handbook of Early Christian Studies*, 641–656.

McKinnon, James W., ed. *Music in Early Christian Literature*. Cambridge: Cambridge University Press, 1987.

McVey, Kathleen. "The Domed Church as Microcosm: Literary Roots of an Architectural Symbol." *DOP* 37 (1983): 91–121.

McVey, Kathleen. "Ephrem the Kitharode and Proponent of Women: Jacob of Serug's Portrait of a Fourth-Century Churchman for the Sixth-Century Viewer and Its Significance for the Twenty-First Century Ecumenist." In *Orthodox and Wesleyan Ecclesiology*, edited by S. T. Kimbrough, 229–253. Crestwood, NY: St. Vladimir's Seminary Press, 2007.

McVey, Kathleen. *Ephrem the Syrian: Hymns*. Mahwah, NJ: Paulist Press, 1989.

McVey, Kathleen. "Images of Joy in Ephrem's Hymns on Paradise: Returning to the Womb and the Breast." *JCSSS* 3 (2003): 1–19.

McVey, Kathleen. "Were the Earliest *Madrase* Songs or Recitations?" In Reinink and Klugkist, *After Bardaisan*, 185–199.

Mengozzi, Alessandro. *L'invenzione del dialogo: Dispute e dialoghi in versi nella letteratura siriaca*. Turin: Paideia, 2020.

Mengozzi, Alessandro. *Religious Poetry in Vernacular Syriac from Northern Iraq (17th–20th Centuries): An Anthology*. CSCO 627–628/Scr. Syr. 240–241. Louvain: Peeters, 2011.

Menn, Esther. *Judah and Tamar (Genesis 38) in Ancient Jewish Exegesis: Studies in Literary Form and Hermeneutics*. Leiden: Brill, 1997.

Merras, Merja. "The Date of the Earliest Syriac Lectionary Br. M. Add. 14528." In Lavenant, *Symposium Syriacum VII*, 575–585.

Miller, Patricia Cox. "The Blazing Body: Ascetic Desire in Jerome's Letter to Eustochium." *JECS* 1.1 (2009): 21–45.

Mitchell, William J. T. ed. *On Narrative*. Chicago: University of Chicago Press, 1981.

Moran, Neil K. *Singers in Late Byzantine and Slavonic Painting*. Leiden: Brill, 1986.

Moss, Cyril. "Jacob of Serugh's Homilies on the Spectacles of the Theater." *Le Muséon* 48 (1935): 87–112.

Moss, Yonatan. "Severus of Antioch on Gender: The Evidence of his *Cathedral Homilies*." *JECS* 33.2 (2025): 249–273.

Muehlberger, Ellen. "Perpetual Adjustment: The *Passion of Perpetua and Felicity* and the Entailments of Authenticity." *JECS* 30.3 (2022): 313–342.

Münz-Manor, Ophir. "All About Sarah: Questions of Gender in Yannai's Poems on Sarah's (and Abraham's) Barrenness." *Prooftexts* 26 (2006): 344–374.

Münz-Manor, Ophir. "Hebrew and Syriac Liturgical Poetry." In *Jews and Syriac Christians*, edited by Aaron Michael Butts and Simcha Gross, 231–253. Tübingen: Mohr Siebeck, 2020.

Münz-Manor, Ophir. "Liturgical Poetry in the Late Antique Near East: A Comparative Approach." *JAJ* 1.3 (2010): 336–361.

Murray, Robert. "Aramaic and Syriac Dispute Poems and Their Connections." In *Studia Aramaica*, edited by M. J. Geller, J. C. Greenfield, and M. P. Weitzman, 157–187. Supplement to *JSS* 4 (1995): 157–187.

Murray, Robert. "Circumcision of the Heart and the Origins of the *Qyama*." In Reinink and Klugkist, *After Bardaisan*, 201–211.

Murray, Robert. "The Exhortation to Candidates for Ascetical Vows at Baptism in the Ancient Syriac Church." *New Testament Studies* 21.1 (1974): 59–80.

Murray, Robert. "'A Marriage for All Eternity': The Consecration of a Syrian Bride of Christ." *Sobornost: Eastern Churches Review* 11 (1989): 65–69.

Murray, Robert. "Mary, the Second Eve in the Early Syriac Fathers." *Eastern Churches Review* 3 (1971): 372–384.

Murray, Robert. "Some Rhetorical Patterns in Early Syriac Literature." In *A Tribute to Arthur Vööbus: Studies in Early Christian Literature and Its Environment, Primarily in the Syrian East*, edited by Robert H. Fischer, 109–131. Chicago: Lutheran School of Theology, 1977.

Murray, Robert. *Symbols of Church and Kingdom: A Study in Early Syriac Tradition*. Rev. ed. Piscataway, NJ: Gorgias Press, 2004.

Murray, Robert. "The Theory of Symbolism in St. Ephrem's Theology." *Parole de l'Orient* 6/7 (1975/1976): 1–20.

Murre-van den Berg, Heleen. "Classical Syriac and the Syriac Churches: A Twentieth-Century History." In Doerfler, Fiano, and Smith, *Syriac Encounters*, 119–147.

Murre-van den Berg, Heleen. "Generous Devotion: Women in the Church of the East Between 1550 and 1850." *Hugoye: Journal of Syriac Studies* 7.1 (2004). https://hugoye .bethmardutho.org/article/hv7n1murre#.

Murre-van den Berg, Heleen. *Scribes and Scriptures: The Church of the East in the Eastern Ottoman Provinces (1500–1850)*. Leuven: Peeters, 2015.

Nedungatt, George. "The Covenanters of the Early Syriac-Speaking Church." *OCP* 39 (1973): 191–215, 419–444.

Neil, Bronwen, and Lynda Garland, eds. *Questions of Gender in Byzantine Society*. Farnham, UK: Ashgate, 2013.

Neyrey, Jerome H. "Jesus, Gender, and the Gospel of Matthew." In *New Testament Masculinities*, edited by Stephen D. Moore and Janice Capel Anderson, 43–66. Atlanta: Society of Biblical Literature, 2003.

Norman, Dawn LaValle. *The Aesthetics of Hope in Late Greek Imperial Literature: Methodius of Olympus' "Symposium" and the Crisis of the Third Century*. Cambridge: Cambridge University Press, 2019.

Norman, Ralph. "Methodius and Methodologies: Ways of Reading Third-Century Christian Sexual Symbolism." *Theology and Sexuality* 13.1 (2006): 79–100.

Oden, Thomas C., and Christopher A. Hall. *Ancient Christian Commentary on Scripture, New Testament*. vol. 2, *Mark*. Downers Grove, IL: InterVarsity Press, 2005.

Olyan, Saul. *Biblical Mourning: Ritual and Social Dimensions*. Oxford: Oxford University Press, 2004.

Önal, Mehmet. *Mosaics of Zeugma*. Istanbul: A Turizm Yayinlari, 2002.

Osiek, Carolyn. "Family Matters." In *A People's History of Christianity*, vol. 1, *Christian Origins*, edited by Richard Horsley, 201–220. Minneapolis: Fortress Press, 2005.

Outtier, Bernard. "Saint Éphrem d'après ses biographies et ses œuvres." *Parole de l'Orient* 4.1–2 (1973): 11–33.

Page, Christopher. *The Christian West and Its Singers: The First Thousand Years*. New Haven, CT: Yale University Press, 2010.

Palmer, Andrew. "The Book of Life in the Syriac Liturgy: An Instrument of Social and Spiritual Survival." *The Harp* 4 (1991): 161–171.

Palmer, Andrew. "The Merchant of Nisibis: Saint Ephraem and His Faithful Quest for Union in Numbers." In den Boeft and Hilhorst, *Early Christian Poetry*, 167–233.

Palmer, Andrew. "A Single Human Being Divided in Himself: Ephraim the Syrian, the Man in the Middle." *Hugoye: Journal of Syriac Studies* 1.2 (1998 [2010]): 119–163.

Palmer, Andrew, and Lyn Rodley. "The Inauguration Anthem of Hagia Sophia in Edessa: A New Edition and Translation with Historical and Architectural Notes and a Comparison with a Contemporary Constantinopolitan Kontakion." *BMGS* 12 (1988): 117–167.

Papaioannou, Stratis. *Christian Novels from the Menologion of Symeon Metaphrastes*. DOML 45. Cambridge, MA: Harvard University Press, 2017.

Papaioannou, Stratis. "Sacred Song." In *The Oxford Handbook of Byzantine Literature*, edited by Stratis Papaioannou, 430–463. Oxford: Oxford University Press, 2021.

Papoutsakis, Emanuel. "Formulaic Language in the Metrical Homilies of Jacob of Serugh." In Lavenant, *Symposium Syriacum VII*, 445–451.

Payne Smith, J. *A Compendious Syriac Dictionary*. Oxford: Oxford University Press, 1903.

Peers, Glenn. "Isaac of Antioch's Organ and the Media of Musical Subjects." *JECS* 26.1 (2018): 75–109.

Penn, Michael. "'Bold and Having No Shame': Ambiguous Widows, Controlling Clergy, and Early Syrian Communities." *Hugoye: Journal of Syriac Studies* 4.2 (2001 [2010]): 159–185.

Penner, Todd, and Caroline Vander Stichele, eds. *Mapping Gender in Ancient Religious Discourses*. Boston: Brill, 2007.

Petit, Madeline. "Exploitations non bibliques des themes de Tamar et de Genèse 38: Philon d'Alexandrie; Textes et traditions juives jusqu'aux Talmudim." In *Alexandrina: Mélanges offerts à Claude Mondésert S.J.*, 77–115. Paris: Éditions du Cerf, 1987.

Petitmangin, Pierre, and the Séminaire d'Histoire des textes, eds. *Pélagie la Pénitente, Metamorphoses d'une légende*. vol. 1. Paris: Études augustiniennes, 1981.

Pétridès, Sophrone. "Spoudæi et Philopones." *Échos d'Orient* 7.49 (1904): 341–348.

Phenix, Robert R., and Cornelia B. Horn, eds. *The Rabbula Corpus: Comprising the Life of Rabbula, His Correspondence, a Homily Delivered in Constantinople, Canons, and Hymns*. Atlanta: Society of Biblical Literature, 2017.

Pierre, Marie-Joseph. "Les 'membres de l'ordre,' d'Aphraate au *Liber Graduum*." In Jullien, *Le monachisme syriaque*, 11–35.

Pino, Tikhon Alexander. "Ephrem Graecus: The Greek Corpus Attributed to St Ephrem the Syrian in Byzantium." In *The Reception of (Pseudo-)Ephremian Writings Outside Syriac Christianity*, edited by A. Hilkens and A. Pirtea. Turnhout: Brepols, (forthcoming).

Porter, Mark. "Back and Forth: Dimensions and Directions of Resonance in Congregational Musicking." *JAAR* 85.2 (2017): 446–469.

Porter, Mark. *Ecologies of Resonance in Christian Musicking*. New York: Oxford University Press, 2020.

Possekel, Ute. "Bardaisan's Influence on Late Antique Christianity." *Hugoye: Journal of Syriac Studies* 21.1 (2018): 81–125.

Possekel, Ute. "'Go and Set Up for Yourselves Beautiful Laws . . . ': The School of Nisibis and Institutional Autonomy in Late Antique Education." In *Griechische Philosophie und Wissenschaft bei den Ostsyrern: Im Gedenken an Mār Addai Scher (1867–1915)*, edited by M. Perkams and A. M. Schilling, 29–47. Berlin: de Gruyter, 2019.

Possekel, Ute. "Orpheus Among the Animals: A New Dated Mosaic from Osrhoene." *Oriens Christianus* 92 (2008): 1–35.

288   BIBLIOGRAPHY

Possekel, Ute. "Selbstverständnis und Bildungsauftrag der Schule von Nisibis." *ZAC* 19.1 (2015): 104–136.

Power, Timothy. "The Sound of the Sacred." In *Sound and the Ancient Senses*, edited by Shane Putler and Sarah Nooter, 15–30. Abingdon: Routledge, 2019.

Price, Simon R. F. *Rituals and Power: The Roman Imperial Cult in Asia Minor*. Cambridge: Cambridge University Press, 1986.

Purpura, Ashley. "Beyond the Binary: Hymnographic Constructions of Eastern Orthodox Gender Identities." *JOR* 97.4 (2017): 525–546.

Puthuparampil, James. *Mariological Thought of Mar Jacob of Serugh (451–521)*. Piscataway, NJ: Gorgias Press, 2012.

Pylvänäinen, Pauliina. *Agents in Liturgy, Charity and Communication: The Tasks of Female Deacons in the Apostolic Constitutions*. Turnhout: Brepols, 2020.

Quasten, Johannes. "The Liturgical Singing of Women in Christian Antiquity." *CHR* 27.2 (1941): 149–165.

Quasten, Johannes. *Music and Worship in Pagan and Christian Antiquity*. Translated by Boniface Ramsey. Washington, DC: National Association of Pastoral Musicians, 1983.

Radle, Gabriel. "The Veiling of Women in Byzantine Liturgy, Hair, and Identity in a Medieval Rite of Passage." *Speculum* 94.4 (2019): 1070–1115.

Ravolainen, Kaija. *The Singer in the Ecclesiastical Hierarchy: The Early History of the Order*. Studia Musica 59. Helsinki: Sibelius Academy, 2014.

Rebillard, Éric. *The Care of the Dead in Late Antiquity*. Ithaca, NY: Cornell University Press, 2009.

Reif, Stefan C. "The Early Liturgy of the Synagogue." In Davies, Sturdy, and Horbury, eds., *The Cambridge History of Judaism*, 3:326–357.

Reinink, G. J., and Alexander C. Klugkist, eds. *After Bardaisan: Studies on Continuity and Change in Syriac Christianity in Honour of Professor Han J. W. Drijvers*. OLA 89. Leuven: Peeters, 1999.

Reinink, G. J., and H. L. J. Vanstiphout, eds. *Dispute Poems and Dialogues in the Ancient and Mediaeval Near East: Forms and Types of Literary Debates in Semitic and Related Literature*. Leuven: Peeters, 1991.

Ricoeur, Paul. "Narrative Time." In Mitchell, *On Narrative*, 165–186.

Rigolio, Alberto. *Christians in Conversation: A Guide to Late Antique Dialogues in Greek and Syriac*. Oxford: Oxford University Press, 2019.

Rives, James B. *Religion in the Roman Empire*. Malden, MA: Blackwell, 2006.

Rizk-Asdourian, Donna. "Women and Their Position Within the Liturgical Life: The Coptic and Oriental Orthodox Churches." In *Rethinking Gender in Orthodox Christianity*, edited by Ashley Purpura, Thomas Arentzen, and Susan Ashbrook Harvey, 182–200. Eugene, OR: Pickwick Publications/Wipf and Stock, 2023.

Roberts, Michael. "Poetry and Hymnography (i): Christian Latin Poetry." In Harvey and Hunter, *The Oxford Handbook of Early Christian Studies*, 608–640.

Rodrigues Pereira, Alphons S. "Two Syriac Verse Homilies on Joseph." *Jaarbericht ex Oriente Lux* 31 (1989–1990): 95–120.

Roller, Matthew B. "Exemplarity in Roman Culture: The Cases of Horatius Cocles and Cloelia." *Classical Philology* 99.1 (2004): 1–56.

Ross, Steven K. *Roman Edessa: Politics and Culture on the Eastern Fringes of the Roman Empire, 114–242 C.E.* London: Routledge, 2001.

Roueché, Charlotte. "Acclamations in the Later Roman Empire: New Evidence from Aphrodisias." *Journal of Roman Studies* 74 (1984): 181–191.

Rousseau, Philip. "The Pious Household and the Virgin Chorus: Reflections on Gregory of Nyssa's *Life of Macrina*." *JECS* 13.2 (2005): 165–186.

Rouwhorst, Gerard A. M. "The Biblical Stories About the Prophet Elijah in Early Syriac-Speaking Christianity." In *Religious Stories in Transformation: Conflict, Revision and Reception*, edited by Alberdina Houtman, Tamar Kadari, Marcel J. H. M. Poorthuis, and Vered Tohar, 165–188. Leiden: Brill, 2016.

Rouwhorst, Gerard A. M. "The Celebration of Holy Week in Early Syriac-Speaking Churches." In Groen, Hawkes-Teeples, and Alexopoulos, *Inquiries into Eastern Christian Worship*, 65–80.

Rouwhorst, Gerard A. M. "Deacons in the Works of Ephrem the Syrian." In *Deacons and Diakonia in Late Antiquity*, edited by Bart J. Koet, Edwina Murphy, and Esako Ryökäs, 188–201. WUNT 2, Reihe 606. Tübingen: Mohr Siebeck, 2024.

Rouwhorst, Gerard A. M. "The Feast of the Epiphany in the Early Syriac Tradition: The Question of the Origins of the Feast of the Epiphany." In *Explorations in Eastern Christian Liturgy*, edited by Nina Glibetic and Gabriel Radle, 185–200. Münster: Aschendorff Verlag, 2022.

Rouwhorst, Gerard A. M. "Hymns and Prayers in the Apocryphal Acts of Thomas." In Leonhard and Löhr, *Literature or Liturgy?* 195–212.

Rouwhorst, Gerard A. M. "Jewish Liturgical Traditions in Early Syriac Christianity." *VC* 51.1 (1997): 72–93.

Rouwhorst, Gerard A. M. "Les lectionaires syriaques." In *La lecture liturgiques des Épîtres catholique dans l'Église ancienne*, edited by Christian-Bernard Amphoux and Jean-Paul Bouhot, 105–140. Lausanne: Éditions du Zèbre, 1996.

Rouwhorst, Gerard A. M. "The Liturgical Reading of the Bible in the Syriac Church." In *Liturgische Bibelrezeption [Liturgical Reception of the Bible]: Dimensionen und Perspektiven interdisziplinärer Forschung [Dimensions and Perspectives of Interdisciplinary Research]*, edited by Harald Buchinger and Clemens Leonhard, 153–168. Göttingen: Vandenhoeck and Ruprecht, 2022.

Rouwhorst, Gerard A. M. "The Original Setting of the Madrashe of Ephrem of Nisibis." In *Let Us Be Attentive: Proceedings of the Seventh International Congress of the Society of Oriental Liturgy*, edited by Martin Lüstraeten et al., 207–223. Münster: Aschendorff Verlag 2020.

Rouwhorst, Gerard A. M. "The Reading of Scripture in Early Christian Liturgy." In *What Athens Has to Do with Jerusalem: Essays on Classical, Jewish, and Early Christian Art and Archaeology in Honor of Gideon Foerster*, edited by Leonard V. Rutgers, 305–331. Leuven: Peeters, 2002.

Rouwhorst, Gerard A. M. "Table Community in Early Christianity." In *Holy People: Jewish and Christian Perspectives on Religious Communal Identity*, edited by M. Poorthuis and J. J. Schwartz, 69–84. Leiden: Brill, 2005.

Rubin, Miri. *Mother of God: A History of the Virgin Mary.* New Haven, CT: Yale University Press, 2009.

Ruether, Rosemary Radford. *Religion and Sexism: Images of Woman in the Jewish and Christian Traditions*. New York: Simon and Schuster, 1974.

Runia, David T. *Philo in Early Christian Literature: A Survey*. Minneapolis: Fortress Press, 1993.

Rush, Alfred C. *Death and Burial in Christian Antiquity*. Washington, DC: The Catholic University of America Press, 1941.

Russell, Donald A. *Greek Declamation*. Cambridge: Cambridge University Press, 1983.

Russell, Tracy L. "The Betrothed of Christ: A Study of the Nuptial Metaphor in Late Ancient Syriac Virgin Martyr Narratives." PhD diss., Saint Louis University, 2023.

Sada, Eve. "Assyrian–Syriac Chants from the Liturgy of the Church of the East." PhD diss., University of Oklahoma, 2021. https://hdl.handle.net/11244/332527.

Salvesen, Alison. "The Exodus Commentary of St. Ephrem: A Fourth-Century Syriac Commentary on the Book of Exodus." Moran 'Etho 8. Piscataway, NJ: Gorgias Press, 2011.

Salvesen, Alison. "Some Themes in Ephrem's Exodus Commentary." *The Harp* 4.1–3 (1991): 21–34.

Samellas, Antigone. *Death in the Eastern Mediterranean (50–600 A.D.): The Christianization of the East; An Interpretation*. Tübingen: Mohr Siebeck, 2002.

Sawicka-Sykes, Sophie. "Demonic Anti-Music and Spiritual Disorder in the Life of Antony." In *Demons and Illnesses from Antiquity to the Early Modern Period*, edited by Siam Bhayro and Catherine Rider, 192–214. Leiden: Brill, 2017.

Schaberg, Jane. *The Illegitimacy of Jesus: A Feminist Theological Interpretation of the Infancy Narratives*. San Francisco: Harper & Row, 1987.

Scholes, Robert. "Language, Narrative, and Anti-Narrative." In Mitchell, *On Narrative*, 200–208.

Searle, Mark. "Ritual." In *Foundations in Ritual Studies: A Reader for Students of Christian Worship*, edited by Paul Bradshaw and John Melloh, 9–16. Grand Rapids, MI: Baker Academic, 2007.

Semaine d'études liturgiques, eds. *Roles in the Liturgical Assembly: The Twenty-Third Liturgical Conference of Saint Serge*. Translated by Matthew J. O'Connell. New York: Pueblo, 1981.

Shaw, Brent. *Sacred Violence: African Christians and Sectarian Hatred in the Age of Augustine*. Cambridge: Cambridge University Press, 2011.

Shaw, Teresa M. *The Burden of the Flesh: Fasting and Sexuality in Early Christianity*. Minneapolis: Fortress Press, 1998.

Sheerin, Daniel. *The Eucharist*. Wilmington, DE: Michael Glazier, 1986.

Sheerin, Daniel. "Eucharistic Liturgy." In Harvey and Hunter, *The Oxford Handbook of Early Christian Studies*, 711–743.

Shelemay, Kay Kaufman. *Let Jasmine Rain Down: Song and Remembrance Among Syrian Jews*. Chicago: University of Chicago Press, 1998.

Shelemay, Kay Kaufman. "The Power of Silent Voices: Women in the Syrian Musical Tradition." In *Music and the Play of Power in the Middle East*, edited by Laudan Nooshin, 269–288. London: Routledge, 2009.

Shepardson, Christine. *Anti-Judaism and Christian Orthodoxy: Ephrem's Hymns in Fourth-Century Syria*. Washington, DC: The Catholic University of America Press, 2008.

Shepardson, Christine. *Controlling Contested Places: Late Antique Antioch and the Spatial Politics of Religious Controversy*. Berkeley: University of California Press, 2014.

Shoemaker, Stephen J. *Mary in Early Christian Faith and Devotion*. New Haven, CT: Yale University Press, 2016.

Shoemaker, Stephen J. "Rethinking the 'Gnostic Mary.'" *JECS* 9 (2001): 555–595.

Siquans, Agnethe, ed. *Biblical Women in Patristic Reception/Biblische Frauen in patristischer Rezeption*. JAJ Supplement 25. Göttingen: Vandenhoeck and Ruprecht, 2017.

Siquans, Agnethe. "'She Dared to Reprove Her Father': Miriam's Image as a Female Prophet in Rabbinic Interpretation." *JAJ* 6.3 (2015): 335–357.

Sissa, Giulia. *Greek Virginity*. Translated by Arthur Goldhammer. Cambridge, MA: Harvard University Press, 1990.

Smelova, Natalia. "Melkite Syriac Hymns to the Mother of God (9th–11th centuries): Manuscripts, Language and Imagery." In *The Cult of the Mother of God in Byzantium: Texts and Images*, edited by Leslie Brubaker and Mary B. Cunningham, 117–131. Farnham, UK: Ashgate, 2011.

Smith, J. A. "The Ancient Synagogue, the Early Church and Singing." *Music and Letters* 65.1 (1984): 1–16.

Smith, J. A. "First-Century Christian Singing and Its Relationship to Contemporary Jewish Religious Song." *Music and Letters* 75.1 (1994): 1–15.

Sodini, Jean-Pierre. "Archéologie des èglises et organization spatiale de la liturgie." In Cassingena-Trévedy and Jurasz, *Les liturgies syriaques*, 229–266.

Sokoloff, Michael. *A Syriac Lexicon: A Translation from the Latin, Correction, Expansion, and Update of C. Brockelmann's Lexicon Syriacum*. Winona Lake, IN/Piscataway, NJ: Eisenbrauns/Gorgias Press, 2009.

Spier, Jeffrey, ed. *Picturing the Bible: The Earliest Christian Art*. New Haven, CT and Fort Worth, TX: Yale University Press, 2007.

Spyrakou, Evangelia. "The Byzantine Choral System Until 1204 (Η Ηχοχρωματική Ποικιλία στην Βυζαντινή Χορωδιακή Πράξη)." In *Byzantine Musical Culture: Papers of the First International Conference of the American Society of Byzantine Music and Hymnology, Attica 10–15 September 2007*. http://www.asbmh.pitt.edu/page12/Spyrakou.pdf.

Spyrakou, Evangelia. "Did Women Chant Professionally in Urban Byzantine Churches?" Paper presented at the International Orthodox Theological Association, Second Mega-Conference, January 11–15, 2023, Volos, Greece.

Spyrakou, Evangelia. Οι Χοροί Ψαλτών κατά την βυζαντινή παράδοση, Ἴδρυμα Βυζαντινής Μουσικολογίας. Μελέται 14. Athens: Institute of Byzantine Musicology, 2008.

Stehle, Eva. *Performance and Gender in Ancient Greece: Nondramatic Poetry in Its Setting*. Princeton, NJ: Princeton University Press, 2014.

Stewart, Columba. "The Ascetic Taxonomy of Antioch and Edessa at the Emergence of Monasticism." *Adamantius* 19 (2013): 207–221.

Swearingen, C. Jan. "A Lover's Discourse: Diotima, Logos, and Desire." In Lunsford, *Reclaiming Rhetorica*, 25–51.

Tabé, Elias. "Les bnay wa bnoth Qyomo." In *Le monachisme syriaque: Aux premiers siècles de l'Église, IIe-début VIIe siècle*, 1:55–60. Patrimonie Syriaque Actes du Colloque V. Antélias, Lebanon: Centre d'Études et de Recherches Orientales, 1998.

Tabory, Joseph. "Maʿamadot: Second Temple Non-Temple Liturgy." In *Liturgical Perspectives: Prayer and Poetry in Light of the Dead Sea Scrolls*, edited by Esther G. Chazon, 235–261. Leiden: Brill, 2003.

Taft, Robert. *The Liturgy of the Hours in East and West: The Origins of the Divine Office and Its Meaning for Today*. Collegeville, MN: Liturgical Press, 1986.

Taft, Robert. "Some Notes on the Bema in the East and West Syrian Traditions." *OCP* 34 (1968): 326–359. Reprinted in Robert Taft, *Liturgy in Byzantium and Beyond*, 326–359. Aldershot, UK: Ashgate/Variorum, 1995.

Taft, Robert F. *Through Their Own Eyes: Liturgy as the Byzantines Saw It*. Berkeley: InterOrthodox Press, 2006.

Taft, Robert F. "Women at Church in Byzantium: Where, When, and Why?" *DOP* 52 (1998): 27–87. Reprinted in *Divine Liturgies—Human Problems in Byzantium, Armenia, Syria and Palestine*, edited by Robert F. Taft, 27–87. Burlington, VT: Ashgate, 2001.

Taitz, Emily. "Kol Ishah—The Voice of Woman: Where Was It Heard in Medieval Europe?" *Conservative Judaism* 38.3 (1986): 46–61.

Talbot, Alice-Mary. "Bluestocking Nuns: Intellectual Life in the Convents of Late Byzantium." In *Okeanos: Essays Presented to Ihor Ševčenko on His Sixtieth Birthday by His Colleagues and Students*, edited by Cyril A. Mango, Omeljan Pritsak, and Uliana M. Pasicznyk, 604–618. Harvard Ukrainian Studies 7. Cambridge, MA: Ukrainian Research Institute, Harvard University, 1983. Reprinted in Alice-Mary Talbot, *Women and Religious Life in Byzantium*, 604–618. Aldershot, UK: Ashgate, 2001.

Talbot, Alice-Mary. "The Devotional Life of Laywomen." In *A People's History of Christianity*, vol. 3, *Byzantine Christianity*, edited by Derek Krueger, 201–220. Minneapolis: Fortress Press, 2006.

Talley, Thomas. *The Origins of the Liturgical Year*. New York: Pueblo, 1986.

Tang, Li. "Christian Communities in Medieval Central Asia: Syriac and Syro-Turkic Inscriptions from Zhetysu and the Chuy Valley (9th–14th Centuries)." In *Silk Road Traces: Studies in Syriac Christianity in China and Central Asia*, edited by Li Tang and Dietmar Winkler, 201–222. Münster: LIT Verlag, 2022.

Tannous, Jack. *The Making of the Medieval Middle East: Religion, Society, and Simple Believers*. Princeton, NJ: Princeton University Press, 2018.

Tavolieri, Claudia. "Body and Soul: The Dangers of Music and Song in Syriac Christianity." In *The Study of Musical Performance in Antiquity: Archaeology and Written Sources*, edited by Agnès Garcia Ventura, Claudia Tavolieri, and Lorenzo Verderame, 247–260. Newcastle-upon-Tyne: Cambridge Scholars Publishing, 2018.

Tavolieri, Claudia. "Una vita tra silenzio e canto: L'importanza dell' educazione musicale delle donne in alcuni e sempi tratti dalla letterature siriaca." In *Proceedings of the International Congress, La vie del sapere in ambito siro-mesopotamico dal III al IX secolo, Rome May 12–13, 2011*, edited by C. Noce, M. Pampaloni, and C. Tavolieri, 351–373. OCA 293. Rome: Pontificio Istituto orientale, 2013.

Taylor, David G. K. "Hagiographie et liturgie syriaque." In Binggeli, *L'hagiographie syriaque*, 77–112.

Tchalenko, Georges. *Villages antiques de la Syrie du Nord*. 3 vols. Paris: Geuthner, 1953–1958.

Thomas, Christine. "Stories Without Texts and Without Authors: The Problem of Fluidity in Ancient Novelistic Texts and Early Christian Literature." In *Ancient Fiction and the*

New Testament, edited by Ronald Hock, J. Bradley Chance, and Judith Perkins, 273–291. Atlanta: Scholars Press, 1998.

Tkacz, Catherine Brown. "Singing Women's Words as Sacramental Mimesis." *Recherches de théologie et philosophie médiévales* 70 (2003): 275–328.

Tkacz, Catherine. "Women as Types of Christ: Susanna and Jephthah's Daughter." *Gregorianum* 85 (2004): 278–311.

Topping, Eva Catafygiotu. *Sacred Songs: Studies in Byzantine Hymnography*. Minneapolis: Light and Life, 1997.

Torjesen, Karen Jo. "Clergy and Laity." In Harvey and Hunter, *The Oxford Handbook of Early Christian Studies*, 389–405.

Torres, Marie-Emmanuelle. "'*Polla eti eis polla*': Some Litanic Practices in Byzantine Imperial Ceremonies?" In *The Litany in Arts and Cultures*, edited by Witold Sadowski and Francesco Marsciani, 101–124. Turnhout: Brepols, 2020.

Upson-Saia, Kristi. "Caught in a Compromising Position: The Biblical Exegesis and Characterization of Biblical Protagonists in the Syriac Dialogue Hymns." *Hugoye: Journal of Syriac Studies* 9.2 (2006): 189–211.

Upson-Saia, Kristi, Carly Daniel-Hughes, and Alicia J. Batten, eds. *Dressing Judeans and Christians in Antiquity*. Burlington, VT: Ashgate, 2014.

Urbano, Arthur P. *The Philosophical Life: Biography and the Crafting of Intellectual Identity in Late Antiquity*. Washington, DC: The Catholic University of America Press, 2013.

van Bekkum, W. J. "Anti-Christian Polemics in Hebrew Liturgical Poetry (Piyyut) of the Sixth and Seventh Centuries." In den Boeft and Hilhorst, *Early Christian Poetry*, 297–308.

van Bekkum, W. J. "The Hebrew Liturgical Poetry of Byzantine Palestine: Recent Research and New Perspectives." *Prooftexts* 28.2 (2008): 232–246.

Van Nijf, Onno. *The Civic World of Professional Associations in the Roman East*. Amsterdam: J.C. Gieben, 1997.

Van Rompay, Lucas. "Antiochene Biblical Interpretation." In *The Book of Genesis in Jewish and Oriental Christian Interpretations*, edited by Judith Frishman and Lucas Van Rompay, 103–123. Leuven: Peeters, 1997.

Van Rompay, Lucas. "The Christian Syriac Tradition of Interpretation." In *Hebrew Bible/Old Testament: The History of Its Interpretation*, I. *From the Beginnings to the Middle Ages (Until 1300)*, 1. *Antiquity*, edited by Magne Saebø, 612–641. Göttingen: Vandenhoeck & Ruprecht, 1996.

Van Rompay, Lucas. "Mallpânâ dilan Suryâyâ: Ephrem in the Works of Philoxenos of Mabbog; Respect and Distance." *Hugoye: Journal of Syriac Studies* 7 (2004 [2010]): 83–105.

Van Rompay, Lucas. "Narsai." In the *Gorgias Encyclopedic Dictionary of the Syriac Heritage*, edited by Sebastian Brock, Aaron Butts, George Kiraz, and Lucas Van Rompay, 303–304. Piscataway, NJ: Gorgias Press, 2011.

Van Rompay, Lucas. "*No Evil Word About Her*: The Two Syriac Versions of the Book of Judith." In *Text, Translation, and Tradition: Studies on the Peshitta and Its Use in the Syriac Tradition Presented to Konrad D. Jenner on the Occasion of His Sixty-Fifth Birthday*, edited by W. T. Van Peursen and R. B. Ter Haar Romeny, 205–230. Leiden: Brill, 2006.

Van Rompay, Lucas. "Society and Community in the Christian East." In *The Cambridge Companion to the Age of Justinian*, edited by Michael Maas, 239–266. Cambridge: Cambridge University Press, 2005.

Varghese, Baby. *The Early History of the Syriac Liturgy: Growth, Adaptation and Inculturation*. Wiesbaden: Harrassowitz Verlag, 2021.

Varghese, Baby. *Ordination of Women in the Syriac Tradition*. Awsar Slawoto 8. Kottayam, Kerala: St. Ephrem Ecumenical Research Institute, 2021.

Varghese, Baby. *West Syrian Liturgical Theology*. Aldershot, UK: Ashgate, 2004.

Velimirović, Miloš. "Christian Chant in Syria, Armenia, Egypt, and Ethiopia." In *The New Oxford History of Music*, vol. 2, *The Early Middle Ages to 1300*, edited by Richard Crocker and David Hiley, 3–9. New York: Oxford University Press, 1990.

Vööbus, Arthur. *Celibacy: A Requirement for the Admission to Baptism in the Early Syrian Church*. PETSE 1. Stockholm: Estonian Theological Society in Exile, 1951.

Walsh, Erin Galgay. "From Sketches to Portraits: The Canaanite Woman Within Late Antique Syriac Poetry." In *Syriac Christian Culture: Beginnings to Renaissance*, edited by Aaron Michael Butts and Robin Darling Young, 66–82. Washington, DC: The Catholic University of America Press, 2020.

Walsh, Erin Galgay. "The Gendered Body in Verse: Jacob of Serugh and Romanos Melodos on the Woman with a Flow of Blood." *Journal of the Bible and Its Reception* 9.1 (2022): 1–26.

Walsh, Erin Galgay. "Giving Voice to Pain: New Testament Narratives of Healing in the Poetry of Jacob of Serugh." *JECH* 12:1 (2022): 96–118.

Walsh, Erin Galgay. "Holy Boldness: Narsai and Jacob of Sarug Preaching the Canaanite Woman." In Wickes and Heal, *Literature, Rhetoric, and Exegesis in Syriac Verse*, 85–97.

Walsh, Erin Galgay. "'How the Weak Rib Prevailed!': Eve and the Canaanite Woman in the Poetry of Narsai." In Butts, Heal, and Kitchen, *Narsai*, 199–226.

Walsh, Erin Galgay. "Mourning Eve: The Homily on Women as Attributed to Jacob of Serugh." *Studia Patristica Nordica* 33 (2018): 31–59.

Ward, Benedicta. *Harlots of the Desert: A Study of Repentance in Early Monastic Sources*. Kalamazoo, MI: Cistercian Publications, 1987.

Webb, Ruth. *Demons and Dancers: Performance in Late Antiquity*. Cambridge, MA: Harvard University Press, 2008.

Webb, Ruth. "Poetry and Rhetoric." In *The Handbook of Classical Rhetoric in the Hellenistic Period 330 BC–AD 400*, edited by Stanley E. Porter, 339–369. New York: Brill, 1997.

White, Hayden. "The Value of Narrativity in the Representation of Reality." In Mitchell, *On Narrative*, 1–24.

Wicker, Kathleen O'Brien. "Mulierum Virtutes (Moralia 242E–263C)." In *Plutarch's Ethical Writings and Early Christian Literature*, edited by Hans Dieter Betz, 106–134. Leiden: Brill, 1978.

Wickes, Jeffrey. "Between Liturgy and School: Reassessing the Performative Context of Ephrem's Madrāšê." *JECS* 26.1 (2018): 25–51.

Wickes, Jeffrey. *Bible and Poetry in Late Antique Mesopotamia: Ephrem's Hymns on Faith*. Oakland: University of California Press, 2019.

Wickes, Jeffrey. "Ephrem's Interpretation of Genesis." *SVTQ* 52.1 (2008): 45–65.

Wickes, Jeffrey, and Kristian S. Heal, eds. *Literature, Rhetoric, and Exegesis in Syriac Verse*. Studia Patristica 78, edited by Markus Vinzent. Leuven: Peeters, 2017.

Wills, Lawrence. *The Jewish Novel in the Ancient World*. Ithaca, NY: Cornell University Press, 1995.

Wilson, Stephen G. "Early Christian Music." In *Common Life in the Early Church: Essays Honoring Graydon F. Snyder*, edited by Julian Victor Hills, Graydon F. Snyder, and Richard B. Gardner, 390–401. Harrisburg, PA: Trinity Press International, 1998.

Wipszycka, Ewa. "Les confréries dans la vie religieuse de l'Égypte chrétienne." In *Proceedings of the Twelfth International Congress of Papyrology*, edited by Deborah H. Samuel, 511–525. Amsterdam: A.M. Hakkert, 1970.

Wolff, P. Maternus. "Drei Begräbnisgesänge Narsais: Kritische Ausgabe im Anschluss an den Nachlass k. Mackes und Übersetzung."*Orient Christianus* 12–14 (1925): 1–29.

Wright, William. *Catalogue of Syriac Manuscripts in the British Museum, Acquired Since the Year 1838*. 3 vols. London, 1870–1872.

Wylie, Amanda Berry. "Musical Aesthetics and Biblical Interpretation in John Chrysostom." *Studia Patristica* 32, edited by E. A. Livingstone, 386–392. Leuven: Peeters, 1997.

Young, Robin Darling. "The 'Church from the Nations' in the Exegesis of Ephrem." In *Symposium Syriacum IV*, edited by H. J. W. Drijvers, R. Lavenant, and C. Molenberg, 111–121. OCA 229. Rome: Pontificium Institutum Studiorum Orientalium, 1987.

Yousif, Pierre. *L'Eucharistie chez saint Éphrem de Nisibe*. OCA 224. Rome: Pontificium Institutum Orientalium Studiorum, 1984.

Zakaraian, David. *Women, Too, Were Blessed: The Portrayal of Women in Early Christian Armenian Texts*. Leiden: Brill, 2021.

This book draws on a number of my earlier essays, although I have revised the material substantially in the process of bringing it all together. I thank the editors and publishers for permission to drawn upon or use portions of the following essays.

Harvey, Susan Ashbrook. "Bearing Witness: New Testament Women in Early Byzantine Hymnography." In *The New Testament in Byzantium*, edited by Derek Krueger and Robert Nelson, 205–221. Washington, DC: Dumbarton Oaks Publications, 2016.

Harvey, Susan Ashbrook. "Bride of Blood, Bride of Light: Biblical Women as Images of Church in Jacob of Serug." In *Malphono w-Rabo d-Malphone: Festschrift for Sebastian P. Brock*, edited by George A. Kiraz, 189–218. Piscataway, NJ: Gorgias Press, 2008.

Harvey, Susan Ashbrook. "Creation, Order, Beauty: Jacob of Serugh on Liturgical Aesthetics." In *The Year of Jacob of Serugh: Essays in Commemoration of the 1500th Anniversary of His Death*, edited by Robert Kitchen and Armando Elkhoury, 155–177. Washington, DC: The Hidden Pearl Press, 2023.

Harvey, Susan Ashbrook. "Encountering Eve in Syriac Tradition." In *Syriac Encounters: Papers from the Sixth North American Syriac Symposium*, edited by Maria Doerfler, Emanuel Fiano, and Kyle Smith, 11–49. Leuven: Peeters, 2015.

Harvey, Susan Ashbrook. "Guiding Grief: Liturgical Poetry and Ritual Lamentation in Early Byzantium." In *Greek Laughter and Tears: Antiquity and After; Proceedings of the 8th A. G. Leventis Conference in Greek, University of Edinburgh, November 2013*, ed. Douglas Cairns and Margaret Alexiou, 199–216. Edinburgh: University of Edinburgh Press, 2017.

Harvey, Susan Ashbrook. "Holy Impudence, Sacred Desire: The Women of Matthew 1:1–16 in Syriac Tradition." In *Studies on Patristic Texts and Archaeology: If These Stones Could Speak; Texts and Contexts*, edited by George Kalantzis and Thomas Martin, 27–48. Lewiston, NY: Edwin Mellen Press, 2009.

Harvey, Susan Ashbrook. "Interior Decorating: Jacob of Serug on Mary's Preparation for the Incarnation." *Studia Patristica* 41, edited by Frances M. Young, Mark Edwards, and Peter Parvis, 23–28. Leuven: Peeters, 2006.

Harvey, Susan Ashbrook. "Liturgy and Ethics in Ancient Syriac Christianity: Two Paradigms." *Studies in Christian Ethics* 26.3 (2013): 300–316.

Harvey, Susan Ashbrook. "On Mary's Voice: Gendered Words in Syriac Marian Tradition." In *The Cultural Turn in Late Ancient Studies: Gender, Asceticism, and Hagiography*, edited by Dale B. Martin and Patricia Cox Miller, 63–86. Durham, NC: Duke University Press, 2005.

Harvey, Susan Ashbrook. "Patristic Worlds." In *Patristic Studies in the Twenty-First Century: Proceedings of an International Conference to Mark the 50th Anniversary of the International Association of Patristic Studies*, edited by Brouria Bitton-Ashkelony, Theodore de Bruyn, and Carol Harrison, 25–53. Turnhout: Brepols, 2015.

Harvey, Susan Ashbrook. "The Poet's Prayer: Invocational Prayers in the Memre of Jacob of Sarug." In *Literature, Rhetoric, and Exegesis in Syriac Verse*, edited by Jeffrey Wickes and Kristian Heal, 51–60. *Studia Patristica* 77, edited by Markus Vinzent. Leuven: Peeters, 2017.

Harvey, Susan Ashbrook. "Revisiting the Daughters of the Covenant: Women's Choirs and Sacred Song in Ancient Syriac Christianity." *Hugoye: Journal of Syriac Studies* 8.2 (2005 [2010]): 125–149.

Harvey, Susan Ashbrook. *Song and Memory: Biblical Women in Syriac Tradition*. Milwaukee: Marquette University Press, 2010.

Harvey, Susan Ashbrook. "Spoken Words, Voiced Silence: Biblical Women in Syriac Tradition." *JECS* 9 (2001): 105–131.

Harvey, Susan Ashbrook. "To Whom Did Jacob Preach?" In *Jacob of Serugh and His Times: Studies in Sixth-Century Syriac Christianity*, edited by George Anton Kiraz, 115–131. Piscataway, NJ: Gorgias Press, 2010.

Harvey, Susan Ashbrook. "Why the Perfume Mattered: The Sinful Woman in Syriac Exegetical Tradition." In *In Dominico Eloquio/In Lordly Eloquence: Essays on Patristic Exegesis in Honor of Robert Wilken*, edited by Paul Blowers, Angela Christman, David Hunter, and Robert Darling Young, 69–89. Grand Rapids, MI: Eerdmans, 2001.

7,   97, 165
7:11-17,   172
7:36-50,   10, 115, 151, 158–160, 180, 240n117,
    241n3, 242n18
10:38-42,   110, 241n4
11:27,   110
14:25-15:10,   30
15:11-32,   161
18:9-14,   161, 242n18
23:39-43,   242n18
23:44,   248n130

John
    4,   110, 113, 165, 242n18
    4:1-26,   241n4
    11,   241n4
    12:3,   240n117
    20,   84, 185

Acts
    2:13,   51

1 Corinthians
    7:9,   25
    14:15,   21
    14:26-40,   244n59
    14:34,   37, 51
    14:34-35,   36

Galatians
    4:22-31,   163

Ephesians
    5:19,   211n180, 21
    5:22-6:9,   244n59

Colossians
    3:16,   21, 211n180
    3:18-4:1,   244n59

1 Timothy
    1:11-12,   36

1 Peter
    2:9,   140, 151
    3:1,   36

Jude
    16,   115
    21:21,   16

Revelation
    5:8-10,   21
    5:9,   230n28
    14:1-5,   64, 67
    14:3,   230n28
    15:3-4,   21

Aaron (priest), 117

Abel (son of Adam and Eve), 180, 182, 185, 250n154. *See also* Eve

Abraham (patriarch), 10, 66, 96, 100, 105, 110–111, 165, 167, 180; Isaac and, 180. *See also* Sarah

Acts of John, 21

Acts of Paul and Thekla, 34

Adam (patriarch), 100, 105, 115, 116*fig.*, 117, 119, 121, 123*fig.*, 124*fig.*, 138, 178, 185, 250n154; Jacob of Sarug, portrayal of, 189–190; Last Judgment and, 123*fig.*, 124*fig.*, 125; Resurrection and, 186*fig.*, 195*fig. See also* lamentation

Ambrose of Milan, 22, 37. *See also* hymns

Anna (prophetess), 66

Anna Komnena, 40

Antioch, 37, 39, 72

Aphrahat, 27, 117–118; biblical history, account of, 117; biblical women, views on, 117–118; *Demonstrations* and, 25–26, 117–118, 121; eschatology and, 25–26; Gentiles and, 118. *See also* daughters of the covenant *(bnat qyama, s. bart qyama)*

ascetics, 3, 8–9, 24–26, 39, 61–62, 77, 102, 104–105, 126, 128, 131, 144, 180; betrothal to Christ, as Heavenly Bridegroom and, 105; choirs, relationship with, 41; clothing and, 76; education and, 34–35; philosophy and, 62; psalmody and, 38, 68, 144; psalms and, 38; women's literacy and, 34. *See also* hymns; *Hymns on the Nativity* (Ephrem the Syrian); Jerome of Stridon; liturgical choirs, female; liturgy; nuns; Shirin; Therapeutae and Therapeutrides; Virgin Mary; women, biblical

Augustine of Hippo, 146, 188

baptism, 23, 25, 28, 37, 53, 57, 105, 108; ecclesiastical canons/rules and, 134. *See also* covenanters *(bnay and bnat qyama)*; deaconesses; Sinful Woman; widows

Bardaisan, 56, 59. *See also* Harmonios; *Life of Ephrem*

Barhadbeshabba, 59; Narsai of Nisibis, account of, 59, 118, 121

Bar Hebraeus, 192, 250n3

Barren Woman (symbolic title), 163. *See also* Elizabeth; Hannah; Rachel; Rebekah; Sarah

Barsauma of Nisibis, 121

Basil of Caesarea, 18, 38, 59. *See also* congregations; psalmody

Bathsheba, 101, 117, 121

Bethlehem, 111; female personifications of, 215n34

Bible, 2, 4–6, 9, 12, 94, 97–98, 135, 156, 163, 198. *See also* Bible (Hebrew); Bible (New Testament); Bible (Old Testament); Bible, books of

Founded in 1893,
UNIVERSITY OF CALIFORNIA PRESS
publishes bold, progressive books and journals
on topics in the arts, humanities, social sciences,
and natural sciences—with a focus on social
justice issues—that inspire thought and action
among readers worldwide.

The UC PRESS FOUNDATION
raises funds to uphold the press's vital role
as an independent, nonprofit publisher, and
receives philanthropic support from a wide
range of individuals and institutions—and from
committed readers like you. To learn more, visit
ucpress.edu/supportus.